# THE HOUSE OF BYRON

'The *Birons* are irresistable.'

*Captain 'Mad Jack' Byron*

Also by Margaret J. Howell
*Byron Tonight*
(Springwood Books, 1982)

# THE HOUSE OF BYRON

*A History of the Family from the Norman Conquest*
*1066–1988*

VIOLET W. WALKER

Revised and Completed

MARGARET J. HOWELL

QUILLER PRESS
London

Published by
Quiller Press Limited
50 Albemarle Street
London W1X 4BD

First published 1988
Copyright © 1988 Violet W. Walker and Margaret J. Howell
Designed and produced by Hugh Tempest-Radford Book Producers
Set in 11 on 12 Baskerville by Galleon Photosetting, Ipswich

ISBN 1 870948 05 X

To

LESLIE A. MARCHAND

and

DORIS LANGLEY MOORE

Printed in Great Britain by St Edmundsbury Press, Bury St Edmunds, Suffolk

# Contents

In memory of

RICHARD NOEL BYRON

# Foreword

*by the Twelfth Lord Byron*

THERE must be something remarkable about a family whose tempestuous history persuades two experienced writers to research and record in such detail the lives of its more prominent members during nine hundred years.

Perhaps the fame of the poet, the sixth Lord Byron, inspired interest because he was very proud of his ancestors. Whatever it was, it remains for me as the head of the Byron family to thank the late Violet Walker and also Margaret Howell and to congratulate them on their work.

While I was reading the typescript of this volume a friend came in, inquired what I was reading, and when told said, 'You are very lucky; so many families would like to know about their ancestors, but are never able'. And indeed we are fortunate; but what about people who are not members of the family? Is there anything of historical interest in it for them?

Indeed there is. With such characters as the many Byron brothers who fought for Charles I in the civil war, The 'Wicked' Lord, 'Foul Weather Jack' and the Poet, it makes absorbing reading. There has always been an adventurous streak in the Byron family. Those who have brought us fame and credit have nearly always been on some sort of active service. Even the poet exhibited this urge—witness his expedition to help the Greeks. Such an adventurous spirit has had its disadvantages: it has seldom brought financial reward and most Byrons have had to struggle with debts, being rescued from time to time by fortunate marriages.

I have often been asked if being a member of an old and historic family has affected my life in any way. I suppose it has. It is rather like wearing a uniform: one feels on no account must that uniform be disgraced.

It is not so easy nowadays to raise a regiment, discover new lands, or be rewarded for lending the monarch some money! Nevertheless it is to be hoped that the history of our House is not finished yet and that the Byrons may still serve their country as in the past.

*Byron*

# Introduction and Acknowledgements

THE former Archivist of the City of Nottingham researched and wrote this monumental family history between 1940 and 1960 in her limited spare time. At the end of this book her colleagues have written eloquently about her work as Archivist, and as writer and researcher; in bestowing just praise on her balanced, reasonable, and energetic life, they evoke the qualities which enabled her to realise the many achievements so eminently represented by this volume. Because she loved her work and did it for its own sake, expecting neither recognition nor reward, her enthusiasm readily communicated itself. In Doris Langley Moore's entertaining novel, *My Caravaggio Style*, Jocasta Leverett meets her at Newstead Abbey:

> We had a special piece of luck which saved us from having to go all round in a large party with a guide. At this lace manufacturers' 'do' the night before, we had the Mayor and a lot of Civic people in the audience, and one of them was the City Archivist. She's a woman and her name's Miss Walker. Well, she happened to be at Newstead today arranging some letters in a glass case, and when I asked her a question about them, she recognised me. So then I told her I had a very particular reason for being interested in Byron, and she seemed surprised and pleased . . . so then she took us and showed us all kinds of things and it was thrilling. . . . Somehow or other we got to talking about whether his hair was naturally curly or not. There's a lock of it in the collection there, and Miss Walker, who's a Byron addict herself, opened the cabinet to let us see it closer.

Characteristically, she wrote *The House of Byron* to contribute to knowledge, but many other responsibilities occupied her and the project remained unfinished by 1960, when she broke off at the poet's life. Upon my undertaking to complete the work, she provided a copy of eight completed chapters and rough drafts of two more, one about the poet, the other about Augusta Leigh and her family. All this was written before Doris Langley Moore, Leslie Marchand, Malcolm Elwin and others had published books and masses of new material on the poet, his father and sister, and the relations between Annabella, Augusta, and others in their circle.

Accordingly I rewrote the chapter on the poet, retaining the outline and scope of the original, but incorporating recent extensive research as concisely as possible, and dropped the chapter on 'Wife, Sister, and Fortune' which skirted ground more widely surveyed since, particularly by Doris Langley Moore and Malcolm Elwin in their publications based on the Lovelace Papers. The 6th Lord Byron's life had to be compacted into a short chapter despite the masses of available documents (his letters alone fill eleven volumes). This book sets the poet in the context of his family and accordingly passes briefly over important material, such as his first travels in the east which, although crucial to his imaginative development, have little bearing on our theme. (His first travels have been treated in full-length works, notably William A. Borst, *Lord Byron's First Pilgrimage*, Yale University Press, 1948, and Gordon Kent Thomas, *Lord Byron's Iberian Pilgrimage*, Brigham Young University Press, 1983.)

Miss Walker also gave me notes and fragments, lists of sources, file cards with notations and quotations, and a few brief notes about Admiral Richard Byron and some of his successors. It was my task to research and write Chapter IX (about the successors to the title) and Chapter X (the Byrons on stage). This last includes large selections from the unpublished autobiography of George Frederick Byron, which illuminates the neglected figure of his notable father, the actor-dramatist. In revising the entire typescript, I made minor adjustments, added or up-dated some material, omitted redundancies, cut some very long quotations, adjusted phrasing occasionally for clarity or brevity, compiled the bibliography, and generally carried through the editing and correction which any author must make in seeing a book through the press. Miss Walker's eight chapters remain substantially as she wrote them. Phrases from the poet's works provide the chapter titles and Miss Walker's original headings remain as sub-titles. The epigraphs for the Prologue and Chapters I to VII stand as she chose them. Her original Chapter I has been re-titled 'Prologue' and the subsequent chapters renumbered, because details about early Byrons are inevitably lacking, and the reader who prefers to join the family in Tudor times may begin at once with the first chapter.

Professor A. L. Rowse published *The Byrons and Trevanions* (London: Weidenfeld and Nicolson, 1978) while the final chapters of this book were being written up. His work presents some of the same material, but it is very different in scope and emphasis. I made no use of it and have not included it in the bibliography.

The opportunity to complete this labour of love has of course been a rare privilege, and one which had to be carried on sporadically, whenever there was time and opportunity to travel or to settle down with the copious documents for an uninterrupted period of writing, which a busy teaching career does not readily allow. It was my great fortune to secure the generous assistance of the late Joan St George Saunders, of Writer's and Speaker's Research, who obtained much information from the Public Record Office, Somerset House, the East India Library, and the British Library. Mrs Brenda Lee took notes in the collection of Lovelace Papers at the Bodleian on my behalf. My own researches took me to various libraries and collections over several years, notably the Folger Shakespeare Library and the Library of Congress in Washington, D.C.; the Theatre Collection at the New York Public Library (Lincoln Centre); the Pierpont Morgan Library (New York); the Harvard College Library Theatre Collection; the Sterling Library (University of London); the British Theatre Museum in Holland Park Road (now in Covent Garden); the Victoria & Albert Museum; the British Library; the Murray MSS collection; and the Roe-Byron collection (Newstead Abbey).

The Curator of the Huntington Library in San Marino, California, provided copies of Henry James Byron's letters and Professor Jane Stedman allowed me to quote from his letters in her private collection. The University of Texas sent copies of playbills, programmes, and letters of Henry James Byron. Mrs Joy E. Byron, of Cheltenham, provided extracts from the unpublished autobiography of George Frederick Byron and information about his branch of the family; and she read and annotated the first draft of Chapter X. The Honourable Robin Byron was particularly generous and enthusiastic: he made available family papers, portraits, and private information, suggested corrections and additions, amplified Chapter IX, on the successors to the title, wrote the 'Epilogue' about his branch of the family, and provided the letter from King Charles II quoted on p. 93.

Others extended considerable help: Professor Leslie A. Marchand, Mrs Doris Langley Moore, O.B.E., and Lt-Colonel Richard Geoffrey Byron, D.S.O. (now 12th Baron Byron) read and commented on the completed typescript. Miss Lucy I. Edwards, M.B.E. assisted with the bibliography and references and in many practical ways, including the tedious checking of the quotations from Huntingdon Plumptre, whose volume of poems was missing from the British Library. Miss Pamela Wood, in charge at Newstead Abbey, supplied photographs, photocopies, and information, and was as generous with her time as her predecessor, Miss Walker herself. I also wish to thank Mrs Elma Dangerfield, O.B.E., Mrs Barbara Harrison, Mr J. D. L. Morrison, Mr John Grey Murray, C.B.E., Mrs Virginia Murray, Mr Michael Rees, Miss Susan Richardson, Mr George Seymour, Mrs Jacqueline Voignier-Marshall, and Mrs Jennifer Yule.

The author and publishers gratefully acknowledge generous grants from the Nottingham City Council and the Nottingham County Council which have made this publication possible.

In his splendid biography of the poet, Thomas Moore observed that pride of ancestry was a decided characteristic of his friend; however, the 6th Lord Byron's writings suggest rather that he was proud of being a peer of England, a member of a distinguished house in general; about particulars he was often inaccurate. As a rebel who loved order, Byron doubtless derived much satisfaction from the idea of his heritage, because he had no close relationship with his relatives, apart from his sister, and never enjoyed settled family life. Knowledge of history, whether personal or national, helps to order the chaos of life; and in following the Byrons through their vicissitudes and victories down the centuries the modern reader, who has only too much cause to be wearied by the changes and chances of this fleeting world, may be comforted and entertained as well as informed by contemplating things past. Life's contrarieties as well as the fluctuating fortunes of the nation are adumbrated in the family story. Here is Hugh, immured in his cell at Kersal, 'that God might avert the scourge of His wrath from him'; foolish Anthony Byron, dying of laughter over a practical joke; Sir John pursuing the Roundhead enemy down a precipice; Sir Nicholas in humorous exasperation 'having no mind to be made a moon-calf, and advantage the King's service nothing by it'; and courageous, amorous Sir Philip declaring 'That never brave man came to any thing, that resolved not either to Conquer or perish'.

Margaret J. Howell

Vancouver, British Columbia
January 1988

# · Prologue ·

## The Escutcheon and Shield: Origins and Early History

Of the mail-cover'd Barons, who, proudly, to battle,
    Led their vassals from Europe to Palestine's plain,
The escutcheon and shield, which with ev'ry blast rattle,
    Are the only sad vestiges now that remain.

No more doth old Robert, with harp-stringing numbers,
    Raise a flame, in the breast, for the war-laurell'd wreath;
Near Askalon's towers, John of Horistan slumbers,
    Unnerv'd is the hand of his minstrel, by death.

Paul and Hubert too sleep in the valley of Cressy;
    For the safety of Edward and England they fell:
My Fathers! the tears of your country redress ye:
    How you fought! how you died! still her annals can tell.

*On Leaving Newstead Abbey*

'I think we [the Byrons] are *very* degenerate! & I have a passion for my Ancestors,' wrote Augusta Leigh, the poet's half-sister, to Miss Mary Ann Cursham in 1832.[1] Their degeneracy is a matter of opinion, and would not readily be admitted by those who consider that the line reached its zenith in the writer's brother; but even a brief survey of the family history will show that her ancestor-worship had ample justification.

By the time of the poet's death, nearly 750 years had passed since the name of Byron first appeared in the records of English history.[2] As in most old families, the earlier members were distinguished mainly for their exploits in war—the periods of peace were too short to allow much scope for distinction in other directions; and even after fighting ceased to be the daily business of noblemen and gentlemen, the traditional Byron courage and gallantry have needed only a spark to ignite them. It is doubtful, however, if they were ever merely brawny warriors: the scholarly and cultured tastes of the first Baron and his Cavalier

[1]

brothers, who fought many bitter years for a lost cause, must have been to some extent an inheritance; and many of their successors were noted for literary or artistic talent—giving promise, as it were, of the gifted poet to come.

*

The name is supposedly derived from Beuron, near Nantes in Normandy, 'which seems to have been the appanage of a younger branch of the Tessons'.[3] In traditional style the Byrons 'came over with the Conqueror' and were duly rewarded with their share of the spoils, as their most famous descendant boasted, 'I can't complain, whose ancestors are there,/Erneis, Radulphus—eight-and-forty manors . . . Were *their* reward for following Billy's banners' (*Don Juan*, X, xxxvi). The exact relationship of Erneis and Ralph de Burun is unknown, but they were probably brothers. The former held lands in Lincolnshire and Yorkshire; from the latter the Barons Byron are descended. In 1086, when the Domesday Book was compiled, Ralph de Burun held in Nottinghamshire manors in Ossington, Calum (Kelham), Costock, Ompton, Hucknall (soon alienated but centuries later to return to the Byrons), Lamcote and Cotgrave; in the town of Nottingham he had thirteen knights' houses, in one of which lived a merchant; and in Derbyshire lands in Weston Underwood, Horsley, Denby, Kirk Hallam, and 'Herdebi'—the last a long-vanished part of the manor of Duffield.

On the manor of Horsley, near Belper, he reputedly built Horestan Castle, which remained the family seat for three generations. The earliest known reference to the castle dates from the reign of Stephen, so that it may have been the work of Ralph's son—one of the many adulterine castles erected by the barons during that stormy period. Ralph must have had some form of manor house and some fortification was almost indispensable, thus he may still be credited with the origin of the building. The scanty ruins were excavated in 1852 by the Reverend Charles Kerry, but so little was left that its size and other features remain conjectural, though Kerry suggested that it 'was a very secure stronghold—more so, perhaps, than Duffield'.[4]

Ralph himself remains shadowy: we do not know his age when he came to England (probably as a young man, to judge from the dates of records connected with his son) whom he married, nor when he died. Estates scattered over two counties (whether by deliberate policy of the Conqueror, or by haphazard assignment of available lands) must have needed much supervision in those unsettled days, and doubtless his time was fully occupied in establishing himself as an English landowner and in learning the manorial customs of his adopted country; for the Norman King was wise enough not to try to uproot all the Saxon ways.

[2]

Ralph's heir, Hugh, stands out a little more clearly as a religious benefactor, more interested in Nottinghamshire than Derbyshire, though known as Lord of Horestan. He was a witness to William Peverell's foundation charter of Lenton Priory, about 1110, which was good policy in view of Peverell's powerful position in the Midlands; and in 1144, jointly with his son and heir, Hugh de Meschines, he gave to the Priory the churches of Dalington and Horsley, and half the church of Cotgrave. 'This was done solemnly in their Chapter-house, before very many witnesses, his younger son, Roger, praising the act.'[5] Three years later, he transferred to the monks the rest of his property in Cotgrave (some of it in exchange for land held by them in Ossington), including Turchetill, his man of Cotgrave, with his children and lands and all things he held of him; and, in return, the canons gave him a war-horse worth ten marks of silver. Finally, 'Hugh de Byron, considering out of the reason given him of God, the life of this sliding age to be short and troublesome, and that he that giveth to the poor of Christ lendeth to God, that day when the Lady Albreda his wife was buried, for her Soul, his own, his Sons and Daughters, and all his Ancestors, by the consent of his sons, Hugh and Roger, gave to the Church of the Holy Trinity at Lenton, his Land of Almeton [Ompton], which gift he and his beloved sons laid on the greater altar, in the presence of Humfr. the Prior & the Covent of Brethren.'[6]

Hugh de Meschines carried his father's religious enthusiasm yet further, unless it was the son's influence that had procured this succession of gifts. Resigning his temporal inheritance to his younger brother, he 'gave his body to God and the church of the Holy Trinity at Lenton, that God might avert the scourge of His wrath from him, due for the very great multitude of his sins,' together with gifts that later led to a law suit with the Hospitallers of St John of Jerusalem.[7]

He spent the rest of his life at the cell of Kersal (in Salford, Lancashire), which was regranted to Lenton by Henry II about 1174–76, being described in the charter as a hermitage which the monks of Lenton are to hold as freely and quietly as Hugh de Buron their monk held it.[8] He was outlived by his brother Roger, who had married Nichola, daughter of Rolland de Verdun. At the beginning of King John's reign, Roger, thinking perhaps that enough had been done for Lenton, granted the monks of Darley Priory the right of estover (taking wood) in Horsley and Kilbourne woods, for the repair of their mills.

If John of Horestan, who is said to slumber near Ascalon's towers, really existed, he must have lived during this period, but contemporary records ignore him: it is not easy to fit him into the family pedigree, unless he was another son of Hugh de Burun. Tradition firmly insists that he was killed at the siege of Ascalon (possibly in 1192—it is uncertain whether he was in the second or the third Crusade) and was buried in the Church of the Holy Sepulchre. At one time, Horestan Castle hill was famous for its daffodils, including a variety identified as the daffodil of Syria, suggesting that someone returned safely from Palestine with a souvenir, but this may have been a later owner, after the Byrons had left Horsley.

Godfrey de Burun, who figures in the Lincolnshire Pipe rolls between 1182 and 1206, was possibly a descendant of Erneis, who owned land in that county. He deserves a brief mention for the fact that, in 1191, he owed money to Aaron the Jew, being thus the first, but emphatically not the last, Byron to resort to moneylenders. As we shall see, it is hardly an exaggeration to say that since 1191 the family has seldom been free of debt.

Roger de Burun was succeeded by his son Robert, who married Cecilia (or Cicely), daughter and heiress of Sir Richard Clayton, of Clayton in Lancashire, and the estate she brought to her husband was the foundation of the family's connection with that county. The Nottinghamshire and Derbyshire estates affording less scope for development, it was evidently considered advisable to concentrate on the new possessions, and in 1198 Peter de Sandiacre, who had married Robert's sister Aeline, paid £100 into the Exchequer for having seisin of Horsley, which he said was of his inheritance, though Horestan Castle does not appear to have been given up until a little later. Some of the land in Lancashire was held of Robert de Grelley, and Farrer suggests, on rather slender grounds, that Robert de Burun married one of Grelley's sisters.[9] If so, she was probably his first wife and Cicilia Clayton his second. In addition to later acquisitions, Clayton Hall remained in the family until early in the seventeenth century. Only a fragment of the original manor house survives, still surrounded by a moat.[10]

The relationships and dates of the various members of the family at this period are so confused that very little can be stated with any degree of certainty. It is disputed, for example, whether Robert junior or Sir Richard was the eldest of Robert senior's four or five sons by Cecilia Clayton; or whether Robert junior surrendered his right to his brother.[11]

In 1232, Richard de Burun was the king's constable of St James de Beuvron, Manche, and in February 1232/3, being then styled as knight, he was entrusted with £104 10s. to pay wages to the knights and serjeants in the Garrison of the Castle there in the time of Randolf, Earl of Chester and Lincoln.[12] In 1254, having killed an unknown man 'by misadventure', he was granted the right of an inquisition into the affair, but the result is not recorded.

Whether he was the eldest son or not, the succession at Clayton was carried on through Robert and his wife Maud. He distinguished himself solely by changing the first vowel in the family name to 'y', and though the spelling was not standardised in its modern form until centuries later, 'u' is rarely found after this date, being replaced generally by 'i'.

Robert's son, Sir John Byron, married Joan or Jennet, daughter of Sir Baldwin Thies or Tyes, a Teutonic knight. She was the widow of Robert Holland, or de Hoyland, and added Rochdale and Butterworth, among other places, to the family possessions. As the estates expanded, the head of the family began to play a more prominent part in public affairs, emerging from comparative obscurity during the period when conflicting claims to the Scottish throne, after the death of the Maid of Norway, were causing trouble for England as well as Scotland. Sir John was a conservator of peace in Lancashire in 1290/1, Governor of Dover about 1290, and of York, 1295/6; and Sheriff of Yorkshire in 1297. He was appointed to perambulate the forests of Sherwood, Inglewood and Galtres in 1300, and in the following year was summoned to the parliament at Lincoln.

His shrievalty was marred by the escape from the gaol of York Castle of William de Ros and other prisoners (presumably taken during the renewal of the Scottish wars), for which he was lucky to obtain the king's pardon, 'by reason of his many cares and occupations at that time, and his diligent pursuit of the fugitives.'[13] An exception to the pardon was made for the escape of Gilbert de Vallibus, a Scot, but the penalty is not stated.

The exact identity of William de Ros is uncertain, but he appears to have been a kinsman of William de Roos of Hamlake, whose daughter Alice, after the death of her first husband, John de Comyn of Ulceby, married Sir James de Byron, of Cadney. The latter was apparently a cousin of Sir John Byron, and one cannot help wondering if family influence was in some degree responsible for the Sheriff's negligence.

There were also military obligations. Sir John was summoned to serve overseas in 1297, when Edward I was preparing to invade Flanders, and as Commissioner of Array for Yorkshire he had to raise 4,000 foot to be sent to Newcastle and against the Scots in 1299. He himself was summoned for the same service in 1300 and 1301. Finally, he was a justice in Lancashire from 1307 to 1316—probably to the time of his death.

Two grants of wardship were used, as was customary, to advance the family fortunes: the first, in 1283, being the wardship of the lands and heir of Oliver de Langeford, whose son had married Byron's daughter. Nine years later, Byron's son, also named John, married the second ward, Alesia (or Alice), granddaughter and heiress of Robert Banastre of Newton-in-Makerfield.[14] John, however, appears to have died young and childless before November 1295 and his widow married Sir John de Langton.

If the younger John died at this date, and his father in 1316, who was the Sir John de Byron who bore, at the battle of Boroughbridge in 1322 against the rebellious Marcher Lords, the arms still used by the family—'argent, three bendlets gules'?[15] The repetition of Christian names leaves much in doubt.

The Sir James de Byron of Cadney who was son-in-law to William de Ros is described in Collins' *Peerage* as the son of Sir Richard Byron and grandson of the Robert who married Cecilia Clayton, though there does not seem to be contemporary evidence that Richard left any children. He saw service against the Welsh in 1277, and had the king's protection for three years in 1283 on going to Jerusalem, renewed for another three years in 1287, again on going to the Holy Land. His lands at Cadney, Kelsey and Kirmington had formerly belonged to Peter of Savoy, one of Henry III's unpopular foreign favourites and uncle of the Queen, Eleanor of Provence, to whom Peter left the Savoy Palace in London. Evidently Sir James died childless between 1295 and 1300, leaving his Lincolnshire estates to his cousin Sir Richard de Byron (Sir John's heir), as the latter is described as Lord of Cadney and Clayton.

In 1308 a commission of oyer and terminer was granted to investigate Richard's complaint that John, Prior of Armston Hospital (with whom Sir James had earlier had dealings), and many others, assaulted him in the High Street of Armston, Northamptonshire, carried away his goods, besieged him in his manor for two days, imprisoned him and assaulted his servants—a tale of woe by no means uncommon in those times. Two years later he had protection on going with the king on his service to Scotland.

By 1318, when Richard had received his knighthood, he had also inherited his father's debts, for the Exchequer was ordered to enrol the king's permission for him to pay off in instalments of 10 marks a year the sum of £205 17s. 0¾d., wherein he was 'held at the Exchequer' for the time when his father was Sheriff of Yorkshire. A large sum, it was neither his first nor his last debt, though one incurred in 1313 jointly with three other men had been paid.

Earlier in 1318, he had acknowledged that he owed £20 to the Prior of Newstead on Ancholme, Lincolnshire, and two years later he acknowledged the debt of £1,000 to William de Bernak, the father of his eldest son's wife. This enormous debt is unexplained, but the £20 owed to the Prior of Newstead was in recompense for a poaching escapade. In June

[6]

of 1318 the Prior had complained that Richard, with his son James and a number of men (some of them from Clayton) broke into his close at Cadney, fished in his various fisheries there, and carried away twelve good swans worth £20. They had also assaulted William de Walden, a canon of the Priory at Cadney. The debt was still unpaid in 1329.

The Lincolnshire estates being a novelty, Richard evidently spent more time on them than on his property in Lancashire. Like his father, he held various offices—being, for example, knight of the shire for Lincolnshire in 1322, commissioner of array for Yorkshire in 1324, and for the parts of Lindsay in Lincolnshire in 1338. He had granted his manors of Cadney, Howsham and Walesby to his sons, James and John, in 1322, perhaps as a precautionary measure, for his debts continued to accumulate, 2,000 marks being owed to Richard, son of John de Crumbwell, in 1335. In 1338, debtor turned creditor for a change when he received payment of a debt of 300 marks from John de Hardredshull.

Richard married twice and had two sons, James and John, by his first wife, Agnes. His second wife, Elizabeth, survived him for at least twelve or thirteen years and married John Colepepper. The parentage of both women remains unknown. John had entered the church and was parson of 'Frengge' (Frenze) in Norfolk in 1318. In 1333 his father gave him the manor of Huddersfield, reserving the right of re-entry if his son should be promoted to a benefice worth 100 marks or more.

Richard's health was evidently failing in 1346, as he was allowed to send a substitute to perform his military service; his death in the same year was followed about four years later by that of his elder son James who, in turn, left two sons, John and Richard, by his wife Elizabeth (daughter of Sir William Barnake or Bernak).

When his grandfather died John was fighting in France under Edward III in the early stages of the Hundred Years War. In the Battle of Crecy (1346) he served under the banner of Richard FitzAlan, Earl of Arundel (whether Paul and Hubert really fell there, and who they were, the poet alone knows) and is said to have been knighted when Calais surrendered to the English in 1347, after nearly twelve months' siege. Since his name does not appear in English records for some years, he probably remained in France until the brief interval of peace that followed the Treaty of Brétigny in 1360. On his return he indulged at intervals in freebooting, a taste he apparently acquired (or encouraged) abroad, without any respect for persons, because in 1361 he was accused of breaking into the Yorkshire parks of Edmund of Langley, Earl of Cambridge and afterwards Duke of York, the King's youngest son. Four years later, Sir Ralph Paynell complained that Sir John Byron and others had broken into his close at Barghton (Broughton) in Lincoln-shire, carried away his goods, and assaulted his servants. In the autumn of 1367 he went abroad again, for desultory fighting still continued, though the war was not formally resumed until 1369.

In February 1373/4 he was appointed to the only English office he appears to have held—commissioner of oyer and terminer in Lincoln-shire—but respectability did not last long. Once more poor Ralph Paynell had to complain of John's depredations, alleging (February 1379/80) that when he was Sheriff of Lincolnshire in the time of Edward III (who died 1377), Sir John Byron and William Sparowe of Glaunfordbrigg (Brigg, Lincolnshire), with other armed men, assaulted him at Kelsey and Howsham, lay in wait to kill him, rescued a notorious malefactor at Kelsey whom he had taken 'for divers mis-prisions', and prevented him from executing his office of sheriff. They also hunted in his free warren there, taking away hares, rabbits, pheasants and partridges, depastured his corn and assaulted his ser-vants. This, however, was Sir John Byron's last fling, for he died in the same year that the complaint was made; and, as he never seems to have found time to marry, or at least, left no heir, the succession devolved on his brother Richard.

Richard may have been much younger than Sir John; records of his life are lacking before 1379, when he was appointed one of the collectors of a subsidy in Nottinghamshire. Two years later he became a Justice of the Peace for the same county, and escheator in Nottinghamshire and Derbyshire. He was knighted, apparently, between 1383 and 1385.

The name of his first wife is unknown, but by his second marriage to Joan, daughter of William de Colwick and heiress to her brother, Thomas de Colwick, he acquired another important estate which brought the family back to one of the counties in which they had been granted lands on their first coming into England, three hundred years earlier. The convenient situation of Colwick—close to the Trent, an important waterway even then and only a few miles from the town of Nottingham—was evidently recognised at once by the Byrons. Although for some time they divided their attention between the new possessions and the older estates in Lancashire and Lincolnshire, Colwick eventually became their principal seat until the purchase of Newstead in 1540.

The medieval manor-house is said to have been built of stone quarried from the foot of the hill to the north of the site and to have been surrounded by a deep moat, the house being approached from the north.[16] The present hall, built in 1776 for John Musters, was in 1892 turned into a racecourse hotel. It was subsequently acquired by the

Home Brewery Company of Nottingham, which in 1978 opened it as a restaurant hotel. The nearby church, long the burial place of the Byrons, remains a roofless ruin.

Proximity to the Trent brought Richard Byron more trouble than profit and the greater part of his married life was vexed by litigation. Between Colwick Hall and the river, a backwater marks the ancient course of an artificial stream or 'trench' diverted from the river to turn the mill-wheel. Sir William de Colwick had constructed a dam which turned so much water into this stream that, in times of drought, boats could not pass up the river but had to discharge their cargoes there, to be carried by land to Nottingham; and, in addition, toll was demanded for the privilege of passing over de Colwick's land to reach the highway. In 1330 an agreement between the Mayor and burgesses of Nottingham and William de Colwick, stipulated the landing-places to be used and the toll to be paid, while Colwick undertook not to maintain the weir. His daughter and son-in-law ignored the agreement after his death, retaining the weir and planting willows and placing piles of timber in the river; they thus diverted the Trent water into the millstream, leaving the river bed dry and choked with obstructions so that for more than nine years boats could not reach the town of Nottingham, nor the King's Castle there. This was not merely inconvenient, but resulted in serious losses of revenue to Nottingham, which by the terms of its charters was entitled to levy toll on boats passing along the river.

Several commissions of enquiry were appointed between 1383 and 1390 and instructions were issued for the demolition of the weir; however, Richard appealed to the King and the order was revoked in 1391. Yet the matter remained unsettled and at another inquest in June of 1392 the Byrons advanced the ingenious plea that the mill-stream was not artificial, but one of two natural courses into which the river divided between Colwick and Nottingham. Their defence meeting with a cold reception, the Sheriff of the county was commanded to remove the weir 'and all other nuisances', which presumably was done as no more is heard of the case.[17]

Richard died five years later. His will, dated at Colwick, 16 June 1397, directed that his body be buried at Cadney and made elaborate provision for the repose of his soul. To the Rector of Colwick, John Godewyn, he left a grey horse as principal (the usual mortuary fee due to the church in lieu of tithes left unpaid) and forty shillings for unpaid or forgotten tithes. Twenty shillings were to be spent on wax candles to be burnt round his corpse, one hundred shillings to be distributed among the poor, and twenty shillings provided for the 'convocation of friends'. He bequeathed all his lands and certain tenements in Cadney

[9]

to William Anty (or Aucy?), chaplain, for the term of his life, enjoining him to celebrate, pray and officiate in Cadney church for the souls of Richard himself, his father, mother and brother, and all his ancestors. His Huddersfield property was to remain in the hands of the feoffees (of whom the Rector of Colwick was one) for twenty years; the issues to be handed over to Richard's executors to pay his debts and to be disposed of as seemed most expedient for the safety of his soul. The residue he left to his executors—his wife Joan, John Godewyn and William Plumptre— again to be disposed of for the benefit of his soul.

Lady Byron survived her husband for thirty years and safeguarded herself from being forced into a second marriage by taking a vow of perpetual chastity before the Archbishop of York in 1397. Her only son, John, was ten at the time of his father's death and in the following October his wardship and marriage were granted to Ralph Radcliff; when Ralph died in 1399, Sir John Assheton obtained the trust.

It remains uncertain whether Radcliff or Assheton arranged a very good marriage for the boy: his bride, Margery, daughter of John Booth of Barton (Lancashire), was a sister of William Booth, Archbishop of York from 1452 to 1464, and half-sister of Laurence Booth, who held the same office from 1476 to 1480; and her sister Alice married Sir Robert Clifton, of Clifton near Nottingham. Although John died about the time when William Booth became Archbishop, Byrons and Booths remained closely linked in both Lancashire and Nottinghamshire, for the Archbishops of York had a mansion at Southwell, whose Minster is the mother church of the latter county. There Laurence Booth died and was buried on the south side of the Minster, in a chapel which was ruthlessly destroyed at the end of the eighteenth century. We will see later that William Booth remembered his great-nieces in his will.

John was married at about thirteen, as appears from an entry in the Lichfield episcopal registers dated 1 June 1400, when the Bishop granted John Byron and Margaret, his wife, licence to have divine service performed by fit chaplains within the oratories of Clayton and Butterworth for three years.[18] It is clear that the Byrons now had a house at Butterworth as well as Clayton but whether it stood on the same site as the later Butterworth Hall is unknown.

The young ward's inheritance and marriage may have received careful attention from his guardians, but his upbringing cannot have included adequate training in filial respect because in 1415 John's widowed mother complained to the Lord Chancellor that her son had forcibly carried her off from Colwick to Lancashire, with an armed band of twenty-eight men, and had forced her into an obligation in £1,000, before the Mayor of Wigan, not to alienate any lands that had descended to her. She may have been one of those exasperating people who keep threatening to change their wills: perhaps there is some excuse for him.

John was knighted in the third year of Henry V's reign (1415/16)[19] and may have fought at Agincourt. He was Knight of the Shire for Lancashire in 1421 and 1429 and for Lincolnshire in 1447; Sheriff of Lancashire (1437–1449), the reversion being granted to his son Nicholas in 1444; and in February 1435/6 he had the doubtful honour of being one of the commissioners appointed to induce the notables of Lancashire to lend the King a considerable sum.

The old lawless spirit still broke out at times: in 1421 he was obliged to agree, on penalty of £160, 'to do or procure no hurt or harm' to Randolph de Coton or any other of the people. Again, some time between 1422 and 1458 the Booths tried to arrest in Manchester Cathedral, Thomas Barbour, one of the clerks, who had offended them in some way. He was protected by the people; whereupon the Booths summoned their kinsman, Sir John Byron, and other gentry, who mustered five hundred armed men and besieged the warden's house. The church remained closed, the clergy not daring to enter.

His official duties, too, could not always be carried out peacefully. In 1440, as Sheriff of Lancashire, he was ordered to distrain on the goods of Sir John Pilkington, who refused to pay his tax of green wax (used to seal exchequer writs), and accordingly seized the defaulter's cattle. Pilkington's brother, Robert, retaliated by seizing some of the Sheriff's cattle and a replevin suit had to be issued. When a writ was granted and the Sheriff's under-bailiff made a seizure of cattle from Robert, Sir John Pilkington sent his brother with a company of Yorkshiremen at night to Rochdale where, after a short fight, they drove off the under-bailiff's cattle. Redress was naturally demanded and finally a settlement was reached. Six years later the Duchy of Lancaster held an inquest into Byron's transgressions, unfortunately unspecified.

On the other hand, Byron's marriage with Margery Booth seems to have revived an interest in the church that had remained largely dormant in the family since the days of Hugh de Burun and Hugh de Meschines. He was among the attendant parishioners when the College of Manchester Church (now the Cathedral) was instituted in 1421 and may have founded the Lady Chapel.[20] Twenty years later he and his wife were granted a papal indult to have a portable altar. He made his most important contribution to the church on 22 January 1449/50, when William Bothe (or Booth), Bishop of Coventry and Lichfield; John Byron, knight; Richard Bothe, Laurence Bothe, clerk; and Seth Worsley were granted licence to found a chantry of two chaplains in the

parish church of St Mary the Virgin at Eccles, Lancashire—to celebrate divine service for the good estate of the King and Bishop, for their
souls after death, and the souls nominated by the founders. It was
called the chantry of St Katherine.

Sir John Byron died between 1450 and 1455 and was buried in
Manchester Cathedral, where the matrix of his monumental brass still
remains in the Lady Chapel that he may have founded. His wife
Margery, who died about 1460, was buried there also, and her brass
was in good condition until recently (and may be still), except for the
loss of the head.[21]

The intervals of Sir John's busy life were, no doubt, fully occupied
with the affairs of his large family, consisting of four sons—Nicholas,
Ralph, Richard, and another Nicholas—and five or six daughters—
Elizabeth, Margaret, Alice(?), Jane, Ellen or Helena, and Catherine.
Possibly Thomas Byron, Archdeacon of Nottingham from 1461 until
his death in 1476, was another son; he is described as a kinsman of
Archbishop Booth, but his parentage is not mentioned.[22] All these
children, except the problematical Thomas, were married, but the
names of their wives or husbands and children are sometimes a matter
of dispute.

Nicholas, the heir, will be taken last. Ralph had a son, Nicholas, who
married a daughter of FitzGeoffrey and left three daughters, Sibbell,
Alice, and Elizabeth.[23] Richard married Lucy, daughter of Sir John
Assheton, by whom he had a son, James, who married Sir Edmund
Trafford's daughter, Joan, and died in 1443 (a year after his father);
and two daughters, Margaret (or Margery), and Joan. On their father's
early death, the girls were placed under the guardianship of their grandfather. Margaret married first Thomas Walsh of Onlepe (Leicestershire)
and secondly Robert Staunton;[24] Joan became the wife of William Basset
of Blore. Richard's widow was married again twice, first to Sir Bertram
Entwysell and then to Sir Ralph Shirley of Brailsford in Derbyshire,
where she was buried in 1481/2.

The life of the younger Nicholas remains in obscurity, though dupli-
cation of names by brothers was sufficiently common in the Middle
Ages to give no reason to doubt his existence. His wife's name is
nowhere mentioned and he is variously described as the father of Helen
who married Sir John Booth of Barton and as the father of Mabel who
married Sir Thomas Gardiner and became the mother of Stephen
Gardiner, the famous Bishop of Winchester. One would like to think
that Byrons and Gardiners were so related, but there seems no reliable
foundation for this pedigree.[25]

Sir John's eldest daughter, Elizabeth, was married to Thomas

Assheton in 1415, when her father settled lands in Droylesden on her. Her husband was a noted alchemist who had King Henry VI's permission to transmute the precious metals; in 1446 a special order encouraged him and Sir Edmund de Trafford to pursue their experiments, forbidding anyone to molest them. Thomas, who had eleven children by Elizabeth, was Sir John Assheton's son by his first wife, Jane Savile; his second wife, according to one account, was Margaret Byron, sister of his daughter-in-law Elizabeth; if true, this must have produced a pretty tangle of relationships, particularly as their brother, Richard Byron, married Assheton's daughter Lucy. Unfortunately, different authorities assign different husbands to Margaret and though she almost certainly had more than one, it is unlikely that all these marriages are correctly attributed to her. A confusion between two generations or a mistake over the bride's Christian name seems likely. She certainly, at some date, became the wife of Sir William Atherton of Atherton who, according to Dugdale's *Visitation of Lancashire*, died before September 1440.[26]

In 1436 a papal mandate to the Bishop of Lichfield revealed that before William Atherton married he allegedly committed fornication with a woman related to Margaret in the third and fourth degrees of kindred and that, having cleared himself of the charge, they were married before the church. As the banns were published in the usual way and no one forbade them, they believed their marriage to be without impediment; but then they feared for their children, particularly the hereditary succession. The Bishop was therefore ordered to investigate and, if he found that William was lawfully cleared of the charge, he was to impose a fit penance on him for the crime, and then decree the marriage true and lawful; if he found otherwise, he must grant William and Margaret a dispensation to remain in the married state and declare their offspring, present or future, to be legitimate.[27]

After Atherton's death Margaret may have married Sir Robert Harcourt or Sir Maurice Herkeley of Wymondham (Leicestershire), who died in 1522.[28] She herself was still living in 1479.

Alice Byron became the wife of Richard, elder son of Richard Barton of Middleton, whose brother John married her niece Margaret. Jane married William Ratcliff; Ellen or Helena was the first wife of Walter Blount, afterwards Lord Montjoy; and Catherine, the youngest, married William Brereton of Lancashire.[29]

Sir John Byron's eldest son and heir, Nicholas, was born in 1415,[30] the year of his eldest sister's marriage. Like his father, he contributed liberally to the church and on 14 February 1455/6, with Laurence Bothe, his uncle; Robert Clyfton, his cousin; and Seth Worsley, he obtained a licence for alienation in mortmain of the advowson of Slaidburn Church, Yorkshire, for the benefit of the chaplains of St Katherine's chantry in Eccles Parish Church. Similarly, in July 1459 the same 'Holy Alliance' gave the advowson of Kneesall Church (Nottinghamshire) to the Chapter of Southwell, and the advowson of Netherwallop (Hampshire) to York Minster. In the following December, this time with the addition of William Bothe, now Archbishop of York, they founded another chantry at Eccles, to be called the chantry of Jesus and St Mary the Virgin, endowing it with the advowson of Beetham, in Westmorland.

Nicholas was Sheriff of Lancashire from 1449 until 1460. His share in public affairs during the stormy period of English history that followed his father's death remains unknown; but he may have taken some part in the early struggles of the Wars of the Roses, apparently on behalf of the Yorkist cause, as he was knighted at the Tower of London in 1461, on the eve of the coronation of Edward IV. The handsome Earl of March, eldest son of the Duke of York, was proclaimed King after defeating the Lancastrians. In the following year Byron was granted the lease of the manor of Rochdale for life.

Some of his Lincolnshire property appears to have been settled, as part of her jointure, on his wife Alice, daughter of Sir John Boteler or Butler, of Bewsey (Lancashire), niece of Sir Thomas Haryngton for, while Nicholas himself held the manorial court at Hibaldstow in 1445 and 1452, it was held by trustees of his widow in 1476.

Sir Nicholas Byron died on 29 April 1462, leaving two sons and four unmarried daughters; and his widow, who was still living in 1489/90, when she had to pay a fine for a writ concerning debt, took a vow of chastity at Southwell, being veiled by her kinsman, Archbishop William Booth. On his own death in 1464, the Archbishop left each of the girls a marriage portion of 250 marks (£166 13s. 4d.), cautiously directing that the total sum of 1,000 marks should be kept in a safe and secure place for that purpose and no other. The elder son, John, received a legacy of 300 marks (£200).

All the girls found husbands: Alice married Henry, son and heir of Sir Robert Sutton of Averham, so becoming the ancestor of Robert, Lord Lexington; Margaret's husband was John, younger son of Richard Barton of Middleton; and the other two, whose names are unknown, married Sir John Savage, K.G. and John Radcliffe of Radcliffe Tower.

John Byron was about fourteen when his father died. In 1473 he was one of a commission appointed to take into the king's hand all the castles and lordships, etc. of the late Sir Thomas Haryngton and Sir John Haryngton. The property of Sir Thomas, uncle of Byron's mother,

Alice Boteler, passed to the crown by reason of the minority of the heiresses, his two granddaughters.

Five years later, at thirty, Byron was elected Member of Parliament for Nottinghamshire, being then described as of Clayton, Lancashire,[31] in which county he is commemorated by a little 'ballad' based on a deed once owned by Colonel Chadwick, of the Lancashire Militia:

### A Trafford and Byron Feud

*by Thomas Barritt*

> In our Fourth Edward's fickle days
> A serious quarrel, story says,
> Took place near Rochdale, we are told,
> 'Twixt Trafford and a Byron bold.
> The cause was this, we understand,
> About some privilege of land.
> Oliver Chadwick, from Chadwick Hall,
> On Byron's part that day did fall;
> But afterwards it came to pass,
> Lord Stanley arbitrator was,
> Who fixed it upon this ground,
> Trafford should pay full sixty pound,
> In holy church at Manchester;
> And from this contract not to err,
> To Chadwick's heirs, to keep them quiet,
> And never more to move a riot:
> Ten marks at birth-day of Sir John,
> And ten at Martin's day upon,
> Each year, until the whole was paid;
> And to be friends again, he said.[32]

Unfortunately the poet does not explain the cause of this dispute.

Edward IV's uneasy reign ended with his death on 9 April 1483 and John Byron was among those summoned by writ to furnish themselves to receive the order of knighthood at the coronation of his twelve-year-old son, Edward V, which was fixed for June 22nd. The ceremony never took place, for the opposition of the Queen Mother's relatives induced the King's uncle, Gloucester, to abandon his role of Protector and to have himself proclaimed King as Richard III after it was established that Edward IV's children were bastards, he having been previously married to Lady Eleanor Butler. Richard's right to the crown was ratified by Parliament. His two nephews were last seen in their residence at the Tower, still a royal palace. Their subsequent fate remains in doubt.

Although rumours that they had been murdered on their uncle's orders may have been whispered, no public accusation was ever made; yet such allegations possibly shortened the King's reign. Two years later, in August of 1485, Henry Tudor, Earl of Richmond, landed at Milford Haven and advanced into the Midlands, while Richard assembled troops at Leicester. The armies met at Bosworth Field; the battle went against the Yorkists through defection of the Stanleys, who were related to Richmond and supported the Lancastrian cause. Richard died fighting bravely on the field and the new King usurped the crown as Henry VII.

Since Byron's Lancashire estates lay within the Stanley's powerful sphere, it was pragmatic for him to follow their lead: there is no good reason to doubt the tradition that he fought in Richmond's army at Bosworth, but the story of his chivalrous efforts to save the estates of Sir Gervase Clifton from confiscation cannot be substantiated, although family tradition holds that this was indeed the origin of the motto 'Crede Byron'—'Henry VII stamped this act of good faith and generous friendship with the motto ever since borne by the family. *Origin of the motto 'Crede Byron'*. Clifton supported King Richard. The legend was related in verse by Sir John Beaumont, elder brother of Francis Beaumont the dramatist:

> . . . If in the midst of such a bloody fight
> The name of friendship be not thought too light,
> Recount my Muse how Byron's faithfull love
> The dying Clifton did itself approve:
> For Clifton fighting bravely in the troope,
> Receives a wound, and now begins to droope:
> Which Byron seeing, though in armes his foe,
> In heart his friend, and hoping that the blow
> Had not been mortall, guards him with his shield
> From second hurts, and cries, 'Deare Clifton, yeeld;
> Thou hither cam'st, led by sinister fate,
> Against my first advice, yet now though late,
> Take this my counsell.' Clifton thus replied:
> 'It is too late, for I must now provide
> To seeke another life: live thou, sweet friend,
> And when thy side obtains a happy end,
> Upon the fortunes of my children looke;
> Remember what a solemne oath we tooke,
> That he whose part should prove the best in fight,
> Would with the conqu'rour trie his utmost might,
> To save the other's lands from rav'nous pawes,
> Which seaze on fragments of a lucklesse cause.
> My father's fall our house had almost drown'd,

[16]

But I by chance a boord in shipwracke found:
May never more such danger threaten mine,
Deale thou for them, as I would doe for thine.'
This said, his senses faile, and pow'rs decay,
While Byron calles; 'Stay, worthy Clifton, stay,
And heare my faithfull promise once againe,
Which if I breake, may all my deeds be vaine.'
But now he knowes, that vitall breath is fled,
And needlesse words are utter'd to the dead:
Into the midst of Richard's strength he flies,
Presenting glorious acts to Henrie's eyes,
And for his service he expects no more,
Than Clifton's sonne from forfeits to restore.[33]

Although this moving story seems worthy of belief, Clifton was not killed at Bosworth (he may have fought there) and if he favoured the losing cause he certainly contrived to make his peace with the victor because his estates were not forfeited and he held various public offices before his death in 1491. Perhaps they took a solemn oath and Sir John Beaumont, hearing the story as a family tradition (Beaumonts, Cliftons and Byrons were related by marriage), versified and dramatised it as fulfilled.

Byron's support for Henry Tudor brought its reward. Exactly a month after the battle, on 22 September 1485, Henry VII granted him for life the offices of Constable of Nottingham Castle and janitor or keeper of its gate; Steward and Keeper of Sherwood Forest; and keeper of various parks and woods in Nottinghamshire, at a yearly wage of 40 marks, with a yearly rent of £9 for the wage of nine foresters whom he was to appoint. Later that year he was appointed Sheriff of Nottinghamshire and Derbyshire for 1486 and was given £100 'as a reward'. During his year of office the Corporation of the Borough of Nottingham paid him their respects several times in the customary way, as the following entries in the Chamberlain's accounts show:

> Item paid, the xxvj. day of Janyver [1485/6], for a potell of swete wyne and a pottel of rede wyne gevyn to Maister Beron etc.       xijd.
> Item paid, ye xth day of Aprill, to Robert Hamerton for iij potelles of wyne gevyn to Maister Beron       xvd.[34]

They had previously given him a gallon of red wine and another of claret on 22 August 1485, probably on his way to or from Bosworth Field. Before Whitsuntide (1486) he received his deferred knighthood when the King was going to York during a tour of the kingdom.

The date of Byron's death is a little uncertain. Collins' *Peerage* quotes the following inscription on his monument at Colwick: 'Here lyes Sir

John Byron, Knt., late constable of Nottingham castle, master of Sherwood forest, custos or lieutenant of the Isle of Man, steward of Manchester colledge. Which John dyed the 3rd of May, in the year of our Lord 1488. On whose soul God have mercy. Amen.' As, however, he was appointed a commissioner to muster archers on 23 December 1488, the date of his death given in the *Victoria History of the County of Lancaster*— 3 January 1488/9—is more likely correct.[35] Like so much else at Colwick, the tomb has vanished and the inscription cannot be checked.

As he died childless and intestate, administration was granted to his widow Margery, daughter of Sir Robert Fowlehurst; and his brother Nicholas—eventually but not immediately—succeeded to the estates. Nicholas, too, had probably fought at Bosworth, and in 1486 his 'good and faithful services' to the new King were rewarded with an annuity of ten marks for life. He was High Sheriff of Nottinghamshire and Derbyshire in 1493.

His brother's death brought him little financial benefit at first, because the absence of a will meant the usual protracted legal delay before he could enjoy his inheritance in peace. Nearly ten years later he was still producing charters to prove his right of free service of Rochdale manor and the inquisition post mortem on his brother's possessions in the Duchy of Lancaster was also deferred until 1498. The statement then recorded that he was thirty years of age, which must be taken as a rough estimate, considering that his father died in 1462, but it suggests he was his brother's junior by some years. Not until 6 March 1500/1 was he granted license of entry, without proof of age, on all John's possessions.

Apparently he was in danger of being defrauded of them, because a month later he appeared before the Mayor and Justices of the Peace of Nottingham, when John Spendlove, a tanner, produced 'a gold ryng called "a signett" wherein is graven the prynt of meremayde with hire combe and hire glasse in eyder hand, and which signet was thoght shuld have bene Sir John Beron's, his broder's that is decessed'. But when an impression was taken the seal proved to be larger and the design reversed. Nicholas renounced his claim, but the seal was ordered to be destroyed. The apparent attempt at forgery had failed.[36]

Several years before, perhaps in pious despondency over his legal and financial worries, he had erected a window in Colwick Church with the inscription:

> PRAY FOR THE SOUL OF THE
> WORTHY MAN NICOLAS
> BYRON ESQ. AND OF JOAN HIS
> CONSORT WHO MADE THIS WINDOW
> IN THE YEAR 1496 AND 12TH OF H. 7TH.[37]

Lady Byron was daughter of Sir John Bussey or Bushey of Haugham, Lincolnshire; presumably he descended from that Sir John Bussey, Speaker, who supported Richard II and was consequently attainted and put to death in 1399 when Henry of Lancaster landed in England. (He makes a brief appearance in Shakespeare's *Richard II*, I, iv; II, ii III, i. He says: 'More welcome is the stroke of death to me/ Than Bolingbroke to England. Lords, farewell' [III, i, 30–31].)

Nicholas Byron became a Knight of the Bath on 17 November 1501, when the fifteen-year-old Arthur, Prince of Wales, was married to Katherine of Aragon. He died 13 January 1503/4 and asked to be buried in Colwick Church. By his will dated 20 December 1503,[38] he left his son 'my blessyng, with such landes as I ame bounden to leve hym in indentours made betwixt me and Rauffe Levyngton of Lughborow [Loughborough], merchaunt'; to his 'enterly belovid wife', for the term of her life, the manor of Over Colwick and the advowson of the church; and all his other lands and tenements in Over Colwick, Nether Colwick, and Adbolton, Nottinghamshire, and in Failsworth, Sunderland, Droylsden and Ancoats, in Lancashire. Although he had five daughters, he made provision for only three, so perhaps two had already married. Each of the three (unnamed in the will) was to have her 'fyndynge honestly' until she should be married, and a dowry of 400 marks. Directions, as usual, were given for the payment of his debts, 'especially . . . to William Perepoyntt and othir,' and Lady Byron was requested to dispose of his goods and chattels to pay for masses for the repose of his soul. To her, too, he entrusted 'ye gude rule, gydynge and preferement of my said childre[n] and heires'. The witnesses included his brother-in-law, Edmund Bussy, and William Elred, parson of Colwick.

Lady Byron was not long a widow: in October of 1505 she and Sir Gervase Clifton of Hodsock were granted a dispensation to marry, despite being twice related in the third degree. Clifton died in 1508 and as his wife survived him at least until 1519 she probably saw all her daughters by Sir Nicholas Byron safely married—Mary to Christopher Wymbish of Nocton (Lincolnshire); Elizabeth to Richard Ratcliff; Ellen to John, son of Thomas Booth; Jane to Matthew, son of Richard Kniveton of Bradley (Derbyshire); and Dorothy to Edmund Pierrepont of Holme Pierrepont, within a few miles of Colwick.

[19]

· I ·

# More the Baron than the Monk:
# The First Byron of Newstead

'The Mansion's self was vast and venerable,
　With more of the monastic than has been
Elsewhere preserved: the cloisters still were stable,
　The cells, too, and Refectory, I ween:
An exquisite small chapel had been able,
　Still unimpaired, to decorate the scene;
The rest had been reformed, replaced, or sunk,
And spoke more of the baron than the monk.

*Don Juan*, XIII, lxvi

DURING the four centuries that had passed since their first coming to England, the Byrons gradually consolidated their position among the county families of the Kingdom and, as a result of judicious marriages with heiresses, they now possessed considerable estates in Nottinghamshire, Lancashire, Yorkshire and Lincolnshire. Details are inevitably lacking, but we do know that they played an honourable part in the almost continual warfare of the Middle Ages; yet their gallantry was tempered by a strong vein of common sense which, without any suggestion of mere self-seeking, prevented them from being drawn into wild-cat schemes of rebellion that would have ruined the family fortunes.

The next John Byron succeeded his father, Sir Nicholas, when the prospects of further advancement were auspicious. Born about 1487, two years after the date often accepted as marking the close of the Middle Ages, and in the year of the battle of Stoke, which ended the hitherto constant internal strife, he grew up at the right moment to enjoy to the full the new and more luxurious style of living that distinguished the Tudor period.

On 10 January 1503/4 this young John began to assume the responsibilities of manhood by riding to Nottingham, apparently to represent his dying father at the Epiphany quarter sessions (Sir Nicholas Byron died three days later); and he was entertained by the Corporation at 'a breykefast the which was eytyn in the chapell on the southside the Chirch of Seynt Mare at the meting of Maister Meyre and his breder and of Maister Perpond and Maister Beryn [Byron] and Maister Nevill with oder'. On this or an earlier visit to the town, he and Master Pierrepont also shared a gallon of wine at William Tybbe's house—a gift which cost the Corporation 8*d*.[1]

Though only sixteen or seventeen, John was already married, for Sir Nicholas Byron had settled the manor of Cadney on his son's wife, Isabel, daughter of Ralph Lemyngton (or Levyngton), the Loughborough merchant named in Sir Nicholas' will, who shared with John's mother the wardship of the heir during his minority. Isabel's parentage does not appear to be given in any records during her life, but some later authorities state that her father was Peter Shelton or Shilton, of Lynne, Norfolk.[2] The Shiltons were related to the Lemyngtons, for a kinswoman named Alice Shilton is mentioned in Ralph's will, and both families were merchants of the wool staple. However, on the tomb erected by Little Sir John Byron to the memory of his father, the latter's first wife is commemorated as 'Isabel Byron daughter of Mr. Lemington' (the inscription surrounds the arms of the merchants of the staple), which makes it hard to understand how the mistake arose.

No doubt she brought her husband a substantial dowry, for Lemyngton was a man of wealth and of considerable standing in his own county, and though his daughter is not named in the published extracts from his will, that is probably because she was already provided for by her marriage settlement.[3]

John Byron had but recently come of age when the austere reign of Henry VII ended and the new young King, handsome and accomplished, was welcomed by his subjects with joyful relief. It was Henry VIII's ambition to play a leading part in the affairs of Europe, and England was soon embroiled again with the traditional enemy—France. England's victory at the Battle of the Spurs in August 1513 caused the French to retaliate by stirring up the Scots, and Byron was appointed one of the Nottinghamshire commissioners for seizing the property of Scotsmen. He may have fought at Flodden the following month.

During the ensuing brief interval of peace with both countries Byron spent some time at Court, where the King maintained a regal splendour in startling and welcome contrast to his father's shabby state. Feasting, dancing, hunting, tournaments, masks and pageantry were the order of the day and night and if Henry VIII, as was only right, outshone all others in richness of costume, the courtiers were not slow to follow his example. When the King spent Christmas at Eltham in 1515–16, a castle of timber was erected in the hall, and William Cornish and the children of the Chapel Royal performed 'the story of Troylous and Pandor richly apparelled'.[4] This was followed by a mock tournament between the knights of the wooden castle and three strange knights, after which there issued in turn from the castle a queen and her six ladies, seven minstrels, six lords and gentlemen, and six ladies, all arrayed in satin, white and green (the colours of the Tudor livery).

John Byron may have taken part in these festivities because by 1519 he had become a squire of the body. In that year he was appointed chief steward of the lordship of Stoke Bardolph (not far from Colwick), steward of the lordship of Rochdale, and one of the four foresters of Sherwood, with the remuneration of fourpence a day. A year later he received a warrant commanding him (as one of several representatives of Nottinghamshire) to wait upon the King with four 'able and seemly persons, well and conveniently apparelled and horsed, himself to appear as to his degree and honor belongeth . . . at the interview to be held between the Kings of France and England in the Marches of Calais.'[5]

Francis I of France and the Emperor Charles V, rival candidates for the crown of the Holy Roman Empire in 1519, were both angling for England's support, Wolsey's policy being to play one against the other. It was arranged, therefore, that after a brief visit to England by Charles in May, 1520, Francis and Henry should meet in June on the plain of Ardres—the meeting which, from its magnificence, was known as the Field of the Cloth of Gold. The chosen site lay between the marvellous summer palace specially erected for Henry at Guisnes and the Castle of Ardres that had been hastily repaired for Francis; and here 'was set a royall rich tent, all of clothe of gold, and riche embroudery of the kyng of Englandes, and diverse other hales and pauilions'; the tent was hung with the richest arras that ever before was seen, and the ground was spread with carpets 'of newe Turkey makyng, all full of beautie'.

On 7 June, Byron presumably rode among the squires who accompanied the King on horseback to the meeting place; the chroniclers have left us dazzling accounts of the rich apparel worn by the procession: 'clothe of golde, clothe of silver, velvettes, tinsins, sattins ambroudered and crymosyn sattens, with chains of gold of great and marvellous weight'—and the horses' trappings were of equal magnificence.[6]

The English King himself was clad in cloth of silver damask, thickly ribbed with cloth of gold, while the costume of the French King was covered with jewels. The splendour was maintained during the ensuing fortnight of feasting and jousting—the last brilliant flare of medieval pageantry before its extinction.

The Field of the Cloth of Gold was immediately followed by another meeting between Henry VIII and the Emperor Charles V at Gravelines, but this was less spectacular and it is unclear whether Byron was present or not.

On his return to England, John evidently remained in favour at Court and, after receiving his knighthood between July 1521 and November 1522, he was appointed to various offices of the kind held by his ancestor. In September 1523 a grant in survivorship of the office of keeper of Bestwood Park, with herbage and pannage and fourpence a day, was issued to Byron and to Sir Thomas Boleyn, the father of Henry's second Queen. Byron was Sheriff of Nottinghamshire and Derbyshire in 1524 and 1528, and in 1526 he was granted a lease for twenty-one years of the manor of Bolsover.

Up to this time, Sir John's domestic affairs have been wrapped in obscurity, but a scandal was brewing. His wife Isabel had not borne him any children (or if she had, none survived), and it is not unfair to assume that she suffered from indifferent health and lived quietly at Colwick while her husband enjoyed the gaieties of the Court or visited his property in Lancashire. We know that Sir Henry Willoughby of Wollaton visited her in November of 1523, when his steward conscientiously entered in his accounts the expenditure of fourpence on 'ale at Notyngam for my Mr. as he comme frome My Lady Beyryns'.[7]

At about this time, Byron formed a liaison with Mrs Elizabeth Halgh, wife of George Halgh of Halgh or Hough Hall, Moston, Lancashire, and daughter of William Consterdine or Casterden, of Blackley in the same county, which resulted in the birth of a son (known to later times as 'Little Sir John with the Great Beard') about 1527—the year in which Byron's royal master made his first application to the Pope for a 'divorce' from Katherine of Aragon. According to Booker, the Consterdines were not of very high status, though among the earliest known residents in Blackley; but at the foot of Sir John's tomb at Newstead are the arms: quarterly, Byron and Clayton, impaling Constantine of Cheshire (or, six fleurs de lys sable).[8]

Although the date of the first Lady Byron's death is unknown (the lettering on the Newstead tomb is almost illegible), it was probably she and not her successor who visited Nottingham Castle in 1529 or 1530, when the Corporation provided her with a pottell of wine at fourpence and a gallon at eightpence; and when the Mayoress and her sisters drank with her at Dalderbury's.[9] The date of George Halgh's death is also a mystery, but certainly the liaison continued for some years before both parties were free to marry, and a daughter, Ann, was also born before their union.

After receiving in 1528 the grant in survivorship (with William West) of the manor of Clipstone and the reversion of the office of warden forester of Thorneywood, both in Sherwood Forest, Sir John Byron appeared in the roll of Parliament in 1529 as member for Nottinghamshire, with Sir John Markham. In the next year he was one of the commissioners appointed to hold an inquisition into the possessions of Cardinal Wolsey, whose recent fall from grace was soon to be followed by his death.

It is to be feared that Byron sometimes misused the powers granted to him because three years later Thomas Cromwell, Wolsey's successor in the King's favour, had in his keeping certain articles touching Sir John's 'misdemeanors for hunting in the King's forest of Sherwood'; but either he had not poached very seriously, or Henry was too much in love to care, for there is no record of his punishment; and in June he was present at the Coronation of Anne Boleyn, being one of the servitors attending 'the Queen's grace, the Bishop, and the ladies sitting at the Queen's board in the Great Hall of Westminster'.[10]

By 1535, the year after the passing of the Act of Supremacy, Cromwell, who as Chancellor and Vicar-General was now all-powerful in matters spiritual and temporal, was preparing his attack on the religious houses, and Sir John Byron was a commissioner for Nottinghamshire to enquire into the tenths of spiritualities. The suppression of the lesser monasteries in 1536 caused serious risings in Lincolnshire. They spread to the north and for many months Byron's time was fully occupied in helping to put down this Pilgrimage of Grace. On 6 October the Earl of Shrewsbury wrote to the King that he had just arrived at his 'poor cot at Herdewyke' (Hardwick), in order to be nearer the King's servants in Derbyshire, whom he had warned to meet him at Nottingham on Monday night (9 October), as this was thought by his son, Francis Talbot, and by Sir John Byron and others to be the meetest time and place. He added a postscript, however, saying that because the rebels were expected at Newark on Sunday, where he could not be ready to meet them, he intended to be in Nottingham on Sunday night with all the force he could.[11] In 1537 the King wrote to Sir John for information on the course of the rebellion in Lancashire. The revolt was put down with great severity, followed by the gradual dissolution of the greater monasteries. Byron was one of the King's representatives who accepted the surrender of Furness Abbey on 5/6 April, and in May he was on the jury for the trial of the northern rebels. 1538 found him occupied with various commissions, and a fortnight's stay in London to answer the Privy Seal about the tithes of Rochdale.

Henry VIII had been a widower since 1537, when Jane Seymour had died after giving birth to the long-desired heir, Prince Edward, and in his loneliness he was easily persuaded by Cromwell to agree to marry Anne of Cleves 'sight unseen'. This time Byron was among the knights who lined her route on Saturday, 30 January 1539/40, when she came from Dartford to Shooter's Hill, Blackheath, at the foot of which was a very gorgeous tent or pavilion, 'and there her Grace entered and shifted her and tarried a certain space banquetting,' while the King marched through the park to meet her.[12] The first sight of his ill-favoured bride was almost too much for Henry; reluctantly he allowed the marriage to take place, but immediately afterwards persuaded poor Anne to agree to a divorce, and consoled himself with the infinitely more attractive Catherine Howard, his 'Rose without a thorn'. Cromwell's error of judgment cost him his head.

Byron, however, was too much occupied with his own affairs to pay much attention to all this. The suppression of the monasteries provided a golden opportunity for the King to replenish his treasury by sales of the confiscated property and for his wealthier subjects to acquire houses and estates that would enable them to live on a far grander scale than hitherto. Newstead Priory, having been surrendered to Dr John London on 21 July 1539, was placed in the custody of Sir John Byron, who was loathe to part with his charge; and after months, doubtless, of negotiation, he received his reward. On 28 May 1540, 'both in consideration of the good, true and faithful service which our beloved servant John Byron of Colewyke . . . knight, has rendered us before this time, and for the sum of eight hundred and ten pounds' Henry VIII granted him 'all the house and site, ground and soil, of the late Monastery or Priory of Newstede within the Forest of Sherewode . . . recently dissolved; and all the church, belfry and cemetery of the same . . . and all our messuages, houses, buildings, barns, stables, dovecotes, pools, fishponds, kitchen gardens, orchards, gardens, lands and soil, both within and without the aforesaid site and adjoining and neer the site, enclosure, ambit, circuit and precinct of the same late Monastery or priory.'[13] With the Priory were granted some 750 acres of land, the adjacent manor of Papplewick, with its stream and fishery, and the rectory of Papplewick church; the common or waste lands of Ravenshead and Kighill [ancient tracts of Sherwood Forest granted by Henry II to Newstead in the foundation deed], Bulwell Wood, and smaller parcels of land, mainly in Linby and Hucknall. All the property was to be held in chief of the King by the service of the tenth part of a knight's fee, with a yearly payment of £4 10s. to the Crown, 3s. to the Archbishop of York for the synodals of Papplewick rectory, 4s. 2d. to the Archdeacon of York for the procuration of the same, and 53s. 4d. for the stipend of a chaplain to serve Papplewick church.

Founded between 1163 and 1173 for Augustinian or Black Canons, the Priory had received many gifts of land in Nottinghamshire and elsewhere during its all but four centuries of existence, and the estate granted to Byron was but a part of its extensive possessions; but Sir John may fairly be said to have made an excellent bargain and, although fifty-three at the time of the purchase, he enjoyed his new property for another quarter century. It was never actually more than a priory, but has been called Newstead Abbey since 1541, perhaps because Sir John was not reluctant to magnify the importance of his acquisition. He must have spent much money in converting it into a private residence, because the buildings were already old and it is unlikely that the canons had spent much on the fabric during their last precarious years. Indeed, Leland, the antiquary, who rode that way from Mansfield about 1540 (probably just before Byron bought it), wrote: 'A little or I cam to the edge of this woodde I left about a quarter of a mile on the right hand the ruines of Newstede, a priory of chanons.'

It was easy for Byron to superintend the work of alteration, as Colwick Hall was only twelve miles away and the old highway from Nottingham to Mansfield ran through the Newstead estate at the back of the Abbey, as Leland described it. He has, inevitably, been accused of vandalism in pulling down the church; yet few people even now would care to have a very large and probably draughty church attached to their house; fewer still could afford its maintenance. Moreover, demolition provided abundant stone that could be used economically to restore the house—more, perhaps, than was actually needed, for carved stones can still be found scattered in the rock gardens. The Angelus bell of the Priory, inscribed 'Ave Maria', Byron is supposed to have given to Hucknall church, where it serves as the treble bell. The destruction of the church was thorough: only the great west front, with the Virgin and Child looking down from the high gable, remains to indicate the beauty that has vanished. Whether Sir John spared this much from superstition or for aesthetic reasons, it is impossible to say; but the charm and dignity of the Abbey depend largely on the survival of this fragment.

Byron preserved the original plan of the domestic quarters of the Abbey. The cloisters still remain almost untouched since they were rebuilt by the monks about 1450, except that the original sloping roofs have been replaced by flat ceilings to carry galleries giving access to the upper rooms. The prior's own rooms and the great hall in which he entertained distinguished guests were available for Byron's use while reconstruction went on; the refectory needed little alteration to transform it into a handsome drawing-room. The east wing required most attention, but Sir John's alterations have been obscured by the work of his descendants, particularly during the Stuart period. At some time the canons' dormitory on the upper floor was sub-divided into large bedrooms; below, the south transept of the church became a secular room and the chapter-house was retained as a private chapel. The Gothic fountain was moved from the cloister garth to the court in front of the Abbey, where it is shown in many engravings until restored to its original position by Colonel Thomas Wildman, who bought Newstead from the poet in 1817.

Newstead was included in the itinerary of Henry VIII's 'summer gests' in 1541, but these tours were planned to extend over several years and few of them materialised, the King's activity being curtailed by increasing ill-health. Because the entertainment of a Tudor monarch meant a heavy drain on the loyal subject's purse, the restoration of the Abbey might have been long delayed by a royal visit. We do not know when Sir John Byron himself began to live there. In the early years of his ownership military duties took him away from home, when France and Scotland renewed their old alliance. He was at home (apparently at Colwick) in September 1542, when J. Chaworth wrote to the Countess of Rutland that Byron was one of the Nottinghamshire captains who were to go under the King to Scotland; on 7 October Sir John Harryngton, as Treasurer of the Wars, was instructed to pay him £93 6s. 8d. for the coats of 560 men and £84 for conduct money of himself, two captains, three petty captains and three hundred soldiers from Colwick to Newcastle—120 miles. At the end of October a similar warrant provided for the return of his troop to Colwick from Ridingburne, in Scotland.[14]

In January 1542/3, when High Sheriff for the third time, he visited the Earl of Rutland or his family at Belvoir, where Lady Byron had been entertained in 1541: ale was brought specially for him 'because he cowd drencke no bere'. A few weeks later the controller of the Earl's household paid 3s. 4d. (quite a handsome tip at that time) 'to Syr Jhon Berynges serwonde [servant] that rode alle nyght to brenge my Laydy a fatte dowe [doe] that was sent to Austen Portter's dowghters marage'.[15] Next year Byron went abroad again, being appointed 'to go in person into France with the King's Majesty in his Grace's battle'.[16] By May 1545 he was living at Newstead with his family, including his Aunt Thomasine, widow of Edmund Bussey of Haydor, Lincolnshire, who then made her will, bequeathing to her nephew and his wife two rings, one set with a diamond, the other with a ruby, he to have the choice with a royal and she the other with a gold angel.[17]

The religious reforms of Edward VI's reign were unlikely to please Byron. Perhaps he was not sorry that advancing years (he was sixty when Henry VIII died in 1547) gave him an excuse to spend more time at home. He was by no means idle, acting as High Sheriff for the fourth and last time in 1552. His lieutenancy of Sherwood frequently brought him into contact with the Earl of Rutland, who had held the Wardenship of the Forest since 1524—an office which became practically hereditary in the Manners family. Sometimes they hunted together. Among the Rutland archives are letters from Byron to the Earl about various business, such as a sale of wood from Sherwood Forest for the repair of the great lodge in Bestwood Park adjoining Newstead. On 10 April 1557 he wrote:

> Your servant Watson has killed a stag which for this time of year is full of flesh. He could not have chosen a better within three miles compass of Newstead. They were so bare of flesh last summer and this winter that many hardly escaped with their lives. I was assessed before you for two hundred marks [£133 6s. 8d.] and twenty pounds, but a servant of my brother Sir Nicholas Sterlay [Strelley] has put me down for two hundred and twenty pounds by oversight. Please have the books amended.[18]

Tax claims and careless clerks are clearly no new thing. His forest duties naturally included attendance at the swanimotes, lesser courts of the forest, where any dryness in his task was counteracted by the usual gift of wine: at the Blidworth 'swynmote' in 1557 he was given a gallon of wine at 1s. 4d.[19]

Byron's alterations at Newstead included the installation of three curious overmantels which, though differing in detail, are alike in general features, bearing heads of men and women in Tudor costume and heads of Moors; some are carved in profile, like medallions, in the compartments of the panelling; others project from it. One or more of them was said to have been at Colwick before being brought to Newstead. The overmantel in the Prior's parlour bears the Byron arms with the inscription, 'Sir Iohn Birron MDLVI', and it is tempting to believe that the bearded head in the centre of the bottom row represents Sir John himself. There have been many conjectures about the significance of the design, which resembles panelling at Smithell's Hall in Lancashire, then owned by the Bartons, who must have been known to Byron in both their northern and Nottinghamshire branches. The profile heads are typical of Italian workmanship of the time, but which owner set the fashion to be envied and copied by his neighbour is a point as yet unsettled. A tradition declares that the carvings commemorate an incident in the Crusades, when a Byron rescued a Christian maiden from a Saracen; and Thomas Moore suggested in his life of the poet that this story was the inspiration of the poet's lines on the 'mail-covered barons'.

Realising that he could no longer hope for legitimate issue, Byron took measures to ensure the succession of his son by Elizabeth Halgh. In 1547 he reached agreement with John Masse and John Arderon touching the manor of Clayton with its appurtenances in Manchester; a fine was levied whereby Byron having acknowledged their right, Masse and Arderon granted the property 'to have and to hold to him and his heirs male of his body, in default to remain to John Byron, bastard son of the said John Byron . . .'. It was a substantial estate, comprising 300 messuages, 3 water-mills, 3 fulling-mills, 4,000 acres of land, 500 acres of meadow, 4,000 acres of pasture, 1,000 acres of wood, 1,000 acres of turbary, 500 acres of furze and heath, 3 dovecotes, £8 of rent, with view of frankpledge, liberties and franchise in Clayton, Manchester, Droyls-den, Failsworth, Blackley, Gorton, Oldham, Crompton, Rochdale, Butterworth, Spotland and Didsbury; so that the younger Byron was placed on a secure footing.

His father's plans for him did not end here, but that was considered sufficient for a while. In 1560, about the time of the birth of his grandson (yet another John), the elder Byron founded Rochdale Grammar School—more or less under compulsion. Archbishop Parker, the patron of Rochdale, had commenced proceedings against Sir John for failing to pay the stipends of the clergy as he had covenanted to do when he became farmer of the tithes of Rochdale, Byron's excuse being that he did not actually enjoy the whole tithes, owing to the existence of certain ancient leases made by the Abbey of Whalley before the Dissolution of the Monasteries. As usual, the parishioners suffered most, because they found it difficult to 'paye the preste his wagis by contrybushon', and were in consequence often deprived of the services of the church. The suit proving long and very expensive, Sir John begged the Archbishop to stay proceedings, to which the Archbishop consented on condition that Byron give, in addition to the annual rent, £17 a year to fund a master and undermaster for a free grammar school to be founded in Rochdale. Sir John willingly agreed and his son gave a promissory note guaranteeing payment of arrears. As usual, the Byrons had difficulty finding the money and in February 1564/5 the Archbishop was obliged to write to the younger Byron:

> After my hearty commendations, gentle Mr. Byron. For that I desire the school to go forward at Rochdale, I would be glad to hear from you what sums ye have in your hands remaining of the stipend of the vicar and curates unpaid, which shall be employed that way, saving to the vicar now thereat from the time of his incumbency his portion due, as also what good help may otherwise be perceived of any of the parish and country agreeably to such expectation as I was partly put in by you and of others,

whereby I shall the rather travail hereafter to extend further any good will to the same, and see cause to give you thanks accordingly. And thus, with commendations to Sir John Byron your father, I commend you to the grace of God as myself. Your friend, M. Cant.[20]

In 1561 came a second family scandal, which Sir John and Lady Byron were in no position to censure. Their daughter Ann evidently inherited her parents' views on marriage, because her husband, Cuthbert Scholfield of Scholfield Hall, Rochdale, brought a suit for adultery against Michael Goodricke in the court of the Bishop of Chester. The principal deponent was a tailor employed at the Hall in 'makeing a gown for Mris. Ann and other apparel for her husband'. Shocked by what he saw and eager, doubtless, to be first with unwelcome news, he went to meet Cuthbert and his mother on their return from Rochdale market. Goodricke made his escape through a window, followed quickly by Ann; Cuthbert 'got to his sword' and would have followed and killed them, but was apparently restrained.[21]

Old Sir John was on the commission of peace for Nottinghamshire (with his son) as late as 1562, in which year he was also *custos rotulorum*. The last record of his activities shows that he was still well enough in the spring of 1565 to dine at Wollaton with Sir Anthony Strelley, two young ladies of Huntingdon, and other visitors to the number of forty. He died two years later (3 May 1567) at what was then considered the great age of about eighty and, in accordance with his wish, he was buried in Colwick church.

His will, made nearly nineteen years earlier, begins with a devout and fervent prayer for the forgiveness of his sins, followed by a long confession of faith, affirming his belief in the Trinity, the doctrine of transubstantiation and the resurrection and his abhorrence of 'the Manaches, Th'arrians, Th'anna-baptists and the Sacramentaries, and all other heretiks with there damnable sectes and opinions'. His lack of sympathy with the Reformation is indicated by his desire 'that an honeste preiste be hyred to synge or saye masse for my soull, &c., within the parishe church of Collwike for 10 years, with 10$^{li}$ for his yearlie stipend'; this has sometimes been quoted as evidence of the latest foundation of a chantry by writers who have ignored the alternative provided in his will which presumably came into force, chantries having been suppressed before his death. With typical Byron commonsense he realised that suppression of chantries might prove permanent and added: 'but if the said stipend by any lawe or lawes heartofore maid and hereafter to be revived be maid to cease, it to go to the poore and nedie people, amendinge and reparinge of highe wayes and briggs [bridges] or other charitable deides'.

[ 31 ]

Other bequests were few and simple:

> To the prisoners in the Common gaole at Nottingham xls., at York,
> Lincoln, and Lancaster, 20*s.* each. . . . To John Byron, my base sonne, all
> my manors, lands, leases, &c., whatsoever, he to be sole executor. My
> verye speciall and trustie cosyns and frendes Sir Jervase Clifton, Sir
> George Perpoynte, Sir John Atherton, knightes, Edmund Ashton of
> Chattertoune, and Edward Holland, Esquiers, to be his coadjutors—each
> to have 10$^{li}$. The right Honorable and my singular good Lord th'erle of
> Ruttland and my brother Sir Nicholas Strelley, knight, supervisors—he
> to have 20$^{li}$, and my brother 10$^{li}$, desiringe my said verie good lorde to
> vouchesaife to take paynes for me herin to accepte that small legacie given
> and bequithed unto hym in good parte althoughe yt be to baise for his
> honor.[22]

· 2 ·

# High Crested Banners:
# Little Sir John and his Successors

The heralds of a warrior's haughty reign,
High crested banners wave thy walls within.

*Elegy on Newstead Abbey*

THE second lay owner of Newstead, famous in his later years as 'Little Sir John with the great beard,'[1] was middle-aged when he succeeded his father, but he had not yet come into any prominence. Although his childhood may have been an uneasy period, at least until his parents were free to marry, his education probably followed the usual course and, as we have seen, by the time he was twenty or twenty-one, his father had begun to make his future inheritance secure.

The only reference to his military service appears in a letter of December from Sir Francis Leek to Robert Cecil, written in December 1559. Leek was commanded by Queen Elizabeth to hire 300 footmen in Derbyshire to serve with him at Berwick; he added in a postscript that, as he heard Mr John Byron would rather that anyone else had the 100 footmen he was appointed to have, he (Leek) was disposed to have them himself, as he had not served with so small a charge for the past fifteen years.

Byron had not yet been knighted nor, indeed, had he held any public office except the minor post of Deputy Ranger of Thorneywood Chase about 1557/8. Some time before 1554 he married Alice, daughter of Sir Nicholas Strelley, on whom her father-in-law settled the manors of Hibaldstow and Cadney, in Lincolnshire; and by 1567 three sons had certainly been born to them and probably also their three daughters. The entire family (with a fourth son, of whose existence this is the only record) is portrayed, dutifully kneeling behind the parents, on the front of the altar tomb that John Byron raised to his father's memory in Colwick Church—a tactful evasion of the dubious status of the deceased's own children, who were customarily shown in this position.

[ 33 ]

Apart from performing the duties of High Sheriff in 1570, Byron quietly managed his new estates and brought up his young family, the eldest of whom, Nicholas, was admitted a Fellow Commoner of Queen's College, Cambridge, in 1571. That same year his father, influenced, no doubt, by the Strelleys, who owned pits in Strelley and Bilborough, began to speculate in coal mining by taking over the lease of Selston manor and its coal resources. How far his venture prospered is not clear. The Strelleys' pits, in the end, brought them more financial embarrassment than profit, and for many years they were in the habit of borrowing from their wealthier kinsman. By 1597 these debts amounted to more than £10,000; Sir Philip Strelley obtained security for this sum by leasing his manors of Strelley and Bilborough to Sir John Byron for twenty-one years at a nominal rent of £2 a year, together with several other manors in Derbyshire and the coal they contained. After making what profit he could from them, Byron sold the remainder of the lease in 1603 to Huntingdon Beaumont of Leicestershire.

John Byron's inheritance was great, but living expenses increased and he conformed to contemporary custom by maintaining a very large household. Lords of the manor were expected, for one thing, to keep open house, particularly at Christmas time, the outstanding example in Nottinghamshire being Byron's contemporary, 'Good Sir William Holles' of Houghton who, from All Hallowtide to Candlemas, allowed anyone to share his bountiful hospitality for three days without being asked who he was or whence he came. The first Sir John Byron of Newstead, in his later years, had replaced his former minstrels (whom the Corporation of Nottingham had rewarded with a shilling in 1537 or 1538) by a troop of players who performed before his guests on special occasions, and at other times toured the neighbourhood as 'Sir John Byron's players'.[2] His son, however, apparently did not care for this novel type of entertainment, as the latest references to the company are dated 1569, when they performed in Nottingham and Leicester. He reverted to 'muscycioners', on whom the Corporation bestowed 6*d.* in 1589 or 1590.

Profits from the mines were not lavished solely on pleasure or ostentation: 1571 saw the foundation of the Byron Charity at Hucknall by John's gift to Lancelot Rolleston and other trustees of Broomhill Close, containing 16 acres of land. (When remeasured in 1871 it was found to contain over 21 acres.) It was to be let yearly to persons who would give the best rent for it; of the rents and profits one-third was to be divided each year among poor people of the parish; one-third to be spent on repairing and beautifying the church; and one-third on any necessary causes 'behooveful, profitable or expedient within and for the town of

Hucknall'. Unlike all too many similar foundations, the Byron Charity has survived and increased greatly in value; and in 1950 £405 was divided equally among the poor, the church, and voluntary institutions. The third share was formerly devoted to hospitals until they were taken over by the state.

*

Domestic affairs claimed much of Byron's attention when his family grew to marriageable age. The will of Sir John Atherton, of Atherton in Lancashire, provided in 1573 for a marriage between his son and heir, John, and one of the daughters of John Byron of Newstead; and the choice fell upon the second girl, Elizabeth. Three years later Byron lost his eldest son, Nicholas, who had probably been admitted at Gray's Inn in 1573. His brother Anthony, who had followed the third son, John, to Queens' College, Cambridge, administered his will that year. In January of 1577 Anthony startled his family and scandalised the University with a secret marriage in the best romantic tradition. The bride was Margaret, daughter of Nicholas Beaumont of Cole-orton in Leicestershire, who at that time was staying with his family in Cambridge in a house very near Trinity Church, where the wedding took place one Thursday[3], without banns or licence, in the presence of two Masters of Art and four members of Mr Beaumont's household. Neither Beaumont nor his wife attended the ceremony, but as they were at home, or at least not out of the town, it was suspected that they were not entirely ignorant of the affair.

The Vice-Chancellor, Dr Roger Goade, after consulting the Heads of Colleges, took the Masters of Art and the minister into custody, but could not deal with the errant bridegroom because he had been secretly whisked away into the country, presumably by the Beaumonts. To make matters worse, it was rumoured that young Anthony Byron had previously become engaged to 'another yonge gentlewoman of the town'. All these details were recounted by the agitated Vice-Chancellor in a letter[4] to Lord Burghley, then Lord Treasurer of England and Chancellor of the University, whose advice and support he desired to enable him to face the natural wrath of Byron senior at the lax supervision of his heir.

Nearly quarter of a century later the scandal was still remembered in Cambridge, being cited as one of the 'contracts and marriages with mean persons of the town' which were encouraged by the town's resistance to the right of search 'for light persons or suspected of evil', claimed by the University. Sir John was so incensed by the marriage that, although he could not entirely disinherit Anthony, he planned to leave an equal part of his estate to his younger son, John; but he was spared this trouble, as we shall see.

On 20 July 1577 John Byron signed the marriage settlement of his eldest daughter, Isabel, and accompanied her in August to Skeffington (in Leicestershire again), the home of her husband Thomas Skeffington who, only twenty-six, had already acted as High Sheriff of his county, to which office he was appointed again in 1588 and 1599. He had another estate at Arley, Warwickshire, and altogether this would appear a satisfactory marriage, in her family's eyes at least. Mary, the youngest daughter, was also comfortably settled either before or very soon after Isabel, marrying Richard Assheton of Middleton, Lancashire, while he was still a minor.[5]

Newstead was by now regarded as the family's principal residence, and Colwick is less frequently mentioned;[6] but periods were also spent at Clayton Hall, near Manchester, and at Royton (or Ryton) Hall, near Oldham, which was largely rebuilt by 'Little' Sir John. (This estate had belonged to the Byrons since 1301 and was sold in 1662. The Hall was 'new fronted' about 1750.) Byron was High Sheriff of Lancashire three times—in 1572, 1580 and 1590—and in his first year of office, when the Earl of Derby was buried, he was one of the eight gentlemen, assisted by eight yeomen, who carried the body from the chariot to the hearse in Ormskirk church.

When at Newstead he continued one of his father's duties by seeing that venison was supplied to the Earl of Rutland, to whom he wrote on 29 December 1575: 'I send by this bearer as good a hind as you are like to have this year out of the forest.'[7] From time to time he was summoned to Nottingham to attend musters of the militia in the Castle yard and shared with his fellow-justices a gallon of Gascony wine and ½ lb of sugar, provided by the Corporation. The Mickletorn (or Leet) Jury complained to the Mayor in 1577 that Alderman Robert Brownlow had not fulfilled his promise to talk with Mr Byron about the tolls and that therefore many burgesses still paid tolls in fairs and markets from which, by the terms of the town's charters, they should be free; but they do not make it clear whether Byron was in any way responsible for the illegal exaction, or whether his influence was sought to redress their grievance.

Having disposed of his daughters satisfactorily, he now felt free to devote more time to public affairs, and was High Sheriff of Nottinghamshire in 1579. He was knighted by Queen Elizabeth at Westminster on Sunday, 24 January 1579/80 but, unlike his father, he does not appear to have spent much, if any, time at court. Not long afterwards he was called upon to administer the estate of his mother who, the scandal of her youth forgotten, was buried on 25 July in the Collegiate Church of Manchester, in which town she had apparently lived since her husband's death. The most costly item in the inventory of her goods (total value £11 7s. 4d.) were a feather bed, bolster and pillow, 30s.; a gown of damask furred through with lamb, 26s. 8d.; and a gentlewoman's saddle with a cover of velvet and bridle, 25s. 8d.; the other household wares were few and of comparatively little worth.

At year's end, when preparing to remove his household to Lancashire for his second turn of duty as High Sheriff, Sir John wrote to the Commissioners for musters asking to be exempt from sending men to the musters in Nottinghamshire. Whether his application was successful or not, the expenses of his year of office were yet sufficiently heavy to compel him to raise a mortgage on some of his lands in Colwick and Sneinton.

His eldest son being dead and his second son childless, Little Sir John gladly welcomed the birth of an heir in 1583 to his third son and namesake, John, for whom he had arranged a very satisfactory and (as it proved) happy marriage, in August 1580, to Margaret FitzWilliam. Her father, Sir William FitzWilliam of Milton in Northamptonshire, was Lord Deputy of Ireland (where he lived like a prince), and her mother one of the Sidneys of Penshurst. (According to some authorities, twin sons were born, John and Nicholas; but the baptism of Nicholas is recorded in the Colwick registers on 6 March 1595/6.)

Before the marriage, Sir John had settled property in Colwick on his son which, if the latter had no heirs, was to go to the scapegrace Anthony for life, and then to the heir apparent of Sir John. Now, however, the line of succession was secured, and before October of 1587 Margaret's husband became his father's heir upon the bizarre death of Anthony Byron.

Hunting one day with his father, he ordered something to be put under the saddle of a young servant's horse, in order to enjoy his alarm when the animal proved restive. The device succeeded only too well, but Anthony laughed so immoderately that he died, 'and turned their mirth into mourning; lieving a sad caveat by his example, to take heed of hazarding men's precious lives for a little sport'.[8]

Summoned from Newstead to Lancashire in September of 1587 by the Earl of Derby, who required him to take his place of squire during the Earl's absence, Sir John Byron attended to his northern estates and, after spending a few days with Lord Derby at Knowsley at the end of the following January, found himself plunged into law suits over the manor of Rochdale. He had obtained a thirty-one year lease from the Crown in 1585 and wanted to improve the wastes to pay his costs; so in February 1588 the Chancellor granted a commission empowering the lord of the manor and the tenants to divide the wastes equally into two.

The coal mines already open were demised to Byron. The matter was not settled easily, however, for in 1594/5 Sir John appeared as plaintiff against David Holt and others about the wastes and commons of Rochdale and, in the end, he probably lost more than he gained.

He visited the Earl of Derby again in January 1589, this time at Lathom House, and later in the year the Earl was instructed by the Privy Council to summon Byron and investigate a complaint made against him by the Earl of Huntingdon that he and his son-in-law, John Atherton, had not performed covenants agreed upon for the Earl's indemnities. Huntingdon had further complained that Sir John's letter to him implied that he (Huntingdon) was inclined to convey Atherton's land to his own use and profit rather than to gratify Atherton, which the Privy Council declared to be unjustified. This occasioned further visits to Knowsley in the autumn. A year later the Council summoned Sir John to London—with what result does not appear. He probably broke his journey to or from town in Nottinghamshire because some time during this year the Mayor and aldermen of Nottingham visited Sir John at Colwick, taking the customary tribute of wine and sugar and dispensing half-a-crown in tips to the butler, cook and porter.

1591 allowed him more tranquil periods at Newstead where, in July, he entertained the fourteen-year-old Roger Manners, fifth Earl of Rutland, on his way to Cambridge. The boy had been there twice in the previous year, when his mother instructed her steward to pay him £3 4s. 4d. for his journey thither and for 'some necessaries'; perhaps he had tipped the servants too lavishly, for on this occasion she restricted his allowance to one shilling. A little later[9] the Earl of Shrewsbury wrote from Sheffield Lodge to his uncles John and Roger Manners at Haddon: 'I am just ready to go a hunting with Sir John Byron's hounds, if the rain will permit.' Byron was Officer of Sherwood Forest for Newstead, Papplewick and Blidworth, and evidently all members of the Manners family came in for their share of venison at Christmas, for this same Roger Manners the elder wrote from the Savoy to his brother on 29 December 1595 that Sir John Byron had sent him four pies of a dainty roe.

Little Sir John's notoriously short stature was by no means a sign of frailty and though he was nearing his seventieth year he still attended musters of the militia, readily contributed rye, malt and money to the relief of the plague-stricken poor, and divided his time between Nottinghamshire and Lancashire. On 29 April 1596 Dr John Dee, Warden of Manchester College, recorded in his diary:

Sir John Byron, Knight, and Mr John Byron, Esquier, dyned with me in colledge. I moved the matter of having xijd. an aker of hay ground of his tenants. He promised well. [The pertinacious Doctor did not let the matter drop, and on Friday, 3 September, added:] I rid to Royton (7 myles from Manchester) to Sir John Byron knight for a quietness . . . to talk with him about the controversy between the Colledg & his tenants, &c. He pretended that we have part of Faylesworth Common within our Newton Heath, which can not be proved I am sure. We wer agreed that James Traves (being his bayly) and Francis Nutthall, his servant for him, shold with me understand all circumstances, and so duely to procede, &c.

In 1597, again High Sheriff of Nottinghamshire, Sir John purchased Bulwell Hill or Rise, enlarging his Bulwell Wood estate on which he had built Bulwell Wood Hall. (A stone in the basement reportedly bore the date 'September 24, 1584' and it is thought to be the first stone mansion erected there, though there may have been earlier buildings. The Hall was destroyed by fire in 1937.) He probably intended it as a residence for younger members of the family—it was conveniently situated a few miles from Newstead. Moreover, he engaged in the popular sport of encroachment and four years later the tenants of the Royal Manor of Bulwell successfully brought a suit against him to recover their right of common in the pasture called Bulwell Moor.

Early in 1599 Sir John suffered the loss of his wife Alice, who was buried at Colwick (doubtless with much pomp and magnificence) on 4 February—a month before the wedding of her eldest grandson. In the same year her husband sat for his portrait—the first Byron of whose features we have an authentic record. The half-length painting, by an unknown artist of no little merit, shows an old but erect and dignified man with a long, white silky beard which amply justifies his nickname. The oval face with high cheekbones and long beaky nose is lit by shrewd, kindly eyes, with a touch of humour. One outstretched hand across his rich but sober costume shows the long, slender fingers characteristic of the family; a ring adorns the little finger. It is easy to understand the impression he made on his contemporaries and the legendary fame that survived him.[10]

In March 1603, when it was clear that Queen Elizabeth could not live much longer, and the claims to the throne of the Lady Arabella Stuart were causing some uneasiness, Sir Henry Brouncker wrote from Hardwick to Sir Robert Cecil:

If her Majesty should miscarry . . . Mr. Wm. Cavendish being indeed but a weak man for such a purpose . . . I do not see how she [Arabella] can be kept in this place two days. . . . Sir John Biren is very old & his son at her devotion & not well reported off; all the gentlemen in these parts as unfit for one respect or other.[11]

The younger Byron, indeed, was so much at her devotion that he allowed her to take his nine-year-old daughter Margaret with her to Court. As it happened, however, the succession of James VI of Scotland was accepted without protest and on 31 March, with ringing of bells, the new monarch was solemnly proclaimed King of England at the Market Cross in Mansfield by Sir John Byron, Roger Ayscough (High Sheriff), Henry Chaworth, John Byron the younger, and other gentlemen.

Three weeks later, on 21 April, the younger Byron was knighted at Worksop by the new King on his way south from Scotland. Queen Anne and the young Prince Henry followed in June and were entertained 'with musicke sweet' at Newstead before passing through Nottingham on their journey to London—a fitting climax to Little Sir John's reputation for magnificent hospitality.

Whatever his son's feelings might be, old Sir John showed himself a loyal supporter of the new monarch when he was called upon by the Privy Council to arrest his neighbour, Sir Griffin Markham, on a charge of 'dangerous practice against his Majesty's person and the state' (conspiring to place Arabella Stuart on the throne). His unsuccessful attempt to execute the warrant was reported to the Bishop of London and the other Commissioners in the following letter dated 16 July 1603:

> Upon the peruse of the Council's warrant and your lordship's letter we endeavoured to be advertised of Sir Griffin Markham's being at his house at Beskwood [Bestwood], so soon as we could possibly assemble together, and had certain intelligence that he did lie this last night at his house at Beskwood, and by his servant's information was this day at home at 8 o'clock and would so remain for anything they knew. Whereupon we went to Beskwood, but when we came thither, his lady informed us he was (as she thought) gone this morning into Leicestershire, but certainly where he was she could not say. Notwithstanding we entered the house and searched the several rooms thereof, but found him not. The causes of our search we alleged was for matter concerning the High Commission, and to this purpose showed your lordship's hand and others, concealing the Lords of the Privy Council's warrant; but for our opinion in the expedition of this service we think it not possible for 1000 men to apprehend him in Beskwood, if he be disposed, for that there is no entrance but at certain gates, locked and kept by his keepers, and his house so seated as cannot be seen until one be near the same. But there be hills far remote from the house which will discover all that enter, whereby he may have warning to forsake his house, and then, such is the spaciousness of that park, being nine miles about, as affordeth no hope of his apprehension. Yet will we do our diligence to apprehend

him, until we may know his Majesty's further command, and to this purpose have sent to know if he be in Leicestershire.—Newstead . . .
P.S. This bearer, the messenger, came hither about 2 o'clock in the afternoon on Friday last. [Signed] John Byron: Brian Lassells: John Thorol.[12]

The unprepossessing description of the wanted man which was circulated to the ports suggests his chances of evading recognition were slender:

Sir Griffin Markham hath a large broad face, of a black complexion, hath a big nose, and one of his hands is maimed by a hurt in his arm, received by shot of a bullet. He hath thin and little hair of his beard.

Eventually he gave himself up and was condemned to death, only to be dramatically reprieved on the scaffold and eventually banished; his property was confiscated.

Neither of the Byrons appears to have been implicated in the Main Plot, also to secure the throne for Arabella Stuart; its failure in the autumn of 1603 resulted in Sir Walter Raleigh's imprisonment in the Tower for twelve years.

The excitements of the past year had told on Little Sir John, but he deferred making his will until the day before his end, on 24 February 1603/4. Over his burial place in Colwick Church his son erected a magnificent alabaster tomb; beneath its canopy the bearded effigy of Sir John lies by that of his wife. He would have deplored the subsequent decay of the church which necessitated the removal of the monument in 1937, but its transfer to the Newstead he loved so well would surely not displease him. So great, indeed, was his attachment to the Abbey that until recent years his ghost has been seen from time to time in the library (the North Gallery), sitting beneath his own portrait, reading a book, in broad daylight. But the North Gallery is no longer a library and since the dispersal of the books and the removal of the portrait to Thrumpton, Little Sir John appears no more.

In 1636 William Sampson of South Leverton, in Nottinghamshire, published a volume of verses entitled *Virtus post funera vivit* which included an elegy 'On the renowned gentleman ould Sir John Byron of Newsteed-Abbey'. They are of little merit, but an excerpt is worth quoting to show that the memory of the man was still green thirty-two years after his death:

Lives he that will not justifie, how fame
Rais'd early Trophees to the BYRONS name?
How by desert, thy nobel vertues shone
In their own orbe, rectifi'd by none.

[ 41 ]

He truely serv'd his Country, nobly the State,
And was for both like *Basills* magistrate,
Free from Corruption, Avarice, or Pride,
His vertues, not his vices, he did hide.
When Roiall *Anne* was pleased for to trie
Diana-like her strong Artillery,
In spatious *Sherwood* famous'd for the fame
Of Robin-hood, whose bowre still beares the name.
Then had you seene our BYRON with what port
He entertaind her *Majesty*, to th' Court
With musicke sweet, as if in harmonie,
The Earth and Heaven's in consort did agree,
To speake a bounteous welcome! such a one
As well might vivifie a hart of stone.
How every office in its owne spheare mov'd,
Admir'd by all, and of the whole Court lov'd,
Freedome, and plenty strove which should exceede,
Bounty proclaim'd full wellcomes to *Newsteede*,
Yet with a free and sparing hand! for shee
Saucde every juncket with sweet temp'rancie.

The Earl of Shrewsbury paid tribute in a letter of condolence to the new heir which also offered pious and practical advice:

Sir John Byron,

I have receaved your lettere by this bearer, & how greivous the losse of so vertuous, kynd, & deere a frend as your father was unto us here, as God best knowethe, so did our teares, which we could not forbeare at the fyrst readyng of your lettere, wyttnes; but as he trule honored & feared God duryng all his lyffe, so are we to gyve him prayse & thankes for his great good blessing extended to him duryng the tyme of his visitacion, & untill his end; and to beseeche his devine Majestie that we may so followe the steps of his vertuous lyffe, as we may joyfully hope to imitate his end when God shall be pleased that we pay our lyke tribute to nature that he hath done.

The offer of your selfe to succeede that good father of yours in his deere & good affection to me I take moste thankfully, & will requite it with assurance of the like good affection to you & yours that I bare to hym, makyng no doubt but that as God hathe lefte you to succede him in his estate & possessions, so you will never fayle to imitate hym in all the good, honest, & vertuous wayes of his lyffe. You saw the great reputacion & love of all honest men that he got by his setteled & steddy course, as well within his house as withoute; abhorring all vice, & lovyng vertue; beyng alwayes constant to his frends, & of a most temperate diett, peaceable & quiett disposition; and, because you intreate me to be unto you as a father, & doe promis to be to me as a son, I will confidently &

freely yet further be bould to advise you, I protest even as thoughe I hadd that naturall intrest in you indeed. I know the estate of that which is left you is good & great, but, withall, I take it you are in great debtts, & have many chyldren to provyde for; so as unles you take some present & speedy course to free your selfe of debtts, which will eate into your state lyke a mothe in your garment, (& untill then shall lyve warely & not to begyn with that state of housekepyng & countenance wher your father left you) you will be further plunged within a shorte tyme, I feare me, then ever you will, perhapps, be able to recover; I doe therefore advise you, that so soone as you have in suche sort as shalbe fytte fynished your father's funeralles, to dispose & dispersse that great household, reducing them to the number of fortye or fyftie, at the moste, of all sorts; &, in my opinion, it wilbe far better for you to lyve for a tyme in Lancashire, rather then in Nottinghamshire, for many good reasons that I can tell you when we mete, fytter for words then wrytynge.

And, because it behovythe you to take some present order in dysposyng & settellyng of your estate, which if it be delayed, & not done spedely, will greatly prejudice you & yours, more than perhaps you can hereafter remedy, I wold not wyshe you to relye uppon the advise of any one or more of thos which served your father or your self, how juste or honest soever you may conceave them to be; but to intreate some one gentellman & friend of yours to be acquainted with your whole estate, as well with your revenewes as all anueties & porcions oute of your lands, with your debtts also, who, beyng made privye to all thos thynges, may freely let you understand his advise & opinion what course will be best & fyttest for you to take in all respectes; and above all men livyng in thos partes, if I were in your case, I protest I wolde intreate Sir John Harpur in this behalfe, who, for the great love & affection that on my owne knowledge he bare to your father that is gone, & to you & your house, I hope will not refuse, uppon your intreatie, to enter into that busynes with you; who for his wysdome, experience, & discredition, is hable to gyve you sounde & good counsell, which may be a good help to the wisest that liveth. His paynes neede to be no more, after his being made perfectly acquaynted with your estate, then to deliver you his advise what course will be best for you to take in all thynges, espetially now at the fyrst, that you may the better put the same in present execution: And hereof yf you lyke, I, uppon notice from you, will write unto him to intreat him to repaire unto you before his comminge up to the Parlament, to afford you the same counsell that he wolde give his owne son in ye lyke case.

Thus you see the liberty I take of your offer, who, as God knoweth, have no peece of thought, or ende therein, then the good & prosperity of you & yours; & thoughe I have wrytten herein playnely what I wyshe, yet if you & I were together but one halfe hower I colde shewe you further reasons to move you to hould this course then is fytt to be committed to paper. And thus, with the remembrance of my wyfe's most hartie comendacions, & the lyke from my selfe, who pray God to put into your harte to performe that which may lene to your owne moste credit, & the happie continuance of all yours in all prosperitie, I will take my leave, & committ you to the Lord Almighty. At Brodstreet, this first of May, 1603.[13]

The large family mentioned by the Earl consisted of two sons—John, nearly twenty-one and himself already a father; Nicholas, the baby of the family, aged eight (another son, George, born in 1597, lived less than a month)—and five or six daughters, two of whom were twins, or rather surviving triplets. Of these, Elizabeth had married Gilbert Armstrong of Thorp-in-le-Clottes (or Thorpe-in-the-Glebe, near Wysall, Notts., since depopulated) in 1602. Alice and Ann were probably also married by this time to Sir John Ratcliffe and John Atherton respectively. The ten-year-old Margaret was in the household of Lady Arabella Stuart; and Mary, now fourteen, remained unmarried. (Some pedigrees mention a Margery, but her existence remains unproved and the name is probably a variant of Margaret.)

How much 'Sir John with the peaked beard' profited by Shrewsbury's good counsel and whether he consulted Sir John Harpur is unknown.[14] His children's marriages meant considerable expense for the customary settlements and the rest of his life was largely a struggle against increasing debt, as the Earl had foreseen.

Hitherto he had been so much overshadowed by his renowned father that little can be gathered about his earlier years. He attended the Earl of Rutland's funeral in 1588 and a year later joined with other gentlemen of Lancashire in signing a document calling upon mayors, churchwardens and others to suppress 'the enormities of the Sabothe'—wakes, fairs, markets, bear-baits, bull-baits, ales, May games, resorting to ale houses in times of divine service, piping and dancing, hunting, and all manner of unlawful gaming—in short, all the activities traditionally associated with 'Merrie England'. He continued the family association with the Willoughbys, with whom he or his son stayed at the newly built Wollaton Hall in August 1599. He took no part in public affairs beyond representing Nottinghamshire in the Parliament of 1597. He remains indistinct, as often happens with the son of a father of such marked personality; but there was an additional and painful reason for his retired way of life.

His wife, Margaret FitzWilliam, was a woman of rare talent and beauty, skilled in the composition of music and poetry, her only weakness being a regret that, since her husband had an elder brother, the latter's wife took precedence of her. This grievance removed by Anthony's early death, the marriage arranged by Little Sir John to counterbalance

[44]

the misalliance of his heir became a union of perfect love and happiness. But after a difficult childbirth, 'wherein she brought forth two daughters which liv'd to be married, and one more that died, I think, as soone or before it was borne', she went out of her mind and never recovered her reason, although 'her ravings were more delightful then other women's most rationall conversations'.[15] Which of the elder daughters were triplets and whether Margery died at birth is not clear; but according to Mrs Hutchinson, Margaret, Nicholas and George, at least, were born after their mother's affliction. Her husband married his eldest son off as early as possible and ultimately devoted himself to the care of his wife, whose insanity 'had left her love and obedience entire to her husband, and he retained the same fondnesse and respect for her . . . as when she was the glory of her age'.

The inquisition post mortem on old Sir John Byron's property was not held until April 1606; this long delay in settling his estate added to his son's difficulties. The first indication of financial embarrassment came in January 1605/6, when he was bound in £200 to William Trinder to save him harmless upon a debt of £88, for which sum Trinder was bound for Sir John's debts. Trinder, a yeoman or husbandman of Sneinton (then a village, now part of Nottingham), became a moneylender on a large scale. Many of the Nottinghamshire gentry were indebted to him at various times and the King himself made use of his services.

A year later, on 26 March 1607, a deed was drawn up to free the Lancashire estates from charges intended for the maintenance of the younger children of Sir John the elder and Sir John the younger, and from all other charges except the jointure of the younger John Byron's wife, Anne, in Clayton. These annuities were to be provided out of the Nottinghamshire estates instead, so that the Lancashire lands might be conveyed to trustees who would sell them to pay the elder Byron's debts, 'amounting to a great Some mencioned in a Schedule to the same Indenture annexed'.[16] Accordingly Ancoats was sold to Oswald Mosley in January 1609 for £750 and the Blackley property was alienated gradually—the sale of a water-mill, a kiln and a house of Joseph Consterdine in 1610 realising £124. Even some detached parts of the Nottinghamshire estates did not escape, for £100 was raised by the sale of a piece of land called Cornerwong, in Basford (near, now in, Nottingham). In spite of this the obliging Trinder was called upon again in October 1609 to join Byron in a new bond to Sir Henry Pierrepont for the loan of £100.

Fortunately, the younger Byron was more securely placed financially and at the end of 1609 the family losses were to some extent counterbalanced by his purchase, for an unspecified sum, of the manor of Linby, adjoining the Newstead and Papplewick estates.[17] The vendors were two London men, Edward Bates and Henry Ellwes, who held it by royal letters patent; it had once belonged to Jasper, Duke of Bedford.

Throughout his reign, James I had continued to mistrust Arabella Stuart as a potential danger to his crown and great was the royal consternation when it became known that she had secretly married William Seymour. The Byrons, too, were perturbed, for good reasons. Margaret was still in Arabella's household, being, indeed, her favourite attendant, and she was one of the witnesses to this ill-fated marriage, which took place about four in the morning of 22 June 1610, at Greenwich. When Arabella was carried away to prison a few weeks later, Margaret's brother, the younger Sir John, hurried south to fetch his sister home to his own house (probably Colwick); 'and there, although his wife, a most prudent and vertuous ladie, labour'd to comfort her with all imaginable kindness, yet soe constant was her friendship to the unfortunate princesse, as I have heard her servants say, even after her marriage she would steale many melancholy houres to sitt and weepe in remembrance of her'.[18]

Some months later the younger Sir John was in trouble himself, apparently in consequence of a duel which obliged him to take refuge abroad, because in March 1611 one Thomas Screven wrote from London to the Earl of Rutland:

> It is certaine that Sir John Biron and Sir John Ratcliff [his brother-in-law] were over seas long since, and it is as sure now that the Lord Scrope with his second—saied to be Sir William Constable—is staied and taken upon the Downes by Sir Thomas Waller, as they were in their jorney passing disguised in an oyster boate, and so his Lordship wilbe in London this night without sayling. The others are sent for, and yt may be some matter of Fleete, or like ponishment, will light upon them all, if but for example sake'.[19]

Evidently the matter, whatever its cause, blew over without very serious results, for in May both the Byrons, with their trustees, signed a deed for the sale of Blackley Chapel (a private oratory of the Byrons dating from 1548) to the inhabitants of Blackley.

A new and serious difficulty now had to be met in connection with the Nottinghamshire estates. Seeking to improve his own revenues, James I continued Queen Elizabeth's practice of appointing Commissioners for compounding for defective titles. Certain of his subjects were accused of being in possession of lands formerly belonging to the Crown, of which they held imperfect grants or no grants at all; and, to prevent costly lawsuits, and out of professed solicitude for his subjects' welfare, the King empowered commissioners to compound with such landowners for specified sums of money, and to issue to them new grants or leases which would put them in secure possession of their estates. The King's suspicion that many estates had been enlarged by illegal encroachment on Crown land was by no means unfounded; on the other hand, some families had held their property for so many generations that the original title deeds had long since disappeared. If they could not prove their title, they must compound for their estates or forfeit them—a case of 'Heads I win, Tails you lose' for the Crown. The estates which Byron was called upon to defend were:[20]

|  | acres | roods | perches |
|---|---|---|---|
| 1. Bulwell Park, containing | 326 | 3 | 2 |
| 2. The Priory of Newstead, with 43 several inclosures, containing | 1813 | 3 | 22 |
| 3. The manor of Colwick and divers grounds thereto belonging, containing | 1190 | 2 | 11 |
| 4. In Linby, divers parcels of ground containing | 0770 | 3 | 34 |
| 5. The manor of Papplewick with divers woods and wastes, containing | 3207 | 0 | 20 |

The defendant replied:

1. That Bulwell Park was part of the possessions of the late Priory of Newstead, and that Henry VIII by letters patent of 28 May 1540 granted it to Byron's grandfather; that it came by lawful conveyance to his father and thence to defendant himself.
2. That the Priory of Newstead was granted to Sir John Byron by the same letters patent.
3. That the manor of Colwick and all the closes thereto belonging are, and for all the time whereof the memory of man is not to the contrary have been, parcel of the manor or lordship of Colwick within the forest of Sherwood and are the defendant's freehold; and that he and his ancestors have been for many hundred years lawfully seized thereof in his and their demesne as of fee or of some other estate of inheritance, 'as he verily believeth'.
4. As for Linby, 180 acres by the forest measure, which were parcel of Linby Hay, were part of the late Priory of Newstead and came to him by the grant of 1540; the rest of the manor he held by descent from his ancestors and by purchase from Queen Elizabeth and from King James I.
5. That the manor of Papplewick was granted by the letters patent of 1540.

The Attorney General cited various commissions, regards and peram-bulations of the Forest to prove that 206 out of the 326 acres of Bulwell

Park were still the king's soil, the only grant to Newstead Priory which could be proved being that of 80 acres by the forest measure, or 120 acres by standard measure, given by Edward I to Philip de Willughby, by him to William de Cossall, and by the last-named to the Priory. He contended, moreover, that the Bulwell Wood named in the grant of 1540 did not mean the whole of Bulwell Rise, but only the 120 acres granted to Willughby. (This may have been true, because in 1601 the tenants of Bulwell won a lawsuit against Little Sir John Byron and others for denying them their right of common on Bulwell Moor.) 1,399 acres of Newstead were claimed as the king's soil, for which Byron must make composition, some allowance being made for the site of the Priory according to its first foundation, 'which is very small'. Of Colwick, the Attorney General concluded by saying (again perhaps with some truth), 'It plainly appeareth that the said Mannor is made great by incroachment.'

The case dragged on for some years, Sir John stubbornly contesting every acre. He commissioned Thomas Longden to draw him a delightful little plan of the wastes of Kighill and Ravenshead (see plate), included in the foundation grant of Newstead Priory, and was doubtless depressed to find what a comparatively small part of the later estate they formed. Eventually he was obliged to compound, and on 30 June 1615 the estates were regranted for £1,000, not to the elder Byron but to 'John Byron junr. knt.'[21] The document begins by naming and granting all the pieces of land in Newstead, Kirkby Annesley, Linby and Linby Hay, Bulwell, Bulwell Park, Wighay, Papplewick, Hucknall Torkard, Lenton, Basford, Annesley, Greasley, Watnall, Nuthall, Adbolton, Colwick, Stoke Bardolph, Gedling, Carlton, Sneinton and Nottingham, which, by an inquisition taken at Papplewick on 4 April 1614 had been found to be assart land and purprestures within the King's Forest of Sherwood, with all the buildings, etc., therein, and all their rights and profits. It then confirms the grant of the other possessions within the Forest of which, by the same inquisition, Byron was found to be lawfully seized—namely, the late Priory of Newstead and all its appurtenances (the manor of Papplewick, Bulwell Wood, etc.), Linby Hay, the manors of Linby and Colwick, and so forth.

Legal costs were not the only drain on the elder Byron's purse during this anxious period. A dowry had to be provided for Margaret when she married Thomas Hutchinson of Owthorpe in the spring of 1612 and later in the year Nicholas went up to Emmanuel College, Cambridge. In August Sir John had the expensive honour of entertaining King James for three days on his way from Rufford to Nottingham. Next year, while Byron was High Sheriff of Nottinghamshire, his daughter Anne Atherton (whose daughter, another Anne, had been born at Newstead) lost her husband. In 1614 the King again visited the Abbey, this time for two days.

Small portions of the Lancashire estates were sold at intervals; when in 1616 the lease of Rochdale expired, it reverted to the Crown, to be recovered by the Byrons some years later.

Although the Nottinghamshire estates were now secured by the composition with the Commissioners, the Crown was keeping a sharp watch for any further attempts at encroachment. On 29 April John Deverell wrote from Langton Arbor (a lodge in Sherwood Forest a few miles from Newstead) to Sir George Manners:

> I lately met old Sir John Byron who told me he had received a letter from Sir John Thornhagh, signifying the King's pleasure that he should forbear imparking his grounds at Newstead until his pleasure was further known; whereupon he told me he gave no directions for enclosure but passed over all to his son. Young Sir John was then in Lancashire, but on his return seemed discontented that stay had been made, and ordered the palings to go forward. I beg you will acquaint my Lord (the Earl of Rutland) therewith.[22]

Passing things over to his son was the elder Byron's usual policy, a course he pursued again in 1619 when his daughter Margaret, Lady Hutchinson, died of a chill at the early age of twenty-five, leaving two little sons, the elder of whom, John, was prominent during the Civil Wars as the Parliamentary Governor of Nottingham Castle.

> She was a lady of a noble famely as any in the county [wrote Lucy Hutchinson years later], of an incomparable shape and beauty, embellisht with the best education those dayes afforded and above all had such a generous virtue joined with attractive sweetenesse, that she captivated the hearts of all that knew her: she was pious, liberall, courteous, patient, kind above an ordinary degree, ingenuous to all things she would applie herself to, and notwithstanding she had had her education att court, was delighted in her own country habitation, and managed all her famely affaires better than any of the home-spun huswives that had been brought up to nothing elce: she was a most affectionate wife, a greate lover of her father's house . . . . She was a wise and bountifull mistresse in her family, a blessing to her tenants and neighbourhood, and had an indulgent tendernesse to her infants. . . . One that was present at her death told me that she had an admirable voyce, and skill to manage it, and that she went away singing a psalme which this maid apprehended she sung with so much more than usual sweetenesse, as if her soul had bene already ascended into the coelestial quire.[23]

When her brother came over to Owthorpe, he found her husband and her sister Alice (Lady Ratcliffe) almost beside themselves with grief;

and to avoid the aggravation of their distress by the customary elaborate funeral, he most sensibly had her buried privately the next morning, without her husband's knowledge. Caring nothing for Sir Thomas's anger, on the following day he carried brother-in-law, sister and three-year-old John away to his own house at Bulwell, leaving the baby George in care of his nurse. To add to their troubles, halfway to Nottingham the horses bolted and overturned the coach, slightly injuring the passengers who, nevertheless, all got out except the maid who was carrying the child. When she saw that the horses were completely beyond control, she wrapped little John in a cloak and flung him into a ploughed field, where the furrows were soft and saved him from harm. He was picked up and carried to Bulwell, 'where his aunt had such a motherly tendernesse for him that he grew and prosper'd in her care . . . every child of the famely lov'd him better than their owne brothers and sisters, and Sir John Biron and my lady were not halfe so fond of any of their owne.[24]

The younger Sir John was at this time trying to re-establish the family fortunes by persuading some of his Lancashire neighbours to join him in coal-mining in the wastes of Oldham manor, 'the gayne of the said coles to be distributed amongst them in proportion to their enclosed land'. His father, on the other hand, was undergoing another financial crisis which resulted in his outlawry—the penalty in civil cases, involving loss of civil rights only—for not appearing to answer a charge in the King's court. It is suspected that Sir John was unable to face creditors who were suing him for debt; whatever the reason, in 1620 one Robert Stokes was granted the benefit of the outlawry of Sir John Byron and Sir John Roades, after payment of the sum due to their creditors, and with the reserve of a tenth part to the King. In the following February father and son (and the latter's wife, whose jointure was concerned) sold to George Chetham, a London grocer, and Humphrey Chetham, a Manchester chapman, Clayton Hall, which had belonged to the Byrons since the marriage of Robert de Burun and Cecilia Clayton at the beginning of the thirteenth century. According to descriptions in old deeds and inventories, it was a spacious manor house with a gate-tower and a private chapel, still surrounded by a moat, and since Newstead Abbey had become the principal family seat, it had served as an occasional residence of the head of the family, or, from time to time, as the home of his eldest son. The Chetham brothers bought all the household and other effects at the same time.[25]

Little more than two years later, on 7 March 1622/3, the elder Byron died on the very same day as the wife whom he had loved with such devotion. The manner of their passing is very beautifully described by their grandson's wife:

> He had two beds in one chamber, and she being a little sick, two weomen watcht by her, some time before she died. It was his custome, as soon as ever he unclos'd his eies, to aske how she did; but one night, he being as they thought in a deepe sleepe, she quietly departed towards the morning. He was that day to have gone a hunting, his usuall exercise for his health, and it was his custome to have his chaplaine pray with him before he went out: the weomen, fearfull to surprize him with the ill newes, knowing his deare affection to her, had stollen out and acquainted the chaplaine, desiring him to informe him of it. Sir John waking, did not that day, as was his custome, ask for her, but call'd the chaplaine to prayers, and joyning with him, in the midst of the prayer, expir'd, and both of them were buried together in the same grave. Whether he perceiv'd her death and would not take notice, or whether some strange sympathy in love or nature, tied up their lives in one, or whether God was pleas'd to exercise an unusuall providence towards them, preventing them both from that bitter sorrow which such separations cause, it can be but conjectur'd; but the thing being not ordinary, and having receiv'd it from the relation of one of his daughters and his grandchild, I thought it not impertinent here to insert.[26]

They were buried at Colwick on 27 March, Sir John's will being proved on the same day.

This document, drawn up on 16 December 1618, when he was still 'of good health and body', represents a gallant attempt to put his tangled affairs into sufficient order to ensure some measure of provision for his younger children. After serious consideration of all his debts which, he admitted, were many and burdensome to him and to his sureties— namely, Nicholas Rolston of Carlton in Gedling, and Gabriel and Vincent Elton of Linby, he appointed these three men his executors, and bequeathed them all his goods and chattels, real and personal, out of which they were to satisfy themselves and all his other sureties, including Roger Haugh, John Lyne and Robert Hawsbroke. For the same purpose they were to receive all his rents, any debts due to him, and the sum of £1,000 which his eldest son had covenanted to pay within a year of his father's death to any person appointed by his will. The remainder of his estate, 'if any be left', after the discharge of his debts and funeral expenses, he bequeathed to his 'loving children Nicholas Byron and Mary Byron, to be equally divided betwixt them'. If anything was indeed left for them, they undoubtedly owed it to their prudent brother rather than their feckless parent.

'Swearing Sir John'[27] did not long survive his father. Though still barely forty at the time of the latter's death (he was baptised at Colwick on Midsummer Day 1583), he probably looked and felt considerably older, his life having been far from carefree. Married at the age of sixteen to an even younger bride[28]—Anne, the eldest daughter of Sir Richard Molyneux of Sefton, in Lancashire—he had ten or eleven sons and either one or two daughters, an unusually large proportion of whom lived to reach maturity. There is little wonder that he saw with dismay his father's financial instability and he soon realised that adequate provision for his children must depend upon his own efforts. Although expected to shoulder the elder Byron's public responsibilities and to come to his rescue in times of domestic trouble, he evidently had no authority to take full control of affairs; and he had barely time to administer his father's estate before he followed him to the grave on 28 September 1625, possibly a victim of the plague that in August had caused Parliament to be adjourned to Oxford. He, too, was buried at Colwick and many years later (apparently after the Civil Wars) his sister Alice, Lady Ratcliffe, erected a monument (now at Newstead) to the joint memory of her parents and of her brother and herself.

The previous lack of a memorial was turned to account by Huntingdon Plumptre in 1629, in his *Epitaphium honoratiss. D. Ioh. Byron eq. aur. nupèr defuncti*:

> *Hic situs\* ad tumulum iaceo Byronus avitum;*
> *Una simul geminum terra cadaver habet;*
> *At tibi, marmor, avi sat erit meminisse perempti;*
> *Ora mihi famam, non monumenta dabunt*
>
> *\* Spendidiss. avi eius sepulchrum quod proximè inhumatus est.*

(Epitaph on the most honourable Sir John Byron, gilded knight, lately deceased: 'Here I, Byron, lie\* by my grandfather's tomb; one plot of earth holds corpses twain; but, o marble, it will suffice for thee to commemorate my dead grandsire; men's lips, not monuments, shall speak my fame.'

\*The grave of his renowned grandfather, very near to which he was buried.)[29]

## · 3 ·

# The Gallant Cavaliers:
# Royalists in the Making

The gallant Cavaliers, who fought in vain
For those who knew not to resign or reign.

*Don Juan*, XIII, lx

AT only twenty-five another John Byron found himself the head of a large family of brothers and at least one sister. Four of these—Richard, William, Thomas and Robert—were more or less grown up, their ages ranging from twenty to about sixteen or seventeen. Philip and Gilbert were between twelve and fifteen, their sister, Anne, about thirteen. Under the terms of their father's will Richard received an annuity of £70, William, Thomas and Philip £40 apiece. The existence of another daughter, Mary, is unproved, and her inclusion in some pedigrees is most probably due to confusion with the unmarried aunt of the younger family, whose name was Mary. George, Francis and Charles all died in infancy, probably before their father, and so did Nicholas, on whom an annuity had been settled out of the Nottinghamshire estates in 1607. He appears to have come between John and Richard and may, in fact, have been John's twin. (The twin relationship mentioned by various writers fits this generation rather than an earlier one; no direct evidence has been found against it.) In addition to these was the late Sir John Byron's youngest brother, Nicholas, not five years older than his eldest nephew and consequently often mistaken for his brother; and indeed he must have seemed more like a brother than an uncle to the elder boys. As we have seen, his father had tried to make some provision for him and he was also heir to his maternal uncle, John Fitzwilliam of Gaynes Park in Essex, who died in 1612[1]—the year in which Nicholas matriculated at Cambridge.

John Byron matriculated at Trinity College, Cambridge, in 1615, took his M.A. degree in 1618, and completed his education by making the fashionable 'grand tour' of Europe, for which a pass was granted him on 14 March 1620, permitting him 'to traveile for three yeares, & to take with him one man together with trunckes of apparrell & other necessaries, not prohibited,' with proviso not to go to Rome.

He had been elected Member of Parliament for the town of Nottingham in 1624 and was chosen Knight of the Shire to represent the county early in 1626 and again in 1628. He attended the coronation of Charles I on 1 February 1626 as 'King's servant of the Privy Chamber' (Gentleman of the Bedchamber), and was created Knight of the Bath— an honour repeatedly celebrated by Huntingdon Plumptre in sycophantic verses; for example:

> *Quod te sulphureae decorant insignibus undae,*
> *   Nomen & à CALIDIS nobile ducis AQUIS?*
> *Nòn fortuna tuos, natura sed auget honores,*
> *   Cùm tibi dent fasces IGNIS & UNDA novos:*
> *Sic te TERRA beet; sic tandem ex AETHERE summo*
> *   Addita sit reliquis quarta corona\* tribus.*

> *\*Allusio ad symbolum huic ordini peculiare, videlicet orbiculum rubrâ fasciâ suspensum, & tribus coronis sub una maiori quasi coeuntibus insignitum; addita hac epigraphe—TRIA IUNCTA IN UNO.*

> (What though sulphureous waves adorn thy crest and thou derivest a noble title from warm waters? Not fate, but nature increases thine honours, since Fire and Water give thee new badges of office: so may Earth bless thee; so at last from the height of Heaven may the fourth crown\* be added to the other three.)

Later in 1626 John was added to the list of commissioners for musters in Nottinghamshire. Clearly his father had not had time to liquidate the debts amassed by Sir John with the Peaked Beard; financial stability could have been restored only by stricter economy and prudence than might reasonably be expected from a young man just released from parental control. He does, indeed, appear to have established his title, disputed by freeholders and copyholders, to the coal beneath their holdings in Rochdale manor;[2] but nearly three years after his father's death it was necessary to obtain counsel's opinion on the late Sir John Byron's will in relation to the manors of Newstead, Cadney, and Howsam; and in 1628 he leased Newstead, Bulwell Park, and other property in Sneinton and Lancashire to his mother and his aunt Alice, Lady Dormer, as security for his debts, for which they were bound jointly with him. A year later he mortgaged the Colwick estate to the Earl of Worcester,

---

\*An allusion to the device peculiar to this order, namely, a little circle hanging from a red cord, and adorned by three crowns linked together, as it were, beneath a larger crown; with this motto: Three united in one.

with little apparent benefit. There were family troubles, too, when Isabel Skeffyngton, John's great-aunt, died, probably at the beginning of 1627; and in the following October Sir John Ratcliffe, husband of Byron's other aunt Alice, was killed at the Isle of Rhé during Buckingham's attempt to relieve the Huguenot rebels besieged by Richelieu.

Although nominally the head of the family, John probably left the control of most domestic affairs in the capable hands of his mother, who had yet another quarter century of life before her. Her eldest son appears to have been devoted to her. Lloyd mentions 'his admirable discourse to his Mother, discovering him as compleat a Scholar, as he was an accomplished Gentleman;'[3] and it was doubtless to please her that in 1627 he commissioned a magnificent heraldic pedigree[4]—some 17 feet long—tracing the descent of her family, Molyneux of Sefton in Lancashire, from William de Molines who came from Normandy in the train of the Conqueror. The name of Lady Byron's father, who died in 1623, was the second on the roll of baronets created in 1611; he was the ancestor of the present Baron Sefton of Croxteth.

Although numerous references to John Byron's scholarly talents exist, no literary work of his is known to exist; it is even uncertain whether any was actually published, or whether his work merely circulated among his friends in manuscript.

Early in 1629 the sixteen-year-old Anne was married at St Andrew's Church, Holborn, to Sir Thomas Lucas, who was nearly twice her age. Although the eldest son, he was, like Little Sir John Byron, born before the marriage of his father, who settled on him the estate of Lexden in Essex. His younger brother, Sir John Lucas, was created Baron Lucas of Shenfield in 1645.

It was in this year (1629) that Huntingdon Plumptre published his *Epigrammaton opusculum*, already quoted; his pious but vague wish for Sir John Byron, 'Par (si qua est) tibi sponsa viro contingat' [May thy bride be the equal (if such there be) of her husband], implies that John was still a bachelor. His marriage to Cecilia (or Cicely), daughter of Thomas West, Lord de la Warr, probably took place not long afterwards. She was the widow of Sir Francis Bindloss of Borwick Hall in Lancashire; he had died in 1628, leaving her with one son, Robert or Robin, then about two years old.

Plumptre was a Nottingham physician descended from a very old family in that town and, in view of his obvious reverence for wealth and rank, it is rather curious that he should have sided with Parliament in the Civil War; but he appears later on to have 'got above himself', for Lucy Hutchinson, while admitting in her *Memoirs* that he 'was a good schollar and had a great deale of witt', adds that he was a 'profest atheist, and so proud insolent a scurrilous fellow, daring to abuse all persons how much soever above him, that he was throwne out of familliarity with the great people of the country, though his excellency in his profession made him to be taken in againe'. He had been widely recommended by Sir Thomas Hutchinson after curing his younger son, George, of epilepsy, and in later years George and his more famous brother, Colonel John Hutchinson (the Byrons' cousins) continued to protect him out of pity and gratitude. In 1629, however, Plumptre was still currying favour and his verses are prefaced by a long, fulsome and pretentious dedication in Latin, 'To Sir John Byron . . . greatly esteemed for his learning, character and courage, and no less distinguished by the stock from which he springs'. The 'shining radiance' of his intellect, the 'heavenly grace' of his countenance, and the general excellence of his character are repeatedly commended in this style; and he was fatuous enough to praise Newstead Abbey for belonging to the Byrons:

> Quòd me dispositae decorant utrínque columnae;
> Alta quòd aetherium culmen in astra fero;
> Tot mea quòd clarae rutilant per septa fenestrae,
> Caelatasq[ue]; frequens ornat imago fores;
> Quisquis es, haud ideò me suspice: forma superbam
> Non facit, in saxis nec mihi tantus honor.
> Maenia [?Moenia] quid iactem, vel opus? colere ista Byronum
> Maius, quàm artifices excoluisse decus.

(What though ranged pillars adorn me on either side; though I rear a lofty gable to the starry heights; though so many clear windows gleam through my walls, and many a figure adorns my carved doorways; whoe'er thou art, look not on me thus: 'tis not my beauty makes me proud, nor in my stones does so much value lie. Why should I boast my walls or workmanship? 'Tis greater honour to revere the property of the Byrons than to pay tribute to the craftsmen.)

The verses addressed to John's Uncle Nicholas and brother Richard become more personal. Nicholas, invoked as 'unique ornament of vernal youth . . . pith of talent [and] darling of wit' is characterised thus:

> Altiùs aethereas Iovis impiger ales in auras
> Carpit iter, celsos ingreditúrque polos:
> Infima sectetur vulgus; mihi summa petenti
> Alta placent; alas mens generosa facit:
> Vilia magnanimus sperno; petit ardua virtus:
> Par fortuna animo sit mihi, Caesar ero.

(The bird of Jove soars strongly to the winds of heaven, and attains the lofty heights: let the baser sort follow a lower course; high places are my pleasure, so seek the highest; a noble spirit makes itself wings; great-souled, I spurn the base; courage seeks trials: if my fate match my soul, I will be a Caesar.)

Two short, cryptic poems about an unknown lady are also addressed to him:

> *Est nigra, quid refert? eadem quoque dives, et ipssam [? ipsam],*
> *Atque simul dotem respice, Cypris [? Cypria] erit.*

(She is black, what matters that? She is also rich, and if you look upon her and her dowry at the same time, she will be Venus herself.)

> *Cur adèo formosa rogas sit Eliza Byrone?*
> *In promptu causam dicere; Eliza nigra est.*

(Do you ask, Byron, why Eliza so fair appears to be?
I will tell you briefly the reason: Eliza Black is she.)[5]

Whether Nicholas was really contemplating marriage with a lady whose fortune was her chief recommendation, it is impossible to say. According to some authorities he married twice, the surname of his first wife, Ann, being unknown. The mother of his children was Sophia, daughter of Charles Lambert of Nimeguen in Holland, Governor of Breda; and as Ernestus, his third son, was born about 1635, any previous marriage can have lasted only a short time.

Both Nicholas and Richard repaid Plumptre by contributing to his book short poems in praise of the author; for example:

### De Authore ad Lectorem

> *Quod legis hic Plumptraeus opus dedit; ille poësis*
> *Plumptraeus Clarij primus in arte chori.*
> *Tantum qui meritâ jam scandit in aethera famâ,*
> *Quantum in Cyrrhaeum scanderat ante jugum.*

> *Nich. Byron*

(To the Reader, concerning the Author, What thou readest here is Plumptre's offered work; he the first Plumptre of the Clarian band in the art of poetry: who, by well-earned fame, now climbs as high into heaven as before he climbed the Cyrrhean peak.)

> *Carmina Phoebeio vis dulce sonantia plectro,*
> *Sublime ingenium, Pieriósque jocos?*
> *Hos lege Plumptraej lusus; qui colligit isto*
> *Quod Charitum, Phoebi est, Aonidúmque libro.*

> *Rich. Byron*

(Do you wish for songs sounding sweetly of Phoebus' lyre, talent of the highest rank, wit of the muses? Read these trifles of Plumptre; who combines in this book what pertains to the Graces, to Phoebus, and to the Aonian Nine.)

Plumptre alludes twice to Richard's short stature, inherited from his famous great-grandfather:

*Ad amiculum D.⁶ Rich. Byron*

*Parva velùt gemma est, & pulchra; ita parvus & ipse*
*Pulcher es: hâc gemmam te ratione putem.*
*Ne te hominem, ne te gemmam (Byrone) negarem;*
*Sis homo, sis idem gemma (Byrone) hominum.*

*(To my little friend Master Rich. Byron*[.] As a gem is small and fair, so small and fair art thou; for this reason would I think thee a gem. I would not say thou wert neither man nor gem, Byron; be thou both man and the gem of men, Byron.)

*In minimo magnum, humano mens corpore; Graius,*
*Si memini, rhetor sic ait Isocrates.*
*Nil de te Isocratis mentitur pagina; cujus*
*Nil animo maius, corpore nil minus est.*

(Great in small compass is the mind in the human frame; so, if I remember rightly, says the Greek Orator Isocrates. Nor does Isocrates' page speak wrong of thee; than whose mind is nothing greater, than whose body nothing smaller.)

Nicholas, who had been admitted at Lincoln's Inn on 19 March 1625, was knighted on 12 February 1630. During the next five years he became father of three sons—Charles, who died before 1639, William and Ernestus. Whether his family lived at Gaynes Park is not clear; he himself was much occupied by military duties abroad and at home even before the upheaval of the Civil War. He seems to have been in the service of the exiled 'Queen of Hearts', Elizabeth of Bohemia, sister of Charles I, from whom he brought a letter to Sir Thomas Roe in 1636. Two years later he was again granted a pass to travel into the Low Countries, being captain of a company there.

Meanwhile, the anti-Puritan measures of Archbishop Laud had roused Scotland to open revolt when the authorities attempted to replace Knox's liturgy by a new liturgy founded on the English Book of Common Prayer. In 1639 Charles I, though short of men and money, ordered the Fleet to sail for the Forth. On 4 April Nicholas prudently made his will, providing for his surviving sons, William and Ernestus, and two little daughters, Frances and Shirtotta. A fortnight later the Justices of the Peace and Deputy-Lieutenants of Norfolk reported to the Earl of Suffolk that

> upon the 15th inst. understanding that the ships appointed for transport were come to Harwich, we drew all our men to a place called Shotly near Harwich, and there Sir Nicholas Byron and the other officers, having reviewed and approved of them, selected according to their several degrees, their own companies, most of which were that night shipped.[7]

On their arrival off Scotland early in May, Nicholas Byron's regiment was landed at Inchkeith, where they were well quartered. Though the Scottish forces under Leslie were ready to offer battle, Charles I realised that he was not strong enough to fight and the 'Bishops' War' was temporarily suspended when he consented to the meeting of a Free Assembly and Parliament. Both armies returned home, but preparations for a renewal of hostilities occupied England for the rest of the year. On 30 December Nicholas was appointed a member of the Council of War, which met on 4 January 1640 to consider a plan of campaign with the Earl of Northumberland. The Council at this time were sitting constantly three mornings a week, and '[plying] their business hard'. On 11 January Nicholas Byron and his niece's husband, Sir Thomas Lucas, were appointed to attend the Earl of Newport to view all the arms in the Tower which had been bought at Hamburg and sent over by Sir Thomas Roe for the King's service.

At the end of the month he was ordered to fetch 100 sergeants and corporals from the Low Countries where, again with Lucas, he was required to procure 500 saddles and he was accordingly at the Hague on 9 March. Early in January rumour had it that he was made Governor of Carlisle, but his commission was not drawn up until February, when he received from Sir William Uvedale, Treasurer at Ware, £960 to provide and furnish 64 horse for the garrison of Carlisle Castle. On 30 March he was granted £500 to make fortifications, but he did not reach Carlisle himself until the end of April. On 2 May Sir Francis Willoughby wrote to Lord Conway and Killultagh:

> Sir Nicholas Byron has come hither to receive from me this command, and I am to retire into Ireland to some other. He has been here a week, but is not willing to receive the charge until we hear something more from the Court.[8]

Little more than a month later he was summoned by the King to London, where he received the formal warrant of his appointment, which allowed him £3 a day. While there, he tried to collect levies for the war, and on 22 June Sir Edward Bashe reported to the Earl of

Rutland that 'our country [Hertfordshire] continues averse to the lieutenants warrants, and no money has been levied, which made Sir Nicholas Byron, who came down yesterday they said to receive it, go off the field in discontent'.[9]

Nicholas was still in the south in July, coping with the usual difficulties of mobilisation, and on the 20th he wrote to thank Lord Conway for sending his goods:

> The rest I have sent by land and hope they will meet you safely at Carlisle if the Scots do not meddle with them by the way, as it is believed at Court they will be in England before the last of this month. But I apprehend far more our own distractions than their threats, valuing them no more than my Lord Lieutenant [of Ireland]'s three blind mice, if we were not so distempered as we are at home. For those that are to go with my Lord Marquis [of Hamilton] have all sworn not to go by sea, if that were all it might go for nothing; but they will have no Papist commanders, and half the chiefs that go with the Marquis are so; we must use no martial law though we have it under the Broad Seal, but such as is Westminster Hall proof, and therefore I was forced to get the trained bands in Herts. to keep them in order, and to send such as were not to the House of Correction there to exercise them daily with the whip till the rest can be brought to obedience to handle their arms well. The 2nd of August we should begin to ship, yet none but my regiment have been exercised, and they so short a time and to so little purpose that it is not worth notice. If these men can be compelled to ship, as I am confident they may, yet when we have them there what shall we do with them? Yet we go on and take the King's money as fast as he can make it, either in the Mint or any where else, insomuch that the brass pots are like to fly if that business be not compounded this day, as the Mint business was before that particular, I refer you to my Lord General who writes at this present. The next news will be that all the soldiers that were with much ado got together are disbanded, since the captains must furnish them with a week's pay by anticipation. How ridiculous it is now to think upon it I leave to your consideration, assuring myself not to ship this year; what I shall do the next I know not. P.S. Your horse shall be continued all this winter, or by God's bread a weak counsel.[10]

The same note of humorous exasperation recurs in a letter to Secretary Vane a month later (21 August):

> I am now come to London, but to boot what I know not as yet though I have been here these 10 days. I would gladly write you some news, but know not where to begin for we are here and in every place in such distraction as if the day of judgment were hourly expected. Hertfordshire [will not] find men nor money, being to go with my Lord Marquis, the King says, 'send Byron to them, he will take order with them'; but Byron

has no mind to be made a moon-calf, and advantage the King's service nothing by it, so has advised to send the Lord Lieutenant [of the county, i.e. the Earl of Salisbury] once more to them, who has wrought them with new projects, which I hear have taken some effect. I have great hopes to see the Earl of Salisbury safely back, though I believe he thought to die no other death. The Lord Lieutenant [of Ireland] has fallen lately into his [old complaint], yet now there is hopes of his recovery.[11]

On 12 December Nicholas borrowed £100 from the Corporation of Carlisle to pay the garrison. There is a gap in the record of his activities during the next year, but by March 1642 financial diffi-culties had become so pressing that he was obliged to petition Parlia-ment for settlement of his account. It was resolved that he should be paid £200 'in discharge of so much of a greater debt due unto him'. Probably the approaching Civil War finished his hopes of receiving a full settlement.

As head of the family, Sir John Byron busied himself with the tasks and duties that had preoccupied many of his forefathers. Newstead Abbey again required some attention: the fine ceiling, reputedly Italian work, in the salon (once the canons' refectory), was completed on 28 March 1633. The reconstruction of the east front, where the so-called royal bedrooms occupy the site of the former dormitory, was probably begun about this time but, owing to the intervention of the war, was not completed until after John's death. Even without the war, he probably could not have continued the work because in 1636 he again mortgaged the Abbey and his property in Papplewick and Hucknall for an unspecified sum to his mother's sister, Alice, Lady Dormer, and Sir William Pennyman, who had married his cousin Anne Atherton. In the deed,[12] in which his mother joined him, he is described as of Bulwell Park; provision was made for the payment of annuities to certain of his brothers under the terms of his father's will.

In 1634 Byron was embroiled with his neighbour, George, Viscount Chaworth, who had obtained a verdict against a forest official named Fenton for poaching in his manor of Annesley, which adjoined the Newstead estate. In his 'answeare to the several untruths contained in the petition of John Chaworth Esqr. [Lord Chaworth's son] lately exhibited to his Majesty', Byron protested that the manor of Annesley was and always had been within the Forest of Sherwood, and the forest officers (the Ranger and the Keeper of Newstead woods) had always, until recently, hunted in Annesley woods, both when the forest was under the command of Byron's ancestors, and after it passed to the Earls of Rutland.

Whereas [continued Byron acidly], the Petitioner alledgeth that Fenton hath used to enter my hounds in his Fathers woods & there to destroy the deere, without respect of season; hee much forgetteth him selfe. For neyther have my hounds ever been entred there (having deere enough of my owne, for that purpose, without troublinge of others) neither hath any unseasonable Deere ever been killed by me: which is a fault so peculiar to his Father & himself (as may appeare by there severall presentments & convictions in the forrest court) that it can not belonge to any els. It is true, indeed, that whilst there was correspondence betwixt the Lord Chaworth & my self, I sometimes followed my hounds into his woods, affording him the like courtesty for his hounds & greyhounds in my libertyes, but since he discourteously stopped my hounds & gave my men ill language, without any cause given on my side; I have not troubled his woods: since which time, Fenton hath hunted as deputy Ranger & by the Earle of Rutlands command & not by my authority.

[And] Whereas the Petitioner affirmeth, that his Father is at grate charge to breed & preserve Deere in his woods I am most certaine that most of the Deere, if not all, which come into those woods are bredd in my own grounds. & for preservation of them, I am sure they have none, but such as bowes & gunnes & greyhounds & notorious Deere-stealers can afford them.

Sir John further complained that Chaworth's verdict against Fenton had been obtained surreptitiously by taking advantage of a delay in the appointment of a warden of the Forest after the death of the late Earl of Rutland.

Chaworth stoutly denied that Annesley was within the Forest, and declared that hunting there had always been forbidden:

Nay, it will be proved that *old Sir John Byron with the Long Beard*, when he was lieutenant of the forest under the Earl of Rutland, was taken up for hunting there by a person yet living, & he was neither sued nor convicted for it, as is now the new fashion.

He challenged Byron to name his ancestors who were in command of Sherwood, and affirmed that he never shot at any deer in the forest, 'nor ever slipped a dog there, which is more than Sir John Byron can say.'[13]

How the matter was settled does not appear, but this friction, already of long standing, was to cause far more serious trouble between the two families a century and more later.

Another dispute with a neighbour arose in the course of Sir John Byron's duties as High Sheriff of Nottinghamshire in 1635, this time with Gervase Markham, never an easy man to get on with. Markham had written to Byron to protest against his assessment for ship-money, declaring that if he had been commanded to present to him his head he would as willingly have done it, and regretting that he was 'so weak in his limbs' that he could not come and expostulate with him.[14] The Sheriff was unimpressed and reported to Edward Nicholas, then Secretary to the Admiralty, on 26 January 1636 that he had expected to be in London before then, and to have paid in all the money, for at the time of the assessment he found no one refractory except Mr Markham, but now that he came to gather up the money very few could pay without distraining. Markham, he continued, taxed him with partiality to Sir Gervase Clifton and others . . .

> who though men of more eminent quality and greater revenues, yet paid not so much as he, but they, though they be men of greater estates, yet live according to their estates and quality, whereas Markham out of £800 per annum in land, and it is thought £40,000 in money, spends not £40 in all manner of expenses, and has none to leave all this to but two bastards that he will not acknowledge.

Nicholas might also perceive, added Byron, by Markham's letter, that Byron was not the only man with this opinion of his wealth: the Sheriff of Yorkshire concurred with him, and 'Lord Newcastle in the knighting business[15] had the like conceit of Markham'.[16]

The general reluctance to pay harrassed Byron beyond the term of his shrievalty: in August he told Secretary Coke that it would be the last week in September before all was gathered in. Subsequently his successor, Sir Hardolph Wasteneys, complained that Byron had sent him neither the names of persons refusing to pay, nor the rest of the £300 due. And after all this the outgoing Sheriff, George Lassells, reported in May 1638 that Sir John Byron refused to pay £3 of his own assessment!

It was truly Byronic to boggle at such a trifling amount and yet, little more than a month later (28 June) to buy the manor of Rochdale from Sir Robert Heath, Attorney-General, for £2,500. The lease of 1585 had expired, it will be remembered, in 1616, when the manor reverted to the Crown and as Heath mortgaged it to the present Sir John Byron soon after he himself acquired it, the period of its alienation from the family was comparatively short. Whether he preferred Lancashire to Nottinghamshire because it was his beloved mother's native county, or whether money troubles forced a change of residence, we may never know;[17] but his intention to make it his principal seat was confirmed by his subsequent choice of Rochdale as his territorial title when he was raised to the peerage a few years later.

Early in 1639 Lady Byron died and on 20 February she was buried, not at Colwick, but in a new vault in Hucknall Church. The tenor bell of the church, cast in this year, may have been given by Byron in her memory. Public duties did not allow him to indulge his grief for long. Like his uncle Nicholas he was soon engaged in the campaign against Scotland—so much so, indeed, that while stationed at Berwick early in 1640 he decided not to stand again for knight of the shire. In June he was quartered near Newcastle and after his return to Berwick he wrote on 24 September to Lord Newburgh that he hoped the effect of the meeting of the Peers with the King would be 'to drive out those vipers we have been too ready to entertain in our bosoms'. He referred to certain wardship lands belonging to his stepson and desired 'that Robin Bindloss may not stir from Cambridge this winter, for till he have more discretion, I believe it best for him to be where he may be most kept in awe'.[18] One may, perhaps, surmise that a military campaign had more attraction for the boy than his studies; nor was this the only occasion on which he did not see eye to eye with his stern stepfather: despite his Royalist upbringing, young Bindloss sided with Parliament in the Civil War.

The general unpopularity of the Bishops' War and the success of the Scots proved too much for Charles I. The Great Council of the Peers at York, mentioned in Byron's letter, was his last attempt to evade the necessity of calling a Parliament. His project did not succeed, however, and he was obliged to abandon the Scottish campaign and summon the two Houses to Westminster—the beginning of the famous Long Parliament.

On 26 December 1641 Sir John Byron was appointed Lieutenant of the Tower of London. His tenure of office was brief and stormy. The King had removed his predecessor, Colonel Lunsford, in response to objections, but the appointment of one so closely attached to His Majesty as Byron was known to be was equally unpopular with a Parliament increasingly anxious to obtain some measure of control over strategic points like the Tower. On 11 January 1642 the Commons asked the Lords to join them in a petition to the King for the removal of Byron from his command and the appointment of Sir John Conyers in his place. They also commanded Byron to attend them at 10 o'clock on the following morning. The Lords declined to join in the petition and Byron, forbidden to leave the Tower without the King's permission, refused to attend Parliament, whereupon food supplies to the Tower were stopped. On the 14th it was reported to be absolutely blocked up. The seamen offered their services to batter it.

On 21 January the Sheriffs of London visited the Tower and acquainted Sir John with an order of the House of Commons, authorising a guard of trained bands to prevent ammunition being taken in or

out without their warrant and to see that no more victuals than usual
were brought in. Ships were ordered to lie at Tower Wharf to keep a
similar guard by water. Byron replied that this was a great violation of
the privileges of the Tower which he was sworn to preserve and, being
commanded also to cashier all the new warders, he pointed out that
they had been increased with the approval of Parliament because the
former number was insufficient to do the duty and that he could not
discharge them without the King's order. Reporting this matter to
Secretary Nicholas, Byron wrote that he had asked the Sheriffs to leave
a copy of the order with him . . .

> but their wisdoms would by no means consent to it. By this, Sir, you may
> see that though I carry myself never so fairly, they are resolved to pick
> quarrels with me. I shall be very careful . . . to give no just causes of
> offence; but truly, if they go about to starve me, or offer any other
> violence, though I cannot promise to keep this place long in the condition
> I am in, yet I will sell both it & my life at as dear a rate as I can.

On 28 January he wrote again to Nicholas, this time about a conspiracy
to surprise the Tower:

> The same day that his Majesty . . . gave me leave to attend the Parlmt.,
> Captain Skippon towards the evening marched very privately when it was
> dark to the backside of the Tower, & stayed at the iron gate with his men,
> which were about 500, where having continued a while with great silence,
> he sent one into the Tower to the Serjeant, who commanded the Hamleters
> that night, that he should march out of the Tower with his men & come to
> him.

On the Serjeant's refusing, Skippon assured him that Byron would
never come into the Tower again as Lieutenant; and then desired him
to draw his men up to the iron gate, and upon the shooting of a musket
to be ready to assist him.

> Whilst these things were in agitation, [continued Byron] I returned from
> the Parlmt., it being almost 10 o'clock at night before I had my dis-
> mission; & so the plot was spoiled.[19]

Parliament, however, did not cease to harry the unfortunate Lieutenant,
who asked to be allowed to resign rather than 'stay to be thrust out by
them'; and eventually on 11 February King Charles consented to the
appointment of Sir John Conyers in his place. At the same time Byron
begged leave to cashier the forty new warders whom the King had
authorised him to retain,

> which would have yielded me above 3,000£ present benefit, yet I have
> forborne to advantage myself that way, considering how unfit it would be to

put his Majesty to 1,000£ yearly charge, in case the Tower should be
disposed of by the Parliament.

The King cannot have had many subjects so considerate of his purse.

The struggle between King and Parliament must soon result in open
war and there was never a moment's doubt where the sympathies of the
Byrons lay. Sir John was willing enough to place his fortune at His
Majesty's disposal, but he had little fortune to place. In April he
pledged some of his plate to Mrs Sarah March or Marshe for £75, to be
retained by her unless he redeemed it within a year. He never recovered
it and subsequently a chest of his plate, weighing 429¾ ounces passed
into the hands of Solomon Smith of St Katherine's near the Tower, to be
haggled over after Byron's death. By now his debts, like those of his
grandfather, amounted to a very large sum—£20,000, including £4,000
owed to his kinsmen the Hutchinsons—and in the course of the year,
together with his brother Richard, he sold Over and Nether Colwick to
Sir James Stonehouse for £23,000. Of this he received either £14,000 or
£16,000, which he distributed among his creditors, promising them the
rest when he received the balance from Stonehouse; but it was never
paid. Having made the best settlement he could, Sir John was one of the
first to join the King at York, whence he wrote on 8 July to the Earl of
Worcester, at the King's command, that he would be ready at Newstead
to receive the money which the Earl had arranged to send there
privately for His Majesty's service. On the 24th, however, he had to
apologise for being absent from home when Sir John Somerset brought
the £5,000 to Newstead, adding that Charles had commanded him to
use it for the levying of 500 horse. He was also employed in collecting
ammunition, for which his uncle Nicholas thanked the Sheriff of
Leicestershire on 5 August; three days later Sir Nicholas himself, with
troops of horse from York, succeeded in removing some ordnance from
the town and castle of Banbury. Unlike many other Royalists, uncle
and nephew had sufficient military experience to make their support of
value. (John, like Nicholas, is said to have campaigned in the Netherlands, but details are lacking.) Nicholas, many years later, was described
as being 'as excellent a Commander of Foot, as Sir John was of Horse
. . . the Life-guard of the World by his Piety, and by His Prudence, a
person whom his late Majesty [Charles I] in all engagements would
have always near him'.[20]

Richard probably had no such experience. To him, John being
childless, had fallen the task of founding a family to ensure the succession
and, though his monument credits him with ten children, rearing them
was, as often in those days, a hazardous proceeding. His wife Elizabeth,

daughter of George Rossell, was the widow of Nicholas Strelley, and at Strelley, within easy distance of Newstead, he made his home. William, his eldest son and heir, appears to have been born about 1635, and on 25 March in the following year his second son, Richard, was buried at Colwick. Dates of birth and death of his eldest daughter, Elizabeth, are lacking; Anne was laid in the new family vault at Hucknall on 12 April 1640, followed by Cecilia or Cecily on 5 May 1641. Of the rest little is known: Catherine grew up to be married; a second Cicely is said[21] to have been buried at Hucknall in 1645; a Lucy Byron who married Edmund Turnor of Panton and Stoke Rochford may have been Richard's daughter, though it remains unproved; Mary's life is a complete blank; but even the name and sex of the tenth child are forgotten. As Richard seems to have kept in closer touch with Nottingham affairs than his brothers he was, presumably, the 'Maister Byron' who, with Sir Thomas Hutchinson, requested the Corporation to appoint Mr Wiggfall, M.A. as usher of the Free School in the town in November 1636.

Robert and Gilbert Byron had both adopted military careers. Robert, eulogised by Lloyd as this 'excellent person, higher in his relation to God by his sacred Birth (*contingit sanguine caelum*) than to his Noble Family by his first', spent much of his life in Ireland, where he had attained the rank of captain by September 1640. In 1641 he was Lieutenant-Colonel in Sir Henry Tichborne's regiment, at first acting without commission, which the King ordered him to receive on 11 May 1642. On 5 March that year he 'had the good fortune to defeat a considerable part of the rebels' army, amongst whom he took prisoner . . . Art Roe McPatrick McArt Moyle McMahowne', for whose head £100 was offered. He was accordingly recommended to the favour of the Lord Lieutenant of Ireland and certificates of his service were later transmitted to the Commissioners for the affairs of Ireland by the Lords Justices and Council, who added that Robert was 'one of the captains who also endured that hard siege [of Drogheda], and merited well in the public services there'.[22] His services at Drogheda were compensated with no more than the normal official delay, but he did not get the reward for his prisoner until after the Restoration. Robert married Lucy, daughter of Thomas West, Lord de la Warr, and therefore sister of Sir John Byron's first wife. All but one of their children died in infancy.

In May of 1639 Gilbert Byron was listed as a lieutenant in the Lieutenant-General's troop—one of six troops of a regiment of horse for the safeguard of the King's person. He served in the Netherlands and in the summer of 1639 or 1640, when he was taking 120 men to Bremen to help the Elector Palatine, the magistrates there refused to let them pass, so that he was forced to take them overland to Amsterdam, at great expense to himself. There 33 were taken by officers of the West India Company, and more at a later date, which cost Gilbert above £600. He therefore petitioned the King for leave to arrest any of the States' ships then in His Majesty's harbours, and to detain them until he received satisfaction for his loss.

There were, however, lighter moments in his career, as for example at the beginning of 1640, when he enjoyed a thrilling hunt in the company of Elizabeth of Bohemia. The Queen's account of it to Sir Thomas Roe runs:

> . . . I must tell you a great exploit achieved here. I did hunt a hare last week with my hounds. It took seven hours, the dogs never being at a fault. I went out with forty horse at least, and there were but five at the death of the hare, myself, your daughter, Honeywood, Stone and Biron. Maurice, Prince Raveuille, the Archduke and many other knight were intreated by their horses to return on foot. I could not but tell you this adventure, for it is very famous here.'[23]

Early in 1641 the same Queen told Sir Thomas Roe that she had had much ado to get Gilbert Byron, who served her, his Uncle (Nicholas)'s company, though he was to quit her service for it. By now, however, he had evidently returned to England and in April was threatening to resign his position as lieutenant to Captain Daniel O'Neale, being weary of the way he was treated by him. A few months later the sum of £100, given to Gilbert by the Earl of Holland for an unspecified purpose, seemed likely to embroil him in a dispute between the Paymaster and the Governor of Carlisle (his uncle Sir Nicholas Byron); but the circumstances are obscure.[24] As one of the Royal bodyguard, he attended King Charles I when that monarch went to the House of Commons on 3 January 1642 to arrest the five members accused of high treason.

Thomas, the fifth Byron brother, who had married Katherine, daughter of Henry Braine, was also in the Army by May 1642, when he was commissioned lieutenant in the Prince of Wales's Regiment of Horse. Nothing is known of the pre-war activities of William and Philip, who were both to give distinguished service to their King.

## · 4 ·

# Against Traitors Contending:
# The Cavalier Brothers at War

On Marston, with Rupert, 'gainst traitors contending,
  Four brothers enrich'd, with their blood, the bleak field;
For the rights of a monarch their country defending,
  Till death their attachment to royalty seal'd.

*On Leaving Newstead Abbey.*

EIGHT years had passed since Charles I paid his first state visit to Nottingham when, rebellion being yet unthought of, he was welcomed with the customary pomp and circumstance, at heavy expense to the town. His second coming in July of 1642 found the town divided: the mace was reluctantly handed to him by a Mayor who had refused to publish royal proclamations and had twice ignored the King's summons to attend him at York. Charles exercised his royal forbearance on this occasion; but why, a few weeks later, he should have chosen Nottingham as his rallying point is unclear: the feeling in the town was predominantly in favour of Parliament. Geographically, however, the site was eminently suitable, lying between the main body of Royalist forces in the northwest and the capital in the south-east, which they hoped to win back from the Roundhead rebels. Moreover, the nobility and gentry of the county, with few exceptions, supported their King and a considerable body of troops and baggage-waggons converged upon Nottingham in response to the proclamation of 12 August, summoning all who could bear arms north of the Trent and twenty miles to the south to rally to the King in ten days.

The allegiance of the seven Byron brothers and their uncle Nicholas was unquestioned, but we do not know how many of them were present at the raising of the standard. The King, with his two sons and 800 horse, entered Nottingham on 19 August and the following day Sir John Byron rode with him to Coventry, intending to secure that town before the Parliamentary forces arrived there. Failing in this, they

returned to Nottingham; on Monday evening, 22 August, in unpro-
pitiously stormy weather, the unwieldy, maypole-like standard was set
up on rising ground to the north of the half-ruined Castle. At the last
minute the King snatched from the herald's hand the denunciation of
the Parliament forces as rebels and made some alterations in it; the
dignity of the proceedings was a little marred by the poor fellow's
consequent difficulty in deciphering the royal handwriting.

While Charles remained in Nottingham until 13 September in the
dwindling hope of obtaining numerous recruits Sir John Byron who,
according to Lloyd, brought 'a great appearance' to the standard, was
dispatched to collect recruits and plate from Oxford. On his way
through Northamptonshire he was surprised by the enemy at Brackley
and forced to retreat.

> In this confusion, [he wrote to a Mr. Clarke of Craughton, near Brackley,]
> one of my Groomes who had charge of my baggage was surprized in the
> towne, another who had a Box, wherein was money, apparrell, and other
> things of Valew, left it in a land of standing Corne, which since hath been
> found, and as I heare brought to you; I have therefore sent this Messenger
> to require the restitution of it; which if you doe, I shall represent it to His
> Majesty as an acceptable service, if not, assure your selfe, I will finde a
> time to repay my selfe with advantage out of your estate; And consider
> that as rebellion is a weed of a hasty growth, so it will decay as suddenly;
> and that there will be a time for the Kings loyall Subjects to repaire their
> losses sustained by rebels and traytors; So I rest in expectation of a speedy
> answer by this bearer,
>
> Your friend and servant,<br>Iohn Byron.

Outraged at being called rebels and traitors, the Parliamentarians
printed this 'insolent' letter and made much capital from it; it seems
unlikely that Byron ever recovered his box. He was to lose much more
before the war ended.

Sir John arrived at Oxford on 28 August and after a fortnight he left
the town, taking much valuable plate and accompanied by about 100
armed scholars as volunteers to join Prince Rupert at Worcester, which
he reached on 16 September. Worcester, being unfortified, was evacu-
ated on the 23rd and Sir John brought a welcome reinforcement of
horse and, says Lloyd, 'a round summe', to the King at Shrewsbury,
where the Royalist forces were being concentrated. Here within a few
days two of his brothers received the honour of knighthood, Thomas on
27 September[1] and Richard on 1 October.

The first big clash of the war took place at Edgehill in Warwickshire
on 23 October. Sir John Byron was present in command of his regiment,

which constituted the only reserve; but when Prince Rupert's charge scattered the enemy Byron impetuously joined in the chase, leaving the foot, which he had been posted to protect, to be taken in the rear. His Uncle Nicholas was wounded, but not seriously. Although morally an advantage to the Royalists, this battle was indecisive and consequently the Earl of Essex's army fell back on Warwick, while the King went on to Oxford which, after an abortive attempt to reach London, he made his headquarters for the winter. Most of the Byrons appear to have been with him, except Robert, who was still in Ireland in December. On 1 November the University bestowed honorary degrees of D.C.L. on John and Nicholas and an M.A. on Richard. According to some accounts, Thomas, Robert and William also received degrees at the same time.

The value of the Byrons to the Royalist cause lay in more than their unswerving allegiance and personal courage. They were not mere boys, plunging with heedless gallantry into the excitement of war, but men in the prime of life with experience of military or civil affairs (or both), and able to realise the gravity and probable intensity of the conflict. They seem, for the most part, to have abandoned their homes entirely; some of their wives shared the nomadic existence of their husbands and played their own parts in the struggle. Sir John Byron's efforts to raise money have already been described; Nicholas's wife, Sophia, in this first November of the war, delivered to Phineas Andrews (presumably as security for a loan) household furniture, clothes, linen, Dutch pictures, agate cups and other rarities to the value of £200. The pictures, acquired (like his bride) in the Netherlands, reveal a discriminating taste in art and this brief enumeration suggests the breaking up of a cultured, comfortable home. That transaction, like the affair of his nephew's plate, led to complications later on.

Meanwhile, a regiment of horse under the command of John Byron and some of his brothers was quartered at Fawley Court, the Buckinghamshire home of Bulstrode Whitelock, who complained bitterly about the ravages of the troops. He admitted that the Byrons had given express orders 'that they should commit no Insolence at my House, nor plunder my Goods; but Soldiers are not easily govern'd against their Plunder, or persuaded to restrain it'. His tale of wanton damage has a familiar ring.

By the year's end Sir John was stationed at Reading. On Saturday, 31 December, with 14 men (according to a contemporary letter) he routed some 2,000 from Cirencester who 'fell into' his quarters at Burford, killing 20 and granting quarter to none. 'In this night service,' says the same account, 'Sir John got a noble scar in the face.'[2] His brother Thomas became a more serious casualty two months later (19 March): while commanding the Prince's Regiment at Hopton Heath he was so severely shot in the thigh that he had to leave the field.

Sir Nicholas Byron was sent to the West in February as Colonel-General of Shropshire and Cheshire, where he conducted a successful skirmish against the rebels on 21 February at Torperley, a village between Chester and Nantwich. On 13 March he was appointed Governor of Chester which, though staunch to the King, had hitherto lacked an adequate garrison and a skilled and experienced officer to direct the defence of the city. The Corporation signified its approval by admitting him gratis to the freedom of the City on 14 April. Although his governorship was short, he became sufficiently popular with the citizens for at least one child to be christened Byron after him—an honour also accorded to his nephew John at a later stage of the siege. Sir Nicholas tried to keep in close touch with the Governor of Shrewsbury, Sir Francis Ottley, whom he shrewdly advised to raise money before anything else, the raising of men being of no use without it. When he wrote this (4 March 1643), Chester was in poor condition, the troops of horse in the city being on the point of departure, while their relief had not yet arrived and, said Nicholas, there was little to be done 'till business be followed in an orderly way'.[3] Being, however (in Clarendon's words), 'a person of great affability and dexterity, as well as martial knowledge', Byron, with help from North Wales, soon raised a force of horse and foot whose skirmishes with the enemy were so frequent and successful that Sir William Brereton was obliged to fortify Nantwich for the Parliament and the rival garrisons competed hotly for the rest of the county. In the latter part of June, Nantwich proved its nuisance value by intercepting Sir Nicholas Byron's letters.

The King was still at Oxford. Sir John Byron appears to have remained in that neighbourhood during the spring months, his most successful skirmish occurring on 7 May when, without losing one of his forty horse, he routed 200 rebels near Bicester, killing their captain and 25 men and taking 12 prisoners. If the Roundheads found him a tough opponent in the field they could, however, strike at his purse and on 27 June the House of Commons ordered the Committee in Lancashire to sequester the estate that Sir John Byron had by right of his wife, of whose son he had the guardianship during the boy's minority; and this may have been the 'very urgent business' upon which he asked Prince Rupert's leave to go to Oxford for one night. He wrote[4] from Brackley, where he was driving the country for horses and cattle and one cannot but wonder if he took the opportunity to avenge the detention of his box by Mr Clarke in the previous summer.

The Cornish rising in May had transferred the main theatre of war to the West where, after a spectacular advance, the Cavaliers' Pyrrhic victory at Lansdowne Hill, Bath, robbed them of their leaders and their foot was penned up in Devizes by what remained of the Roundhead force under Sir William Waller. On 12 July Sir John Byron and Prince Maurice accompanied the army sent to their relief under Wilmott, and the great Royalist victory of Roundway Down was in large measure due to the charge of Byron's brigade, which put to flight Sir Arthur Haselrig's formidable regiment of cuirassiers. In his official report to the Secretary about the battle (printed at York), Sir John described vividly how they

> swept their whole Body of Horse out of the Field, and left their Foot naked, and pursued them neare three Miles over the Downes in Bristoll way till they came to a precipice, where their Feare made them so valiant that they gallop't down as if it had been plain ground, and many of them brake both their own and their Horses necks.

The speedy surrender of Bristol gave the Royalists mastery of the West, but the troops, whose pay was always in arrears, were ever ready to desert or mutiny for plunder. On 27 July, Byron warned Prince Rupert that he foresaw a mutiny unless the soldiers received some benefit from His Highness's victory at Bristol.

Emboldened by this success, the Earl of Newcastle in the North summoned the town and castle of Nottingham to surrender, safe-conduct for the messenger, Major Cartwright, being requested on 7 August by Sir Richard Byron who some time between March and August had succeeded Sir John Henderson as Governor of Newark, the Royalist stronghold in Nottinghamshire. Nottingham's reply to Newcastle was but a more polite version of George Hutchinson's unofficial retort to Cartwright that 'If my Lord would have that poor castle he must wade to it in blood'.

The Governor of Nottingham at this time was Colonel John Hutchinson, cousin of the Byrons, who were naturally upset by his support of Parliament, and perhaps because, as Lucy Hutchinson suggests, 'the dissention of brethren is allwayes most spitefully persued', he and Sir Richard Byron were to each other the 'most uncivil enemies' imaginable. Nevertheless, through the medium of a Mr Ayscough, Richard now, 'out of love and tender compassion to him', begged Hutchinson to surrender, promising that he would find means to save his rents for the present and his estate for the future. To this Hutchinson replied that 'except he found his owne heart prone to such treachery, he might consider there was, if nothing elce, so much of a Biron's blood in him, that he should very much scorne to betray or quitt a trust that he had undertaken'.[5] A Royalist force from Newark raided Nottingham on 18 September and caused much trouble before they were driven out five days later. Colonel Hutchinson's brother George fell in with a troop under Sir Richard Byron and although his men were outnumbered they got Sir Richard down and captured his hat. He himself escaped, but his horse was so badly wounded that it fell dead in the next street.

Slowly the balance of fortune was being turned by the firmness of the Parliamentary leaders. The siege of Gloucester was raised by Essex and the indecisive result of the first battle of Newbury on 20 September, where Sir John Byron commanded the horse of the right wing, attached to a brigade of infantry under his Uncle Nicholas, further weakened the Royalist hold on the West. By 16 October Sir John was back at Oxford, asking Colonel Aldrich, the Governor of Aylesbury, for a trusty go-between, by whom he would propose something to Aldrich's advantage. On 24 October his services to the King were rewarded by the grant of a peerage. He chose to be styled Baron Byron of Rochdale—the only estate he had any hope of retaining after the war—and as he had no child the title was granted with remainder to his six surviving brothers, Richard, William, Thomas, Robert, Gilbert and Philip.

Returning to Brackley, which seemed to have a curious attraction for him, Lord Byron wrote to Prince Rupert on 6 November to ask for pay for his regiment and reported that a 'poor woman go-between' at Aylesbury (doubtless the one he had asked Colonel Aldrich to provide a few weeks earlier) had been taken by the enemy and probably hanged. He wrote again the following day to accept Rupert's offer of the sole command in Lancashire, provided that he was given time to get his regiment in fit condition for such a long march; he was informed by friends that he might be appointed Governor to the Prince of Wales in place of Lord Hertford and he asked the Prince 'to bee a meanes to make that sure to mee before I goe; this beeinge but a tenporary, that an employment likely to continue to my advantage, when this warr is ended'.[6]

As a result of Ormonde's truce, the soldiers engaged in suppressing Irish rebels were set free for service elsewhere and by the end of November Lord Byron had marched westward by way of Bridgnorth (where the Corporation hospitably refreshed him with a pottle of sack and a sugar loaf) to meet detachments brought over from Ireland with the object of sweeping Cheshire and Lancashire clear of the enemy. With this welcome aid his army is described as rolling like a flood up to the walls of Nantwich, the only garrison held by the Parliament in Cheshire; but it was not an easy objective. Further reinforcements from

Ireland followed, Colonel Robert Byron among them. He left Dublin on 1 December with orders to land, if possible, at Chester. A fortnight previously his services in the defence of Drogheda and elsewhere had been rewarded by a royal grant of the town, castle and lands of Ballygarth and the towns of Inglandstone and Moorechurch, Co. Meath.

Although Nantwich remained untaken, Lord Byron's army had some success in the neighbourhood; but, on Saturday 23 December, occurred an episode which greatly sullied his reputation. A detachment of his troops under Major Connaught entered Barthomley Church, where about twenty men from the surrounding district had taken refuge in the steeple, and by burning forms, pews and rushes smoked them out, forcing them to call for quarter. When Connaught had them in his power, however, 'he caused them all to be stripped stark naked, and most barbarously and contrary to the laws of arms murdered, stabbed and cut the throats of 12 of them . . . and wounded all the rest, leaving many of them for dead'.[7] It is unclear in the contemporary records whether the victims (who included the village schoolmaster) were armed or not, but the episode cannot be discounted as a mere atrocity story, for Lord Byron, though not apparently present in person, showed his approval of the horrible business by writing to the Marquis of Newcastle:

> The Rebels had possessed themselves of a Church at Bartumley, but wee presently beat them forth of it, and put them all to the sword, which I find to be the best way to proceed with their kind of people, for mercy to them is cruelty.

Unfortunately, his letter fell into enemy hands; they gleefully printed it for propaganda and any material advantage derived from the exploit was offset by the natural indignation it caused. This condoning of savagery in one whom contemporary writers present as a gallant and chivalrous gentleman is hard to understand. If it were an isolated incident, we might assume that Byron's wholehearted devotion to the King's cause, which cost him home and fortune and the bitterness of exile, bordered on fanaticism: the mounting strength of the Round-heads was becoming perceptible; perhaps he was frenzied by a fore-boding of the King's defeat—a possibility never previously entertained. However, this was not the only time that he was accused of cruelty and even so staunch a Royalist as Randle Holme said that his barbarity was so great that 'he prospered not'. He apparently had a streak of latent cruelty which the stress of war brought to the surface. Significantly, his brother Robert mentions the affair approvingly in a letter to the Marquis of Ormonde.[8]

[ 75 ]

This unhappy affair was but the foreshadowing of a cloud of misfortune gathering over the Byrons. Sir Robert Byron's aforementioned letter was dispatched on 9 January 1644 to give Ormonde news of an encounter at Middlewich on 26 December, when the Irish Royalist troops won a notable victory over Sir William Brereton's forces, with small loss to themselves; Robert himself was wounded, however, and apologised for not sending Ormonde other news because 'the anguish of my hurt made me heedless of [every]thing: this being the first day, I have been able to sit up, which I a little forced myself unto, that I might not seem unthinking in my respects to your Excellency'.

The very day after this letter was written Newstead Abbey was pillaged by a party of Roundheads sent from Nottingham to collect food and money from Mansfield. The raid was greatly magnified later by the sixth Baron in his *Elegy on Leaving Newstead Abbey* ('War's dread machines o'erhang thy threat'ning brow'), but when Colonel Wildman, who bought the Abbey from the poet, was questioned about the possibility of a siege, he replied dryly, 'As a soldier I should say it must have been a very short one!—at least, if Old Noll commanded in person'.[9] Any resistance must have been slight. Although the family plate had been removed, other goods of value which remained were loaded into carts to accompany the booty from Mansfield. But the Royalists in Derbyshire heard of the raid and *en route* to Nottingham the convoy was attacked by 100 horse from Wingfield Manor under Colonel John Frescheville, who had what he called a 'little scuffle' with the rebels in a narrow lane near Bestwood Park. He was driven off after a sharp fight, with casualties on both sides. Even so, some of the plunder did not reach the official rebel coffers, for in 1647 Capt.-Lieut. Roe and Ensign James Rotherham (both Parliamentary officers) were accused of misappropriating goods and jewels seized on this occasion. The Abbey for a time was held as a Parliamentary garrison under the command of Colonel Francis Pierrepont; but the tradition that the Roundheads did further damage to the remains of the church and destroyed the images of saints that once stood in the niches, though possible, is unsupported by evidence.

The Parliament army under Sir Thomas Fairfax was believed to be on the way to Lancashire, where the Royalist headquarters at Oxford hoped he would receive 'a sharp entertainment' from Lord Byron with his Irish regiments. On 14 January, however, John had to report to Prince Rupert that two days previously his Uncle Nicholas, while travelling from Shrewsbury to Chester with his wife in company with Sir Richard Willis, was surprised by Colonel Mitton at Ellesmere on a dark and stormy night, and taken prisoner with others of his party. He was committed to the Tower on 10 February.

Further reverses followed. A determined assault was made on Nantwich on 18 January; but a sudden thaw swelled a little river that ran between two sections of the Royalist army and after making a detour of four or five miles, Byron's division arrived to find that the other section had been defeated by Fairfax, who captured the chief officers, 1,500 soldiers, and all the artillery. Every regiment except Sir Robert Byron's lost its colours.

John Byron retired to Chester. As usual the Cavaliers were acutely in need of money and on 20 February he borrowed £60 from the Corporation. With this aid he held the menaced city until the arrival of Prince Rupert put fresh heart into the garrison. On Monday 11 March, accompanied by Lord Byron and others, the Prince rode through the streets lined with soldiers to be welcomed at the Cross by the Mayor, Randle Holme, who, being lame, came in a coach, and by the Corporation, resplendent in their robes of office. The next morning he rode round the city to inspect its defence works; and either then or shortly afterwards Byron was appointed Governor of Chester in place of Sir Abraham Shipman.

The first gap in the ranks of the Cavalier brothers was opened by the death at Oxford of Sir Thomas Byron, victim of a senseless murder. On 7 December 1643, after a dispute about pay, he was attacked in the street by Captain Hurst of his own regiment. At first there seemed a chance of his recovery, but after lingering in agony for nearly two months he died on 5 February 1643/4 and was buried four days later in Christchurch Cathedral, 'on the left side of the grave of Wm. Lord Grandison, in a little isle joyning on the south side of the choir'. His murderer had already been executed—'shot to death with five carbines'—a week after the attack. About thirty-seven, Thomas was considered a very valuable and experienced officer and was, in practice, the leader of the Prince of Wales's Regiment of Horse, under the titular command of the Earl of Cumberland. Both his sons are said to have died before him, but John possibly survived.[11] His widow Katherine proved herself equally a Cavalier in spirit by acting as a secret service agent in the King's cause.

Several northern gentlemen of Sir Thomas Byron's regiment were assigned, after his death, to Lord Wentworth. Not liking this they decided to return home, but on their way they were attacked by a party from Colonel Hutchinson's garrison at Nottingham, who took eight of them prisoners. When the news reached Sir Richard Byron at Newark, for the sake of his brother's memory he promptly exchanged them for prisoners taken in Nottingham during the raid of the previous September. Newark, too, was feeling the pressure of Parliamentary strength, particularly on the Lincolnshire side, and the difficulty of obtaining provisions had already obliged the Governor to ask Lord Loughborough for help. From the postscript to Richard's letter it seems that the shortage of cheese worried him most. The position was actually serious since Newcastle's retreat into Yorkshire, because Newark was now the only Royalist stronghold in the East Midlands and blocked the north-ward advance of the Parliamentary forces. The Roundheads had already occupied villages within three or four miles of the town and on 29 February Sir John Meldrum began the siege in earnest. Most of the Royalist horse was sent away before this, leaving a garrison of fewer than 2,000 men; yet with this small force Sir Richard Byron contrived to hold the town against greatly superior numbers until it was relieved—a gallant defence which sufficiently refutes the assertion of Gervase Holles that he was 'a person of a narrow soule and every way unequall to the charge he undertooke'.[12]

By 6 March, when the Muskham fort was captured by Meldrum, the town was completely encircled and the Governor sending out desperate appeals for help. With some difficulty Prince Rupert was made to realise the urgency of the occasion. On 12 March, accordingly, having finished his tour of Chester, Rupert set out for Newark, collecting reinforcements on the way. His attack on Meldrum's army resulted in a spectacular Royalist victory and by the 22nd Newark was once more free. Sir Richard Byron was for some time busily employed in disposing of his prisoners.

The main scene of battle now shifted to Yorkshire, where the Marquis of Newcastle was besieged in York by the Scots and the Roundhead forces under Lord Fairfax and his son, Sir Thomas Fairfax, who were joined in May by the Earl of Manchester and Oliver Cromwell. Once more Prince Rupert marched to the relief and on 2 July came the great clash at Marston Moor. Of the four brothers who, according to tradition, took part in the battle, John was indubitably one, Philip almost certainly another; and the other two were probably William and Gilbert. Robert, who had been knighted at Oxford on 12 May, seems to have been left to govern Liverpool when Rupert took the city before march-ing into Yorkshire; and Newark still claimed Sir Richard Byron's attention.

At Marston Moor, Lord Byron's impetuosity led him into the same error he had committed at Edgehill. His regiment was on the right wing, in the front rank of Prince Rupert's division, and instead of waiting for Cromwell's cavalry to reach him, he charged across the ditch behind which he was stationed to fight on less favourable ground, with disastrous results, for although Prince Rupert brought his whole force to the rescue, they were completely swept from the field. The Royalist left at first was more successful, routing Fairfax's horse, but when faced by the relieving force of Cromwell's well-disciplined cavalry, they shared the fate of the right wing, and the infantry of the centre were soon equally overwhelmed. When night came, the Royalists had suffered a crushing defeat and though Prince Rupert escaped, to be joined by some of his officers in York, Newcastle's army was wiped out. Lord Byron's thoughts must have been bitter as he rode from the field, but there was no trace in them of the defeatist attitude that sent Newcastle scurrying abroad to ignominious safety.

Attempts to gloss over the disaster did not deceive Sir Richard Byron, for though he wrote to Lord Loughborough that 'the supposed victory we had in the north over the rebels proves (as their own side calls it) an Edgehill battle', i.e. indecisive, which was putting it mildly, after cautiously telling Prince Rupert that 'the success of your Highness's late encounter with the great body of the rebels we have understood in the general only', he continued more boldly, 'we have thought it our duty to consider how we might recruit your Highness with some considerable force'. Two days later (8 July) he urged upon Loughborough that 'It is most necessary that we should draw your forces, ours, and the rest we expect from the other garrisons into a body, but we cannot conceive fit to move until we hear from the Prince'.[13]

Retreating with what remained of his horse, Rupert left York as well garrisoned and provisioned as he could and the enemy promptly resumed the siege, which lasted little more than a week. During the final storming of the city on 16 July, Sir Philip Byron was killed when Lord Manchester's troops attacked the Manor House, and he was buried in York Minster on the following day. Though the records of his life are scanty, Lloyd's curious little character sketch is tantalisingly suggestive:

> Sir Philip Biron, a gentleman of a wide and capacious soul to grasp much, and of an enlarged heart to communicate it; θεραπωνεπωτος, a Servant of Love; a great Master of 'ερωτικὴτεκνὴ, the Art of Love, as if, with Socrates, he that knew every thing, knew nothing but how to love. After many signal services in York-shire, in each whereof there was always observed something of a judicious stratagem, in a general Storm by the whole Parliament Army upon York, he was killed in the Head of his Regiment, which never went out, but he would tell them, *That never brave man came to any thing, that resolved not either to Conquer or perish* [—a thoroughly Byronic maxim].[14]

What Lloyd implies by 'Servant of Love, Master of the art of love,' it is impossible to say. Philip's marriage seems to have been a war-time romance that ended all too soon in tragedy. His wife was a Miss Heskett or Hesketh—her Christian name is forgotten, but she may have been one of the Heskeths of Rufford Old Hall in Lancashire—and though we do not know when or where they were married, it was probably after the outbreak of the war. After Sir Philip's death, his young widow was living in Chester, of which her brother-in-law, Lord Byron, was Governor (except for a short time in the autumn of 1644, when he was superseded by William Legge); and here on 27 August, little more than a month after the death of her husband, her brother Henry was buried in Holy Trinity Church. She followed him to the grave on 16 November, leaving a little daughter, Anne, baptised but a week before, who survived her mother only another week and was laid to rest in the same church on 24 November.

*

After the battle of Marston Moor, Lord Byron had returned to his command in the west; in August he was involved in the defeat of Sir Marmaduke Langdale's northern horse near Ormskirk, as they marched southward. Byron had come from Liverpool, mounted 'on a pacing nag, and thinking of nothing less than fighting that day'; and in trying to rally his regiment, which was thrown into confusion by the flight of Lord Molyneux's brigade, he was unhorsed and nearly captured. He was rescued by Langdale, who brought off his own men without trouble. In the following month (18 September) he was defeated by Sir William Brereton in an attempt to regain Montgomery Castle, which Lord Herbert of Cherbury had surrendered to Parliament, thereby impeding Byron's contact with Shrewsbury. Again he had a narrow escape, being saved this time by the quality of his horse; with 300 cavalry and some remaining infantry he retreated towards Shrewsbury. The Royalists suffered another heavy blow on 1 November, when Sir Robert Byron was obliged to surrender Liverpool.

By this time many were wavering in their allegiance to the King. Although the officers were still, for the most part, ready to endure anything, lack of pay provoked mutiny in the ranks and daily desertions. There was friction in Chester between Lord Byron and Governor Legge, each blaming the other for contributing to the Royalist reverses, and in October Byron was grumbling at not having, as before, sole charge in Prince Rupert's absence. Though he did not mind Legge's being Governor of Chester, he objected to his command being extended to cover Cheshire, Flint and Denbigh, and he even begged to be recalled if he was not worthy of the command he formerly held. He remained in favour, however, and in his capacity as Gentleman of the Robes to James, Duke of York, was directed to receive £5,000 for defraying the expenses of the Duke's robes and privy purse.

Despite his military preoccupations, some time during 1644 John Byron found time to marry again. He was forty-four and his new wife, Eleanor, daughter of Robert Needham, Viscount Kilmorey, only seventeen; but she was already a widow, having been married at the age of eleven to Peter Warburton of Arley in Cheshire, who died at Oxford of smallpox in August 1641, aged nineteen. Her noted beauty was to bring her a somewhat invidious distinction after Lord Byron's death.

The early months of 1645 were no more auspicious for the Byrons individually than for the Royalist cause as a whole. John remained near Chester and at the beginning of February 'Bloody Byron' (the epithet recalling the episode at Barthomley) was reported to be in Beeston Castle. Early in January, Joseph Rhodes was sent to Newark with Lieutenant-Colonel Whichcote, who carried a letter to Sir Richard Byron from his mother, then at Merton College, Oxford, 'which letter opened of itself[!], being slightly made fast by a cover of paper'. In it she warned her son that the Prince had appointed Rhodes to share the governorship of Newark with him and urged him either to contest the appointment or resign his commission. 'I would advise you,' she continued, 'to get Sir Jervase Clifton and the rest of your friends to write to the King and Prince Rupert that they will not have Rhodes to govern there.' The letter was copied before it was delivered to the Governor, and on 10 January Rhodes reported the matter to Prince Rupert, adding that he was told Sir Richard Byron would not mind another person being appointed to control the surrounding district, providing that he himself retained the command within the walls. Before the end of the month Richard was superseded as Governor by Sir Richard Willis, but the exact reason for his downfall was evidently as obscure to earlier writers as it is to us. In Warburton's *Memoirs of Prince Rupert* it is attributed to slackness and incompetence; and Whitelock records that he was suspected of corresponding with the Parliamentary party—a charge which sounds like enemy propaganda. Mrs Hutchinson is probably nearer the mark when she speaks of 'high discontents' between the Governor and the King's Commissioners at Newark. Dr Wood has pointed out that Prince Rupert's vigorous championship of Willis later on suggests he was responsible for his appointment as Governor;[15] and Rhodes's intriguing letter had thus probably borne fruit, we may assume, but not to the writer's personal advantage. Sir Richard Byron's active part in the war was almost at an end. He appears to have joined his brothers in the west. In April he and Robert were taken prisoners at Chester by Sir William Brereton. In September Richard was living in the Parliament's quarters, where he remained until the following June.

On 23 January 1645, Parliament ordered that 'Lieutenant-Colonel

Byron [presumably either Gilbert or William] now prisoner at Manchester, be neither exchanged nor released without the Privity and Consent of this House'. He was soon followed into captivity by Sir Nicholas, who was taken at Shrewsbury on 22 February and sent to Nantwich; but both Nicholas and Robert had regained their freedom before the summer came.

The net was tightening around Chester. On 26 April, about a week after the capture of his brothers, John Byron gave Lord Digby, the Principal Secretary, a dismal account of the condition of the city, urging the need for speedy and powerful relief. He had no thought of surrender, however, assuring him that 'For these poor means I have left to maintain this place. . . . I shall improve them to the utmost, and how unfortunate soever I may be, [you] shall have an account of my charge befitting an honest man & one whom I hope you shall not blush to own'.[16] His appeal was heeded, for the King set out to relieve Chester on his way north to join Montrose, who had defeated the rebels in Scotland; but Byron was able to meet him at Stone, in Staffordshire, with the welcome news that the enemy had, temporarily at least, retired. Charles accordingly turned east and captured Leicester instead—his last success, as it proved, for Fairfax, fearing that the King might threaten London or the eastern counties, abandoned the siege of Oxford and hurried on his track.

The armies met at Naseby, near Northampton, and on 14 June the Royalists suffered a crushing defeat which virtually ended the war. For the remaining months of his freedom King Charles was a fugitive with but a handful of his army—among them, at first, Sir Robert Byron, who had commanded his regiment in the battle. At the end of the year he returned to Ireland. Sir Nicholas was probably with the King also: later in the summer he tried to collect reinforcements in Ireland, returning in September with the news that six thousand Irishmen were to follow him. Further disasters followed, however. On 10 September Prince Rupert surrendered Bristol to Fairfax and a fortnight later the King, who had made his way to Chester, watched from a tower another defeat of his troops by Poyntz at Rowton Heath, two miles away. Charles withdrew to Newark, urging Lord Byron to hold Chester eight days longer. He held it for nearly twenty weeks, and his success in persuading the garrison to endure their very great hardships was even more remarkable than his resistance to the enemy's attacks. Breaches in the walls were stopped up with packs of coarse wool; malcontents who grumbled at the meagre rations were entertained by the Governor to dinner, when they shared his own fare of boiled wheat and spring water. (If Lloyd is to be believed, this Spartan diet later deteriorated into 'Cats, Dogs, yea, and those failing . . . but one meal in three dayes'). And summonses to surrender received contemptuous replies. By 10 October the Parliamentary forces reported to Lenthall that the town was so strictly besieged that none could get in or out, as Byron complained in letters to one of his brothers and to the Archbishop of York, which the enemy had just intercepted. They also captured a messenger who carried a commission appointing Byron Governor of Conway and Field Marshall General of all North Wales—a barren honour for one who could not stir out of Chester, although the Royalists in those parts were struggling to collect sufficient troops to relieve the city and Colonel Gilbert Byron commanded some 500 or 600 men in Carnarvonshire. Early in December, Eleanor Lady Byron went to Oxford and personally begged the King to send relief to her husband. Charles promised to do his utmost, but circumstances were now beyond his control.

At the end of the year, when Brereton complained that Roundhead prisoners in Chester were being starved, Lord Byron replied that they had been far better provided than Royalist prisoners in Brereton's custody:

> We shall so far remember charity begins at home and as your design is to reduce us by starving, not to suffer the plentiful provision of prisoners to straighten those who faithfully serve in the garrison. If you send any provision for them, it shall be faithfully given.

Unwilling to do this, Brereton proposed the exchange of an equal number of prisoners.

By 17 January 1646, Byron was obliged to admit to Lord Astley that Chester could not hold out above nineteen days at most, yet to Brereton's offer of harder terms than those on which he was prepared to surrender he answered (on 27 January) with unabated haughtiness:

> Those demands of mine, which you term unparalleled, have been heretofore granted by far less Commanders than yourself, no disparagement to you, to places in a far worse condition than, God be thanked, this is yet. . . . As for your conceit in demanding of myself and the rest of the commanders and officers, to be your prisoners, I would have you know that we esteem our honor so far above our lives, that no extremity whatsoever can put so mean thoughts into the meanest of us all.[17]

His persistence was rewarded; when the city finally capitulated on 6 February it was on the most honourable terms. Lord Byron himself was to go free with his horse and arms and ten mounted and armed attendants; also his wife and servants, with two coaches (each drawn by four horses) to accommodate them and such other ladies and gentlemen as he thought fit. He was allowed to take eighty of his books and all the 'deeds and evidences, manuscripts and wrytings' in his possession; but neither he, Lady Byron, nor any of their attendants might take among them all more than £40 in money and £20 in plate. Together with the entire garrison they were at liberty to march to Conway, with a convoy of 200 horse, and five days were allowed for the journey. The sick and wounded were to be cared for and the citizens must not be plundered.

Undaunted by his recent hardships, Lord Byron marched from Conway to Carnarvon Castle and although everyone seemed to be making peace with Parliament he and Sir Jacob Ashley, the Governor of Worcester, tried to raise sufficient men to join the King at Oxford. Before the end of March 1646, however, it was clear that Charles could not keep Oxford much longer and he was already negotiating with Parliament and the Scots. All Byron could do was to hold Carnarvon and there he continued until all fortresses were surrendered after the King had given himself up to the Scots at Southwell on 5 May. The articles of surrender of Carnarvon, dated 4 June, were no less favourable than those he had obtained at Chester and, according to Lloyd, he enjoyed the benefit of them,

> with a notable escape or two, to rally the decayed and scattered spirits of the Kingdom into further attempts for his Majesty, travelling invisibly and with incredible speed from place to place for a year together, not sleeping four nights together in a place for a year, till the fatal drowsiness hanging over the Kingdom, put him upon taking his rest too, and withdrawing to France to follow his ingenious Studies, which the War had interrupted in the course, but not in the effect of them.[18]

Scattered, indeed, were the Cavalier brothers and their movements in this disastrous period uncertain. Robert, who had returned to Ireland, continued in his command until 1647. Gilbert, the only member of the family who was not knighted, was appointed Governor of Rhuddlan Castle sometime in 1645 and remained there until the general surrender of fortresses, when he was allowed three months to make his peace with Parliament or go abroad. In April 1645, Sir William Byron, at the head of 400 horse, was defeated in a brisk skirmish near Holt Castle in Denbighshire by a Colonel Jones and was himself taken prisoner. No more is heard of him until 25 February 1646 when he was knighted at Oxford and it is likely that he had only just been released, for two months later Colonel Mytton was reprimanded by the Committee of both Kingdoms for having given a pass to Sir William Byron and two servants to go to the King. They completely forbade the granting of any more passes, 'conceiving that it may prove very prejudicial to the state'. William joined his brother in Carnarvon and was named as entitled to benefit by the articles of surrender. After this he disappears from view, except for a tradition that he was drowned in the Irish Channel before 1652. He apparently never married.

After the King's surrender most Royalists laid down their arms and prepared to make what terms they could with Parliament. Lord Byron's exertions in the lost cause and his personal devotion to King Charles were too well known to be passed over by the enemy and he knew that he must expect little mercy. Being childless, he could indulge his loyalty and follow the Court into exile. To his brother Richard, heir to the peerage and father of a considerable family, fell the task of retrieving the family fortunes. Richard was first of the Byrons to compound for his sequestered estates, on 2 June 1646, when he was still living in the Parliament's quarters; perhaps he had spent the previous months making useful contacts: on 10 July his fine was assessed at 1/10th the pre-war value of his estate—the lowest rate—amounting to £120. He was followed on 1 October by Gilbert (youngest of the surviving brothers) who, on the contrary, was fined at the highest rate—one-half—which meant he had to pay £350.

Extortion of this kind could never reconcile the Cavaliers to defeat. Many paid their fines only by selling land, for which there were few prospective buyers. Throughout 1647 the country smouldered with discontent and quarrels between Parliament and the Roundhead army encouraged the Royalists to watch for an opportunity to renew the war. On 26 December 1647, King Charles signed an Engagement with the Scots which undertook to restore him to the throne provided he recognised presbyterianism in England for three years. Revolts broke out in the wake of this agreement. Lord Byron returned from Paris and for some months, despite a reward offered for his capture, made secret preparations to help the Scottish invasion. To the Earl of Lanerick he wrote on 10 March 1648:

> My Lord, Since my coming into the Parliament parts I have negotiated with some eminent persons of the adverse party with so good success that I doubt not but upon the first [entrance] of your army in England the greatest part of Lancashire, Cheshire, and North Wales will declare for the King, and that the principall places of strength in these countries will be secured for his service. I have likewise laid a design for the surprisall of Nottingham Castle and the Cittie of Oxford at the same time, and had I but a reasonable some of money, I should not doubt to make all sure, but unless hast[e] bee made on your side all our endeavours will bee [in vain], order being now given to secure all the King's party. It will be requisite likewise for the prevention of all feares and jealousies and satisfaction of the people that a declaration usher in your army, and that care bee taken

for the dispersing a competent number of coppies. Thus much I have made boulde to signifie to your Lo^PP by Colonell Chesnall, who will deserve your Lord^PS favour and respect. I humbly desire as speedily as may be to heare from your Lo^PP. This comes from Lord Biron, who is, My Lord, Your most humble faithfull servant.[19]

A week later he wrote that he had received a commission from the Prince of Wales confirming his previous appointment by the King as Commander in Chief of Cheshire, Lancashire, Shropshire and North Wales, and again he urged on Lanerick the necessity for speed. His brother Gilbert was already working on Nottingham Castle, which had been held by Captain Thomas Poulton since Colonel Hutchinson's retirement to Owthorpe. Colonel Gilbert Byron tried to bribe Poulton to surrender the fortress and Poulton, knowing the weakness and discontent of his garrison, dared not reject the offer outright. After consulting Hutchinson, therefore, he temporised until he could get reinforcements from London and then, according to one account, promised to deliver up the Castle in the deliberate hope of trapping the Royalists. An attack was certainly made on the Castle early in June, when the Royalists were driven off, and some were captured. In view of his heavy fine, Gilbert had much to win and little to lose and he threw himself wholeheartedly into the revolt. If he was present in person at this attack, which is uncertain, he appears soon afterwards to have gone to Pontefract Castle, which had been seized by the Royalists on 3 June. When the garrison grew to unmanageable proportions Byron, Sir Philip Monckton, and Michael Stanhope withdrew to Doncaster with 300 horse and, their numbers soon increased to 500, proceeded to plunder Lincolnshire. They then decided to join Royalist forces of other counties and marched towards Leicestershire. Their route lay through Owthorpe where, by Gilbert's command, they took only provisions and two horses, with a groom. Indeed, chivalrous scruples apart, they were so closely pursued by the enemy that they dared not stay to plunder and on the next day (5 July) at Willoughby Field, within a few miles of Owthorpe, they were utterly defeated by a Parliamentary force under Colonel Rossiter's command. Gilbert Byron was taken prisoner and conveyed to Belvoir Castle, whereupon Colonel Hutchinson, handsomely remembering the ties of blood that bound them and grateful for the forbearance shown at Owthorpe, sent a sum of money for his immediate relief and afterwards procured his release and composition with Parliament.

After the Restoration (1660), when his widow petitioned for a pension, she declared that Gilbert had tried to get into Colchester while the Royalists held it against the besieging forces of Fairfax, but was captured and received such severe wounds that he eventually died of their effect. As Colchester surrendered at the end of August 1648 this does not easily fit in with the chronology of Mrs Hutchinson's story, unless he was released from Belvoir very quickly. Mrs Hutchinson presented her husband favourably; on the other hand, petitioners' stories were often inaccurate—sometimes, no doubt, because memories had grown dim but at others through a deliberate exaggeration in hope of obtaining a larger pension.

In the West, Lord Byron tried to effect a rising in Shropshire. This failing, he turned his attention to North Wales and in August, when the Scottish army under the Duke of Hamilton was defeated in Lancashire, Byron took up his quarters in Anglesey until his forces, which were still receiving recruits from the neighbouring counties, should be strong enough to take the field. On 17 September he was reported to have taken Carnarvon Castle and to be holding his own. However, a dispute between Byron and Lord Bulkeley caused an uproar that allowed Mitton to storm the island in October. The two Royalist leaders escaped to the Isle of Man; Byron went on to Ireland to make a last vain bid for Irish help. In November his name was included by Parliament in the list of seven persons excepted from pardon, the Lords substituting Byron and Sir George Ratcliffe for the Earl of Newcastle and Sir John Winter.

On 6 May 1648, the Solicitor General for sequestrations in Nottinghamshire was ordered to secure Richard Byron's goods and stop the payment of his rents as being one of the persons bound for money lent for the maintenance of Newark, which must have been a serious setback to his attempts to re-establish his family. Sir Nicholas Byron's disappearance from the records after 1646 may have been due to failing health. In December of that year his wife recovered some, but not all, the goods she had deposited in 1642 with Phineas Andrews; the rest Andrews had seized on pretence of debt. Her husband's estates in Essex were sequestered in March of 1648 and before the end of the year he was dead and was thus spared any knowledge of the execution of the King he had served and loved so well.

He was scarcely buried when creditors swooped on his estate. Sophia, Lady Byron, wisely renounced probate of his will and on 15 December administration was granted to Sir Thomas Alcocke of St Martin's Lane who, on 4 January 1649, begged to compound for a debt or bond of £1,500 which Sir Nicholas Byron had owed him. He explained that the administration of Byron's will had revealed that a debt of £1,000 was due, which he intended to recover at his own cost towards the satisfaction of his own debt, having no other means to save himself from ruin. The Committee for Compounding directed his fine to be set at 1/10, payable when the debt was recovered. Eighteen months later he was still trying to collect his money.

Alcocke was not the only creditor, however: on 15 January the Essex Commissioners were ordered to suspend the sequestration of Sir Nicholas Byron's estate, which had been secured by John Fountaine, a barrister of Lincoln's Inn, to pay a debt of £500 for which he had compounded. Under these circumstances Sophia had little hope of benefit from her husband's property and although on 26 December 1649 she was said to be entitled to an annuity of £460 and arrears, it does not appear that she received it.[20] On 18 July 1651 she obtained a pass to travel, with two servants, to her native Flanders; but she may have returned to England before her death in 1653 or 1654. Administration of her will was granted on 10 November 1654 to her third son, Ernestus.

*

The execution of King Charles I on 30 January 1649 completely shattered what was left of the Royalist cause. Some took refuge abroad, sharing the hand-to-mouth existence of Charles II's court. For those who remained in England the lean years of the Commonwealth meant a no less bitter struggle for survival. The Byrons, like everyone else, were preoccupied with financial embarrassments. Thanks to Colonel Hutchinson's intervention, Gilbert came off comparatively well: on 22 May his fine was reduced to 1/6th, amounting to £146 13*s.* 4*d.*, which was paid off in July and his estate discharged. Shortly afterwards he begged a saving to compound for a debt of £240 (the arrears of his annuity), most of which he recovered before March 1651. He was allowed to compound for it for £40. A further assessment of £80 made on him the following September was not acted upon and he seems to have had no further trouble.

The manor of Colwick and lands there and in Sneinton belonging to John, Lord Byron, had been sold to Sir James Stonehouse and on 26 December 1649 his mother Anne, Lady Byron, was ordered by the Committee for Compounding to appear before them to show by what right she claimed a dower of £2,100 in the property. Since she did not appear even after a repeated command the prosecutors begged an order that she might not afterwards challenge any such dower right. The Committee referred the case to Brereton. An order in Chancery was eventually made (28 May 1651), requiring her to assign the lease to her husband's creditors and on 9 July she executed a deed accordingly.

That is the latest date on which Anne, Lady Byron is known to have been alive. The date and place of her death are unknown. About this time Lord Byron's Aunt Alice, Lady Ratcliffe, directed that a monument be erected in Colwick Church to her father and mother, who died in 1623. The bottom part of this wall-tomb commemorates her brother, the Sir John who died in 1625, and herself, but it omits the date of her death. Presumably she is represented as kneeling opposite Sir John, whose wife is not mentioned in the inscription.

Sir Thomas Byron's widow, Katherine, as we have seen, was not content with a passive role in the war: on 17 May 1650, a warrant was issued for her arrest on a charge of corresponding with the enemies of the Commonwealth and for her committal to Peterhouse, so that she might be examined by the Council of State. On 20 June she was bound over for £200 for her good behaviour. She was then living at Newstead. Her sister-in-law, Anne, was in Ireland, where her husband, Sir Thomas Lucas, died some time between 18 March 1649, when he made his will,[21] and 28 June 1650 when, as his widow, she tried to recover two statutes staple for £600 and £400 extended on the lands of Lord Byron and his mother. Her husband had included these in the particulars for which he compounded, but had received no benefit because of the sequestration.

The next applicant for money was Lord Byron's unmarried aunt, Mary, who begged for payment of £1,000 or interest on it, settled by her grandfather on his lands as her portion. She had received £80 a year until the wars, then very little, and nothing at all since the sequestration of Lord Byron's estates. Now she was sixty years old and had no other livelihood; but the poor woman's request was refused because she had omitted to sign the petition.

Sir Robert Byron, who had been a member of the council of war that resolved to defend Drogheda in August 1649, now apparently came over to Newstead to settle his own affairs. He had not been sequestered, but his small estate was liable and on 6 February 1650/1 he was informed against by one Major Blackmore and begged to compound. His case was referred, but nothing, apparently, was done; however, he was arrested in Dublin some time that year and imprisoned briefly.

The exiles who toiled unceasingly to restore their new King found many sympathisers abroad who had been outraged by the fate of King Charles I. When Lord Byron was driven out of the Isle of Man to Ireland he attached himself to the forces of the Marquis of Ormonde who, after the King's execution, sent him to invite Charles II to Ireland. Byron's activities were closely watched by Parliament: on 14 March, four days after his arrival at the Hague, he and all who plotted or assisted rebellion in Ireland were ordered proscribed and banished as enemies and traitors and to die without mercy wherever they should be found within the limits of the nation; their estates were to be confiscated, an order likely to carry little weight with one who had long since lost all his estates and was already exempted from pardon. The King did not accept the Irish invitation and Byron returned to the Queen's court in Paris, where Henrietta Maria was living modestly. There he found that he had been supplanted in his absence in the confidence of his charge, the Duke of York, but he accompanied the Duke on a visit to Brussels. Byron spent much of 1650 travelling.

The Scots offered help to the King and though Byron's approval evoked an acid comment from Hyde: 'If Lord Byron has become a presbyterian, he will be sorry for it,' this invitation was accepted. Charles landed in Scotland on 23 June and was declared King. Byron's wanderings were probably determined by the desire to seek reinforcements. In August he was in Jersey, intending soon to go to Paris and then to the Low Countries; but in September, incredibly, considering the price on his head, he was in London. A month later he was in Brussels, no longer Governor but officer to the Duke of York, now permitted to choose his own attendants. There is no evidence that Lord Byron took an active part in the Royalist invasion of England which culminated in Charles II's defeat at Worcester in September of 1651 and the King's subsequent dramatic flight. The English court spent Christmas in Paris. On Christmas Day Evelyn noted in his diary, 'The King and Duke receiv'd the Sacrament first by themselves, ye Lords Biron and Wilmot holding ye long towell all along the altar.'

It was his last recorded service to the King. Before 13 August 1652 he died in Paris, aged fifty-two, 'an irreparable loss', as even his critic, Hyde, admitted. He was a 'A true Englishman' indeed; the public life of 'Honest Sir John Biron (as Kings called him)'[22] might serve as a pattern for the true Cavalier. Yet the man himself remains enigmatic. The Barthomley episode clashes disagreeably with the chivalrous conduct contemporaries ascribe to him. His many surviving letters give a straightforward account of his war activities but they reveal little of his private life; they lack literary charm and also the humour that enlivens Sir Nicholas Byron's correspondence. We know nothing of his relations with either of his wives and nothing that explains his second marriage to a girl less than half his age who loyally shared his hardships at the siege of Chester and the discomforts of exile in France.

One relic of this Cavalier Byron was reverently handed down to his successors. In April 1816 Mrs Augusta Leigh, at the request of her half-brother, the poet Byron, sent Lady Byron a ring containing the hair of Charles I and the first Baron, to be kept for his daughter. A few days later (14 April 1816) Lord Byron himself wrote to his estranged wife, 'The ring is of no lapidary value—but it contains the hair of a king and an ancestor—which I should wish to preserve to Miss Byron.'

[ 90 ]

## · 5 ·

# The Hospitable Pale:
# Commonwealth to Early Georgian

Again, the Master on his tenure dwells,
  Enjoy'd, from absence, with enraptur'd zest.

Vassals, within thy hospitable pale,
  Loudly carousing, bless their Lord's return;
Culture, again, adorns the gladdening vale,
  And matrons, once lamenting, cease to mourn.

*Elegy on Newstead Abbey.*

THERE was little prospect of 'enraptur'd zest' when the second Lord Byron succeeded his brother: the Commonwealth still had eight years to run. Most of the Royalists found their struggle for mere existence complicated by plots and attempted risings that disturbed the latter part of this period. Rather unexpectedly Richard abandoned his former circumspection after the death of his brother: he was implicated in one plot after another, as if, on becoming head of the family, he had inherited the obligation to subordinate personal and family interests to the service of the King. His eldest son, William, had survived the perils of infancy and was about seventeen, but even if he died before his father, Richard still had at least two brothers and several nephews to succeed him, should his own family fail; the tenure of estates under the Commonwealth was in any case very uncertain and the Byrons were obviously willing to risk them for a noble cause.

The Royalists had established a secret council of seven (the Sealed Knot), with agents in the various counties to collect arms and prepare for revolt. The failure of the first Protectorate Parliament and its dissolution by Cromwell in January of 1655 encouraged their hopes: despite leakages of information, resulting in many arrests, a Royalist rising was planned for 8 March. Richard, Lord Byron, was appointed leader in Nottinghamshire and told Wilmot that he was very much pleased his county had so much confidence in his little carcase as to choose him for their leader; but the affair was badly bungled: when the time came he was away in London, and so was Sir George Savile of Rufford Abbey, whose house was a centre of the conspiracy. Nevertheless, on the appointed date about 300 Royalists converged upon Rufford and a cartload of arms was brought from Thurgarton Priory by the Coopers; but on hearing that the rising in Yorkshire which they intended to join had already collapsed, the Nottinghamshire conspirators flung the arms into a pond and dispersed with prudent rapidity. Despite his absence, Lord Byron was arrested near Covent Garden on 21 May and committed to the Tower with his son. He was later removed to St James's and was still in custody in December, when General Worsley asked the government for directions about the confiscation of his estates. Exactly what happened to them remains unclear; between August 1655 and April 1656 Richard was party to a complicated series of deeds with his dead brother's creditors, by which the lease of 1628 was freed from trusts which might benefit him. Portions of the mortgaged estates were assigned to various people for the residue of the term of eighty years and these, in turn, assigned them to Adriana de Mayerne, Marchioness of Mon Povillon, daughter of Dame Isabella de Mayerne whose husband, Sir Theodore, had been Charles I's physician. The idea probably was to get the property into the hands of Royalist sympathisers who would be willing to return them to Lord Byron when he could pay off the mortgages. We do not know when Richard was released from custody. His wife, Elizabeth, died in 1657 and, according to the monument erected to Richard's memory years later, was buried in Hucknall church; the date is not recorded in the register. Some time before 1663 he married another Elizabeth, the youngest daughter of Sir George Booth of Dunham Massey, Cheshire.

Rochdale, to which the first Baron had clung until his sequestration, was the first estate to be recovered, at least in part, by his heir. On 4 July 1658 a London merchant named Rowland Alcocke conveyed the manor to Christopher Cratford of Covent Garden; on the same day Cratford, who appears to have been Richard's attorney, leased it for eleven years to Lord Byron who, for the first seven years, was to pay £80 annually 'in the common dining hall in the Middle Temple', and afterwards one peppercorn yearly if demanded.

The death of Protector Cromwell the following September revived Royalist hopes. The Roundheads had no leader strong enough to hold together the discontented factions; Richard Cromwell held his father's place a bare eight months before being obliged to abdicate. A Royalist revolt was accordingly planned for 1 August 1659 and although leakage of information again led to the arrest of some of its leaders, the rising took place in Cheshire under the Earl of Derby and Sir George Booth, Lord Byron's actual or prospective brother-in-law.

The King himself wrote to Richard Byron:

'Brussells, 17th July 1659

This honest bearer hath delivered what you sent me, for which I thank you, and if he had not assured me from your selfe that you do not enough my mynde in particulars, I should have been very confident that you had not stood in neede of any advertisements, and I am confident you have before this time received advice from my frindes that you are to do, together with Commissions, since I am sure they depende as much upon your interest and concurrance, as upon any mans; however that you may not be without Commissions which the bearer sayes positively you were when he left you, he would deliver you as much as are necessary for the beginning, and then all thinges will afterwards be quickly supplyed and I know you will be ready to do as your neighbours and frindes shall, and by the healpe of God wee shall shortly meete, and you may be sure you shall alwayes finde me to be

Your very affectionate frinde,
Charles R.'[1]

Blunders and betrayals wrecked Richard's plans to lead the movement in Nottinghamshire. Knowing that he was under suspicion, he dared not fetch from the carrier's a trunk-full of pistols that he had had brought down from London so, rather coolly, he begged his cousin, John Hutchinson, to send for them and keep them in his own house. When Hutchinson, despite his disapproval of the government, refused, Richard bribed a ruined Cavalier to go to the Colonel's house with fifty men and bring away any weapons they could find. This scheme, too, was betrayed, and Mrs Hutchinson appealed for help to the captain of the county troop, but by then the rising had already failed. Early on 12 August, Lord Byron had assembled between 60 and 120 men in Sansom Wood in Sherwood Forest, two or three miles south-east of Newstead Abbey, intending to attack the militia at Southwell and then proceed to Newark. But, unnerved by the news that the militia under Captain Cludd had been reinforced, they made for Nottingham instead, pursued by Cludd, who captured their colours, took many prisoners, and effectually dispersed the rest of the small force. Again the Byron estates, such as they were, were in jeopardy; on 25 October the Commissioners for sequestrations informed the Committee for Nottinghamshire that a Mr Crouch had claimed Lord Byron's goods, and the case had been referred to counsel. They instructed the Committee to take care that the state was not defrauded and also to examine the claim of William Byron to his father's real estate. On 3 December Richard was formally accused of complicity in Booth's rebellion and two days later the Nottinghamshire Committee reported that in failing to appear he had confessed himself a delinquent by default. However, his danger was more apparent than real, for by this time the entire country was seething with revolt, and on 2 January 1660, General Monk crossed the Border on his way south to effect the Restoration. On 8 May Charles II was proclaimed King in London.

*

Before pursuing the history of the main line, however, we will follow the fortunes of the other surviving Byrons during this exciting time.

Sir Nicholas Byron left two sons, William and Ernestus, the elder of whom died at the early age of twenty-three or twenty-four, some time before 9 February 1657, when his brother and heir petitioned the House of Commons on the ground that, since he came of age, no one had been authorised to compound with him for his father's estate. In due course (6 March) a committee of Parliament reported that the Commissioners for managing estates under sequestration, sitting at Haberdashers' Hall, should be empowered to compound with him at a tenth and it was resolved accordingly. Under a warrant[2] of 30 July 1659, Ernestus was arrested for complicity in Booth's rising and remained in custody until 27 February 1659/60, when he was ordered to be discharged from 'the Gatehouse', and the sequestration of his estate was suspended until further orders from Parliament. He may have celebrated his personal freedom and the restoration of the monarchy by getting married to Isabella, daughter of William Stanley. The date of his marriage remains unknown, but in about 1661 his wife bore him a son, Edward, who was followed by three daughters—Susanna, Isabella, and Sophia.

No sooner was Charles II safely settled on the throne than he was besieged by impoverished Royalists clamouring for money. Although owners of sequestered estates were quickly enabled to resume possession, other Royalists had been obliged by heavy fines to part with some of their lands at low prices, for which they now demanded compensation or the cancellation of sales; and those who had no lands claimed pensions for their loyal services. The exchequer being (not unnaturally) practically empty, and the cancellation of forced sales rejected as impracticable, a money-raising method much favoured by distressed Cavaliers was to lay information about goods in the possession of enemies of the state, for which they either received a reward or were allowed to retain the goods when seized. In some cases this was sheer gambling, as when (for example) a man gave information about an enemy ship lying in an English harbour, in the hope that the cargo would be valuable enough to pay for his trouble. The Crown was similarly occupied in recovering its own possessions that had come into private hands and on 22 August 1660 Ernestus Byron and three other men who had discovered where certain goods of the late King and Queen were detained were authorised by the Lord Chamberlain to seize them. A little later he was empowered to secure books which concerned a 'great discovery' in the Prize Office, made known by Abraham Johnson; and he petitioned for a grant of a proposed discovery on his own account in December 1665. Two years later he was appointed escheator in Barbadoes and all the Caribee Islands (acting through a deputy on the spot), and held this office until his death in 1672, at the age of about thirty-seven. He was buried at Lambeth on 5 October. Isabella survived him for many years and in time married off her three daughters, Susanna to a Mr Povey, Isabella to Mr Holt, and Sophia to Mr Moseley.

Edward Byron, aged about eleven when his father died, chose a military career; by June 1685 he was a cornet in Captain Richard Hamilton's Dragoons. A reward of £50 granted to him on the following Michaelmas day for secret services suggests that he may have played some part in suppressing Monmouth's recent rebellion. Four years later he was a captain in Wharton's Foot, and subsequently commanded a company in Colonel Richard Brewer's regiment of foot from about the beginning of 1692 to the end of 1696. The following year he petitioned for an allowance of forfeited lands, and after the Duke of Shrewsbury had reported to the Treasury that the King was disposed to take a favourable view of his request, a warrant was issued on 19 April to the Lords Justices of Ireland for the grant to Sir Edward Byron for 99 years of such portion of specified forfeited lands in that country as should amount to the yearly fee of £100, being 1,216 acres. The Lords Justices demurred that the lands in Edward's list were worth about £400 and that they could advise no grant until his petition was regularly referred to Ireland. This was done and eventually on 8 July 1698 the earlier warrant was annulled and 1,216 acres of other land to the clear yearly value of £104 3s. 8d. were allotted to him for 99 years at the quit rents and crown rents payable therefrom before their forfeiture, 'in consideration of many good and acceptable services by him performed'.

The reward came too late to benefit him much, for he died unmarried before the end of the year at about the same age as his father. His will, 'all written with my owne hand',[3] made in the previous April and proved 16 January 1698/9, sheds light on his relations with his family. Some years before he had made a previous will and entrusted it to his eldest sister, Susanna Povey, who afterwards refused to give it back to him, for which reason he now left her only five pounds. The second girl, Isabella Holt, stood higher in favour and received £50. The rest of his estate went to the youngest—his 'dear sister Sophia Moseley'—who was to pay half the yearly income from it to his 'Dear Mother' during her life and to receive the whole herself after Lady Byron's death.

Eleanor, Lady Byron, the widow of the first Baron, left Paris soon after her husband's death and returned to her father's house at Dutton in Cheshire. On 22 March 1652/3 the County Committee for Chester reported to the Committee for Compounding that she now for the first time claimed her jointure out of the estate of George Warburton of Arley, brother and heir of her first husband, Peter Warburton, to whom she had brought a marriage portion of £2,000 or £3,000. They referred to her second marriage to Lord Byron during the siege of Chester and her travels with him in England, France, Ireland and elsewhere, and asked whether they were to pay the jointure and whether with arrears, which it appeared she might have arranged with George Warburton not to claim, as they were on affectionate terms. As the decision is not recorded, she doubtless despaired of getting her money; poverty may well have seemed easier to bear among friends in the exiled English Court than in the oppressive gloom of Puritan England. She returned to France to become, if John Evelyn were accurate, 'the King's seventeenth whore abroad',[4] and no more is heard of her affairs until the Restoration, when she joined the throng of claimants.

For one who stood high in royal favour recognition of services to the Crown was prompt and in March 1661 Lady Byron was granted an annuity of £300; a warrant was issued for payment of a year's pension on 25 June. Unfortunately the Exchequer was soon drained and by the end of 1662 Eleanor's pension was already in arrears. In haphazard fashion, orders were given from time to time for her annuity to be paid from money in the hands of assessment collectors, fines payable to the Receiver of the Duchy of Cornwall, and any other likely source of revenue and it is not surprising that actually she received very little after the first payment. Charles II was embarrassed by the number of his friends. Evelyn hinted to Pepys in 1667 that delays in making royal gifts were deliberate and instanced the case of 'that whore my Lady Byron', who gave Charles no peace until she had persuaded him to order £4,000 worth of plate to be made for her; 'but by delays, thanks be to God! she died before she had it'.[5]

Just before Christmas 1663 Eleanor was in Chester, where she died a month later, and was buried in Holy Trinity Church on 26 January 1663/4. Her death must have been very sudden, because on 20 January, only six days before the funeral, her step-mother, the Viscountess Dowager of Kilmorey,[6] made her will and left Eleanor £5. Lady Byron's own will (made on 23 January) was proved on the 29th by her sister Katherine Needham, the sole executrix. To her cousin Penelope Beverley she left two of her best gowns and divided the rest of her wearing apparel between Penelope and her servant Frances Harrison, who also received £10. Honoro, another servant, was given £20. All the rest of Lady Byron's goods—plate, jewels and the money due from the Exchequer—were divided into four equal parts, one share going to her brother, one to her step-sister, the wife of Sir Peter Leycester, one to her sister Katherine, and the fourth part shared equally by her sister Screven, Mr Lane, and Penelope Beverley's son, Thomas. As her pension from the Crown had not been paid for 2½ years, the arrears amounted to £1,125 and a warrant was issued for payment of this sum to her executor on 17 March. The Needhams seem to have been an affectionate family: in her own will made in April 1663 Katherine had left Eleanor £50 and a gilt cup and plate; after Eleanor's death she transferred the £50 to her brother and bequeathed to her sister Penelope Egerton a miniature of Lady Byron. When Thomas Needham died in 1690, the inventory of his goods at Dutton Lodge included, 'in the best Chamber . . . The Lady Byrons picturs'; but there is nothing to show if they were portraits of her or merely pictures once owned by her.

The high favour Lady Byron enjoyed at Court is attested by the inclusion of her portrait by Sir Peter Lely in the famous series of Restoration ladies at Hampton Court, where she is shown in the guise of St Catherine. The identity of this picture has been disputed, but another portrait of Eleanor Byron, by Greenhill, belonging to the twelfth Lord Byron, which differs in pose and style, is nevertheless very obviously the same woman. In the Lely portrait, particularly, the delicate beauty of her pale oval face, framed in dark hair, triumphs over the fluctuations of aesthetic standards; she is one of the few women of that period who appear really beautiful to modern eyes. She was also very charming: the uncharitable gossip of Evelyn and Pepys is offset by the assertion of the famous Cheshire antiquary, Sir Peter Leycester (her step-brother-in-law),[7] that she was a 'Person of such comely Carriage and Presence, Handsomeness, sweet Disposition, Honour and general Repute in the World, that she hath scarce left her equal behind'.

It is uncertain whether the binding over of Sir Thomas Byron's widow, Katherine, in 1650, put an end to that dauntless lady's activities in the Royalist cause. A reference to Charles II's correspondence with 'Lady Bise' (the code name for Lady Byron) by Daniel O'Neill when writing to the King on 8 March 1655 may apply to her, but possibly

Eleanor was meant. Nothing definite is known of Katherine's movements until after the Restoration, when (on 5 September 1660) she joined the throng of claimants by petitioning for repayment of £700 which her husband had advanced for the King's own regiment and for a pension for her own services 'in carrying secret letters and intelligence, for which she was plundered, sequestered, and endured cruel imprisonment'—which may well have been true; it may equally well have been a heightened version of the episode already mentioned.[8] John Ashburnham certified that the late King had promised £400 in part satisfaction of the debt, but that it had never been paid. The Earl of Southampton, as Lord Treasurer, reported that, although the certificate was no proof of the debt, yet from his own knowledge of Sir Thomas Byron's merits and the necessities of his family, he advised that the petition be granted and said he would try to pay it by instalments of £100 or £200 a year which, in the present state of the Exchequer, must serve instead of a pension. Payment was not forthcoming immediately; in the following February she petitioned again, declaring that she had been dependent on charity since her husband's death. Warrants were duly issued for the promised instalments of £200 and she was lucky to receive them; but naturally she still considered that her own work should be rewarded. In 1665, when the £700 was paid off—and, no doubt, spent—she asked again for 'some bounty or a pension for her old age', without success; on 10 June 1668 her petition for a grant of what she could discover of four vessels employed to Tangiers, of which the King was being defrauded, was referred to the Commissioners concerned. At some unspecified time she and several other petitioners were granted a patent of all plate and other lotteries (except the Royal Oak lottery or any resembling it), but it did not bring them much relief, because too many people were qualified to receive the benefit; so, on 12 August 1674, they asked for the patent to be renewed for a further thirteen years and this was granted in the following month. Little as it was, it probably sufficed for the short span of life remaining to her: on 11 February 1676 she was buried in the cloisters of Westminster Abbey.

The standard peerages and pedigrees may be wrong in declaring that Thomas and John (perhaps born in 1643), the sons of Sir Thomas and Katherine, Lady Byron, both died in infancy. During the Restoration period a John Byron was described as nephew of Sir Robert; his parentage is not mentioned, but it is difficult to fit him in elsewhere. He first appears in 1662 (24 April), when the Duke of Ormonde was directed by royal warrant to issue a commission to (*inter alios*) Ensign John Byron, in the King's Regiment of Guards in Ireland; on 28 July following he was in Major Edward Billingsley's company. Two years later he was commissioned lieutenant to Major Richard Broughton. When Sir Robert Byron was at the point of death, on 12 October 1673, the Lord Lieutenant of Ireland wrote to Lord Arlington that he designed Sir Robert's company 'for his nephew John Byron, who is now in England, but is one of the eldest lieutenants of the Regiment of Guards, and has applied himself industriously to that trade, and made himself fit for command. Besides that family has deserved as well as any of the King'.[9] A week or two later he signed the commission accordingly.

Captain Byron dined with Sir George Rawdon at Lisburn on 30 November 1677, before leaving the same evening for Belfast, and in the following January he was stationed with the Life Guards at Drogheda, where his uncle Robert had distinguished himself many years before. His company was again at Lisburn in June 1679. This is his last appearance in the records, unless he is the Mr John Byron who, in 1694, recommended certain persons for passes to go to Holland. Where he lived then, when he died, and whether his military duties left him time for any private life are all alike unknown; but the Lord Lieutenant's description leaves no doubt that he was a genuine Byron.

When Gilbert Byron had compounded for his estates in the spring of 1651, he settled down to enjoy, as far as failing health permitted, a brief period of family life. The date of his marriage and the parentage of his wife, Dorothy, are unknown, and only two of their five children appear in the registers of Hucknall Church, where Alice was baptised on 13 April 1652 and Lucy on 30 October 1654. Less than eighteen months later their father died as a result of the wounds he had received in the war[10] and he was buried at Hucknall on 16 March 1656, leaving his widow to face a bitter struggle with her young family. Even before her husband's death they were living on Dorothy's money and the rest of her estate was soon spent on the children; but neither poverty nor misfortune could break the spirit of a Byron's wife, and somehow she contrived to manage until the Restoration.

Her first petition to the Crown failed, obliging her to disperse her children among friends, but in 1661 she again implored the King to give her a pension 'to enable her to call them back, and bring them up to serve God and the King'. This time she was granted an annuity of £200 and a warrant was issued for the first half-yearly instalment on 3 May. Grateful as she was, it was barely sufficient for their needs and a year later, returning thanks for this 'relief for her and her miserable infants from their perishing condition', she asked to be appointed Keeper of the Sweet Coffers or Dresser to the Queen. She was described as 'Lady Byron' in orders for her pension in 1669 and 1670, which may indicate that she obtained the post of Dresser, though the appointment is not recorded.[11]

As usual, her pension was frequently in arrears and on 13 March 1668 she persuaded her brother-in-law, Lord Byron, to accompany her to the Treasury to try the effect of a personal appeal, but she had to be content with a promise that she would be considered when there was any money! The excuse was doubtless genuine and the promise was partly fulfilled by an order for £200 on money from the hearth tax on 5 June.[12]

Dorothy Byron died in 1671 and in June of that year her daughters Alice and Lucy petitioned successfully for the continuance to them of her pension, as they had no other support; in September they were formally granted £100 a year each. By jogging the Royal memory occasionally they obtained the money down to October 1674, but what became of them after that is a mystery. It may be that Lucy was the 'daughter of — Byron' who was left a widow in 1679 by the death of Edmund Turnor of Panton and Stoke Rochford;[13] perhaps Alice, too, had found a husband.

An even deeper obscurity envelops the remaining three grandchildren. Were they the James, Adam and John Byron whose guardians tried in November 1670 to get a bill passed to enable them to make leases of certain tenements?[14] Or was one of them the Richard Byron who was a naval officer between about 1673 and 1708? He first appears in the State Papers in July 1683, when he was a lieutenant in the *Pearl*, and from 1702 (or earlier) he commanded the King's yacht, the *Fubbs* (so christened years before by Charles II in honour of his favourite, the Duchess of Portsmouth, when she returned uncommonly plump from a holiday in France). He received orders from Vice-Admiral Robson on 21 August 1702 to sail in company with the *Bedford* to Tangier Road, and after carrying letters to the Alcaid of Alcaçar, to let Captain Haughton know that he was ready to join the fleet. Two years later, when the Jacobites were giving the Government some uneasy moments, Lord Godolphin suggested to Robert Harley that Captain Byron ought to be examined as to his reasons for refusing the four musketeers that Lucan had demanded for the seizing of Sir George Maxwell and his companions. 'I find,' wrote Godolphin, 'it seemed to him that he could not answer the doing it, but I confess it seems to me that it is harder to answer the not doing it'.[15] On 1 July 1704, accordingly, he signed (*Ri Biron*) a statement in Harley's writing that he had recently spent a week in Rotterdam, during which he often saw Sir George Maxwell, Mr Hayes and a Scotsman called Sir James. Captain Byron dined with them several times at the Rose and Crown Ordinary. No one asked him to seize Sir George Maxwell and his followers, but he asked Mr Vernon if such seizure was justifiable. Vernon thought so, if it could be done out of the town; but they escaped out of his reach. Richard Byron gave Harley further details the next day, enlarging on the difficulty of arresting these people at Rotterdam without full authority from the States General to the Governor of the town. 'It is a great mortification to him,' added Harley, 'to have any crime laid to his charge after having served 31 years in the royal navy, and he hopes for a favourable construction upon what he has done in the matter'.[16]

He seems to have remained under a cloud for a time: his petition in 1706 for payment of his share of the Vigo booty was refused. The following year he proved his loyalty by reporting that he had arrested a well-known French Roman Catholic who had come on board the *Fubbs* at Sheerness as passenger to Rotterdam, whence that yacht was taking Mr Vernon, envoy to Denmark. In January 1708 he was in command of the *Cleveland* yacht and after that no more is heard of him. Richard's private life remains a blank; indeed there is no proof he was one of the Newstead Byrons, but the dates of his career make it possible that he was a son of Gilbert and Dorothy Byron.

Other Byrons are even more difficult to place. Was the Thomas Byron who, on 8 March 1663/4, was commissioned lieutenant to Sir Robert Byron's company of foot, in the King's Regiment of Guards, the other son of Sir Thomas Byron who, like John, is said to have died in infancy? Was he identical with the Thomas Byron, 'gent., Londoner,' who was buried at Hucknall on 15 August in that same year? Who was the Thomas Byron of Bermondsey, who died 18 May 1685, aged 41 years and 8 months, having had twelve children, one of whom, Joanna (named after her mother), died 18 March 1695, aged ten?[17] Again, an Edmund Byron was installed as prebendary of White Lackington in 1708 and died in 1710, holding the vicarage of Lydiard Episcopi. The details are scanty, but it is likely that some of them, at least, were children or grandchildren of the Cavalier Byrons who had to make their own ways in life after the Civil Wars and had gradually lost touch with the main line of the family.

About others there is no doubt. Anne, the only sister of the Cavalier brothers, continued to live in Ireland after the death of her husband, Sir Thomas Lucas; between 1650 and 1653 she married Edward Sutton of Cloncurry, Co. Kildare. He was knighted at Whitehall in 1660 and later received a baronetcy. She, too, petitioned for compensation and on 11 November 1663, after receiving several grants which proved ineffectual, she was recommended to Secretary Bennet by the Lord Lieutenant of Ireland, who said that 'her sufferings and those of her family merit the King's special consideration'. As her husband was appointed Gentleman of the Privy Chamber in 1667 they must have spent some time in

England; but Anne died in Ireland on 22 May 1679 and was buried two days later in St Peter's church, Drogheda. Sutton survived her till 1695, when he was interred in Westminster Abbey.

Richard and Sir Robert were the only Cavalier Byrons who lived to see the Restoration. A letter to Thurloe from 'Andrew Butler' (the pseudonym of Manning, a Royalist traitor who earned £1,200 a year by supplying the Protector with information about Charles II) in May 1655 expresses surprise that Sir Robert Byron, Compton, and Sir Richard Willis were not taken: this implies that Robert had taken part in the recent rising. Possibly he escaped to Ireland, where military duties obliged him to make his home. He lay low until the King's return and on 2 August 1660 his 'humble petition' was read in the House of Commons. Consequently the Lords Justices were instructed (29 January 1660/1) to pass patents granting him the castle and lordship of Enniscorthy and other lands formerly belonging to Robert Wallop, which Charles I had intended to give him when they were forfeited to the Crown by reason of their owner's rebellion.

A few weeks earlier Robert had joined the other captains of the old establishment in Ireland in praying to be restored to the commands they had held until 1647 when, the Marquis of Ormonde having given up the government, they lost their posts and were imprisoned and 'prosecuted for their lives'. Byron doubtless considered this mere formality. Already Charles II needed him: on 22 February he informed the Lords Justices that Sir Robert had to leave Ireland on important service for the King in England and that during his absence his 'entertainment' in Ireland must suffer no check.

On 27 March 1662, Byron's name appeared in the list of trustees appointed by Ormonde and Albemarle for arrears of pay due to commissioned officers who served the King or his father in the wars in Ireland before 5 June 1649. He was stationed in Kilkenny at the beginning of August but three weeks later, on the grounds of ill-health, he was given permission to be absent from his command as Colonel of a regiment of foot in the standing army in Ireland and to stay in Dublin for two months, where he was undergoing a 'course of physic'. His illness was aggravated by financial difficulties; in October he and his fellow officers were obliged to be content with a moiety of ten months' arrears of their pay in satisfaction of the whole. There was a hitch, too, in the Enniscorthy grant, the property having been transferred to the Earl of Southampton and others and on 12 November his petition for other lands instead was referred to Ormonde. Property in England was allotted to him, but this also proved ineffectual, so in 1663 he asked to be given lands which the Act of Settlement showed clearly to be in His

Majesty's hands; on 21 August the King directed the Lord Lieutenant to grant him a lease of Ardgowl More in County Limerick. It was followed (possibly in 1664) by a grant of one-third of certain lapsed money (under the Act of Settlement) and one-third of various lands set out in lieu thereof.

Meanwhile Robert had resumed his military duties and on 14 October 1663 his company was ordered to winter at Carrickfergus; but his name had been put forward for the post of Master of the Ordnance in Ireland and on this very day the Lord Lieutenant was writing to Secretary Bennet that, while he had no objection to Sir Robert Byron, he thought the King had overlooked the economy that would result from the appointment of Lord Dungannon (ranger of Ulster, 1660, and Member of the Irish Privy Council). Sir Robert Byron was preferred and had entered on his new duties by the beginning of December.

Early in 1664 he was in London, where by a curious chance he was in Secretary Bennet's room while Mrs Hutchinson was vainly pleading for permission for her imprisoned husband (Byron's cousin) to receive visitors on business. When she had gone, Bennet told Sir Robert that he had heard Mrs Hutchinson relate the sad condition of her husband and his house and urged him to 'take notice how the justice of God pursues those murtherers, that, though the king pardon'd both his life and estate, by the hand of the devine justice they were now like to come to ruine for that crime'.[18] A good Cavalier, Byron may have appreciated such sentiments, but he could hardly have remained unmoved by the plight of one whom he had looked upon as a brother.

Even in London Byron found himself liable for military duty, being ordered to march early one morning (3 March) to Southwark, with two companies of the Guards, to preserve the peace in that borough.

When the Earl of Kildare died, Sir Robert applied for his troop, but it went to the Lord Lieutenant and he had to be content with a promise of the next vacancy. He was directed to be sworn a member of the Irish Privy Council on 31 August. Later in the year he pointed out that the low condition of the Treasury had prevented his receiving the reward of £400 for the capture of a notorious Irish rebel in 1642;[19] in November the King ordered him to be paid from any funds found due to the Crown in Ireland, but not from any other revenue.

During the summer of 1665 Robert made a grand tour of garrisons, forts and stores in Ireland. He spent most of June and July in putting Kinsale 'in a reasonable good posture of defence' before leaving for Limerick and Galway. After this, his routine for the next four years was broken only by such minor affairs as the consideration of requests for the removal of his troops by various aggrieved petitioners; but in

November 1671 his admission that he owed the Crown £700 brought him into conflict with the Commissioners of Accounts. The Lord Lieutenant warned Lord Arlington that, if the debt were remitted, 'we may, considering how vast sums have been remitted already, shut up our shops here'.[20] Nor was this his only financial difficulty: a week or two later he and about twenty other officers presented to the Lord Lieutenant and Council a petition for three months pay which was in dispute between them and the new farmers. While it was under consideration, a certain Roger Jones got hold of a copy of the petition and sent it to Lord Ranelagh, the Vice-Treasurer of Ireland, who hastened to get his petition to the King in first and so aggravated the affair that all the officers concerned were dismissed from their commands as 'mutineers' and summoned to England; Byron, Lord Power, and Sir Henry Ingoldsby were also suspended from the Council Board. On arriving in London, they were forbidden the Court, except some who had rendered eminent service to the King. Sir Robert Byron naturally came under this heading and three months later returned to Ireland to resume his command, but whether with or without the disputed pay does not appear. In August 1672 he was on a committee appointed by the Lord Lieutenant to draw up a model scheme for the quartering of the Army so as to make the best use of it, considering its weak state after the rest of the troops had been sent to England.

Robert was now sixty-one and the strain of a lifetime's military service was telling on his health. Accordingly, when Lord Conway approached him about buying his place as Master of the Ordnance, he admitted that he was willing to part with it, but would not make a positive declaration until he had heard from someone in England to whom he had written. Conway decided that Byron's correspondent was probably Lord Arlington and passed the information on to the Lord Lieutenant, who urged Arlington to promote the exchange.

> The place requires a more active man than Sir Robert Byron, [he wrote on 1 October 1672,] and that office cannot be in so good order as it ought till a more diligent and younger man be at the head of it, and I believe Lord Conway would do very well in that employment. . . . I am confident 'twill be much for the King's service, and it will be a convenience to Sir Robert Byron, for Lord Conway is willing to give him a good compensation.[21]

Either the terms were not approved or Robert, like many elderly men, could not make up his mind to retire and in the event he died in harness. He was seriously ill in April 1673, when the Lord Lieutenant again asked Lord Arlington to consider Conway his successor, adding that the latter was willing to give £1,000 to Lady Byron, who would be left in great want; but he lingered for six months and died between 12 and 15 October, a few miles from Dublin. Conway was disappointed, for after some delay the coveted post was annexed to the office of Master of the Ordnance in England. Lady Byron was presumably left to manage as best she could. All their children died young except Cicely, who in 1665 had married Charles Balfour of Castle Balfour, co. Fermanagh. They had one child, Lucy, who became the wife of Hugh McGill and, after his death, of Blayney Towneley of Towneley Hall.

*

For the second Lord Byron the restoration of the monarchy inaugurated a busy and anxious period of post-war reconstruction—with the familiar problems of repair of damage and dilapidations, claims for compensation, and a general shortage of money. Although he was now about fifty-five and had known little rest for twenty years, Richard once again proved that his small frame concealed a disproportionately large stock of energy and courage and he lost no time in reassembling his scattered property. The Newstead and Papplewick estates had been assigned to Elizabeth, daughter of John, Viscount Chaworth, on 6 May 1659, and on 5 October 1660 Richard's heir, William, obtained a licence to marry her. The wedding did not take place for another year, but Lord Byron could feel reasonably assured that that part of his property would ultimately be restored to his family.

Faced with the prospect of raising enough money to buy out the persons to whom Adriana de Mayerne had assigned the rest of his estates, he now (October 1660) applied for a grant of the manors of Chillerton, in Hampshire, and Holt, in Wiltshire, both of which had belonged to John Lisle, now attainted for treason. Neither this nor a similar petition for a share of lands in Ireland appear to have been granted, but somehow Lord Byron found means to retrieve his inheritance. The court roll of Rochdale shows him as lord of the manor by 9 October 1661 (four days after his son's marriage); on 16 January 1661/2 he covenanted to pay the de Mayerne assigns all the money that would be due on 14 February upon principal and interest of all mortgages or estates, amounting to £4,905. The next step was to obtain sufficient money for repairs and improvements. First, Richard petitioned the King for a patent to revive the office granted by Charles I to Thomas Bushell and Thomas Carleton, to rectify the abuses in silk dyeing, 'which not only continue but increase'. No more is heard of this, but in another direction he was evidently more successful, because on 12 December an order was made to pay him £600 in consideration of his surrender of a grant made to him by the late King of three hundred of the best trees growing in Sherwood Forest.

Lord Byron was also involved, with the other commissioners for Nottinghamshire, in settling the debts they had incurred long ago in the defence of Newark; and on 21 July 1662 they agreed to remit nearly £5,000 and out of the £10,000 remaining due from the Crown to satisfy every creditor who had put forward a claim. He was still prepared to take up arms again for his present sovereign, if required, and on 1 October was given a commission as Major and Captain of a troop of 100 horse in the regiment of the Earl of Lindsay, the Lord Great Chamberlain.

On reviewing his financial position, however, Richard decided that some part of his property must be sacrificed for the benefit of the rest, so the Royton estate in Lancashire was sold this year to Thomas Percival of Gorton. He then boldly asked for a grant of £2,000 a year from the estates of those who had disturbed the peace or hindered the King's restoration, but was refused because these lands were appointed for reprisals and were vested in the King for those uses only.

In 1663 a bill was introduced into Parliament 'for supplying the Loss of certain Evidences in the Time of the late Troubles, belonging to the Estate of Richard Lord Byron'. As a petition from John Musters was considered with it, this bill must have been required to safeguard Musters' title to the Colwick estate, which the first Lord Byron had sold to Sir James Stonehouse just before the Civil War and which was afterwards sequestered.

On the outbreak of war with Holland in 1665 the requirements of the Navy brought an urgent demand for timber for shipbuilding. Realising this, Richard Byron proposed to deliver 'at certain prices' 2,000 loads of timber from the Newstead woods which John Russell reported to the Navy Commissioners to be 'good and fit for the service'. A note of his contract was written down by Samuel Pepys on 29 June 1665. With estate repairs in mind, Richard Byron became buyer as well as seller, desiring to be sole purchaser of 'lops and tops' and other refuse wood, useless for the Navy, felled in Birkland and Billhagh—two tracts of Sherwood Forest near the place where he was felling a great quantity of his own wood for the Navy. On 17 January 1665/6, accordingly, the King instructed Lord Treasurer Southampton to sell Lord Byron this refuse at the best price received for such wood in that forest since the Restoration.

Transporting timber was problematical for the Navy because good roads were almost unknown. Fortunately, Sherwood Forest is not far from the Trent and somehow the great trunks were dragged across country to Gunthorpe, conveyed down the river to Stockwith, from there to the mouth of the Humber and thence by sea to the naval dockyards. Boats were rarely available when required. Early in 1665/6 Lord Byron discovered that 'hazards at sea' caused the shippers to demand exorbitant rates for carriage that almost equalled the price he was to receive for his timber and therefore he asked the King to order the Commissioners of Prizes to lend him the *Friendship* and the *Leif* of Rotterdam to convey his 2,000 loads of timber to Harwich, Woolwich, Deptford and Chatham. These two prize ships were ordered to be sold, but on 27 February the Commissioners were instructed to lend him two other ships then at Harwich, 'he giving due caution for their restoration'. This satisfactory arrangement for the latter part of the journey was, however, invalidated by a bottle-neck at an earlier stage, presumably caused by insufficient barges; and on 7 May John Russell wrote from Edwinstowe to tell the Navy Commissioners that Lord Byron refused to fell any more trees, having so much timber and plank still lying at Gunthorpe, which he did not know how to get to Stockwith.

A spell of military duty this summer afforded a welcome break. Some time during the year he was granted a commission (confirmed in 1667) as captain of his own troop of horse—one of the non-regimental troops of 80 men (officers included) raised for home defence in view of the Dutch menace. Towards the end of August Lord Byron's troop passed through King's Lynn *en route* to the neighbouring coast towns.

The following year (1667) Richard was at Plymouth, doubtless on naval business and in May the ships for which he had a previous warrant were otherwise disposed of and he petitioned successfully for the loan of two other condemned prizes, the *St John Evangelist* of Amsterdam and the *St Peter* of Rotterdam. His supply of timber was, indeed, so highly appreciated that a month later Charles II 'being pleased to allow him to retain [the ships], in consideration of his services and suffering,' directed the Commissioners to cancel the security which Richard had entered into for their redelivery. In October and November 1667 he was pressing the Customs for payment of various tallies and, according to Lord Lexington, by 17 January 1667/8 he had succeeded in getting tallies for the money he had spent on the garrison of Newark. It is not surprising that Dorothy Byron should have invoked the aid of a relative so skilled in extracting money from the Government when her pension was in arrears.[22]

For the next few years offal wood appears to have been his chief concern and transport for timber proceeded smoothly, except that in July 1669 he had to borrow another boat, the *Chick*, from John Russell to carry plank from Stockwith to Hull, where he had a ship loading.

Four years later Lord Byron obtained an annuity of £500 for life; it was paid fairly regularly until a few months before his death. He was also granted £500 in December 1674 as royal bounty by way of compensation for wood in Sherwood Forest to which he had a claim. Nevertheless, he energetically resisted an assessment of £102 16*s.* on the manor of Newstead, claiming that his accounts showed that this sum, or the greatest part of it, had been duly paid by a former servant. Process was accordingly stayed on 6 December 1676 to give him time to satisfy the Treasurer of it and on 23 March 1678/9 the amount was quit-claimed by the Crown because Lord Byron's former steward had died and the acquittances for it were either lost or so mislaid that they could not be produced for his discharge. This did not prevent a subsequent renewal of the claim, which continued to give Richard's heirs trouble for years.

When John Evelyn passed Newstead Abbey in August 1654 he remarked that 'situated much like Fontaine-bleau in France, [it is] capable of being made a noble seate, accommodated as it is with brave woods and streames; it has yet remaining the front of a glorious abby church'. Richard Byron could not afford to do much more than restore it to a habitable condition after the years of wartime neglect, but he may be credited with rebuilding part of the east front. The upper portion, over the chapter-house and the south transept of the long-vanished church, is divided into large bedrooms with a range of later attics above and may have been started in the reign of Charles I and completed in the time of Charles II. These handsome 'Royal bedrooms' are known as Edward III's room, Henry VII's lodging, Charles II's room, and the Duke of Sussex's room, because it is supposed these distinguished guests slept in them. However, Edward III can hardly have slept in the canons' dormitory, which in his day occupied the site. Apart from the nineteenth-century Duke of Sussex, who certainly stayed at Newstead more than once when Colonel Wildman owned the Abbey, there is no authentic record of these visits, nor is it known when the names were first attached to the rooms. Henry VII's lodging is mentioned by Thoroton in his great history of Nottinghamshire published in 1677. We may hope that Richard Byron's services to his King were rewarded by a personal visit from Charles II, who may be imagined strolling along the terraces above the Eagle Pond, but it is unlikely that indefatigable monarch spared the time. The local tradition which associates him with the neighbouring estate of Bestwood, granted to his son by Nell Gwynn, is likewise unsupported by evidence.

On 4 October 1679, Lord Byron died at the age of seventy-three and was buried in Hucknall church in the vault with his first wife. His widow[23] erected a monument with a long epitaph in the chancel. After recalling the services and sufferings of his family in the Civil Wars it continues:

> *Yet it pleased God [so] to bless the honest endeavours of*
> *the said Richard Lord Byron, that he repurchased part of*
> *their ancient inheritance, which he left to his posterity,*
> *with a laudable memory for great piety and charity.*

However, despite his considerable qualities, Richard was not popular: perhaps he had a sharp tongue which easily provoked enmity; but whatever his faults, he worked unceasingly for King, country, and family, and secured for his line a second spell of prosperity and renown.

Another epitaph was appended to verses entitled *Merit Rewarded*, addressed by the Nottinghamshire poet, Thomas Shipman, to Richard's heir:

> Illustrious Byron Justice found;
>   Being four times crown'd.
> 1. From noble Ancestors did get
>      A Coronet.
> 2. Then loyal Valour did bequeath
>      A Lawrel wreath.
> 3. His suff'rings Martyr's glory found
>      With Roses crown'd.
> 4. Nothing can add to his great Story
>      But that of Glory.
>   My Lord,
> I shall not vainly mourn his doom,
> Since he dropt fully ripe into his Tomb:
> Yet loaded more with Glory than with Days. . . .

Indeed, Richard outlived all his own generation, his sister Anne having died the previous May; and of his ten children only one son and one daughter are positively known to have survived him. Catherine had married William Stanhope (knighted at Windsor 26 July 1683) at Papplewick on 3 July 1677; but nothing is known about her sisters, Elizabeth and Mary, and the others had died long before their father.

At the age of forty-four, William, third Lord Byron, came into a far better inheritance than he could have dared to hope. A child when the Civil War broke out, he was old enough during the Commonwealth to share his father's tribulations, and it was his good fortune that the Restoration came before he had lost all the optimism and resilience of youth.

The Chaworths of Annesley and the Byrons of Newstead had long been close, though not always friendly neighbours, but the memory of poaching feuds was obliterated by the sterner conflict in which both families had served their King to the end. We shall probably never know whether love or convenience was primarily responsible for the transfer of the mortgaged Newstead estate to Elizabeth Chaworth who, when William Byron obtained the marriage licence, was living with her grandmother, the dowager Lady Campden at Brooke House, in Rutland. She was about twenty-six—his senior by a year or two—and neither would be considered young in those days of early marriages; but, as we have seen,[24] the wedding was delayed, probably by financial difficulties. Eventually it took place at Papplewick church (about 1½ miles from Newstead) on 18 October 1661, so uniting two families that were to be estranged by tragedy and linked again by romance in succeeding generations.

They went to live at Bulwell Wood Hall, the recognised home of the Byron heir, and set about raising a family. Their first child,[25] sometimes called William, was either still-born or lived but a short time and was buried at Hucknall on 13 April 1664. We do not know whether joyful expectation of his birth or grief at his death prompted his mother's gift of a silver-gilt chalice and paten, still treasured by the church. The chalice (originally a steeple-cup) and its cover bear the London hall-marks for 1608–9 and 1609–10 respectively. The inscription runs:

> *This cup was given to the Church of Hucknall Torkard*
> *by the honorable Elizabeth Byron, anno 1664.*

It bears the Byron arms impaling those of Chaworth. The paten, a plain silver-gilt with the hall-mark for 1663–4, has the same arms and is inscribed:

> *This plate and cup was given to ye Church of Hucknall*
> *Torkard by ye honble Elizabeth Byron daughter of ye*
> *Right honble Lord Viscount Chaworth anno: 1664*

A second son, baptised Richard on 17 March 1665, was buried less than a year later (8 March 1666) and the third boy, John, christened 18 July 1666, also died young. Elizabeth, their reputed first daughter (if she ever existed) went unrecorded in the registers,[26] and Henrietta Maria, baptised 17 March 1667/8, was fated to enjoy less than three and a half years of life.[27] Then at last the luck changed.

Few county families (particularly of Royalist sympathies) did not consult Dr Robert Thoroton, most prominent physician in Nottinghamshire. Living at Car Colston, twelve miles east of Nottingham on the south side of the river, he could not visit very frequently his patients in the northern part of the shire, so they wrote him long letters describing their symptoms and ailments in frank and simple detail; he appears to have treated them by correspondence course. An ardent antiquary, he frugally jotted down on the blank backs of these letters pedigrees, notes on family history, descriptions of tombs and armorial windows, all in preparation for his master work, *The Antiquities of Nottinghamshire*, published in 1677, which has rightly earned him the title of 'the father of Nottinghamshire history'. These notes, now in the muniment room of the Nottingham County Libraries, would startle and perhaps horrify the good doctor, if he knew how much confidential information about his patients he unwittingly preserved for posterity. Thus his patient, the young Mrs Byron, wrote to her 'esteemed friend', apparently just after Christmas 1668, expecting another child:

> I have waited all this while for a piece of venison, [she begins in friendly fashion,] which will come now very unseasonable, for the keepers' luck hath been so ill that of 2 braces of does we could not have one pasty all this Christmas. I hoped, according to your promise to Mr By[ron], I should have seen you before this. I bless God I have been better of this great belly than ever I was of any, & eat my meat better, digest it well; only suppers does not agree with me, & most spoon meats turns sourish on my stomach; but boiled milk is much my diet at a night, but if you think it not good for me, I shall forbear it. I have not above a fortnight or few days more to reckon, & cannot hear of a Nurse that will come in time, & if you cannot help me to one, I must bring it up with the spoon. [After further details of her condition and that of two servants, on which she asks advice, the letter ends,] I pray for patience for you to read all this scribble. . . . Mr. Byron presents you his service; both ours, pray, to your lady.[28]

Dr Thoroton's treatment was justified by the birth, on 4 January 1668/9, of a fourth son, William (baptised at Hucknall 26 February), who lived to be his father's heir. He was soon followed by Juliana, baptised at Hucknall 19 May 1670, and Catherine, both of whom lived to a normal age. The two youngest children, however, were no luckier than the eldest: Ernestus was buried 9 March 1671/2, four days after his baptism; and Anne, baptised at Hucknall 7 July 1673, was buried 5 April 1675.

William Byron had other preoccupations. His income soon proved insufficient and evidently he lacked his father's flair for business, since he was outlawed for debt in 1667, when a lease of some of his lands was granted to a Thomas Bayly. By 1669, however, he had recovered his position sufficiently to be appointed governor of the grammar school founded at Bulwell two years before by his kinsman, George Strelley;

[111]

and in 1675 he was granted thirteen trees from the Forest—one for each year that he had held the office of Bowbearer of Sherwood since succeeding his father in 1662. In 1667 he was a commissioner for levying the army tax in Nottinghamshire. In this year, too, he wrote verses (which the change of fashion permitted to be in English rather than Latin), returning thanks to Thomas Shipman of Scarrington, who sent a present to 'the most beautiful Ladies his Daughters' (i.e. Catherine and Juliana, about six and seven years old) in the following lines:

### CREDE BYRON. 1677

You, like the gen'rous Sun, do still dispence,
To those that merit least, your influence.
Your Obligations have that pow'rful charm;
They need must conquer, when they first disarm.
The Favours, you so freely have bestow'd,
Are such we ne'r deserv'd, nor you e're ow'd,
The Debt is mine I own; I ought to pay;
But, like a Bankrupt, beg a longer Day:
They're brisk, and young; and can another way.
My Muse I should excuse, she's dull and rude;
Those that do write to you in Verse intrude;
Were not her Products all from Gratitude.
Presumption is a crime, but worse despair;
One errs in boldness, and the other fear.
But I presume you'l[l] pardon the first Fault:
The Man's a Coward that ne'r makes Assault.
In such Atchievements if I chance to dye;
I live in fame, if in your memory.
My whole ambition only does extend
To gain the name of Shipman's faithful Friend.
And tho I cannot amply speak your praise;
I'le wear the myrtle, tho you wear the Bayes.

W.B.[29]

Of Shipman's long response the most interesting passage runs:

Was't not enough your Ancestors did aid
The mighty Norman, when he did invade?
Whose noble Acts increast their former store,
And here confirm'd those Honours they brought o're?
Is't not enough that this Illustrious Line
Succeeds in you, and you maintain the Shine?
Diff'ring but thus fro' th' glory they have won,

[112]

They were the Morning, you the Mid-day Sun?
Is't not enough the Byrons all excell,
As much in loving, as in fighting well?
Witness their Motto, prov'd in Bosworth Field,
Where Truth did their triumphant Chariot gild.
Is not that fame enough your Noble Sire,
With his six noble Brothers, did acquire?
All valiant Knights! whose Title was not bought,
But under Charl[e]s his Royal standard sought.
Is't not enough that Brittish Coronet
Circles your head, your Ancestors did get?
But you must thirst after inferiour praise,
And from the Brittish Bards too gain the Bayes? . . .

Here, again, is a tantalising and inexplicable reference to the Byrons'
prowess in love. Shipman also, in *The Plunder*, begged from William
Byron 'verses he pleas'd to write upon my Tragedy of Henry the
fourth'. A pleasant life, indeed, when country squires had leisure—and
ability—to exchange verses in this way. In 1679 Mrs Byron was
similarly honoured by the poet, who addressed her in *The Mirror* and
*The Hieroglyphic*, both pieces included in his volume *Carolina: or, Loyal
Poems* (1683):

### THE HIEROGLIPHIC. 1679

To the Honourable Mrs. Byron, having pleas'd to send me
curious and significant Draughts of her Ladiships own
hand, in way of Hieroglifics.

Could I, like you, my Pencil use;
Or had command of such a Muse;
All other Artists I'd out-do,
By coming som[e]thing near to you.
But as poor Dreamers oft conceit,
Were they in fortune rich and great,
They'd live, and spend at such a rate.
So had I your Estate in Wit,
Like you, methinks, I'd manage it.

. . .

Your drops of Ink, like those i'th' Spring
Both Violets, Roses, Lillies, bring.
Your Fruit-trees equal Wonders shew;
Both bear at once and blossom too;
The Spring and Autumn's both in you.

[113]

Your planted Vines, i'th'infant Stems,
Seem to bud forth their blushing Gems.
Apelle's self would be mista'en;
Both Birds and He could not refrain.
When you, with Grass, cloath fancy'd fields,
They feed those Flocks your Pencil yields.
And what does greater Wonders show,
Your Ink's the Milk that makes them grow.
When you draw Birds we wond'ring stand,
And swear they fly from out your hand.

. . .

The death of William Byron's father that October brought a temporary
halt to such courteous exchanges. Administration of Richard's will
having been granted on 30 April 1680, the new Baron transferred his
wife and three surviving children to Newstead and took over the management of that estate. On the very day of Richard's death, the
renewed claim for an unpaid assessment on Newstead was once more
deferred on the understanding that it would be settled by 20 November; but William had no more intention of paying it than had his
father, and on 19 September 1683, after further fruitless enquiries and
adjournments, he at last won a reluctant discharge of the sum from
the Treasury.

He was now able to live comfortably on a scale befitting his rank. His
household included a Chaplain, the Reverend Thomas Sheppey, B.A.,
formerly of Pembroke College, Cambridge, who in 1682 published an
assize sermon entitled, Τὰ Πρὸς 'Ειγήνην: *The things that belong unto
peace*,[30] which he had recently delivered before the judges in St Mary's
Church, Nottingham. He prefixed to it this dedication to his patron:

> . . . Your Lordship was pleased to honour this Discourse with your
> Presence, and . . . with your Approbation. . . . My design in Publishing
> these Papers (next to Gods Glory) is to evidence my self a sincere and
> Loyal Protestant [he was formerly a papist—a very dangerous and
> unpopular persuasion at that time] against all Exceptions: and to
> Demonstrate that your Lordship could not give a more convincing argu-
> ment of your Zeal for the Church of England, than by receiving into your
> Protection one that shall consecrate his Life and Studies to the service of
> his Holy Mother; and his Noble Patron. . . .

These turbulent last years of Charles II's reign were a dangerous
period for the King's supporters and if Lord Byron took much active
share in public affairs, he was singularly successful in covering his
traces. As he grew older he probably reverted to his ancestors' policy of

loyalty with moderation, and lived as quietly as he could at home. He was not entirely immersed in local concerns, however. As a supporter of the Court or Tory party, he went to Oxford in March 1681, when the King summoned Parliament in that city, and while there he was visited by Viscount Latimer or his brother, whose father, Lord Danby, the lately-fallen Treasurer, still lay in the Tower, where he had been hustled on a charge of high treason two years before, at the time of the 'Popish Plot' scare. If his sons were soliciting their father's friends to effect his release they were unsuccessful: Danby remained in custody until 1684.

Lady Byron was buried at Hucknall on 20 June 1683 and two years later, at the age of fifty, her widower celebrated the beginning of a new reign by getting married in Westminster Abbey on 25 June 1685;[31] his second bride—another Elizabeth, nine years his senior—was the eldest daughter of Sir George Stonehouse, third baronet, of Radley in Berkshire, and the widow of Sir Richard Stydolph, baronet, of Norbury in Surrey, who had died in February 1676/7.

When Lord Byron's son, William, grew up he seems to have been put in charge of the Lancashire property, following the family custom of pre-Civil War days, for on 16 July 1688 he was among the gentlemen appointed at Ormskirk quarter sessions to inspect the work of overseers of highways in Sefton. Neither father nor son is known to have played an active part in the Revolution of 1688. Lord Byron was a Tory of staunch Royalist stock; but he was neither fanatic nor papist and by this time many Tories were as anxious as Whigs to rescue the country from the disastrous results of James II's policy. Indeed, William's friend Lord Danby had become the King's bitter opponent and since his release from the Tower was leading a revolt in Yorkshire. On the other hand, Byron was old enough to remember the Civil Wars and shrank from action tending to renew such miseries. As no detailed list of the Earl of Devonshire's supporters in the Nottinghamshire rising has survived, his neutrality cannot be taken for granted and he may have gone so far as to pay his respects to the Princess Anne, James's younger daughter, when she spent a few days in Nottingham that December on her way to join her brother-in-law the Prince of Orange, whom even she supported against her father.

Certainly the Byrons accepted the new regime without question and probably with relief and they held minor offices from time to time. The younger William was a commmissioner for levying in Nottinghamshire the tax for war against France in 1690, and both of them were appointed Deputy Lieutenants for the county in May 1692 and September 1694.

In 1692 Lord Byron's younger daughter, Catherine, who was nearly twenty-one, was married in the chapel of St Peter ad Vincula in the Tower of London to Sir Arthur Cole, Baronet, who in the following year, when he was twenty-four, was elected Member of Parliament for Inniskillen and in 1695 for Roscommon.[32] Her father died on 13 November 1695 and was buried in the family vault at Hucknall three days later; but for some reason administration of his will was not granted to his son until 12 December 1696.

Juliana Byron went to Ireland[33] to join her sister, Lady Cole, with whom she seems to have spent the rest of her life. The widowed Lady Byron appears to have returned to London, for she was living in the parish of St Giles-in-the-Fields in October 1699, when she took over from William Beaumont and William Edwards the remainder of a term of eighty years in the parsonage and manor of Much Dunmowe in Essex, for the sum of £800.[34] She died on 28 December 1703 at the age of seventy-six and was buried with her first husband at Mickleham.

*

Although the fourth Lord Byron took his seat in the House of Lords on 21 January 1696, his attendance was so irregular that in November an order was made for his attachment if he was not present on certain days. Little is known of his activities for more than three years after his father's death and he may well have been abroad for part of the time. Certainly in August 1699 he spent two days with Tom Mansell at Loo in Flanders where, wrote Robert Jennens,[35] 'they hunted once, which proved a damned chace, so that I believe they won't give a very good character of our sport'.

It was, however, high time that he paid some attention to estate affairs at home, for the Government was challenging his right to cut down trees in Sherwood Forest. Appearing at the Treasury on 24 May 1700, he declared that he was authorised to fell timber by 'ancient grants' which he would show to the Steward of the Forest Court; and as the matter then dropped, he must have proved his case.

In the House of Lords Byron showed himself a good Tory by voting on 17 June 1701 for the acquittal of Lord Somers, the late Lord Chancellor, who was impeached for his share in the Partition Treaties.

His appointment again as Deputy Lieutenant of Nottinghamshire in September 1702 indicates that he intended to spend more time in Newstead. In fact, William was at last contemplating marriage—with Lady Mary Egerton, daughter of the third Earl of Bridgwater—and after so many years without a mistress, the Abbey must have needed a good deal of attention. For the bridal chamber he chose Charles II's bedroom and had the ceiling painted according to the fashion of the

Sir John Byron. 'Little Sir John with the Great Beard', founder of the Byron Charity in 1571. Old, but erect and dignified, he made a deep impression on his contemporaries and legendary fame survived him.

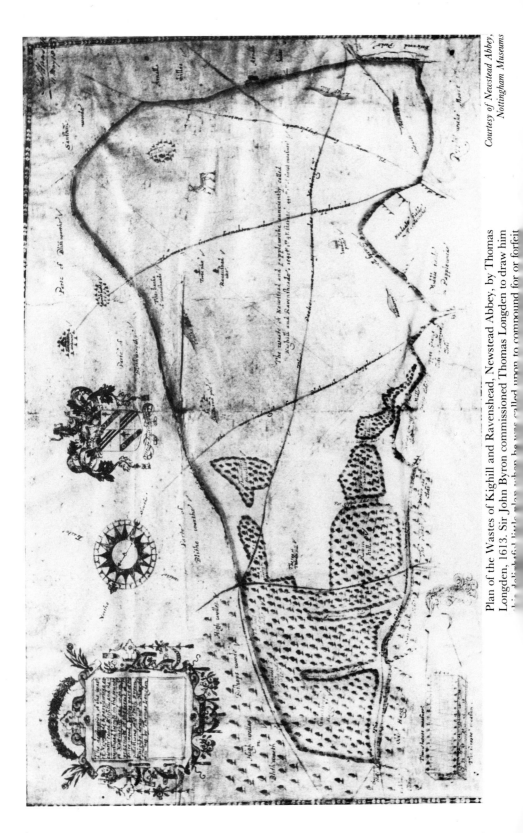

Plan of the Wastes of Kighill and Ravenshead, Newstead Abbey, by Thomas Longden, 1613. Sir John Byron commissioned Thomas Longden to draw him this plan in 1613. Early also when he was called upon to compound for or forfeit

*Courtesy of Newstead Abbey, Nottingham Museums*

*Courtesy of University of Manchester, Tabley Collection*

John, 1st Lord Byron, by William Dobson. A brave but impetuous commander, his exertions in the Civil War and his personal loyalty were well known. He followed the court into exile.

Eleanor, Lady Byron, second wife of 1st Lord Byron, she was born in 1627 and married at the age of eleven Peter Warburton of Arley in Cheshire who died of smallpox in 1641. Married for the second time to Lord Byron in 1644 when she was seventeen, she was widowed again in 1652 but later found favour at court and is recorded by Pepys as having been mistress to Charles II.

*Courtesy of Newstead Abbey, Nottingham Museums*

Sir Nicholas Byron. His sense of humour enlivens his correspondence. According to Clarendon, he was 'of great affability and dexterity, as well as martial knowledge'.

Sir Thomas Byron. A very valuable and experienced officer, murdered by a captain of his regiment in 1643.

Richard, 2nd Lord Byron, by Cornelius Johnson.

The Hon. Maria, Patrick and Elizabeth Chaworth, children of John 2nd Viscount Chaworth. Elizabeth, born 1632, married William, 3rd Lord Byron in 1661. She had ten children, only three of whom survived into adulthood, including William, 4th Lord Byron. She died in 1683. Patrick became 3rd Viscount Chaworth and Maria married Michael Armine.

William, 4th Lord Byron, by Sir Godfrey Kneller. Gentleman of the Bed-chamber to George, Prince of Denmark, he married three times and was survived by five children by his third wife Frances, daughter of Lord Berkeley of Stratton. An amateur artist, he studied under the Flemish painter Peter Tillemans. Newstead was restored under his affectionate care.

Mary Egerton, first wife of William, 4th Lord Byron by Sir Godfrey Kneller.
After only eleven weeks of marriage she died of smallpox.

The Hon. George and Frances Byron, children of 4th Lord Byron by his second wife, Frances Williamina, daughter of 1st Earl of Portland. George died in 1720 aged twelve; Frances died in 1724 aged thirteen.

William, 4th Lord Byron, Frances, Lady Byron and William, John and
Richard as infants at Newstead Abbey 1726, by Peter Tillemans.

West View of Newstead Abbey near Mansfield, by Samuel Buck, 1726.

Pair of watercolours by William, 5th Lord Byron.

Admiral the Hon. John Byron, 'Foulweather Jack', the poet's grandfather, by Sir Joshua Reynolds. 'He had no rest at sea'.

Sophia Trevanion, wife of Admiral the Hon. John Byron, by Rosalba. The poet's grandmother for whom, as a beauty in her younger days, 'Men would have willingly run thro' Fire'.

The Hon. Richard Byron. Third son of 4th Lord Byron. Self-portrait aged sixteen.

Newstead Abbey by Wooten

day: an oval centre, pale blue flecked with white, representing the sky, with a border of allegorical figures between the arms of Byron and Bridgwater and, in the corners, the monogram EMB i.e. Mary Egerton Byron. The wedding took place in February 1703, when he was thirty-four and she twenty-six;[36] but their married life was brief. Eleven weeks later (11 or 12 April) Lady Mary died of small-pox and was buried at Hucknall in the Byron vault.

After three and a half years of seclusion, either at home or abroad, Lord Byron decided to risk a second venture, and on 19 December 1706 he married Frances Williamina, the third daughter of William, first Earl of Portland. The Bentinck arms were added to the painted ceiling, but the rest was left untouched and one would like to know the second Lady Byron's thoughts as her gaze rested on the arms and monogram of her short-lived predecessor. Their eldest son, born 1 October 1707, was christened George after the Prince of Denmark, Queen Anne's husband, to whom Lord Byron was Gentleman of the Bedchamber, and whose funeral procession he attended in that capacity on 13 November 1708. Two more boys—William, born 6 July 1709, and William Henry, born 23 October 1710, lived only a short time. They were followed by a daughter, Frances, on 10 August 1711; she appeared to have a better chance of surviving; but not many months elapsed before the family vault was opened again (7 April 1712), this time to admit the body of her mother. Lady Byron's untimely death on 31 March, so soon after that of two children, set tongues wagging, and the day after the funeral Lady Strafford relayed to her husband the rumour that 'she died of a distemper her Lord gave her'.[37]

Satisfied that he had done his duty by begetting an heir, Lord Byron consoled himself by improving his estate and applied to the Crown for a grant of five hundred trees out of the royal woods of Birkland and Billhagh in Sherwood Forest, for the repair of Newstead Abbey and the enlargement of the park.[38] Unfortunately, the details of his alterations are unknown, except for the repair of the stone Gothic fountain, on the lower part of which are his initials, W.B., and the date, 1720.

Apart from this, his activities during the eight years that followed his wife's death are wrapped in obscurity and if he took any share in suppressing the Jacobite rising of 1715, it passed unnoticed; but in the summer of 1720 he was aroused from his seclusion by the death of the twelve-year-old George on 6 July; he was buried at Hucknall on 8 July. Determined to have an heir, William looked about him for a healthy young woman to supply the need and on 1 November Lord Berkeley of Stratton wrote to the Earl of Strafford:

I am going to dispose of one of my daughters [Frances] to Lord Byron, a disproportionate match as to their ages, but marriages not offering every day, I would not miss an opportunity, though attended with never so many inconveniences.[39]

This marriage of convenience took place at Kensington on 3 December 1720, apparently without elaborate preparations, for the painted ceiling this time was left untouched and one can only hope that, if the bride disliked it, she was allowed to choose another room. In due course the bridegroom's hopes were amply fulfilled by a family of five boys and one girl, of whom all but one lived to reach old age. Psychologically, however, the amalgam of Byron and Berkeley blood produced a crop of strangely assorted characters: two sons so unlike that they might be labelled 'villain' and 'hero'; a clergyman-artist; and a daughter whose peculiar conduct excited comment even in that golden age of eccentrics. It was perhaps just as well that neither parent lived to see the full fruits of their union.

Their first child, Isabella, born 10 November 1721, preceded the much-desired heir by less than a year and the 5th of November (1722) was a most appropriate birthday for one of such explosive temperament that William manifested in his later years. The orderly pattern was preserved by John's appearance on 8 November 1723, but Richard rather spoilt the effect by arriving on 28 October 1724; even so, four birthday celebrations in a fortnight must have upset nursery routine. The latest brood had the nursery entirely to themselves by this time: Frances, the last survivor of her father's second marriage, died on 21 or 22 September 1724, aged thirteen.[40] Lord Byron now felt sufficiently secure to make his will on 17 April 1725, and Lady Byron could afford to relax a little; nearly eighteen months elapsed before the birth of Charles on 6 April 1726, while George, the youngest, did not appear until 22 April 1730. Although he was to prove the least distinguished member of the family, he began his life under the auspices of a royal god-father and on 25 June the Master of the Jewel House was ordered to give Lord Byron 110 ounces of gilt plate (amounting to £65 or thereabouts) as a gift from King George II on the christening of his son. All the children were born at Newstead and baptised in the private chapel there; their names and dates of birth were written by their mother on a pane of glass on one of the windows of the Abbey.[41] This unusual record has unfortunately disappeared.

Charles died when he was five, on 16 May 1731, but the rest were reared without difficulty. They were, perhaps, rather too healthy and lively for an elderly father; certainly the older boys were sent off to

Westminster School at the earliest possible moment—William and John in February 1732, when they were nine and eight respectively, and poor little Richard the following June, aged seven. It proved too soon in his case, for he had to be withdrawn three years later.

The King's gift to George shows that Lord Byron was in favour at Court. From 1729 until his death he received a £1,000 pension from the Crown. He still appeared occasionally in the House of Lords where, on 6 May 1731, he voted against taking off the duty on Irish yarn. We cannot say how he divided his time between London and Newstead. Lady Byron seems to have preferred town life and she may have lived in London as much as her husband would permit. She certainly disliked the Abbey, for when Elizabeth, Lady North, visited Papplewick in 1739 she wrote to her mother, Lady Kaye, 'We were yesterday at Lord Byron's, a glorious fine park, and a fine old house. I am amazed how my Lady could hate it so much'.[42]

From the few records of his work we may infer that Newstead was renewed under the fourth Lord's loving care: his solicitude for his estate appears in a letter written from Newstead to the Earl of Oxford on 24 July 1728:

> Hearing that Brigadier Sutton has been endeavouring to procure a lease of Harloe and Lindhurst for 61 years of your Lordship, and that his demands have not been agreed to; as your estate of Kirkby joins to mine at Newstead, and Harloe and Lindhurst is but half a mile from me, I should be sorry to have that command in any other hands but yours, which would be very prejudicial to me and my family. And I hope you will never let those grounds for the use of red deer, which feed constantly upon your own tenants and this neighbourhood to the great prejudice of many poor families. Therefore if you be disposed to let Harloe and Lindhurst I should be very proud of being your tenant for the same at your own terms. I beg pardon for the trouble I have here given you.[43]

Harlow Wood borders the east side of the present main road between Newstead and Mansfield; and Lindhurst, which lies behind its north-east corner, was the site of the lodge or pavilion built for James I when he hunted in Sherwood Forest. The fourth Lord Byron was well acquainted with it, for a stone pillar marks the spot where, at a meeting of the Attachment Court of the Forest in September 1702, he had taken his oath of office as Bowbearer in company with the Duke of Newcastle, Lord Warden; Scrope, Lord Howe, Chief Ranger; and other officers. A note on this interesting pillar is appended to this chapter.

The earliest known view of Newstead is the engraving of the West Front published by Samuel Buck in 1726 and dedicated to Lord Byron, showing the Gothic fountain that William had repaired in 1720 standing in front of the house. Clearly he was still engaged in alterations, for the large chimney shown in the centre of the west wall does not appear in the fine picture of the Abbey painted by Pieter Tillemans a few years later (*c.* 1730; Tillemans died 1734). Tillemans, a Flemish artist who enjoyed Lord Byron's patronage for some time, also, according to Horace Walpole,

> . . . had the honour of instructing [him], who did great credit to his master, as may be seen by several of his lordship's drawings at his beautiful and venerable seat at Newstead abbey . . . and where Tillemans himself must have improved amidst so many fine pictures of animals and huntings. [To this is added a note:] Several coloured sketches which were drawn by Tillemans, and the copies by William, Lord Byron, when his pupil, are now in the possession of Captain R. Byron, R.N., his lordship's grandson. He has likewise a view in oil, of the abbey and lake at Newstead, a large picture, by the same artist. . . . There is a very scarce print of John West, first Earl of Delawarre, from a drawing by that Lord Byron.[44]

Tillemans' painting hangs in the Abbey once again and a charming watercolour showing Lord Byron at Newstead with his wife Frances, and three infant children, William, John and Richard, is in the possession of the twelfth Lord Byron. A version exists in oil which is believed to have been copied by the fourth Lord from Tillemans' watercolour. Lord Byron's other works are scattered: the British Museum has two small landscapes by him, one in watercolours and body colours, the other in India ink with pen outlines, touched in places with watercolours, and though not unpleasing, they suggest that, *pace* Horace Walpole, his lordship did not rise above amateur standard. Still, with his painting, building and care of the estate, he may be assumed to have spent his latter years happily enough until he died at Newstead on 8 August 1736 at the age of sixty-seven. He was buried at Hucknall four days later. Of his own generation only one sister outlived him. Juliana, who never married, had been buried at West Dean in Wiltshire nearly three years before (30 August 1733); but Catherine, whose husband had been raised to the Irish peerage as Baron Ranelagh, survived until November 1746, when she was nearly seventy-five.

\*

## NOTE ON THE LINDHURST STONE

This pillar has a curious history. Originally it had a brass plate bearing the following inscription:

> Foresta de Shirwood in Com. Nott. *Memorandum.* At the Attachment Court held for the said Forest in this Place called Lincoln dale in Mansfield walk the [blank] day of September in the first year of the Raigne of our [blank] Lady Queen Anne over England &c. Anno Dom 1702—John Digby and John Neal Esqrs, Two of her Majesties Verderers of the said Forest, Then & there the Right Noble John Duke of Newcastle Lord warden of the said Forest, The Right Honble William, Lord Byron Bowbearer of the said Forest, The Rt. Honble Scroop Lord How chief Ranger of the said Forest And Keeper of the Several walks call'd Birkland and Bilhaigh, George Savile Esqr Keeper of the Offices of Mansfield woodhouse and No Manswood, Thos. How Esqr. Keeper of Mansfield & Lindhurst, Took the several Oathes appertaining to their Respective Offices, Administered by Francis Wyld Gent, Clark of the said Forest. Attending then these Deputy Keepers, Wm Gosling Senr., Wm Gosling Junr, James Moor, Wm. Clark, Gent: John Key, Thos Westyngton & John Bagulie, Gent.

The inscription was copied by B. Wilcocks in 1741 and in 1813 his version was transcribed by a surveyor named James Dowland, who added that the brass plate bearing the inscription was said to have been stolen many years before by some tinkers.[45] The stone had fallen before about 1775, when S. H. Grimm drew it lying on the ground, but it had evidently been set up again before Dowland saw it, as he gave its height as 6' 2" from the ground.

At the beginning of the twentieth century what had come to be known as the 'Keeper's stone' was visited by two local antiquaries, who found it standing, but upside down. The inscription was forgotten and the existence of Dowland's copy unknown to them. After much discussion about the origin of the pillar, they evolved a theory to their satisfaction, but unfortunately, when the late Duke of Portland had the stone re-erected right way up and protected by a railing, their theory was incorporated in the inscription on the new bronze plate affixed, which reads:

### Forest Stone | Lyndhurst

> This stone from the ancient market house of Mansfield was placed here A.D. 1752 by Henrietta Cavendish Holles Harley, Countess of Oxford, & Lady of the Manor, to mark the site of the Great Forest Court & Swainmote.
>
> On this place the justices in eyre met the great officers of the Forest every seven years for the administration of its affairs, & here also the verderers met the swains or freeholders in a moot three times a year for the purpose of renting the pasturage.

\*

[ 121 ]

# · 6 ·

# The Sword that Slew Him:
# The Wicked Lord

'Tis fifty years, and three to boot,
Since, hand to hand, and foot to foot,
And heart to heart, and sword to sword,
One of our Ancestors was gored.
I've seen the sword that slew him; he,
The slain, stood in a like degree
To thee, as he, the Slayer, stood
(Oh had it been but other blood!)
In kin and Chieftainship to me.
Thus came the heritage to thee.

*The Duel* (addressed to Miss Chaworth) 1818

O N the death of the artistic fourth Baron the succession devolved on a boy of such turbulent character that his long, mis-spent life has become a part of folk lore. We cannot determine how early the 'Wicked' Lord Byron acquired his sinister title, but in 1823 his great-nephew was moved to make a mild protest against a passage in Amédée Pichot's *Essai sur le Génie et le Caractère de Lord Byron*, prefixed to the fourth edition of his French translation of the poet's works. Pichot declared that the 'murderer' of William Chaworth retired after the famous duel to Newstead Abbey, where he lived in retirement, hated by his tenants, at war with his neighbours, holding no communication with his family, disposing of several of his estates, and allowing the home of his ancestors to fall into ruins.

The poet, writing to J. J. Coulmann in July of 1823, remarked:

As to Lord Byron, who killed Mr. Chaworth in a duel, so far from retiring from the world, he made the tour of Europe, and was appointed Master of the Stag-hounds after that event, and did not give up society until his son had offended him by marrying in a manner contrary to his duty. So far from feeling any remorse for having killed Mr. Chaworth, who was a

[ 122 ]

fire-eater (*spadassin*), and celebrated for his quarrelsome disposition, he always kept the sword which he used upon that occasion in his bed-chamber, where it still was *when he died*. It is singular enough, that when very young, I formed a strong attachment for the grand-niece and heiress of Mr. Chaworth, who stood in the same degree of relationship as myself to Lord Byron; and at one time it was thought that the two families would have been united in us.[1]

Pichot's is the earliest printed version of the legend, which was amplified in 1830 by Thomas Moore who, in his *Life, Letters and Journals of Lord Byron*, rehearsed the tales then current around Newstead—how 'the old Lord' flung his wife into a pond, how he shot his coachman and threw the corpse into the carriage where Lady Byron was sitting, and then mounted the box himself and drove off; how he always went armed and how, in his later years, his only companions were two servants—Joe Murray and 'Lady Betty' (Elizabeth Hardstaff)—and a colony of crickets which, on the day of his death, all left the house at once. Moore admitted that these and many other stories were gross fictions, while relating them with relish, and the legends persisted. Since the time of his great-nephew (who certainly owed little to him) few people have said even a qualified good word for 'Devil Byron' or 'The Wicked Lord'.

That the poet's account was most correct is confirmed by hitherto unpublished documents deposited in the Nottingham County Libraries by Mr and Miss Truman of Nuthall. These papers came into the Truman family with the grandmother of the owners; she was the great-granddaughter of William Daws, steward to the fifth Lord Byron for more than forty years. They consist of two books of general accounts for the Newstead Estate 1754–1798, with one retrospective entry for 1748; a smaller book for the Gringley estate, 1754–1773; a few miscellaneous documents; and a file of 389 business letters, mainly addressed to Daws, from about 1763 to 1773, including thirteen from Lord Byron himself and four from Lady Byron. Before examining these papers, however, we must consider William's early years.

He was not fourteen when his father died, but already beyond the control of his young mother, who was left sole executrix of her husband's will.[2] His formal education came to an abrupt end and he entered the Navy where, it may have been hoped, he would at least find some scope for his adventurous energy. He was appointed Lieutenant in *H.M.S. Falkland* in May 1738 and served later in the *Victory*, which he allegedly left just before she was lost in a storm on 5 October 1744. Presumably, having come of age in November 1743, he was expected to leave the hazards of a naval career to his brother John, the future Admiral, and to settle down to the responsibilities of his position; but these, as we shall see, weighed very lightly with him in comparison with the pleasures and privileges of his rank. Certainly, he subscribed 200 guineas to the Duke of Kingston's Light Horse in 1745;[3] and he even accompanied the Duke into Lancashire to help suppress the Jacobite rising; but, this danger over, he is next heard of in London, leading the life of a fashionable, if not very reputable, man-about-town.

By this time the family was widely scattered. The widowed Lady Byron had, in 1740, become the second wife of Sir Thomas Hay of Alderston, East Lothian; and three years later Isabella married the Earl of Carlisle. John was still a prisoner in South America, where he was shipwrecked on his first long voyage in 1741; Richard was at Oxford and George still at Westminster School. The fifth Baron was expected to establish his own family and his courtship was soon the subject of so much gossip that on 12 September 1746 the following entry appeared in White's betting book:

> Mr. James Jeffreys betts Mr. John Jeffreys One hundred Guineas to Fifty Gs. that Lord Byron is married to Miss Shaw before Michaelmas One thousand seven Hundred and forty eight.
> If Ld. Byron or Miss Shaw Dye or either of them married to any other person before that time, Mr. James Jeffreys loses his Hundred Guineas.[4]

Three weeks later (20 October), James Jeffreys was emboldened to lay a further wager of fifty guineas with Mr Fanshawe that the marriage would take place before next Lady Day and Captain Draper ventured five guineas with him, but they narrowly lost their bets.

Unfortunately William was not content with an orthodox wooing. In her memoirs George Anne Bellamy, the actress, tells an extraordinary tale of her abduction by an unnamed Earl on behalf of his friend, Lord Byron:

> Among those who paid me the greatest degree of attention was Lord Byron, a nobleman who had little to boast of but a title, and an agreeable face . . . and as his vanity was hurt at my rejecting him, he formed a resolution to be revenged of me for my insensibility. His Lordship was very intimate with a person who was a disgrace to nobility; and whose name I shall conceal through tenderness to his family. . . . To this friend Lord Byron committed the execution of his revenge. [One Sunday evening, accordingly, she was abducted in a coach by the Earl, who told her that she had better consent to make his friend Lord Byron happy, and be happy herself, than oppose her good fortune.] To this he added that, his friend was shortly to be married to Miss Shaw, a young lady possessed of a very large fortune, which would enable him to provide handsomely for me. I was so struck with the insolence of this proposal, that I remained for some time quite silent.

Fortunately for Miss Bellamy, her brother witnessed the abduction; he went to the Earl and to Lord Byron's house in Great Marlborough Street; but the latter denied any knowledge of the matter, 'as indeed he could do with a greater degree of truth, that he had not seen me that evening'; the brother believed him and transferred his wrath to his sister, who was further mortified to discover that her elopement was grossly misrepresented by the newspapers. She found it prudent to retire from the world for a while.

She is an unreliable authority, but one cannot believe that she invented the entire episode, which is the more distasteful because it happened just before Byron's marriage. (Her chronology is a little vague, but it seems to have been in January 1747.) Indeed her persecution continued after it: she writes that on 22 May, when she reappeared at Covent Garden Theatre as Athenais in *Theodosius*:

> I had no sooner come upon the stage ... than the first object that presented itself to my view was Lord Byron, who had placed himself in the stage-box. The tremor I was thrown into by seeing a person so near who had been the cause of so much disquietude to me, entirely deprived me of all my powers, and I stood for some time motionless. Mr. [John] Rich ... [Manager of Covent Garden Theatre, 1732–1761] came immediately behind the scenes to enquire the reason of it. His Lordship had by this time quitted his seat, and placed himself against one of the side scenes, in sight of the audience. Mr. Rich ... found his Lordship in this situation, and was no longer at a loss to account for my trepidation. As Lord Byron knew that our proprietor had in his youthful days been a man of gallantry, he accosted him with an assured look, and said, 'Well, Rich; I am come to take away your Athenais!' [Rich, however, reproved him, and desired him to quit the stage, whereupon] his Lordship ... very prudently retired to his seat in the stage-box, meditating revenge. But he was no sooner seated there than the audience, who generally engage on the side that humanity points out, took the alarm, and obliged his Lordship to retire from thence to the front boxes, in the back part of which he concealed himself from further insult.

The next evening, while she was at supper, a letter was brought in:

> Upon opening the scrawl, we found it came from Lord Byron; who, though he was lately married to one of the best and loveliest of her sex, made me therein an offer of a settlement. His Lordship concluded with swearing that if I did not consent to his proposal, he would pursue me till I took shelter in another's arms. As soon as Mr. Quin had read the letter, he called for pen and ink, and sent the following answer to it. 'Lieutenant O'Hara's compliments to Lord Byron, and if he ever dares to insult his sister again, it shall not be either his title or cowardice that shall preserve him from chastisement.' This fortunate impromptu of Mr. Quin so

frightened his Lordship, that the waiter came soon after to let us know he was gone. And we found that this valiant nobleman actually set off the next morning for Nottinghamshire. Nor have I ever since been troubled with his attacks. Lady Byron, some time after, came to my benefit, and honoured me with marks of her generosity, which were the more pleasing to me as they likewise afforded a proof of the liberality of her sentiments.[5]

Elizabeth Shaw who, at the age of eighteen,[6] became Lady Byron on 28 March 1747, was the only daughter and heiress of Charles Shaw[7] of Besthorpe Hall, Norfolk, and his wife Frances Lightfoot; and she brought her husband a fortune of £70,000, the greater part of which he squandered before her death. Her inheritance consisted of estates in East Dereham, Wymondham and Tibbenham in Norfolk, Stretham in the Isle of Ely, and Gringley in Nottinghamshire. Her few surviving letters show that she was gentle and kindly; her conduct to George Anne Bellamy shows remarkable courage in facing a distressing situation so soon after her marriage and indeed she needed courage because her unsuitable husband gave her little happiness in return for her wealth.

Shortly before his final repulse by Miss Bellamy, Lord Byron was elected Grand Master of the Freemasons of England (30 April 1747) and on 16 May he attended a special performance at Drury Lane, when three rows of the pit were railed off for the Masons, who were 'desired to meet His Lordship cloath'd at the Rose Tavern, the corner of Bridges Street, Covent Garden'. At the Grand Master's particular request, the programme included a song by John Coustos, the hero of the moment for having endured a long imprisonment by the Inquisition in Lisbon, where he was tortured nine times without either renouncing his religion or revealing the secrets of freemasonry. His *sufferings* were published in 1746, illustrated by his portrait and three 'plates of tortures', and evidently Lord Byron had been much impressed by the book.[8] His enthusiasm for freemasonry soon waned, however, and he did not attend another meeting until 16 March 1752, when he nominated Lord Carysfoot as his successor and came to the latter's installation four days later. He allegedly went abroad for several years and it is likely that he travelled for at least part of that time.

Little is known about the Byrons' early married life. Their first child, William, born 7 June 1748, was buried eleven months later (7 May 1749); a second William arrived on 27 October of that year; Henrietta Diana was baptised at Newstead on 30 August 1751; and the youngest, Caroline, was born 17 January 1755.

Although Newstead Abbey had been lovingly cared for by the fourth Baron, it was probably neglected after his death when his son was in the Navy or in London. By 1749, however, the fifth Lord Byron was taking sufficient interest to build a curious structure known (unofficially) as Folly Castle. The date was carved over the porch. The craze for erecting ready-made ruins was still to come, but almost every owner of any real standing adorned his property with some more or less useless erection, inevitably dubbed 'So-and-so's Folly'. Folly Castle, a small tower on rising ground beyond the Upper Lake, was intended to serve a useful if not very creditable purpose: it was the scene of many concerts and gay parties that tradition has inevitably translated into unspeakable orgies. Inevitably, too, it became a haunted spot and even after its prosaic use as a school in later times it retained such a sinister reputation that it was demolished in the late nineteenth century. That seems a pity now; it was a genuine period piece. Although there may be some truth in the legends, we must credit William with providing a separate building for his orgies, rather than inflicting them on his wife in their own house.

We may look for truth in the dispassionate accounts of the estate mentioned earlier. They begin in 1754. Those for the Gringley property contain little of general interest; but from the Newstead estate books more can be gathered. At first, money came in and went out freely. The Dowager Lady Byron (now Lady Hay) was receiving £600 and the present Lady Byron's mother, Mrs Shaw, £300 a year. The latter was also entitled to one-third of a moiety of the rents and fines of East Dereham and Wymondham of the Queen, which in March 1755 came to £54 10s. 5½d. At the end of 1754 Lord Byron paid an unprecedented £1,000 into the account—a payment that was not repeated.

William had not lost his interest in nautical matters when he left the Navy for, like the Duke of Kingston at Thoresby, he kept a 20-gun ship and other boats on the lake at Newstead and engaged them in mimic warfare. (A cabin door from one of his boats remains at Newstead.) Among early entries in the accounts are the payments, in 1755, of board wages for six weeks (at 4s. per week) to Joseph Murray 'the sailor boy' and for twelve weeks at 5s. to Barnard White 'the sailor'. Joe Murray served Lord Byron faithfully in many capacities to the end, was taken over by his successor, the poet, and on the sale of the Abbey in 1817 he passed with it into the service of Colonel Wildman. On 4 October 1756 Thomas Beardall was paid for the carriage of guns for the tiny forts on the Upper Lake, shown with the ships on many engravings of the period. 'Two silly forts', Horace Walpole called them after his visit to the Abbey in 1760, adding, 'the present Lord has lost large sums and paid part in old oaks, five thousand pounds worth of which have been cut near the house. In recompense he has built two baby forts, to pay his country in castles for the damage done to the navy'. Arthur Young, who visited some years later, thought it unfortunate that the cannon should be levelled at the parlour windows.

Not content with one large lake, Lord Byron planned another in the direction of Papplewick, and in July 1756 rent was paid for land taken out of Towndro meadow to enlarge 'the great pond'. This Lower or Sherwood Lake was still under construction at the time of Young's visit, but was never completed; the pile of stones, called 'the Ragged Rock', which Byron intended to rise from its centre, stands high and dry on the bank. Another water feature, on a smaller scale, was a 'jet d'eau perpetuel' which, according to Horace Walpole, the fifth Baron installed in the cloister garth before 1760, on the site where the Gothic fountain formerly stood and now stands again. Walpole added that Lord Byron was going to make three Venetian windows in the Great Drawing Room or Refectory, but fortunately these did not materialise.

In addition to these extraordinary expenses, there are payments for catching the large crayfish then preserved in the little River Leen that feeds the Newstead Lakes; for keeping the deer; for repairs to Bulwell Wood Hall and the chancel of Hucknall Church; for household supplies; and for many other normal concerns of a large estate. The steward's duty did not end with these; although Rochdale and the Newstead property were under separate management, Daws received their accounts annually and kept in close touch by correspondence with the agents for those estates. Sometimes personal visits were necessary, as in July 1755 when he travelled to Rochdale to prepare for Lord Byron's arrival there; and again in September, when he went to let the coal mines. In April 1757 he journeyed to London 'with cash for the jewels' and doubtless the increase in his salary from £30 to £50 a year was well earned.

Lord Byron's own movements during this period are obscure, but he seems to have spent some time in London; when his eight-year-old daughter, Henrietta Diana, died on 1 June 1760, she was buried at St James's, Westminster. Two charges on the estates were removed in 1757 by the deaths of Lord Byron's mother-in-law, Mrs Shaw, and his mother, Lady Hay, who was buried at Twickenham on 21 September (she died 13 September; the last payment to Mrs Shaw was made on 5 May.) But any financial relief their deaths accorded him was temporary. From 1759 onwards certain changes in the accounts suggest straitened financial circumstances, resulting in reduced expenditure, although Byron personally was frequently calling on Daws for large sums. Racing and cock-fighting appear to have been his extravagances: he was reported to be one of a 'very gay and numerous assemblage of the nobility and gentry' that favoured Nottingham with their attendance at the races and cocking in July 1763.

He spent the early part of the following winter in London; on 1 December he wrote to his steward: 'Daws, I wou'd have you send in a brewing of Malt, I hope to be down at Newstead next week—Yours Byron'. He was back in town in February, when Daws travelled up to see him there, but apparently he intended to amuse himself with his 'navy' during the summer, as in April the steward and the sailor went to Gainsborough and Stockwith to buy materials for the ship. Absent or present, Byron did not allow any liberties to be taken with his property, and on 3 June 1764, the following advertisement appeared in the local newspapers:

> This is to give notice, that whereas the Rector of Linby has for several years made a practice of angling, lading, groping, and every other method of killing and destroying fish, and likewise of shooting in the manors of Bulwell, Newstead, Hucknall and Blidworth: therefore whoever will detect and give information against the aforesaid Rector to Mr. William Dawes, of Hucknall, shall, upon conviction receive five guineas reward over and above what they are entitled to by Act of Parliament. Byron.[9]

The poet Byron was mistaken in supposing that his great-uncle was appointed Master of the Royal Staghounds after the duel: actually he held that position from December 1763 to July 1765, when the Tories went out of office. Perhaps the most popular moment of his career came in November 1764 when he turned out a fine stag on the Nottingham race-course (then on the Forest), before thousands of spectators. The stag ran thirty miles in less than three hours, over very rough country, crossing the Leen, the Erewash and the Trent. It was taken while trying to cross the Soar, in the presence of nearly fifty horsemen, but it is not known whether Byron himself was among them.

A typical instance of William's high-handed treatment of his neighbours occurred during his Mastership and is told in a little book, *Original Anecdotes of the late Duke of Kingston and Miss Chudleigh*, by Thomas Whitehead, for many years servant to the Duke. Speaking of Thoresby, Whitehead writes:

> The park was stocked with plenty of deer. . . . There were likewise about eight or ten head of red deer, but these latter often straying in the forest of Sherwood, Lord Byron, who then kept the King's stag-hounds, would pursue them into Thoresby Park, which so disturbed the herd that his Grace was at last determined to destroy them, which he did. Before this happened, his lordship's hounds had driven one of the outlying red deer into the lake; this was while his grace was at dinner. As the stag baffled their utmost attempts to take him, Lord Byron sent to the duke to lend a boat for that purpose. His grace ordered the captain of his vessel to lend no boat, or any other assistance, saying, 'As the hounds had driven him

in, they might drive him out again'. His lordship was not much beloved of the duke or any of his neighbours. His grace could not forget the death of his friend, Mr. Chaworth.

Nevertheless, they had been friendly in earlier days, when both Byron and Chaworth frequently visited Kingston's house at Holme Pierrepont to play bowls on the green, which was considered one of the finest in England.

The story of the duel itself has been told many times. On 26 January 1765 the gentlemen of the Nottinghamshire Club[10] held their weekly dinner at the Star and Garter Tavern in Pall Mall; and at about seven o'clock in the evening a dispute arose between Lord Byron and Mr William Chaworth of Annesley about the preservation of game. Chaworth advocated strictness as the only effectual method with the country people, but when Byron argued that it might only prompt them to do more mischief,[11] he declared heatedly that Byron would not have a single hare on his estate if it were not for the care taken by himself and Sir Charles Sedley to preserve the game on their manors. Lord Byron offered to bet £100 that he had more game in an acre than either of them, but the wager was not taken. He then asked what manors of Sir Charles Sedley he meant; when Chaworth answered Nuthall and Bulwell, Byron replied that he knew Nuthall was Sedley's, but Bulwell Park was his. After some further bickering Chaworth retorted, 'If your Lordship wants any further information about his manors, Sir Charles Sedley lives in Dean Street, and your Lordship knows where to find me in Berkeley Row'.[12] This was the first hint of any serious quarrel, but as no more was said at the time, the company thought little of it.

About an hour later, however, Chaworth went out of the room with George Donston and asked him if he thought he had gone far enough in the matter. Donston sensibly replied that he thought Chaworth had said rather more than was necessary upon so trifling an occasion, and that he did not believe that either Lord Byron or the rest of the company would think any more about it. As he went back into the room, he passed Byron going out, which made him rather uneasy, and his fears were soon justified.

Whether the meeting of the antagonists on the stairs was intentional or fortuitous is uncertain, but it proved disastrous. At the request of one of them, they were shown by a waiter into an empty room on the floor below the dining room, lit only by 'a poor little tallow candle' and a dull fire. As Chaworth turned from bolting the door, Byron, with his sword half-drawn, called 'Draw!' Chaworth made the first pass and, entangling his sword in Byron's waistcoat, thought he had wounded him, but

Byron, unhurt, shortened his sword and ran him through. He then rang
for assistance and helped his adversary to a chair, but admitted at his
trial, 'I could not help observing that, he might thank himself for what
had happened, as he had been the Aggressor; that I supposed he took
me for a Coward, but I hoped I had as much Courage as another Man!'

When the alarm was given, the members of the Club found Chaworth
in a chair, bleeding from a body wound six inches deep. The eminent
surgeon Caesar Hawkins[13] was summoned and after some delay the
wounded man was carried home, where he died at nine o'clock the
following morning, having made a will in favour of his mistress.[14] He
dictated a statement in the presence of his uncle, William Levinz. From
witnesses' accounts of Chaworth's remarks after the duel, it is unclear
whether he really believed that Byron had attacked him unfairly.
Levinz, rightly or wrongly, held that view and urged the prosecution of
the assailant.

Lord Byron scorned to take refuge abroad, as was frequently done
in such cases, and was committed to the Tower to await his trial.
Contemporary letters make several references to the affair, particularly
those addressed to Horace Walpole's friend George Selwyn, and it is
significant that the correspondents never suggested ostracising Byron
and were, in fact, slightly amused at the public sensation caused by the
trial.

'If you are curious about [the trial], I can secure you a ticket for Lord
Lincoln's gallery,' wrote Horace Walpole on 19 February to George
Montagu, who replied that he would not be a spectator of such a scene
for anything.[15] Selwyn's niece, Mary Townshend, informed him on
8 February that 'Mr. Chaworth was a much more popular man than his
adversary, which I believe has inclined people to give hints which they
had not much foundation for . . . there is no reason to doubt the duel
having been a fair one'.[16] Selwyn, for whom deathbeds and executions
had a morbid attraction (or so his friends pretended), was then in Paris
and the approaching event was used by several of his correspondents as
bait to entice him home. 'Though you have but little chance of an
execution,' wrote Richard Rigby on 12 March, 'yet, if that event does
not bring you, I shall despair of ever seeing you again'.[17] Four days later
Gilly Williams declared, 'There is not the least chance of either hempen
or silken halter in Byron's process, though it will last three days, and
probably be as well attended as if the fate of the country depended upon
it. He is in Wilkins's apartment, walks about the garrison with a warder,
and makes public dinners for Lady Falmouth and Miss Sennisheri,
three days in a week. How different from the recluse life we have known
passed in those walls'.[18]

The trial took place before the House of Lords in Westminster Hall on 16 and 17 April. Owing, it may be presumed, to excellent legal advice, Lord Byron's statement, which he asked to have read by the Clerk, 'as my Voice is very low,' was remarkable for its restraint and expression of proper feeling. The impartial evidence of the Club members leaves no doubt that, whoever may have been the aggressor, both were equally ready to pick a quarrel and the prisoner was accordingly found Not Guilty of murder, but Guilty of manslaughter.[19] Claiming the benefit of the statute of Edward VI he was discharged after payment of the fees.

Among the large and fashionable audience was Thomas Percy, who accompanied Lady Northumberland's son. 'A grand sight,' he entered in his journal; and in a letter to the Reverend Richard Farmer, whose sister Mary was later to marry Lord Byron's brother Richard, he added: '. . . he was justly acquitted, there being nothing in the Evidence that bore hard upon him; bating that I think the act of duelling itself criminal, and therefore to be discouraged'.[20] His opinion was shared by Horace Walpole who, with somewhat unusual charitableness, wrote to Lord Hertford on the day after the trial: 'The prisoner behaved with great decorum, and seemed thoroughly shocked and mortified. Indeed, the bitterness of the world against him has been great, and the stories they have revived or invented to load him, very grievous'.[21]

The trial, though not directly mentioned, is reflected in the Newstead accounts. Daws was summoned to London in February and again in April and Lord Byron drew on him for two sums of money amounting to more than £700. £75 of this he actually paid back afterwards—a very unusual thing, which perhaps shows that the ordeal had shaken even his nerve a little. There is a letter to Daws from Isaac Spratt, agent for the Norfolk estates, beginning, 'In the first place, give me leave to congratulate you on the happy success of the House of Lords determination on Lord Byron's affair with Chaworth'.

Before Bulwell Wood Hall was burnt down a painting of a white horse hung there. On it, the story ran, Lord Byron, immediately after his acquittal, rode home from London without stopping, the horse dropping dead at the last fence. This picturesque tradition is belied by evidence in the accounts that he was still in London on 25 April. He did spend some time in Nottingham shortly thereafter, for in May, Daws had to meet him at Gringley to 'look over affairs there'; and the Gringley tenants afterwards received a pleasant souvenir of his visit in the form of a buck, with two guineas for drink to go with it. Apparently he 'looked over' Newstead rather critically, too, as in July Richard Hardstaff was paid for pulling down the upper part of the old kitchen and clearing the rubbish away. In August Lord Byron was abroad, but had returned by 11 September, when he signed the half-yearly account; but far from retiring from the world he continued to divide his time between town and country as before. After staying in London in the spring of 1766 he spent part of the summer at Ashworth, near Rochdale, where Daws had taken a house for him, in order to 'look over' his Lancashire property, and to arrange a new lease of the coal mines, which was causing trouble. He returned to Newstead in the autumn and on 1 November wrote to Daws (in London) that he proposed to be in town the latter end of the next week. August 1767 saw the arrival of the family at Newstead and in November Byron was again in town. On 11 April 1768 Lady Mary Coke wrote in her journal:

> I then went to an Auction [in London], where I mett Lord Byron, who told me his niece, Lady Frances Howard,[22] was to be married thursday or friday, & that he was then going to Ly Carlisle's to inquire which of the days was fixt on. I asked if the wolf he bought three years ago at Spa was still alive; he said it was, & tho' grown a great animal, was so tame that it play'd with the Cows, & run about with the dogs.

This is not the life of a recluse or an ostracised man.

For some time after the trial, however, though Byron continued to draw heavily on account, he took a more direct personal part in managing his estates. The rents collected from the Hucknall and Newstead tenants (about £1,200 a year) were entered by Daws for the first time. His keen supervision of detail is illustrated by a letter to the steward sent from Ashworth on 31 July 1766:

> Daws, When you go to Nottingham I wou'd have you ask Mr Evans if He received my Letter[.] in your next I woud have you inform me who has been at Newstead, you dont mention wheather Mr Stanley has finish'd ye Gutters on the Kitchen Roof, I hope by this you have got most of the hay Byron.

His vigilance had not abated two years later, when he wrote to Daws from London:

> I have inclos'd a Bill of £20 to pay what I order'd when I left [News]tead, I intend being down on ye 6th of next Month & tell every Body that is at work that I expect to see something done when I come down, for I declare ye last time I came I cou'd hardly perceive they had been at Work    Byron

His interest in the lease of the Rochdale mines was of course prompted by his chronic need of money; so were the sales of timber and raising of the Norfolk rents: but at the same time, there are payments for fencing Newstead Park, for supplies of stone and repairs of various kinds, which show that the welfare of the estate was emphatically not being neglected as yet.

The Newstead 'navy' was still maintained: a boat was brought from Gunthorpe in 1767, and two cobles were built at Bridlington in 1771, though it is doubtful if they were ever paid for. According to a local legend, while one of the vessels was being conveyed on wheels through the park, some of the country people who disliked Lord Byron remembered Mother Shipton's prophecy that when a boat laden with heather should pass through Sherwood Forest Newstead would pass away from the Byrons. Accordingly they gathered the ling that grows near the Abbey and heaped it on the vessel as it went by; but unfortunately for their hopes the prophecy took about fifty years to work.

Much of the correspondence is devoted to neglected payments to tradesmen, ranging from humble and pitiful requests to emphatic and infuriated demands, even as the sums involved ranged from 1*s*. 6*d*. on a parcel left at the Hutt[23] by the Mansfield coach to £170 19*s*. 7*d*. due to the grocers at Mansfield, who found themselves obliged to decline his Lordship's favours. He had not always been so dilatory. Ann Clay, writing from Handsworth in 1767 to ask for payment for trees supplied in 1764 and 1767 said, 'Till this bill neither my Father nor I was ever above half a year out of our money for goods sold to his Lordship; when his Lordship was at Newstead he paid the money upon receipt of the trees'.

The financial situation was obviously deteriorating rapidly and as extravagant fathers rarely like their sons to follow their example, Lord Byron was naturally very much annoyed when his son also ran into debt. Young William Byron, now eighteen and a half years old, was completing his education in France and had drawn on M. de Pignerolles of Anger for £240, which exceeded the allowance that Daws had arranged for him to receive. Informed of this by a letter from Abel Smith, the Nottingham banker, in February 1768, Lord Byron characteristically ignored it and later communications on the subject and in March 1769 M. de Pignerolles was still clamouring for his money: 'I believe it is his Lordship's Intention to pay his Son's debts,' he wrote, 'as Lady Byron order'd him that I should draw for what money I should want on his Account. Though this £150 will not be sufficient to pay all he owes . . .'.

Lord Byron was having sufficient difficulty raising money for his own purposes. In March 1768 he borrowed £1,200 from Lady Byron's cousin, Charles Gould, to whom he mortgaged the Wymondham and Tibbenham estates (Besthorpe had been sold) as security for £600. At the same time he tried to sell this property outright, but purchasers were shy and the need for clarifying the title to the estates produced one of Byron's most characteristically peremptory letters: 'I wou'd have you send me by the first Coach an Act of parliament,' he wrote to Daws on 17 January 1769, 'if you have not one by you, I woud have you go to Mr Sterrop & get one from him'—the unfortunate steward apparently being expected to know by instinct that he referred to the private Act for settling the estates passed at the time of Lord Byron's marriage; this is explained in a letter from the Norfolk agent. In September Messrs Lazarus and Salomon wrote that they would try to find some one to advance the sum required by his Lordship but, if they were successful, it was insufficient to stem the rising tide of debt. Soon Thomas Townsend was pressing for arrears of fee farm rent for Gringley that had been accumulating for four years, and Peter Stoughton, the Norfolk agent, was becoming most uneasy about the security for £500 that he had rashly volunteered to lend his Lordship until young William Byron came of age, which happened in October 1770. In November Gould advanced £1,600, half of which, as before, was secured on the Norfolk estates.

The crisis came in 1771—the year in which the younger William defied his father by marrying his cousin Juliana Elizabeth, one of Admiral John Byron's daughters, and it is hardly surprising if the combination of domestic and financial upheavals had a disastrous effect upon Lord Byron's easily roused temper and even upon his health, for there are references in the estate correspondence to his indisposition in July. It was easy enough to quarrel with his son, but unfortunately that young man's consent was needed for the sale of the Norfolk estates to pay off the debts and this he steadily refused. Although in July Lord Byron, through the medium of Daws, informed Charles Gould that he hoped he now had a scheme to raise money without troubling his son, this was probably bluff; a few weeks later Gould complained that 'His Lordship's Conduct towards me is very extraordinary: he is sensible that I have not only undertaken to purchase the Annuitys granted to Sir Abraham Jansson, but have taken upon me to discharge the *Arrears* purely to accommodate his Lordship's affairs; and yet his Lordship takes no heed towards securing the Repayment; and seems equally indifferent about making me a Title to the Stretham Estate, which he has expressly engaged to do'.

Moreover, having come to some sort of terms with the father, Gould found the son equally unaccommodating, and on 17 October he informed Daws that

Mr Byron having now given me an absolute denial of carrying the agreement for the Sale of the Stretham Estate into execution, as well as of repaying any part of the Money advanced, I stand in a very precarious Situation, and as I am bound in honor to make good the Purchase of the annuitys and to discharge the Arrears to Mr. Robson . . . I have given in your name to Mr. Sharpe to be appointed Receiver of the Rents of the Estates charged with those annuities by a Deed to be executed by my Lord, which will save his Lordship the expence of an appointment by Order of the Court of Chancery. My Lord, whom I saw this day, Sets out to morrow for Newstead, and will execute the Deed at his return to London the middle of next Month.

A little later we learn from Howard, the attorney, that Daws was also to receive the arrears due to Mr Evelyn on his annuity of £450.

The details of these transactions are obscure, as there is a gap in the account books between July 1771 and October 1772, only partially supplied by a summary account on a loose sheet of paper; but the deed was duly executed. Daws was appointed receiver and from 1772 to 1773 his accounts were returned to the Court of Chancery instead of to Lord Byron. It was doubtless a busy and anxious time for the conscientious steward, who was in London for five months, yet somehow the arrears were paid off and financial affairs reverted to a more or less normal condition.

We do not know when all the Norfolk estates were sold: the sixth Baron was giving directions about Wymondham as late as 1811; but Gringley, after several possible purchasers had been approached (Lord Middleton, for one, replied that he had no money to part with), was sold in 1774 to the Duke of Devonshire, who also bought the manor of Hucknall.

Sales of land and timber were not the only way to raise money: one of Gould's letters reveals that the plate had been pledged for £550 and in these desperate straits it is likely that Lord Byron snatched even at the straw offered by J. Newton, who wrote to Daws on 9 January 1772: 'I have been informed there is in Lord Byrons Stove a larger Quantity of Pine Plants than can . . . bring their Fruit to Perfection. . . . [If it is true] shd. be glad to have the Opportunity of purchasing a few Plants'.

Much more profitable to his Lordship, however, was the five days' sale of more than 460 pictures from Newstead, which took place at Christie's, 20–25 March 1772, and realised nearly £3,300. To us the prices seem ridiculously small: the highest bid for a picture was £66 3s. for 'A rural view in Italy, a warm and clear picture,' by Swaneveldt, while 'A den of lions, extreamly capital,' by Rubens, brought only £57 15s. And the largest amount (£195 7s.) was paid for 'An elegant Cabinet, representing the Temple of Love with its emblems and attributes, elaborately embost in silver'.[24] But allowing for the differences in the value of money, Byron did quite well.

The sale, nevertheless, was a tragedy for the Abbey, which had been one of the show-places of Nottinghamshire throughout the eighteenth century: many visitors had praised those pictures. Horace Walpole wrote in 1760: 'In the hall is a very good collection of pictures, all animals; the refectory, now the great-drawing-room, is full of Byrons'.[25] Eight years later an anonymous tourist approved 'the very fine collection of paintings, and the taste that is shewn in placing them to the greatest advantage';[26] and in 1771 Arthur Young was equally appreciative. Almost the whole of these, eloquently described in the catalogue as 'collected by his Lordship and noble Father during the Course of a great Number of Years with great Speculation and vast Expence', were ruthlessly swept away; the loss was irreparable. The family portraits were not included, but their subsequent fate is uncertain. Some may have remained at the Abbey a little longer, and certainly one—Little Sir John Byron—is definitely known to have been there in the poet's time.

On 6 August 1805 the poet wrote to his sister, Augusta Leigh, complaining about his mother, who had forbidden them to correspond:

> 'You may figure to yourself, for your amusement, my solemn countenance on the occasion, and the *meek Lamb-like* demeanour of her Ladyship, which contrasted with my *saintlike* visage, forms a *striking family painting*, whilst in the background, the portraits of my Great Grandfather and Grandmother suspended in their frames, seem to look with an eye of pity on their *unfortunate descendant. . .'.*[27]

He may well have been referring to the portraits of William, fourth Lord Byron, and his first wife Mary (by Kneller) which still belong to the family (although the poet was not, of course, descended from the first wife of the fourth Lord but from his third wife, Frances). The only other portraits painted before this time that have remained the possession of the family are those of Eleanor, second wife of the first Baron, George and Frances (children of the fourth Lord's second marriage), a watercolour by Tillemans of the fourth Lord and his third wife, Frances, with their three eldest children at Newstead, and a large oil portrait of Elizabeth Chaworth (first wife of the third Lord) together with Patrick and Maria Chaworth (her brother and sister). These are all now in the possession of the twelfth Lord Byron but the exact history of their descent is unknown.

After the first explosion of rage at his son's marriage, the fifth Baron cooled down sufficiently to draft proposals for the settlement of his estate in Nottinghamshire and Lancashire, the yearly value of which he assessed at £1,903 2s.[28] He offered to charge Rochdale with £100 a year to Mrs Juliana Byron until her marriage or death, with £2,000 payable upon either event. To his daughter 'Frances' (presumably Caroline is meant) he would secure £7,000, payable at her majority or marriage, but not until after her father's death. He proposed to settle the whole estate on himself for life and to debar himself from cutting timber on the Newstead estate (other than for necessary repairs). Provision was also suggested for the children of Juliana's marriage. This document was apparently never carried into effect, but paved the way for further negotiations. Early in February 1772 the Norfolk agent heard with pleasure the prospect of 'a reconciliation between my Lord, his Son and the Commodore [later Admiral]'; and a month later Walter Mather, tenant of Bulwell Forge, wrote to Daws: 'I was yesterday with his Lordship, who told me that he was reconciled to Mr. Byron. I was very glad to hear [this]', he added, 'for I always had a great regard for the Familay'. They had, in fact, executed a deed of covenant on 18 January whereby the father agreed to pay the son, during their joint lives, an annuity of £700 from the following Michaelmas, clear of all taxes, etc. and a sum of £2,000; the son undertook to join in a recovery of a moiety of the manor of Stretham and of the manors of Gringley and Tibbenham, to raise money for discharging outstanding annuities and mortgages. Perhaps Lord Byron was further appeased by the birth of a grandson (William John Byron) in May, and he may in time have come to realise that, even if he did not get on well with his brother John, the Admiral's child was not a completely ineligible daughter-in-law, for in 1773 John received a legacy of lands worth £20,000, with £5,000 for his daughters, under the will of his maternal uncle, Lord Berkeley of Stratton.

Temporarily in funds after all these drastic expedients, Lord Byron went off to France in the summer of 1772 for what he doubtless considered a well-earned holiday, leaving his wife and family in England. From Petersham, near Twickenham, Lady Byron dispatched to Daws (1 October) one of her courteous letters that differed so strikingly from her husband's peremptory notes:

> Daws, I recd. yrs. this day & have wrote to My Ld directly About it. I am Extreamly sorry to hear Poor Nanny is so bad; her Sister sets out for Newstead this day; by whom I send this letter. I hope yr. Wife & Family are well & Am Yr. Friend E Byron.

Poor Nanny appears to have been the housekeeper at Newstead, for on 9 October Lady Byron wrote again:

> My Ld is come to England & is now wth me; he desires I will tell you he shall be at Newsd. on Monday ye 19th at Dinner. —As Poor Nanny is so bad & desirous to go to her Friends we think she had better set out as

soon as she can After you recieve this; & my Ld will leave Some Money with me for her when she gets to Town—My Ld Imagens yr. Lettrs. are gon to France as he has not heard from you lately. E. Byron. [Overleaf:] My Lord desires you will take ye Inventory that Nanny has & Likewise ye Keys of ye Cellars & Every place. If poor Nanny sd want a little money for her Journey my Ld says you must let her have it.

Keeping well out of his father's range, young William Byron settled in Middlesex at Pinner and in October 1774 was elected M.P. for Morpeth through the influence of his cousin, the Earl of Carlisle, who was lord of that manor. He died in June 1776, however, at the early age of twenty-six, and was buried at Twickenham on the 24th, leaving a four-year-old son. Juliana's widowhood was lightened by the company of her unmarried sister Sophia Barbara who, having quarrelled with her mother, lived with her sister until 1783, when the still young Mrs Byron became the second wife of Sir Robert Wilmot of Osmaston, in Derbyshire. This marriage, however, lasted no longer than the first, for she died on 15 March 1788, when her eldest son, William John Byron, was in his third year at Rugby. She had other children by Wilmot.

After 1772 Lord Byron continued drawing funds from Daws carelessly, with the inevitable result that ominous clouds reappeared on his financial horizon. At some unknown date the piece of water behind the Abbey was drained and a brass eagle lectern and two candlesticks were found; they had been thrown there by the canons of Newstead when the Priory was dissolved in 1539. Two chests believed to contain treasure were also seen, but before they were got out of the mud a message was received from Lord Byron that the pond (later known as the Eagle Pond) must be refilled at once: he was coming to Newstead in his usual hurry. The treasure (if it exists) has never been recovered, but in 1775 Lord Byron converted the lectern and candlesticks into much-needed cash; on 12 December Sir Richard Kaye (later Dean of Lincoln and Archdeacon of Nottingham) wrote triumphantly to the Duke of Portland:

> I have bought Lord Byron's strong beer for my parish, and his brass Eagle for Southwell, at very good bargains; he is dismantling the whole. I have also got his Orange and Lemon trees. . . . The messages are very civil between the buyer and the seller, tho' we never met in our lives.

Curiously enough, Southwell had to wait thirty years before receiving the lectern, which Kaye presented to the Minster in 1805.

Dismantling apparently proceeded piecemeal for some time, culminating in a six days' sale at Newstead between 15 and 20 June 1778, which marked the break-up of home and family alike. Almost every room, from the 'Little Nursery' and the kitchen to the 'Great Dining

Room' was stripped of its furniture and of such pictures and ornaments as remained (including 'Ten very fine Plaister Statutes [*sic*], as large as Life'); and the ransacking of attics and storerooms brought to light such ill-assorted oddments as two pairs of French horns, a collection of animals in spirits, twenty arrows and three bows, six steel crossbows, and five birdcages. Several lots of books on architecture had doubtless belonged to the fourth Baron, and a 'Port Folio, with several curious Plans, Elevations &c.', contained the early 17th century designs by John and Huntingdon Smithson, which were purchased at the sale by the Reverend D'Ewes Coke, of Brookhill Hall in Derbyshire, and are now in possession of the Royal Institute of British Architects.

Husband and wife had long been drifting apart and the surviving records do not show whether the breaking up of their home was the result or the final cause of their formal agreement to separate. On 9 September 1778 Lord Byron executed a release of Newstead to the long-suffering Gould and George Stubbs, in trust to provide an annuity of £500 for Caroline, his only surviving child; on 18 May 1779 he consented to pay Lady Byron £100 a year, with an additional £50 if Caroline did not wish to live in the same house with her mother. As only £100 is entered yearly in the accounts we may infer that they lived together until Caroline's death at the age of thirty on 15 November 1784, probably after a long illness as she had made her will on the 20th of the preceding January. Like her brother, she was buried at Twickenham, the resting-place of her grandmother's family, the Berkeleys.

The income from her father, which was to continue during his life, she left in trust to Gould and Stubbs to pay £100 yearly for the education and maintenance of her godson, Robert William Shirley,and his sister Frances, children of Washington and Frances Shirley, with remainder to their mother; £100 went to her cousin Isabella, George Byron's daughter, and £300 to Lady Byron or to such persons as her mother should direct, with remainder to Isabella. Caroline's portion of £5,000 under her parents' marriage settlement was similarly divided among the same persons; and she gave £100 each to her cousins George (the Admiral's younger son), and Frederick (Isabella's brother). The not unusual stipulation that the legacy to her 'dear Mother' was not to be 'subject to the debts, receipts, control or intermeddling of Lord Byron' had a very real meaning in this case, for both Caroline and her brother were spirited enough to stand up to their autocratic father and to go their own respective ways.

Lady Byron survived her daughter by three-and-a-half years, dying in London (at Somerset Street) on 5 July 1788; eleven days afterwards she was buried in the same grave as her parents at Besthorpe. All her servants received varying sums of money under her will,[29] and numerous little bequests to friends and relatives are characteristic of her kindness and consideration; as, for example: 'To Mrs. E. Booth . . . my 6 gilt tea spoons and sugar tongs, as they were her present to me; also my pinchbeck watch;' and to 'Miss Lyford, eldest daughter of my Cousin Chas. Lyford of Winchester, my *Gold Watch* and my diamond rings, and my diamond pin for to pin a handkerchief'. To 'my worthy friend Elizabeth Booth (who now resides with me)' she also left the rents and profits from the Wymondham property for life, and George Byron's eldest son, John, received £100. The greater part of her estate she left in trust for her grandson William John, with remainder to her cousin Sir Charles Gould if her grandson did not reach his majority. As William John was twenty-two when he died unmarried, presumably his estate would pass to his grandfather, which was the last thing poor Lady Byron would have wished.

We do not know how Lord Byron passed his time after his wife and daughter left him. The accounts reveal his frequent London visits between 1778 and 1782—he went continually at one period, judging by the numerous journeys Daws made to see him—but his activities there are a mystery: he may well have hidden from his creditors. In 1779 he even suggested to Daws that 'a little money might be maid [*sic*] from the inside of Newstead, such as Chimney Pieces Brass locks flooring Wenscote &c &c, tho I cant Pull down the House I have a pouer to sell all materials in the inside also the Game . . .'[30] A curious little entry in the accounts in October of that year records: 'Paid William Bell for searching in the cloisters, etc., at Newstead for a vault or cellar, etc., 14*s*. 6*d*.' When Washington Irving stayed at the Abbey with Colonel Wildman more than fifty years later, old Nanny Smith, the former housekeeper, recalled that 'One time, Lord Byron [meaning the poet] took a notion that there was a deal of money buried about the Abbey by the monks in old times, and nothing would serve him but he must have the flagging taken up in the cloisters; and they digged and digged, but found nothing but stone coffins full of bones'.[31] Possibly the old lady was confusing the two lords and really meant this search, unless the poet also heard of it and tried his luck. Neither found the treasure, which may be there still!

In 1783 three suggestive payments were made: two, totalling £3 16*s*. 10*d*., were to John Oscroft and Hardstaff for mending the Old Dam Head; the third, five guineas, to Mr Robinson, 'being your Lordship's allowance towards repairing the Nether Dam Head after broke'. These recall a legend of which two versions exist. According to Augusta Z. Fraser, there was once another large stretch of water above the present great lake, with an old mill standing on a dam between the two. The Wicked Lord having given the miller notice to quit, the latter took his revenge by secretly cutting the dam. The mill was swept away and for the damage caused by the floods between Newstead and Nottingham Lord Byron had to pay £60,000 in compensation, which ruined him.[32] It is highly improbable that he could have raised such a sum, but Albert Brecknock, on the other hand, relates in his *Pilgrim Poet* that the fifth Baron had a passion for forming large ponds by damming streams, regardless of the damage done to the water mills lower down the Leen. When a law suit was begun by the owner of the cotton-mill at Papplewick, he borrowed money to fight the case from William Beardall, the tenant of Abbey Fields farm, who deducted an annual sum from his rent until the debt was liquidated. To revenge himself for the loss of the case, Lord Byron, aided by friends, cut through the back of Reid Pond (later called the Gas House Pond), which was then the largest on the estate, hoping that the mills would be destroyed. But the banks of the lower ponds withstood the pressure, and the waters went over them like a weir, without damaging the mills.

The exact truth is difficult to determine, but although the small sums actually paid for repairs suggest that incidents have been magnified beyond recognition, additional evidence shows they probably had some foundation. On 9 April 1785 the following advertisement appeared in *Creswell and Burbage's Nottingham Journal*:

> Whereas it having been represented to me, that some Person or Persons did on Saturday the 26th Inst. draw up the Shuttle of the Flood-Gates of my lower Lake, in Newstead Park, in the County of Nottingham;
> Notice is hereby given,
> That such Person or Persons, and all other Person and Persons, who shall in any Manner interfere or meddle with the said Lake, or any of my Lakes or Waters in my said Park or in any other Part of my Estate in the said County; or who shall interfere or meddle with any of the Shuttle or Shuttles, or any other Appurtenances belonging to the said Lakes or Waters, or any of them, shall be prosecuted with the utmost Rigour of the Law.
> —Given under my Hand and Seal this 31st Day of March, 1785.
> Byron.

And on 14 May, the same paper reported:

> On Sunday last [8 May], an Express arrived at Messrs. Robinsons, of Papplewick, in this County, with the News of their having obtained an Injunction from the Lord Chancellor against Lord Byron and his agents, for stopping the Current of the Leen in Newstead Park.—This welcome Intelligence was soon communicated to the neighbouring villages, where

it was received with the greatest pleasure, and the two following Days were spent in Expressions of sincere and decent Joy. This event has blasted the eager Hopes of arbitrary Extortion,—unfettered the Operations of spirited Ingenuity,—and restored to many Hundreds of Industrious Poor—THEIR DAILY BREAD.

Emphatically, Lord Byron was not popular in that quarter. All the same, he was not entirely careless of his own property. Fencing and hedging continued between 1779 and 1784, and there was still sufficient game on the estate for Daws to despatch many hampers of it to London in 1784—some of which were perhaps intended for Caroline in her last illness. That Lord Byron still regarded Newstead as a source of pleasure as well as income is evident from the entry in October 1784: 'Paid Mr. Kendall for three pictures in the study and two statues in the garden— £15 15s.' (Other statues formerly in the garden were included in the sale of 1778.) These are the well-known statues of a male and female satyr in the Devil's Wood, as it was called by the country people, who regarded the effigies with superstitious horror and fear. Possibly the Wicked Lord had a sardonic humour that conceived this original method of discouraging trespassers in his garden. The effect was decidedly eerie, but now that the grove has been cut down, the terrace where the statues stand among lavender bushes and Siberian crab-apple trees, above the Eagle Pond, is one of the loveliest parts of the Newstead gardens.

During his frequent and prolonged absences in town, Lord Byron had allowed tenants the privilege (for a consideration) of laying corn in some of the low rooms at the Abbey, but the mention of pictures for the study implies his intended return, which is confirmed by his letter to Daws, 24 December 1784:

Daws, As I intend being at Newstead on the 8th or 10th of next month, I would have you order in a load of coals, and tell Bell to put up a few bricks in the Hall fire place that I may have a fire there. I would have John Hardstaff do the carpenter's work that is wanted. I am informed that John Lee is imployed at Newstead by Twig and that he stops the earths for Mr. Musters; the instant I get down I will discharge Mr. Musters and send John Lee to gaol. Tell Bell to have everything in readiness to put up the Hall chimneypiece whilst I am down. Do you see that there is a good road to the Park gates, and down to the House. Byron.

He was content to fare frugally while he was there: later Daws entered his expenditure for bread, cheese, butter and ale 'to Newstead Hall the time your Lordship was there'.

Much carpentry was undertaken. Other payments in 1785 suggest that Lord Byron was preparing to settle in the country and it seems likely that his life of seclusion began about this time—twenty years after the duel that was popularly supposed to be the cause and fourteen years after the marriage of his son, which Byron the poet believed to be the reason. He was about sixty-three. His daughter's death probably made him realise his age keenly and on 27 May 1785 he made his will—a peculiar document.

To Robert Aisley, his London attorney (the sole executor) he bequeathed all his household goods, furniture, plate, linen, china, carriages, horses and all other effects in his house on Hampstead Heath and Newstead Abbey, and all monies and securities, in trust to convert them into cash as soon as possible and to reimburse himself for money owed to him by Lord Byron and for business carried out. Aisley was also to retain £50 for a ring, 'as a token of the sense I have of the Friendship, attention and good offices of the said Robert Aisley to me and my concerns for a long series of years'. The only legacies to relatives were £25 each to John and Frederick George Byron, sons of his brother George who lived in Nottingham. This brother's children are the only members of his family with whom he seems to have remained on speaking terms; it is pleasant to imagine these young men riding over to Newstead occasionally to beard their formidable uncle and still more pleasant to know that he appreciated their attention. Unhappily, Frederick did not live to enjoy his legacy.

The residue of his estate the fifth Baron left to 'Elizabeth Hardstaff (my servant) . . . as a recompense for her faithful and long services'. The country people called her 'Lady Betty' to signify their interpretation of her relations with her master.

He was not quite penniless and content with an annual income of about £250; but in 1791 he allowed himself the luxury of filing a bill in Chancery to stop the lessees of the Rochdale property from getting coals—a suit which, as usual, dragged on for years and remained unsettled until his successor's time. The steward drew no salary from 1786 until his death in 1794 at the age of seventy-six. His work was taken over by his son, William Daws junior, also without reward, but from 1791 to 1798 the accounts are very brief, payments being limited almost entirely to annuities and taxes.

In 1794 the fifth Baron's grandson and heir was killed in Corsica at the early age of twenty-two. The island was in revolt against France, led by General Paoli, whose many years of exile had given him such a favourable opinion of England that he proposed to annex Corsica to the British Crown. Operations were accordingly begun, but on 31 July William John Byron was killed during the siege of Calvi, in the course of which Nelson lost his right eye.

The legal consequences of this failure of his direct heirs roused Lord Byron to make one more visit to London in pursuit of what he had no doubt persuaded himself were his rights. In 1796 or 1797 he suddenly appeared in the office of John Hanson, later the legal adviser of the sixth Baron, and submitted his case. When the settlement of his property was made after his son's marriage in 1771, the ultimate reversion of the fee-simple was limited to the heirs of the son, instead of being left in the father, which made him merely the tenant for life, without the power of raising money on the estate. Conveniently forgetting that this had been his own proposal or, more probably, hoping that at this distance of time no one would remember the circumstances, he now blamed this arangement on the negligence of the lawyers, professed to have made the settlement gladly 'as any other father would do' (in actuality he had been obliged to submit to his son if he wished to get his own way in other respects) and painted a heart-rending picture of his inability even to cut down a tree—though after the timber-felling exploits censured by Walpole as far back as the 1760s, it is doubtful whether any remained to be cut. Day after day he poured forth his lamentations, bowed down by his 'most painful and pitiable load of distress', which so deeply impressed a young lawyer[33] who had a seat in Hanson's chambers that in later years he quoted Lord Byron's misfortune as authority for correcting a similar proposal in an intended settlement. Hanson, one suspects, was less sympathetic and, his case being adjudged past remedy, Lord Byron reluctantly returned home.

As Admiral John Byron died in 1786, George in 1789, and Isabella, Countess of Carlisle, in 1794, Lord Byron outlived all his relatives except his brother Richard. His own end came on 21 May 1798 and he was buried in the family vault at Hucknall on 16 June, to be succeeded in the title by the 'little boy in Aberdeen', whom he had ignored.

According to tradition, his last days were spent mainly in the kitchen, feeding the crickets with which the Abbey swarmed and which were said to know his voice and came when he called them. The night of his death they trooped out of the house in a long procession. This, as Mrs Fraser has justly remarked,[34] was a very harmless and inexpensive distraction, but most of the legends that swelled to such vast proportions in the years after his death are less amusing. Naturally the spirit of the Wicked Lord joined the Abbey ghosts and the manner of his haunting made a romantic story. He is supposed to have had a sister who disgraced herself by marrying a gamekeeper and was consequently disowned by her family—so effectively indeed that her existence cannot be traced, yet to this unsuitable marriage was ascribed the existence of

Sophia Hyatt, the mysterious but real 'Little White Lady' who frequented the neighbourhood of the Abbey in Colonel Wildman's time. Every year on a late autumn day, when the leaves fly in the wind, an invisible horse can be heard galloping through the park, while a woman's voice cries repeatedly: 'Speak to me, my Lord Byron, only speak to me!' Nearly fifty years later this provoked a ludicrous, long ballad from the pen of Ebenezer Elliott, who should have stuck to his corn law rhymes.

### 'DEVIL BYRON': A BALLAD

#### Ebenezer Elliott

A strange man own'd yon Abbey once,
　Men call'd him 'Devil Byron';
Yet he a sister had, who lov'd
　Well that Man of iron.

And well he lov'd that sister—Love
　Is strong in rugged bosoms;
Ev'n as the barren-seeming bough
　Oft hoards richest blossoms.

Yet from his heart, when she espous'd
　A peasant, he dismiss'd her;
And thenceforth 'Devil Byron' spoke
　Never to his sister!

Therefore, whene'er he drove abroad,
　She chas'd the Man of iron;
Rode by his wheels, and riding cried,
　'Speak to me, Lord Byron!'

Thus, at his chariot's side, she pray'd;
　For was he not her brother?
'Do speak to me, my Lord!' she said;
　Was he not her brother?

Her quivering hand, her voice, her looks,
　Might wring soft speech from iron;
But he speaks not!—her heart will break:
　He is 'Devil Byron'.

Yet down his cheeks tears shoot like hail;
　Then speak, thou Angel's brother!
Why struggle, in thy burning soul,
　Wordless fire to smother?

Oh, power is cruel. Wilful Man!
  Why kill thy helpless sister?
Relent! repent! already, lo,
  Beauteous blight hath kiss'd her!

Men say, a spectre with thee walks,
  And will not from thee sever;
A shadow,—not, alas, thy own!
  Pointing at thee ever:

Oh, think of Chaworth, rashly slain,
  And wrath, too late repenting!
Think of the kiss men give the dead!
  Vainly, then, relenting.

. . .

As rainbows fade, she perish'd. Then,
  How far'd the stubborn-hearted?
With her—the wrong'd and lost—he lived;
  Never to be parted!

He lik'd the Abbot's garden well,
  But there a shape was sighing;
There in each pale reproachful flower,
  Sinless love seem'd dying.

. . .

Dying, he saw her dying face;
  And, as with poison'd lashes,
It look'd forgiveness, its slow smile,
  Smote him—He is ashes.

Well sleep the dead: in holy ground
  Well sleeps the Heart of iron;
The worm that pares his sister's cheek,
  What cares it for Byron?

Yet when her night of death comes round,
  They ride and drive together;
And ever, when they drive and ride,
  Wilful is the weather.

On mighty winds, in spectre-coach,
  Fast speeds the Heart of iron;
On spectre-steed, the spectre-dame—
  Side by side with Byron.

Which is most sad of saddest things?
    The laughter? or the weeping?
Laughs Chaworth, while her Feast of Sighs
    Love-in-Death is keeping?

            . . .

He does not speak, he cannot speak!
    Then break, thou Heart of iron!
It cannot break, it cannot break!
    I can weep for Byron.[35]

Six more verses rub in the moral.

Headstrong, extravagant, violent, the fifth Baron certainly was; he was also an overbearing father and a most unsuitable husband for the gentle Lady Byron. But he cannot have been entirely wicked because in his penurious old age he retained the services of an unpaid but able steward and at least two faithful servants—Joe Murray, once the 'sailor-boy'; and Elizabeth Hardstaff, the housekeeper. Whether Elizabeth benefited from her legacy after all her master's debts were settled is doubtful, but she was loyal enough to his memory to try to persuade Tom Moore that the sinister legends attached to his name were distorted versions of harmless episodes. She explained, for example, that the tale about throwing his wife into a lake or pond originated in a playful push given to a young lady visiting the Abbey, which caused her to lose her balance and fall into the water; and doubtless many similar stories had no more substantial foundation.

Ebenezer Elliott based his melodramatic ballad on stories from old Luke Adams, who as a young man worked as a charcoal burner near Newstead and who gave the 'Wicked Lord' a surprisingly good character. His refusal to prosecute poachers was a strong point in his favour locally, and if Chaworth was the more popular man in London society, he stood far lower in the esteem of the Nottinghamshire tenantry, who considered Byron as little to be blamed for the duel.

## · 7 ·

# Foulweather Jack:
# Admiral John and the Others

He had no rest at sea. . . .

—*Epistle to Augusta*

YEARS before the fifth Baron's death, his brothers and sister had
had little to do with their incalculable kinsman and tacitly regarded
the second son, John, as head of the family. Leaving Westminster
School in 1737, John followed William into the Navy and on his first
long voyage the seventeen-year-old midshipman was plunged headlong
into adventure. His own *Narrative*, compiled many years later, reads like
a diary written up from day to day.[1]

In 1740 a squadron was fitted out under the command of Commodore
(afterwards Lord) Anson to attack the Spanish settlements in the
Pacific Ocean. But, as John Byron remarked,

> a strange infatuation seemed to prevail in the whole conduct of this
> embarkation. For though it was unaccountably detained, till the season
> for its sailing was past, no proper use was made of that time, which should
> have been employed in providing a suitable force of sailors and soldiers;
> nor was there a due attention given to other requisites for so peculiar and
> extensive a destination.

English officialdom was running true to form. His own ship, the *Wager*,
was an old Indiaman fitted out as a man-of-war; intended also as a
store-ship, it was heavily laden with supplies and 'crowded with bale
goods and encumbered with merchandise'. The crew were men pressed
from long voyages and 'all her land forces were no more than a poor
detachment of infirm and decrepid invalids from Chelsea hospital,
desponding under the apprehensions of a long voyage'. Even the commanding officer, Captain Kid, died shortly after the ship left England;
he was succeeded by Captain Cheap.

For a time all went well, although the *Wager* was nearly wrecked on

Staten Island; but shortly afterwards, while they were trying to round Cape Horn by way of Strait Le Maire, the mizzen-mast carried away and consequently they lost sight of the squadron and were drifting on a lee shore. Against the advice of his officers, Captain Cheap persisted in making as directly as possible for the rendezvous at the island of Socoro and could not be brought to recognise their danger until too late. Before nightfall on 17 May 1741 the wind increased to hurricane force; inasmuch as only twelve hands remained fit for duty, it is hardly surprising that at about four o'clock in the morning the ship struck.

Byron's graphic account of the terrible scenes that followed is too long to quote in full and too good to be quoted in snippets. After much confusion and despair the boats were got out, the Captain was induced to leave the ship, and about 140 of the crew struggled ashore to find themselves in so desolate a region that they considered their new situation little better. Their only shelter at first was an abandoned native hut, supplemented later by a makeshift contrivance rigged up by the carpenter; very little food had been saved from the wreck; and what Byron aptly termed 'the most unprofitable spot on the globe of the earth' provided only a few sea-fowl and shell-fish. Fortunately, the Indians who appeared a few days later proved friendly. Factions appeared among the crew; whereupon, says John,

> seeing it was the fashion, and liking none of their parties, I built a little hut just big enough for myself and a poor Indian dog I found in the woods, who could shift for himself along shore, at low water, by getting limpets. This creature grew so fond of me and faithful, that he would suffer nobody to come near the hut without biting them.

Before long, however, despite John's protests, this unlucky animal was commandeered to provide a meal, 'upon which, thinking that I had at least as good a right to share as the rest, I sat down with them and partook of their repast'—an episode revived by his grandson when he described the shipwreck of Don Juan.

One desperate party sailed away up a lagoon and were never heard of again. The Captain did not improve matters by over-hastily shooting a midshipman whom he suspected of attempted mutiny. Another party set off in the long boat, hoping to make their way home through the Straits of Magellan, but John, finding that they did not take the Captain with them, left the vessel and rejoined Captain Cheap, one Mr Hamilton of the Marines, and the surgeon, on the land they had named Wager's Island. They reckoned they were about ninety leagues north of the western mouth of the Straits of Magellan; the Captain hoped that by travelling north they might seize an enemy ship and rejoin their squadron. The return of one of the seceding groups who had settled on the other side of the lagoon increased their numbers to twenty and they repaired the remaining two boats. On 15 December the whole party set out; but after two months of hardship and misery they had lost the yawl and left four marines behind; they could make no further progress and returned to Wager's Island. A few days later the Indians reappeared with a Spanish-speaking cacique (native chief) from the neighbourhood of Chiloe; he was persuaded to guide them to the Spanish settlements.

Their numbers were now reduced to thirteen; they set out again in the barge with the cacique and his servant, escorted by two Indian canoes; but their guide provided food only for Captain Cheap, so the suffering of the company continued. The extraordinary Captain disgraced himself by refusing food to a seaman dying of starvation, although he had a large piece of boiled seal, which he shared only with the surgeon.

The next calamity was the loss of the barge in which six men had absconded with such few clothes, muskets and ammunition as they had saved from the wreck, leaving the rest of the party to their fate. When the Indian guide, who had left them for a few days to hunt seal, came back, he was enraged at the loss of the boat, which had been promised to him for his services; but eventually he consented to take Captain Cheap and John Byron in his canoe in search of other Indians. When they eventually reached a native encampment, John was left to shift for himself and was luckily befriended by the Indian women, who supplied him with food and shelter. He rejoined the surgeon and the rest of the party, which embarked once more with the Indians about the middle of March. After weeks of incredible toil and hardship, during which the surgeon died and Mr Hamilton was left behind, Byron, Captain Cheap and Mr Campbell reached the island of Chiloe, where they were hospitably received by the natives and at last able to eat their fill. At the Jesuits' College at Castro, to which they were conducted by a Spanish guard, a further treat awaited them—'an old ragged shirt apiece but clean, which was of infinite service to us; nor did eating at first give me half the satisfaction this treasure of an old shirt did'.

After a week's stay there, they proceeded to the governor's so-called palace at Chaco, and they were allowed to go as they pleased about the town, where every house was open to them. John Byron must have had his full share of the family charm: he had been befriended already by Indian women; now he spent three weeks with an old lady who took a fancy to him and begged the governor to allow him to visit her; and finally the niece and heiress of the richest priest on the island promised to convert and marry him. The old man approved; he displayed his niece's fine clothes. His own wardrobe, which should be John's when the old man died, and a piece of linen, which he offered to have made into a shirt for his prospective nephew-in-law, were additional inducements: 'I own this last article was a great temptation to me,' wrote John; 'however I had the resolution to withstand it, and made the best excuses I could for not excepting [*sic*] of the honour they intended me.'

When the annual ship arrived in December, the Englishmen were taken to Valparaiso, where their reception was very different. Here they were lodged in the condemned hole, swarming with fleas and with an armed sentry outside who 'made a pretty penny' by taking money from everyone who wished to see the prisoners. Only the kindness of a soldier who supplemented their scanty official ration without payment saved them from starvation. So they survived to be transferred to Santiago and were there permitted to lodge with a Scottish physician, Don Patrico Gedd, who treated them very kindly during the two years they stayed with him.

In December of 1744 they embarked on a French ship bound for Spain, which, however, they never reached. After more storms, misadventures and delays, followed by three months' detention in France, they were released at last and landed at Dover with insufficient funds to pay their charges to London. John accordingly rode all the way there without food, defrauding the turnpikes by jumping the gates, ignoring all calls to stop. In London he took a coach to Great Marlborough Street, but was dismayed to find the family house there shut up. However a draper, at whose shop the Byrons had dealt, obligingly paid the coachman and informed John that his sister had married Lord Carlisle and lived in Soho Square. At that house his disreputable appearance roused the porter's suspicions; but eventually the wanderer was admitted:

> I need not acquaint my readers with what surprise and joy my sister received me. She immediately furnished me with money sufficient to appear like the rest of my countrymen; till that time I could not be properly said to have finished all the extraordinary scenes which a series of unfortunate adventures had kept me in for the space of five years and upwards.

He had arrived home in February of 1746, when the country seethed with excitement over the last stages of the Jacobite rising. Lord Byron was probably still in the north with Kingston's Light Horse. Richard was at Christ Church, Oxford (he had matriculated 27 June 1743); and George was approaching the end of his schooldays at Westminster. John was relieved to find them all alive; his only surprise was the discovery that his sister had for nearly three years been the second wife of the fourth Earl of Carlisle, her senior by some twenty-seven years.

John had been promoted lieutenant during his absence and on 30 December 1746 he was appointed Captain of the *Syren* frigate. The War of the Austrian Succession, the cause of his first long voyage, was drawing to its close and on 8 September 1748 he took advantage of the approaching peace to marry Sophia Trevanion, daughter of John Trevanion of Carhays in Cornwall. The private ceremony in the Trevanions' family chapel occasioned some difficulty for his grandson, the poet, who was required to prove this marriage before taking his seat in the House of Lords: by 1809 the chapel was in ruins and the wedding was remembered only by some aged villagers, including an old woman who had helped to cook the wedding dinner.

They had little time together; soon after the Peace of Aix-la-Chapelle (October 1748) John was in command of the *St Albans* on the Guinea Coast, from which he passed to the *Augusta* guardship at Plymouth in 1753; and thence to the *Vanguard* in 1755. Of their six (some say seven) daughters, Sophia (born 2 June 1750), died ten months later (10 April 1751) and was buried in St Andrew's Church, Plymouth. Frances, Juliana Elizabeth and Sophia Barbara survived; Charlotte (born 3 November 1760) and buried at Plymouth 17 April 1761, had a more fortunate successor named Augusta Charlotte. John, the elder son, arrived on 7 February 1756—nearly seven and a half years after his parents' marriage; George Anson was born 30 November 1758.

The children saw little of their father during their early days. A futile expedition against Rochefort in 1757, while he was in command of the *America* (60 guns) preceded a more successful cruise along the French coast; the next year John Byron served in the fleet off Brest under his old commander, Anson, after whom his younger son was named. Two years later, in the *Fame*, he led a small squadron to Canada to superintend the demolition of the fortifications of Louisburg; and in due course he reported to the Admiralty a successful action against the French in the Bay of Chaleurs in Restigouche River and duly received the King's approval. A memorial column with plaque later commemorated the skirmish there. According to Margaret Sillars—

> In the Spring of 1760, a small French squadron, under Sieur de la Girandais, sent to the relief of Quebec, sought shelter in the Restygouche [*sic*] river. Here with the aid of shore batteries, they bravely withstood an attack by a superior British squadron under commander the Hon. John Byron, 'Foulweather Jack', from 20 June to 11 July before they were completely defeated.[2]

Peace seldom meant relaxation for Commodore Byron. On 2 July 1764 he sailed from Plymouth in the *Dolphin* (the first English naval vessel to be sheathed with copper), accompanied by the *Tamar*—ostensibly as Commander-in-Chief of all His Majesty's ships in the East Indies. The commission was a blind; actually he was bound for a voyage of discovery in the South Seas. To avoid arousing Spanish jealousy, the secret was kept until they were further south than necessary for the Cape of Good Hope; and the crew readily forgave the deception when informed they would receive double pay. Continuing to the south they encountered a rare race of giants on the shores of Terra del Fuego—a discovery subsequently dismissed as a mere traveller's tale because no trace of these outsize natives has since been found. Scepticism was perhaps increased by an exaggerated description of their height (7½ to 8 feet for the women, and 9 feet or more for the men) in a popular account of the voyage published anonymously in 1767.[3] Byron's estimate was more moderate: 'One of them . . . came towards me[;] . . . he was of a gigantic stature. . . . I did not measure him, but if I may judge of his height by the proportion of his stature to my own, it could not be much less than seven feet'. He remarks that they were not lanky, but broad in proportion to their height, and therefore truly to be reckoned as giants. Unfortunately his Journal was not published until 1773, in Hawkesworth's collection of voyages, and doubtless it had fewer readers than the earlier popular version, so that Byron was unjustly derided for an exaggeration he did not make. Since he was not given to false claims, we may assume he indeed saw an unusual tribe, which has since become extinct. The anonymous author may also have exaggerated when he wrote: 'The Commodore himself measures full six feet', since the Byrons were remarkable for their lack of inches.

On 12 January John sighted the Falkland Islands and after taking bearings and soundings he sent the boats in to look for a harbour. On the 15th they found a fine one which Byron named Port Egmont after the Earl of Egmont, 1st Lord of the Admiralty. The Falkland Islands had been discovered in 1592 by Capt. John Davies and in the following year Hawkins had taken formal possession of them in the name of Her Majesty Queen Elizabeth. Subsequently French settlers had spent a short time on the island, but at the time of Byron's visit they remained uninhabited. He took formal possession of them in the name of George III—an event which has assumed some significance in recent years.

Byron now passed through the Straits of Magellan, taking two months to do so because of the severity of the weather. On reaching Cape Pillar, Byron should have turned north but instead sailed out into the Pacific.

He voyaged far but missed much; because he sailed due west, instead of zigzagging or quartering over the ocean, Sir John Knox Laughton inferred that he 'was wanting in the instinct and the hound-like perseverance which go to make up the great discoverer'.[4] It is clear, however, that he was handicapped by sickness among the crew and that he tried to find healthy places where the men could recuperate. The anonymous officer already quoted has much to say about the Commodore's humanity and solicitude for his men—he insisted on their wearing cork jackets when swimming through the surf; distributed cloth to make them long waistcoats during the rainy season; and took great care of their diet when they were attacked by the dreaded scurvy, with the result that they lost fewer men than any other ship in such a voyage. Such conduct makes an exemplary commander but not, perhaps, the most successful explorer.

The *Dolphin* and the *Tamar* reached England on 9 May 1766, and for two years the Commodore enjoyed sufficient leisure to indulge in literary composition. In 1768 he published his *Narrative*, quoted earlier. It was an immediate success: a dozen editions or reprints were issued at intervals down to 1925 and the book has been rightly praised by critics of widely differing tastes. John Wesley, staying in Dublin in 1769, entered in his Journal (30 April):

> My scraps of time this week I employed in reading the account of Commodore Byron. I never before read of any who endured such hardships and survived them. Sure, no novel in the world can be more affecting or more surprising than this history.

And a modern American author has written: 'As an exciting picture of brave men fighting almost overwhelming hardships for years, this surpasses *Robinson Crusoe*'.[5]

In January of 1769 John Byron was appointed Governor of Newfoundland, but as much of his time there was occupied with disputes about fishery regulations between the French ambassador and the merchants of Poole, his office brought more vexation than pleasure. He was superseded by Molineux Shuldham in February 1772, leaving his mark on Canada in the name of Byron Bay, on the coast of Labrador.

In England he was harassed by domestic cares: his children were growing up and going their own ways. The younger boy, George Anson, had already followed his father into the Navy; and on 27 March 1772 John, the elder, who like his parent had been educated at Westminster (and afterwards at a French military academy) was appointed ensign in the 68th Foot. Frances had married Charles (afterwards General) Leigh on 11 July 1770, presumably with her father's approval; but the

[155]

marriage of Juliana to her cousin, William, involved the Commodore in a quarrel with his brother, Lord Byron; their disagreement was inflamed by the latter's sale of the Newstead pictures and the break-up of his household. John's sympathies lay with Lady Byron and her children, to whom he proved a good friend; probably indignation at the spoiling of his old home decided him to buy some of those family portraits, as we have seen. Fortunately he was relieved from financial anxiety the following year when his mother's brother, John, Lord Berkeley of Stratton, left him a legacy of lands worth £20,000 in Yorkshire and Hampshire; the Commodore's daughters received £5,000 and each son £2,000.

He was now able to buy the little country place for which so many sailors long. His choice of site is explained by one of the romantic traditions the Byrons have a knack of attracting. According to the story, he was travelling to Portsmouth to embark for some wild and savage land, where he intended to settle, but was held up by highwaymen at Pirbright in Surrey; or (another version runs) he lost his way. Anyway, he allegedly thought there was enough savagery and wildness in Pirbright without going abroad, so he purchased an estate known in the seventeenth century as Mansland. He rebuilt the house almost entirely between 1774 and 1775, renaming it Byron Lodge; the rising ground behind became Mount Byron. By 1816, however, it was called Pirbright Lodge and eventually became simply The Lodge.[6] Before his death he planted a mile-long avenue of Scotch firs, known today as The Admiral's Walk.

The outbreak of war with the American colonies in 1775 recalled Byron to active service. He was promoted to be Rear-Admiral of the Blue on 31 March, and in September was offered an appointment as Second-in-Command in North America; but thirty-five years in the Navy had sapped his strength and in September he wrote to Lord Sandwich:

> I hope your Lordship is convinced that as I never yet declined any service, so I should embrace this offered me now with infinite satisfaction, did my health permit; but in its present impaired state, I am much afraid I should not prove equal to the task. I shall do myself the honour of waiting upon your Lordship as soon as you return to town.

This reply, communicated to King George III, evoked a royal compliment:

> He is too gallant an officer [wrote the King] to pretend illness without sufficient reason; therefore I expect, when you see him, that he will not change his opinion; in which case I am clear that Sir Peter Parker is the properest person you can pitch upon.[7]

Byron's active career was not over. In April 1777 he was appointed Rear-Admiral of the White and from Rear-Admiral of the Red (23 January 1778) he advanced within a week to Vice-Admiral of the Blue (29 January). His health improved, so that he could assure Lord Sandwich of his readiness to go anywhere, and he was soon taken at his word.

> By a letter from Mr. Stephens late last night [he wrote on 1 May] I received your Lordship [Sandwich]'s commands, and as soon as I could procure post horses came immediately to town, but too late for the Levée; however, I had the honour of a long conference with His Majesty, who was pleased to point out to me the service I am intended for. I find it is expected I should sail directly. As I thought myself certain of going to India many things I sent by Captain Vandeput in the Asia, and what I have left [are] all here in town, so that I think I have a chance of going to sea with only a purser's kit, though I have hired a waggon to carry them to Plymouth.

He was actually under orders for New York in command of the West Indies fleet, his exact destination to vary according to the intelligence received of the French Admiral D'Estaing's movements. But on 8 July Byron's fleet was dismasted, scattered and crippled by one of those tempests that dogged his career and gained him the name 'Foulweather Jack'. By the end of September his squadron had assembled at Sandy Hook and on 18 October they put to sea in search of the enemy, only to be overtaken and dispersed by another violent storm. 'I look upon myself as the most unlucky fellow that ever was,' wrote the Admiral to his nephew Lord Carlisle on 9 November, 'and shall have no thoughts of home till I have had one fair meeting with D'Estaing. . . .'[8] Refitting at Rhode Island, they were not ready to sail until 13 December, when the French fleet, now in strength, was sheltering off Martinique. Byron arrived at St Lucia in the *Princess Royal* on 6 January 1779 and a fortnight later he superseded his friend Barrington in command of the squadron. On 19 March he was promoted to be Vice-Admiral of the White—the highest rank he attained.

The English fleet kept the French bottled up off Martinique for six months, but in June, when Admiral Byron departed for St Christopher's to see a convoy of trade vessels safely off for England, D'Estaing seized the opportunity to go south, and having taking Grenada without much trouble, allowed that town to be pillaged. Byron followed in haste, hoping to protect Grenada and thinking he had the advantage in numbers; he gave the signal to engage, but the French had been reinforced by ten ships of the line and the British attack was a fiasco. Fortunately for them, however, D'Estaing did not want to prolong the

[ 157 ]

fight, rightly believing his enemy was too weak to capture Grenada, and he retreated into the bay. Byron returned to St Kit's with the remnant of his sadly shattered fleet. D'Estaing reappeared a fortnight later while Byron lay in Basseterre Roads, but after some random gunfire the French vanished again taking the prospect of any decisive engagement with them.

Exhausted by this long series of storms, disappointments, and reverses, Admiral Byron's health now broke down again, so seriously that Captain Johnstone reported to Lord Sandwich:

> Since I wrote to your Lordship concerning Mr. Byron, I learn that this unfortunate man was struck with disorder and disease that deprived him of his reason, of which he was hardly recovered when they took the *General Glover* privateer.[9]

He was accordingly given permission to relinquish his command to Rear-Admiral Parker and return home. His reverse at Grenada had provoked hostile criticism in England; on 1 September Mrs Thrale reported that her flighty friend, Mrs Byron ('whom I love better than she deserves'), was wild with grief because her husband was supposed to have forborne fighting in the Grenada affair. However, his long career had given him comparatively little experience of fighting; courage and good seamanship unsupported by sound practical tactics do not often win naval victories, and the criticism was unduly harsh.

Certainly Byron's naval colleagues dissented from the popular verdict; on 15 September Mrs Thrale was able to add: 'This however prov'd a false Alarm, for here is Barrington come over, & gives Byron the best of Characters'.[10] This is corroborated by passages in many letters. 'Byron is a brave but unfortunate man,' was the verdict of Thomas Bromley; and some went further. '[Admiral Barrington] speaks highly of Byron, and of all the Officers, but the neglects from home and difficultys there, are, he says, amazing and unsurmountable.' So wrote Lord Pembroke to Lord Herbert on 10 September; and again on 24 September: 'Adl. Barrington is returned, & speaks highly of Biron, who has, he says, a fleet to victual without provisions, to equip without stores, & man without men'. Lord Pembroke, who had an Admiral cousin just home from the West Indies, took a personal interest and championed Byron in letters to his son, clinching the matter with the declaration that 'Byron & Barrington know one another, & therefore love, & respect one another'.[11] Barrington himself wrote to the Bishop of Llandaff on 30 October:

> You have heard how my poor friend Byron has been abused, and I verily believe some folks would have been happy could they have laid the blame

of the capture of Grenada on him. However after a great deal of bustle about nothing, he has not only been graciously received, but the following answer sent by the Admiralty to his letter: '. . . I have it in command from their Lordships to acquaint you, that they very well approve of your proceeding and animated conduct [etc.]'.[12]

Despite this vindication, Admiral Byron took no further part in the war and after the declaration of peace in 1783 he declined an offered command in the Mediterranean and he was not employed again. His family provided ample distraction—not always of a welcome kind— and possibly news of a scandal involving his eldest son contributed to his breakdown.

About a year after entering the Army the younger John had been appointed ensign in the Coldstream Guards (26 July 1773). He was promoted Lieutenant and Captain, 1 May 1777, held the rank of Adjutant, from 30 July 1778 to 20 June 1779, and after the outbreak of war in 1775 served in America where, according to his son, he had 'the reputation of a good officer, and showed himself such'. But unfortunately, though, he was not only 'of an extremely amiable and (*enjoué*) joyous character, but careless (*insouciant*) and dissipated'.[13] His son, the poet, never knew the full sordid story, however. 'Mad Jack's' return to England prefigured scandal that led to his ruin.

Some time in 1778 John became acquainted with Amelia, Lady Carmarthen, daughter of Robert, Earl of Holdernesse, on whose death (in May of that year) she succeeded to the title of Baroness Conyers. In 1773, aged only nineteen, she had married the Marquis of Carmarthen (later Duke of Leeds), by whom she had two sons and a daughter in rapid succession. By November 1778 her acquaintance with John Byron had become a love affair conducted with reckless folly on both sides. When the Marquis came back from the country on 13 December, the servants could no longer be silenced by bribes. Lady Carmarthen was out when her husband arrived and discovering, on her return, that he had questioned the household, she exclaimed, 'Then I cannot think of staying here!' Ordering a sedan chair, she was carried to Admiral Byron's house in Bolton Street (then occupied only by servants) and sent her footman to Green Street, Grosvenor Square (where Mrs Byron lived during the Admiral's absence in the West Indies), to fetch Captain Byron. John joined her immediately and after a short stay in his father's house they travelled together to Chislehurst and Rotting-dean, among other places. Lady Carmarthen's trial for adultery resulted in the pronouncement of divorce at Doctors' Commons on 26 March 1779 and on 9 June the lovers were married at St George's, Hanover Square. This legal formality can hardly have lessened the Admiral's annoyance at the cool use of his house for their affair and it was perhaps as well that Jack (who retired from the Army on 14 September 1780) and his wife made their home in Paris, where their children were afterwards born.

The Admiral's wife, Sophia, was considered a beauty in her younger days, endowed with 'a Style of prettiness that inspired Passion more than symmetrical Proportion is ever found to do, in short [a Woman] for whom . . . Men would have willingly run thro' Fire'.[14] Her zest for social life was unshared by her husband. During the early years of their marriage, her frequent spells of grass widowhood were fully occupied in bearing and rearing or burying her eight or nine children; but by 1778, when all the survivors were grown up and only the youngest daughter, Augusta, remained at home, Mrs Byron had become friendly with Fanny Burney and Mrs Thrale, who mention her frequently in their diaries. The other unmarried girl, Sophia (Augusta told Miss Burney), had quarrelled with her mother, and since she enjoyed financial independence, thanks to the legacy from Lord Berkeley, she lived with Juliana, who had married Lord Byron's son, William.

> Ah! Miss Burney, [Augusta would say,] if you knew Sophy, you would never bear me! she is so much better than I am,—and so handsome, and so good, and so clever—and I used to talk to her of you by the hour together. She longs so to know you! 'Come!' she says, 'now tell me something more about your darling, Miss Burney! But I ought to hope you may never see her, for if you did I should be so jealous!'[15]

Fired by the prevalent craze for analysing characters and dissecting feelings, Mrs Thrale attempted to assess her friends by giving points, which resulted in this 'score' for Mrs Byron:

| | |
|---|---|
| Worth of Heart | — |
| Conversation Powers | 15 |
| Person Mien and Manner | 16 |
| Good humour | 17 |
| Useful knowledge | 18 |
| Ornamental knowledge | 5 |
| | 71 |

She came second only to that paragon, Mrs Montagu, who scored 101. Mrs Thrale explained her system:

> − = I do not know well enough to decide; by Good humour is meant only the Good humour necessary to Conversation . . . it is general Appearance rather than Beauty that is meant by Person Mien and Manner . . . By ye ornamental [knowledge] is meant Singing Dancing Painting & suchlike.

They also diverted themselves with Goldsmith's idea of everybody's being like some dish of meat: Mrs Byron became 'Provincial Toast'; and for comparison with some animal they put her down as the zebra—which all seems to add up to something more like a chimaera![16] And although Mrs Thrale reluctantly deplored her friend's taste in lending her a poem on the geranium (by the Hon. Andrew Erskine) 'so obscene' that she refused to pollute her book with it, and returned it without comment, their friendship remained undisturbed.

When the Byrons and the Thrales were at Brighton in the autumn of 1778, Mrs Thrale, in a letter to Dr Johnson, gently teased him for his indifference to Mrs Byron, who said she had 'tryed hard for [his] heart one Day at Stretham [the Thrales' home], but found it impregnable'. Johnson's blunt reply that he did not remember her gave Sophia more amusement than offence; in due time her persistence was rewarded. The scandal of her elder son's elopement and the prolonged controversy over her husband's conduct in the West Indies played such havoc with Mrs Byron's health and nerves that by 1779 she welcomed the annual visit to Brighton as an opportunity to seek comfort and sympathy from Mrs Thrale. Johnson said, approvingly, that she could not do better, though he was obviously far from clear what all the fuss was about, since her husband seemed well spoken of and to have done everything he could; he scorned Mrs Thrale's insinuation that her friend's emotional state would displease him:

> You shall not hide Mrs. [Byron] from me [he wrote on 8 November]. For if she be a feeler, I can bear a feeler as well as you; and hope, that in tenderness for what she feels from nature, I am able to forgive or neglect what she feels by affectation. I pity her as one in a state to which all must come, and I think well of her judgement in chusing you to be the depository of her troubles and easer of her bosom. [He added a week later:] It is well that she has yet power to feel. Fiction durst not have driven upon a few months such a conflux of misery.[17]

The following spring found Mrs Byron still so far from well that early in April, accompanied by Augusta, she went to Bath where Fanny Burney, visiting them at the Belvidere two days after their arrival, found her friend already improved by the change, 'and she rattled and shone away with all the fire and brilliancy of vigorous health'.[18] She had been married long enough to discover that the wife and mother of Byrons rarely enjoyed prolonged, unruffled happiness; nevertheless she was shocked when her younger son, George Anson, suddenly returned from Barbadoes with a wife he had met only ten days before the end of his three weeks' stay there. Mrs Thrale, of course, was called upon for consolation, and George's mother and sister spent an afternoon recounting this fresh misfortune to Fanny's ears, also.

> Poor Mrs. Byron seems destined for mortification and humiliation [commiserated the diarist] yet such is her native fire, and so wonderful are her spirits, that she bears up against all calamity, and though half mad one day with sorrow and vexation, is fit the next to entertain an assembly of company—and so to entertain them as to make the happiest person in the company, by comparison with herself, seem sad.

She appreciated Dr Johnson's good wishes, but her mercurial temperament hardly justified his solemn reflection that 'Declining life is a very awful scene'.[19]

Although the abrupt marriage became the favourite topic of Bath gossip for weeks, Mrs Byron's resilience and Augusta's youthful optimism overrode all embarrassments and they went the social round as usual.

Augusta Byron was inseparable from Fanny Burney, who loved her 'romantically-partial young friend . . . a very aimiably-ingenious girl, and I love her the more for her love of her sisters'. In May they went to see *The Merchant of Venice*; on 4 June they met a party at the Pump Room before going to a public breakfast in Spring Gardens. There Augusta noticed Captain Bouchier, who had danced with her—'and he plagued me to death'—and who was not her only admirer. At another ball Augusta left her mother at the upper end of the room (according to her rank) to sit by Miss Burney, who had the lowest place; she was soon followed by Captain Brisbane, 'a young officer who had met her in Spring Gardens, and seemed much struck with her'. Fortunately, the romance made little progress and the young man departed in search of easier conquests. Fanny seems smug in her professed astonishment at Mrs Thrale's account of a certain Miss M—being taken in by Captain B—:

> Mrs. Byron has lost too little to have anything to lament, except, indeed, the time she sacrificed to foolish conversation, and the civilities she threw away upon so worthless a subject. Augusta has nothing to reproach herself with, and riches and wisdom must be rare indeed if she fares not as well with respect to both, as she would have done with an adventurer whose pocket, it seems, was as empty as his head.[20]

Their friendship with Fanny was ruffled at this time by the jealousy of Mrs Thrale, who declared that Mrs Byron was disgusted at Miss Burney's behaviour to her, after receiving such friendship and kindness; she classed Mrs Byron among the women she *loved* best, whereas Fanny ranked only among those she *liked* best. She protested that not mere vanity led her to fancy she had helped forward Mrs Byron's salvation.

Mrs Thrale's quibbles left Mrs Byron undisturbed and she remained on affectionate terms with both ladies. Later in the summer, when the wheel of fashion whirled Byrons, Thrales and Burneys to Brighton, Fanny and Miss Thrale called on Augusta, 'but found her invisible with this influenza'. However, Mrs Byron entertained them for two hours and promised to introduce Miss Burney to the Admiral, which Fanny realised was a great privilege—he always avoided his wife's women friends (Mrs Thrale concluded), 'from some odd peculiarity of disposition'. Nevertheless, he had enjoyed *Evelina*: during their stay at Bath Augusta reported that her father very often talked of Captain Mirvan, 'and though the book is very high in his favour, is not half pleased with the Captain's being such a brute'.[21] Miss Burney mentions no meeting with the Admiral, so perhaps Sophia was unable to fulfil her promise, but by 6 February 1781 Mrs Thrale could boast of stealing a march on her rival: 'Mrs. Byron rejoices,' she wrote to Fanny, 'that her Admiral and I agree so well; the way to his heart is connoisseurship it seems, and for a background a contorno, who comes up to Mrs. Thrale, you know.'[22]

Despite her animated elegance, Sophia was a staunch friend and she was apprehensive of trouble in the Thrale household. Henry Thrale was an unsatisfactory husband—he vexed his wife, among other ways, by flirting with Sophy Streatfield, a pretty fool acidly summed up by Mrs Byron as 'Everybody's admiration and nobody's Choice'. Despite, or perhaps because of, precarious health, Thrale wanted to prepare for a visit to Italy in the spring, but his wife insisted that Mrs Byron would be heartbroken at their departure. Sophia was even more troubled, however, by Mrs Thrale's friendship with Gabriel Piozzi, an Italian musician whom she had first met at the Burneys' house in 1778. 'I suppose that you *know* that man is in love with you,' she said during her farewell visit on the eve of the Thrales' intended departure; and she was but partly reassured by her friend's reply that she was too miserable to care. All was changed, however, by Henry Thrale's sudden death a few hours later. Sophia played the rôle of comforter, which she gallantly sustained through weary months of legal and domestic difficulties that followed; but before the end of the year she herself was again involved in some mysterious trouble that prompted Johnson to write in sympathy: 'Dear Mrs. [Byron] she has the courage becoming an Admirals Lady, but courage is no virtue in her cause.' His judgment was not based solely on chance meetings at Streatham, for at least once he paid her the honour of a visit.[23]

Henry Thrale's widow was not expected to remain inconsolable for long and soon her love for Piozzi was openly declared; but her intention to accompany him to Italy raised stormy disapproval. Sadly Hester concluded that if even Dr Johnson cared nothing for the loss of her friendship and company, no other hearts were likely to be broken, though 'my sweet Burney and Mrs. Byron will perhaps think they are sorry'.[24] She delayed her plans to arrange for the care of her children and in April 1783 she settled at Bath, where her daughter Sophy became seriously ill in the autumn. 'Mrs. Byron has been with me to day,' wrote Dr Johnson to Mrs Thrale on 27 November, 'to enquire after Sophy. I sent her away free from the anxiety which she brought with her.'[25] His own health was failing and we hear of no further meetings with Mrs Byron before his death in December 1784. By that time Hester Thrale had married Piozzi and was in Italy with him. Her friendship with Mrs Byron necessarily suffered a long interruption.

We hear little of the Admiral's family for the next few years. George saw active service against the French fleet in the West Indies and on his return to England in 1782 had the unpleasant task of reporting the burial at sea of the Duke of Rutland's brother, Lord Robert Manners, who had been killed in action. 'I firmly believe,' he wrote, 'there never was a more awful melancholy burial.'[26] A year or two later Augusta married (Vice-Admiral) Christopher Parker, son of Admiral Sir Peter Parker whom the King had once suggested as a suitable substitute for Admiral Byron in the American war. Their son, born about 1785, was named Peter after his grandfather.

Meanwhile, Captain John Byron's brief spell of comparative respectability had ended with the untimely death of his wife on 27 January 1784, from consumption said to have been caused by accompanying her husband to a hunt too soon after the birth of their second daughter, Augusta Mary. She was buried at Hornby, Yorkshire. Their first daughter, Sophia Georgina, had also died and their only son had lived for an hour; so the surviving girl was taken over by her maternal grandmother, Lady Holdernesse, while her handsome, penniless father repaired to the happy hunting ground of Bath in search of another rich wife. There he married Catherine Gordon of Gight, a plump Scottish heiress worth more than £23,000, on 13 May 1785 in St Michael's Church.

His parents were now alone and the Admiral's health failed rapidly. In addition to family troubles, they seem to have had money worries and to have suffered from the law's delay. On 19 December 1785 Sophia wrote impatiently to James Sykes, the family lawyer, about their account, wondering that anyone but himself could suppose she could exist for three months 'in expectation of what was to be paid me by stipulation at the end of that period' and concluding resentfully that 'you seem to have forgot you was not always the great man you are now become—and that you have heretofore wanted money still more than I do—'.[27] She made her will that year, appointing the Admiral a trustee for her grandson, William John, but her husband pre-deceased her on 5 or 6 April 1786 and was buried at Twickenham on the 10th. By his will, made 12 July 1785, Sir John Wodehouse of Lexham, Norfolk, was sole executor; he left his wife an annuity of £480 (in augmentation of her marriage settlement) from his copyhold estates at Crowdall (Hampshire) and Pirbright (Surrey) and his property near Pickering (Yorkshire) held on lease from the Duchy of Lancaster. The surplus rents and profits were to be divided equally among his son, George Anson, and his daughters, Frances Leigh, Sophia Barbara Byron, and Augusta Charlotte Parker. After his wife's death the estates were to be sold and the money likewise divided among these children, who were also to share the residue of his personal estate. He had already advanced considerable sums to John and Juliana (Lady Wilmot) and therefore left the former only £500 which, it eventually appeared, he had already signed away,[28] and the latter £2,000. His bequest of the interest on £100 for the benefit of Sarah Smith, daughter of John Smith, a Pirbright potter, for her maintenance and education until she was twenty-one or married, and afterwards to be held in trust for her, is inexplicable. A codicil, dated 17 March 1786, predictably made bequests of £100 to his friend James Sykes, £100 to his servant Sarah Prarn, and £40 to her husband, William Prarn. Unfortunately, he forgot the need for witnesses to the codicil and his writing had to be confirmed by affidavit.

The task of compiling inventories was entrusted to Sykes, who had witnessed the will. Mrs Byron wrote to him from Bolton Row on Friday, 7 April 1786:

> I find I made a mistake for you must be here at eight *not nine* o'Clock next Monday morning—and Sir John W[odehouse] intends you shall go down as well and with Mr. Wike to take inventorys & discharge Ser[van]ts— but as He must take one of Furniture here Tuesday—that I may not have the pain of it when I am in the House—I beg you not to go down to Pirbright till Wednesday—
>
> Your humble Sert.
> S. Byron
>
> . . . I will leave orders Breakfast shall be ready for you on Monday if you & Captn M. will come in time to eat it in this room.[29]

Mrs Byron's annuity was inaccurately magnified to Mrs Piozzi as £1,600, which may have been her total income (the amount of her jointure is not mentioned). She was doubtless well provided for and the bequest of £500 to 'that scapegrace Jack who has behaved in a most shocking manner to his Mother, & goes on as usual like a Rascal'[30] was generally considered magnanimous treatment. Despite his reputed irascibility, the Admiral had been a kind and fair husband and father, but 'Mad Jack' avoided dealing with him, preferring to pester his mother with begging letters, as when, to take one typical example, he wrote to Sykes from Frankfurt on 14 March 1784:

> I have taken the Liberty to draw upon you for forty-four pounds. I intended to have sent the Bill to my mother but they would not give me mon[e]y on a Bill drawn on my Mother[.] Therefore I was obliged to draw on you, I have wrote to Grosvenor Square about it. I desir'd my Mother to repay my Father, whom I hope will be so good as to advance the sum for me Till my Affairs are settled.[31]

The end of Mrs Byron's first year of lonely widowhood coincided with Mrs Piozzi's return from Italy. She was welcomed gladly and a few months of Piozzi's assiduous attention converted Mrs Byron's cordial hatred into genuine liking for him. The resumption of this friendship was perhaps Sophia's last real pleasure: the death of Juliana, Lady Wilmot, on 15 March 1788, was a blow from which she never fully recovered. Neither of her other daughters ever went near her and George Anson 'the only Son that Should be her Comfort' was in India. Old and infirm, she retained enough of her former self to make Mrs Piozzi marvel at the different affects of age on women:

> Mrs. Byron has lost all Face, but retains that elegance of Form & Manner—that still strikes you with the Idea of a decay'd Belle, a Lady of Quality more battered by Sickness than subdued by Age.

This she attributed to her having been born a woman of fashion, whereas her contemporary, Mrs Cholmondelay, sister of the actress Peg Woffington and daughter of a bricklayer, 'became one at 15 years old—yet you see that was not early enough'.[32]

Sophia was growing hard to please, though, coveting her neighbours' servants and boring unwilling listeners with tedious stories of domestic difficulties. She seemed to be failing rapidly in June of 1790, but lingered on until 6 November, when she died at Bath and was buried there in the Abbey on the 12th, 'by Dr. Davis' stone'. Almost her last act was to write 'in a scrawled and painful hand' to her old friend:

> Don't be *overcome* with the *little cant* of grief of my daughter [in-law] Mrs. G. B. when I am no more. Tell Her black becomes Her and she will forget it all—once more—adieu—Think I have not many more Hours to love thank and beg you never to forget your S.B. [P.S.] It's a hard struggle and Mr Grant will tell you my sufferings.[33]

Mrs Byron's death spared her further grief on account of her sons.

The reckless, vapid John was to die in exile, debt and disgrace. George Anson, who did not share his brother's faults, yet had little further happiness in store for him. After serving with distinction in the West Indies, he applied for a transfer to the East; early in 1789 he sailed for India in command of the *Phoenix* to join the campaign against Tippoo Sahib. There he promptly intercepted that potentate's transports, loaded with military stores, and was mentioned in dispatches for his assistance in reducing a fortress on the coast of Malabar. Shortly thereafter, when his ship lay off the mouth of a river up which he was to convey part of the army, he had to have an interview with General Abercrombie, who was marching towards Seringapatam. Although a fresh wind caused a heavy sea on the bar of the river, 'danger disappeared before his eagerness'. He set out in a boat, which was soon overturned, and the gunwale struck him twice violently on the breast. He was not expected to survive the shock, but the doctors ordered him back to England, hoping he would live long enough to reach it. He arrived home in 1792, to be overwhelmed in a few months by the loss of his wife, Henrietta Charlotte, who died at Bath on 26 February 1793, at the early age of twenty-nine, and was buried in the Abbey on 1 March. She probably died in childbirth: a son named John James was also buried there on 2 April.

Her wretched husband took the two surviving children, George Anson, Junior, nearly four, and Julia Maria Charlotte, a year or two old, to Dawlish, where he himself died on 11 June at the age of thirty-four. The obituary notice, written by a friend whose stilted language does not obscure admiration and sincere sorrow, described him in the *Gentleman's Magazine* as

> brave, active and skilful, his Majesty has lost in him an excellent and loyal officer. In his private character he was devout without the appearance of it, fond of his family, constant in his friendships, generous and humane.

George's cousin, Lord Carlisle, exerted himself to obtain Government pensions for the orphaned children; in April 1794 they were granted £50 a year each. The East India Company was recommended to pay them additional pensions of the same amount.

\*

The fifth Lord Byron's only sister, Isabella, resembled him in attracting public attention by eccentricity. She married Henry, fourth Earl of Carlisle, at St George's, Hanover Square, on 8 June 1743, when she was twenty-one and he a widower of forty-nine. Three children by his first wife were still living (the eldest boy had died of consumption in 1741); but the second son, Robert, died three months after his father's second wedding; and the elder daughter was already married, leaving only Diana at home, so the duties of the stepmother were not onerous. Isabella's own family expanded rapidly. To their mother's dismay, the first three children were girls—Anne (1744), Frances (1745), and Elizabeth (1746); the urgently needed heir, Frederick, did not arrive until 1748, to be followed by yet another daughter, Juliana. A well-stocked nursery and the marriage of Diana in 1748 brought comparative release at last.

Lady Mary Wortley Montagu, who knew Isabella soon after her marriage, thought her very agreeable, but inclined to be gay. Child-bearing had effectually curbed any such inclination for some time and she naturally wanted to enjoy herself again, but details of this time in her life are few. She was at York races in July 1753 and in Passion Week of 1758 Horace Walpole attended a great concert at the Carlisles' London House in Soho Square, where he was amused to see Dr John Brown, who professed to dislike opera, 'singing the *Romish Stabat Mater* with the Mingotti [an opera singer] behind a harpsichord'.[34] These were perfectly normal amusements for anyone of Isabella's rank, but Lady Mary declared, soon after Lord Carlisle's death in the following September, that he showed his uncommon probity and good nature 'by the disposition of his will in the favour of a lady he had no reason to esteem'—a puzzling comment.[35]

Lady Louisa Stuart, on the other hand, believed that Isabella began with great strictness of conduct and principle and 'preserved an unspotted reputation through the whole of her married life; what might be fairly termed her career.' She added that in her autumn time Isabella 'surprised her acquaintance by seeming to relax and grow gay; re-entered the world, after quitting her weeds, like a lover of the dress and diversions she had formerly professed to dislike & blame'.[36]

On 10 December 1759 Isabella, now thirty-eight, reversed the balance of age in her previous marriage by becoming the wife of William Musgrave[37] of Hayton Castle, Cumberland; he was only twenty-four, but she pretended he was ten years older. This, of course, made a considerable stir. 'Well,' said Lady Blandford, 'I have not patience with that woman; at her time of her life, and with daughters grown or growing up round her, to go and marry a young fellow she must buy breeches for'.[38] Male comment was even franker; when Lord Temple importuned King George III for the Garter left vacant by the death of Lord Carlisle, Charles Townsend said that he should have proceeded by degrees—if he had been content to ask first for *Lady* Carlisle's garter, no doubt he would have obtained it! Isabella remained unperturbed and moved freely in the circles frequented by Horace Walpole who, delighting in her oddity, told George Montagu that she thought Thomas Gray extremely like him (Walpole) in manner, to which Montagu retorted, 'I delight in Lady Carlisle's judgment that finds a perfect resemblance between Gray's sage taciturnity and your bold intrepid impetuosity; 'tis very like a whale or a camel'.[39]

When her daughters grew up Isabella combined duty with pleasure by chaperoning them to Almack's and other assemblies. In 1768 Lady Anne was appointed Lady of the Bedchamber to Princess Amelia, who was well pleased with her; and in April Lady Frances married John Radcliffe. Isabella spent some weeks in August with the Duchess of Northumberland at Alnwick Castle, where she found a congenial companion in the Reverend Thomas Percy,[40] who shared her 'great taste for Antiquities and every other Branch of literature', and who acted as her guide on many country rides. One day they went in her postchaise to see Warkworth Castle and Hermitage, which gave Percy his long-sought opportunity to speak of Mary Farmer, who had recently married Richard Byron. Percy was a friend of Mary's brother, the Reverend Richard Farmer of Emmanuel College, Cambridge and impressed on Lady Carlisle how much Mary's family was respected at Leicester and said all he could to impress her favourably with her new sister-in-law. He had heard that Isabella and Richard were not always on the best terms and was therefore delighted to hear her say that she was glad to hear her brother had such a prospect of happiness and that she intended to show Mrs Byron every friendship and regard. She believed they were then in Northumberland and wished they would visit Alnwick on some public day while she was there; but they did not, and Percy had to send his news by post to Farmer.[41]

Isabella's third daughter, Elizabeth or Betty, became the wife of Peter Delmé in 1769 and in the following year a comfortable home for Anne and Julia (who remained single) was ensured by Frederick's marriage to Margaret Caroline, daughter of the first Marquis of Stafford. When eventually Peter Delmé died in 1789, Juliana (usually called Julia) went to live with her widowed sister.

Musgrave, for all his youth, had sober tastes. Isabella's rather ill-assorted union lasted longer than anyone had expected, but gradually the ties between them loosened and when she knew her children were well settled Isabella washed her hands of domestic responsibilities and went abroad, to the helpless consternation of her family who remained on good terms with their stepfather, showing that they did not blame him for the separation. Musgrave found a multitude of public and private interests to occupy him. Called to the Bar in 1758, he became a Bencher of Middle Temple in 1789 and Treasurer in 1795. In 1763 he was appointed a commissioner for customs and in 1785 a commissioner for auditing public accounts. He was Vice-President of the Royal Society (1786) and the Society of Antiquaries (1786), and became a Trustee of the British Museum in 1783. In these diverse offices he proved able and attentive and his talents and pleasant manners won him many friends. In later years, when his health broke down, he philosophically spent his enforced leisure compiling the *Obituaries* for which many genealogists since have blessed his name; and he also enjoyed the fine collection of engravings which were advertised for sale shortly before his death in 1800.[42]

Meanwhile his errant wife in France became entangled with one 'Baron' after another and, being a true Byron, got into many money difficulties. For years travellers returning from the Continent were asked for scandal about her. In 1774 Lady Mary Coke stayed in a house in Lyons where Isabella had lodged for some time with her Baron of the hour (probably the adventurer who called himself the Baron de Wenheim; his real name was Monsieur Larcher). The landlady reported that they had behaved with all decency, the Baron keeping her Lady-ship company during the day and attending her when she went out, but always retiring to his own room at night; but, she added, to be sure 'people talk'd a great deal'.[43] Four years later she was staying in the Chaillot district and visiting Madame du Deffand, who could not make her out at all and appealed to Horace Walpole for enlightenment: 'I don't know that she is a very sensible woman . . .', she wrote on 17 June 1778, 'she talks a lot and speaks good French; there is nothing objectionable and nothing interesting in her'. On 29 July Madame complained that she did not know what to say to her tiring visitor and was glad that her calls were rare. Isabella was enjoying herself at Chaillot, despite having no news of her son, a member of the Commission then treating with the American Colonies, or of her brother, the Admiral. She had heard once from Lord Carlisle's friend, George Selwyn, however, and not long afterwards she told Madame that she had had a letter from her son, written from Philadelphia.[44]

She left Chaillot for Avignon early in November and on 2 December dined in Paris with the Reverend Dr Warner, who told Selwyn that 'she is very tranquil; reposing all her care and confidence in you, and says as kind things of you as I suppose she wrote to you by the last post'. If Lady Louisa Stuart is right, Isabella disliked George Selwyn, but wanted to borrow money from him and thus found it politic to keep in with Lord Carlisle's greatest friend. Selwyn, for his part, felt obliged to keep an eye on her during the Earl's absence in America, and deputed Dr Warner to try (unsuccessfully) to persuade her to return to England. She was confident of help from the Maréchal de Biron, with whom she had probably claimed kinship—the kind of claim, as Lady Louisa remarked, that the French were prompt to acknowledge with important English people who could boast a Norman surname.

On 13 June 1781 Selwyn, returning from Bedford House, met Admiral John Byron, who said his wife had received letters from Lady Carlisle in which she talked of coming home:

> He spoke to me about her with great good nature and reason [wrote Selwyn to Lord Carlisle], but said that the correspondence was between his wife and her, and seemed to hint, if he was himself consulted, she should advise her better. . . . What a fracas we shall have when my Lady Dowager arrives; and if she does not, I see no end of her vexations.[45]

However, Lady Carlisle remained abroad for another ten years.

Isabella devoted intervals in her pursuit of pleasure to art and literature. Walpole says that Isabella and Richard 'copied the etchings of Rembrandt in a masterly style' and that her etchings from un-published Italian masters were highly coveted by contemporary collectors.[46] She was 'ever more scribbling' too, and wrote an 'Answer to Mrs. Greville's *Ode for Indifference*' (wrongly attributed to her daughter-in-law) beginning:

> Is that your wish, to lose all sense
> In dull lethargic ease;
> And, wrapt in cold Indifference,
> But half be pleased or please?

The poem deserved Lady Louisa Stuart's dismissal as a 'poor enough answer'. With advancing years Isabella turned to more serious topics in prose. In 1789, apparently unconscious of any incongruity, she published an edifying treatise, *Thoughts in the form of maxims addressed to young ladies on their first establishment in the world*, which would find few respectful young readers today.

A few years later Lady Carlisle returned to England at last. Of her own family, only the fifth Lord Byron and Richard still lived; but as the former was shut up at Newstead and the latter living far away in Northumberland, she may never have seen them again. She was almost a stranger to her own children and perhaps not a very welcome one; so she went to Bath, where Lady Middleton, with whom she tried to renew acquaintance, was asked, 'What Baron attends upon her now?' But Isabella could no longer maintain the pretence of youth. She died shortly afterwards, on 22 January 1795, at the age of seventy-three.

*

In the history of this odd family few things are more surprising than the third son's undeviating respectability. Sent, like his brothers, to Westminster School before he was eight, Richard seems to have left three years later, at least for a while, but apparently returned because his self-portrait, painted when he was sixteen, identifies him as 'a scholar at Westminster'.

Richard matriculated at Christ Church, Oxford, in June 1743, took his B.A. degree in 1747, and the M.A. in 1750; and then he established a family precedent by taking Holy Orders. On 2 October 1758 he was instituted as Vicar of Eglingham in Northumberland. He spent the rest of his long life in the north of England, as far removed as possible from the brothers and sister with whom he had little in common. He had inherited the financial aptitude of his name-sake, the second Lord Byron, and petitioned the Government for a grant of lands in Nova Scotia; on 5 June 1764 he was granted 10,000 acres at a quit rent of a farthing an acre, on the conditions that within two years one white settler be introduced for every 200 acres and that one rood in every 1,000 acres be devoted to hemp. Gold, silver, coal mines, and fishing rights on the coast, were reserved.

This venture prospered well enough to enable him to marry (14 January 1768) Mary Farmer, one of the daughters of a respected maltster in Leicester. We do not know how Richard Byron became acquainted with her family. The obvious link was Mary's brother, Richard, a scholar of distinction, who was nearly eleven years younger than Byron and graduated from Cambridge; however he was fast becoming so eccentric in manners and dress that strangers thought him half crazy. He had made his mark by publishing an *Essay on the Learning of Shakespeare* (1766) and he issued proposals for printing a history of his native town; but the labour needed was too much for one of his easygoing habits and eventually he passed his materials over to John Nichols. He could not be induced to remove from Emmanuel College and declined a bishopric because 'One that enjoyed the Theatre, and the Queen's Head in the evening would have made but an indifferent Bishop'.

Although Thomas Percy had not known Mrs Byron personally when he was extolling her family to Lady Carlisle, he was corresponding with Richard by June of 1770, when he told Farmer that he had many things for him, particularly the curiosities deposited in his hands by Mr Byron.[47] These may have been museum specimens of some sort, or perhaps Richard was contributing to Percy's collection of ballads.

The Byrons' eldest son, Richard, was born on 30 July 1769; and on 11 November his father was collated to Ryton in Durham. The Rectory, dating from the late fifteenth century, but largely rebuilt about 1709, was a comfortable, roomy house with a fine oak staircase and a pleasant sheltered garden for the children to play in. From the adjoining church-yard the ground sloped gently down to the Tyne; on the far side it rose sharply to a considerable height; to the east was a wide view over the vale to the hills above Newcastle.

Here their second son, John, was possibly born, about 1771, to be followed by a brother, Henry, in about 1776.[48] Henry, who went to Cambridge in 1793, followed his father into Holy Orders and eventually became grandfather of a famous actor-dramatist. He was preceded at Cambridge by John (Emmanuel College, 18 June 1788), who then went into the army, but died early at his father's house in Haughton-le-Skerne on 18 February 1805.

As his boys grew up, Richard tried to increase his income through practical business ventures. In 1787 the Bishop of Lincoln confirmed his lease of mines, collieries and seams of coal in Ryton to David Crawford, a Newcastle goldsmith, and Robert Erdington of Stella. In his leisure he was an amateur artist, a talent which in common with Isabella he had inherited from their father, the fourth Lord Byron. His self portrait, done at the age of sixteen shows that he had already surpassed his father in terms of ability; later he copied Rembrandt's famous etching of the *Three Trees* so cleverly that it passed in a sale for the original print. The family still own a delightful book on flowers, presented to his wife Mary, 'Coloured in my own hand'. He was reportedly an excellent draughtsman and was credited with several other things 'of his own invention'.[49]

In April of 1795, when his boys were grown-up and Richard was seventy, he moved from the northern bounds of Durham to Haughton-le-Skerne in the extreme south, 1½ miles from Darlington, where stood the mill of John Kendrew, the first spinner of flax by machinery. Apart from the death of his son, John, his days here passed uneventfully, and indeed time dealt so gently with him that he made his will only when he was eighty-five. He died at last on 5 October 1811, three weeks before his eighty-seventh birthday, and was buried to the left of the church porch. His hatchment, impaling his wife's arms with his own, is still preserved in the church.[50] Mary, probably some years younger, sur-vived him by sixteen years.

Richard was the first modern Byron to enter the Church. Through his younger son he was great-grandfather of a noted dramatist; and from his elder son were descended the eventual heirs to the Barony. His life in retrospect seems a circle of quiet amid the turbulent ebb and flow of a stormy family's life.

Neither marked eccentricity nor blameless respectability attached to George Byron, the youngest of this brood, who failed to live up to the honour of his royal christening gift. He was well-meaning but weak, and chronically hard-up, a liability to his exasperated relatives, who from time to time did what they could for his children, realising that he was incapable of doing anything himself.

Leaving Westminster in 1746, he began well enough by entering the Army, aged sixteen, as Ensign in the 19th Foot. In 1747 he was appointed Cornet in the Duke of Cumberland's Dragoons; he was Lieutenant in the 14th Foot in 1749; and after six-and-a-half years' service advanced to the rank of Lieutenant and Captain in the 1st Foot Guards. But his heart remained in the Midlands where he was born and where he was already planning to settle down. He was enrolled as an Honorary Burgess of Nottingham on 20 September 1754 and a month afterwards (26 October) he married, at St Mary's Church, Frances Levett, daughter of a well-known Nottingham surgeon, Elton Levett, who had died about ten years before. Her mother was the daughter of John Rickard, a former alderman of the town. Frances, aged eighteen, had an elder sister, Anne, married to George Parkyns of Bunny (a son of the famous 'Wrestling Baronet'), who received the freedom of Nottingham on the same day as George Byron.

Nottingham was a pleasant town before the industrial revolution turned it into the huddle of slums that disgraced it in the nineteenth century; most of the great county families had a house there in which they spent the winter months. George Byron could afford none of the fine mansions in the most fashionable quarter along Low Pavement and Castle Gate, overlooking the Meadows—purple with crocuses in spring— that stretched between town and the River Trent. The three-gabled house in which he spent most of his married life stood on the south side of Gridlesmith Gate (now called Pelham Street), just before it opens into Swine Green (later Carlton Street). It was demolished about 1872. One of Mrs Byron's uncles, Thomas Levett of Westminster, left his niece a house in King Street, St James's, in 1785, which she probably let, since she and her husband seem to have been more in need of ready money than a London residence for occasional use.

Their first child, Isabella, born on 20 October 1755, was baptised at St Mary's on the anniversary of her parents' wedding. As a family man George decided to retire from the Army on half-pay in Jordan's 8th Marines. Twin sons, William and George, baptised 2 September 1756, survived but a fortnight before being conveyed to the family burial-place at Hucknall; an entry in the Newstead accounts, a few weeks later, of payment for a coffin, suggests that the funeral expenses fell on

Lord Byron. John, born 14 September 1758, was followed after six years by Frederick George (21 November 1764).

Many years later, during the hearing of a Nottingham election petition, John was called to give evidence about previous elections he had seen: the first he remembered was that of October 1774, when he was sixteen. Nottingham elections were usually memorable for riots; but John had particularly bitter personal reasons to recall that month, because on 6 October, a few days before polling began, his father had been ordered by the Court of Quarter Sessions to pay for the maintenance of a female bastard child born about three months previously to Mary Goddard, an unmarried woman, of which George was adjudged the father. His wife's eventual forgiveness resulted in the birth of one more legitimate boy, Francis, who disappears completely after his baptism at St Mary's on 4 February 1777.

Apart from his affair with Mary Goddard, the latter part of George's life is a complete blank. He did not hold any municipal office and his amusements must have been restricted to those available in the neighbourhood without much expense. He probably met and borrowed money from his eldest brother at the local races and cockfights and could have taken part in the famous stag hunt of 1764. Nottingham's theatre in St Mary's Gate (built about 1760) was not a costly entertainment; and doubtless George took his wife occasionally to the fashionable Assembly Rooms on Low Pavement, for Byrons could not patronise the tradesmen's assembly at Thurland Hall.

So he drifted along until he died at Paddington on 5 or 6 May 1789; he was buried near his brother the Admiral at Twickenham on the 10th. The only notable fact the writer of his obituary could discover was that he fathered 'the gentleman whose comic pencil has lately enlivened the polite arts'.

George probably availed himself of his privilege as a burgess to have his two boys educated at the Free Grammar School in Stoney Street, founded by Dame Agnes Mellers in 1513, then under the mastership of Dr Timothy Wylde. John subsequently entered the Army, and by 1803 had risen to the rank of Major in the 1st Regiment of the Royal Lancashire Militia. Giving evidence in that year before the select committee on the Nottingham election petition, he described himself as a friend of Admiral Sir John Borlase Warren, whose home was at Stapleford Hall in Nottinghamshire. Legacies of £100 from Lady Byron in 1788 and £25 from Lord Byron in 1798 were insufficient to allow him to marry. The rest of his career is as obscure as his father's. He died at the age of sixty-five in his own rooms in Charles Street, St James's Square, London, on 30 June 1824.

The comic pencil mentioned in George Byron's obituary notice was the tool of his younger son, Frederick George, who inherited in full measure the artistic gift that had hitherto made but tentative appearances in the family. He had a good sense of humour and his talent naturally found an outlet in the social caricature that so vividly presents life in the later eighteenth and early nineteenth centuries. His sense of public obligation satisfied by a short spell of service at the early age of seventeen, as Lieutenant in the Nottingham Militia, Frederick next turned to more congenial pursuits. He was only twenty when engravings of his drawings began to appear, one of his earliest efforts being a view of the interior of the Pantheon when Lunardi's balloon was exhibited there soon after his first ascent in September 1784.[51] *The Prince's Boy*, a forerunner of the strip cartoon, was published by William Holland of 50, Oxford Street, on 17 March 1788; it was followed in April by *English Slavery*, which is almost certainly his work, although his name does not appear on it. 1789 produced (10 April) *Old Maids at a Cat's Funeral*, engraved by John Pettitt; and (29 July) *The Ghost*, engraved by J. Parks—a high-spirited picture of the consternation among a convivial party at the appearance of a traditionally-sheeted spook.

Encouraged and, we hope, enriched by success, Frederick made a tour of France in 1790 or 1791, which produced his best work: *Inn Yard at Calais, Breakfast at Breteuil, Changing Horses near Clermont, Visit to the Convent at Amiens*, and *Returning from a Review at the Champ de Mars in Paris*. Rich in the humours of travel, this fine series of coloured aquatints also indicates his ability as a topographical draughtsman, which appears again in his view of the West Front of Newstead Abbey—a drawing good enough to please even the captious owner of Newstead. Like the French series, it was not published until after Frederick's death. The last work to appear in his lifetime was an etching of G. M. Woodward's drawing, dated 8 December 1791, *The Clerical Exercise*.

Frederick was barely twenty-seven when illness drove him to 'Bristol Hotwells' in a vain attempt to recover his health; but there, in February 1792, death cut short his promising career and denied him the fame enjoyed by his contemporary satirists, Thomas Rowlandson and James Gillray. The view of Newstead was published 1 January 1793, but the outbreak of the Revolutionary wars in that year ruined the market for the French prints, which did not appear until between 1801 and 1803, when the Peace of Amiens brought a horde of tourists to the Continent.

Frederick's original sketches have unfortunately disappeared. They probably passed to his mother, for a cousin of the artist, George Isham Parkyns (son of George and Anne Parkyns), was engraver and co-publisher of the Newstead print, described as 'drawn by J. C. Barrow,

F.S.A., from a correct Sketch taken upon the spot by the late F. Byron Esqr.'; but their subsequent fate remains unknown. His sketch books must have contained other drawings that would be of great topographical interest now; the humour of his satirical sketches is less exaggerated than the grotesquerie of many of his contemporaries. As it is, his slender output and the rarity of his prints have made them 'collectors' pieces' for the discerning few.

Isabella Byron, the eldest of George's family and the only daughter, was the most fortunate financially, if not in other respects. In an age when girls of good social standing had small chance of marriage without dowry or settlement, she seemed determined to remain single; but in 1784, when she was twenty-nine, her cousin Caroline, Lord Byron's daughter, came to the rescue by leaving her £1,000 and an annuity of £100, with an additional £1,000 and £300 a year after Lady Byron's death, which occurred in 1788. This altered matters completely, and before very long Isabella became the wife of Count Paravicini-Capelli, whose provenance is as mysterious, if not as dubious, as that of Lady Carlisle's young 'Barons'. He may have been descended from a Count Paravicini who had once made glass in Nottingham, where he died in 1735, leaving his mark on the town in the name of Paravicini Row, later changed to Count Street (and since swept away by street improvements).

The poet Byron thought that Isabella married a Count Palavicini, and when informed that the Marquis Palavicini wished to make his acquaintance at Genoa in 1823, he wrote:

> He may be a sort of connection for aught that I know—for a Palavicini of *Bologna* I believe married a distant relative of mine half a century ago.—I happen to know the fact as he and his sposa had an annuity of five hundred pounds on my Uncle's property—which ceased at his demise— though I recollect hearing that they attempted—naturally enough—to make it survive him.[52]

He seems to be referring to Caroline's bequest; but he gives the amount of the annuity incorrectly and therefore his accuracy about the name may also be doubtful.[53] The loss of their income when the fifth Lord Byron died in 1798 must certainly have been very unpleasant for the Paravicinis. They fade from the scene after this and no more is heard of them until Isabella died at Tunbridge Wells on 16 August 1834, when she was nearly seventy-nine.

[177]

## · 8 ·

# Byron the Poet:
# The Last Baron of Newstead

> I twine
> My hopes of being remembered in my line
> With my land's language.
>
> *Childe Harold's Pilgrimage*, IV, ix

WHEN the heiress of Gight flouted superstition by marrying 'Mad Jack' Byron on the thirteenth day of a month traditionally shunned by brides, the gossips of Aberdeenshire correctly foretold that her fortune would soon be as utterly lost as her heart. The only child of George Gordon of Gight and Catherine Innes of Rosieburn, both of whom died during her infancy, Catherine was brought up by her grandmother, who tried to give her a better education than she herself had received, and succeeded in fostering a love of books; but Catherine was inclined to be stout, retained her Scotch accent, and lacked sophisticated polish—attributes which shamed her son later on. At twenty she was thus ill-equipped to resist the easy charm of the handsome ex-Guardsman, whom she met at a Bath assembly. The Admiral, perhaps with some misgivings, was a party to the marriage settlement signed the day before his son's wedding, but it is surprising that Lady Gight, as she was popularly called, allowed her granddaughter to marry while under age, for Captain Byron's shady past was no secret. She may have thought that any husband was better than none: her granddaughter, though she could, and did, boast her descent from Princess Annabella Stewart, daughter of King James I of Scotland, was no beauty. In any case, Catherine must have had her way, for she was desperately in love and (despite bitter disillusionment) never fell out of love with her recklessly irresponsible but captivating husband.

Jack Byron added his heiress's surname to his own and settled down with her at Gight to squander her fortune. His debts, on a Byronic scale, soon ate up most of her £23,000. After eighteen months the estate was sold to Lord Aberdeen and Mrs Byron was left with the income from £4,200, from which she had to pay her grandmother an annuity. They eluded the Captain's creditors by escaping to France, his former refuge. There Catherine, who was pregnant, nursed Jack's little daughter, Augusta, through serious illness. Although Captain George Anson Byron, living at Chantilly, paid some of his worthless brother's debts, Jack Byron's extravagance continued, to the increasing distress of his wife.

In December of 1787 Catherine returned to London, where she had taken lodgings for her confinement. Augusta, who accompanied her, was soon afterwards sent to live with her grandmother, Lady Holdernesse, and to be brought up by aristocratic relations. Catherine awaited the birth of her son in rented rooms at 16 Holles Street, which connects Oxford Street and Cavendish Square. Arriving in England early in January, Captain Byron avoided his creditors by hiding in the country and was probably not with his wife when her son, George Gordon, was born on 22 January. On the 26th he wrote from Edinburgh to his wife's agent, James Watson, that she was 'brought to bed of a son on Monday last, and is far from well'.[1]

This was hardly surprising. Her disillusionment pervades her own letter to Watson:

> Holles Street, Febry 28 1788.
>
> Sir
>
> I shall make Mr Becket give you an account of all Mr Byrons Debts that we know of as soon as possible but I hope the money wont be given to him but to have some body to pay them for he will only pay what he is obliged to pay and there will be still more debts coming in & more demands for money. I am very sorry he is getting a new Carriage the money Mr. Leslie gave me is not sufficient to clear all my expenses but I will let you know exactly what I shall want in a few days and what I shall want to keep me in London for two months longer as I have taken a House for that time. . . . I will not go to Bath nor will I leave this till Mr. Byron gets a house & is fixed for I am tired of so many journeys. . . .
>
> I want Money to be sent me to keep me while in Town and I must have it, as if Mr. Byron gets it it will be thrown away in some foolish way or other. . . .
>
> My little boy is to be named George   dont show Mr Byron this. . . .[2]

Catherine would have waited for ever for her volatile husband to get a house and become 'fixed'. As London was too expensive for her diminished income she soon returned to Scotland and settled in Aberdeen.

On 21 March Jack wrote to condole his sister, Frances Leigh

(separated from her husband, General Charles Leigh), on the death of their sister, Lady Wilmot, and to complain that his income was settled on Mrs Byron and that he was obliged to live in a narrow circle! By September of 1790 he had abandoned his unfortunate wife altogether and joined Frances, who had a house at Valenciennes in France. When their mother's death recalled her to England, he was left to deal with her creditors and his own, writing letters to her which strongly suggest sexual as well as fraternal intimacy. Full of self-pity and bravado, they describe his brutal behaviour to the servants, who could not get their wages, and even to the besieging creditors. But he was kind to animals (one of his few merits), giving news of Fanny, his dog, '& your little bird is [in] good health, & I take the whole care of him, as Josephine [the servant] has never been sober'.[3] He boasted about his mistresses in the crudest terms:

> As for me I have more upon my hands than I can do, as La Henry, who does the business well, is always after me, & I love to oblige her *Dames* now & then. As for La Marigny, she is as wide as a Church Door, & I really was resolved [not] to do it with her, because Renaud said that one must give her mony, & quoted the P[rince] de Ligne. Altho not so young nor so handsome as him, still the *Birons* are irresistable. You know that Fanny.
>
> As for La *Henry* she told me that I did it so well, that she always *spent* twice every time. I know this will make you laugh, but she is the best piece I ever—[4]

On 15 December he wrote: 'I declare I can find no Woman so handsome as you. I have tried several, but when I do any thing *extraordinary* I always think of you.' He told his sister that his amours were all finished and then boasted of having 'one third of Valenciennes', including a girl he had seduced by promising her employment if Josephine left (22 December); and on Christmas Day he described how he had kicked the unfortunate Josephine downstairs.

He had quarrelled disastrously with his few friends, but although reduced at last to such poverty that he contemplated escaping from Valenciennes, for which he would have needed a disguise, he maintained his sister's box at the theatre, where one night he started off a riot. His letters to Fanny became angrier and more desperate, for he was left to bear the consequences of their extravagance. He had been counting on £500 from his mother's will, but on 8 February Fanny wrote to say that he had already signed it away. His reaction to this disastrous news has been aptly captured by Doris Langley Moore:

> He could not see how it had happened, though he acknowledged he had put his signature to 'a paper at Deal . . . for the 500£' which a lawyer well

known to the family had drawn up; but whoever was taking advantage of that must be 'the greatest Rascal on earth'. . . . He did not seem to grasp that, if he had assigned his £500, it was not in Fanny's power to collect it, and he went so far, in a later letter, as to say he would die in the King's Bench rather than forfeit it.[5]

On 16 February he again begged Fanny for money and remarked: 'I am glad she [Mrs Byron] writes to you. She is very amiable at a distance, but I defy you and all the Apostles to live with her two months, for if any body could live with her, it was me. . . . For my son, I am happy to hear he is well: but for his walking, 'tis impossible, as he is club-footed'.[6] This last inaccurate assertion has been taken as evidence about Byron's lameness, but the Captain had little knowledge of and small interest in his son, preferring to inquire about his daughter, who lived with rich relations.

He declined steadily after that, finally reduced to making plans for enlistment in the French army, even as a private, a dismal outlook for an aristocrat who defied the mob's liking for democratic plays at the theatre. Tuberculosis seems to have fastened upon him: he wrote of a cold which had long troubled him. He could not shake it off and had to keep to his room. He was left with few clothes and without the means to buy food, because bailiffs had seized the goods and the unpaid servants were stealing from him. He became alternately angry and fawning with his sister, who was apparently detained in London by a lover, and who wrote remonstrating letters. He replied to her for the last time on 8 June 1791:

My Dearest Sister

Your letter has made me too unhappy to say much, as you reproach me with *Ingratitude* which God knows I do not want towards you. If you knew my situation! You will forgive me when you know it.

I beg you will take what comes to me for yourself as it is your *due*. . . . I must try to shift for myself. As for the *friend* that told me you liv'd with the Marquis de [illegible name], the same who wrote you *word* of it was the same who informed me—

. . . I have not a shirt to my Back nor a Coat, as the one I had here is totally used.

You say every thing you do displeases me. I once more repeat that my situation is such, that if I utter'd any thing in my letters that has offended you, I am sorry for it, as my intention was never to cause the least uneasiness to you. For your own sake do not listen too much to those who write you all the news.

When he dictated his will to two French notaries, he appointed Fanny his executrix and ordered the penniless little boy in Aberdeen, in whom he had taken slight interest, to pay his debts and funeral expenses.

Jack Byron died on 2 August, aged thirty-five. It has been assumed that he committed suicide, but as Fanny apparently returned to his deathbed, he may well have succumbed to consumption, undernourished and desperate as he was during his last months. Fanny broke the news to Catherine, who replied that she doubted she would ever recover from the shock:

> You wrong me very much when you suppose I would not lament Mr. Byron's death. It has made me very miserable, and the more so that I had not the melancholy satisfaction of seeing him before his death. If I had known of his illness, I would have come to him ... necessity, not inclination, parted us, at least on my part ... and notwithstanding all his foibles, for they deserve no worse name, I ever sincerely loved him.... I have the greatest regard and affection for you, for the very kind part you have acted to poor Mr Byron, and it is a great comfort to me that he was with so kind a friend at the time of his death. You say he was sensible to the last. Did he ever mention me? Was he long ill, and where was he buried? ... also send me some of his hair.... George is well. I shall be happy to let him be with you some times, but at present he is my only comfort.... I hope, if anything should happen to me, you will take care of him.[7]

Unconscious of any irony, Catherine was lonely and naturally anxious to stay in touch with her husband's family, particularly when she heard that the fifth Baron's grandson, William John Byron, had died in battle at Calvi on 31 July 1794, so that her own son was now heir to the title. The dead heir apparent had been much taken with Jack Byron's charm, after sailing with him off the Kentish coast during the summer of 1789, but none of the family troubled to tell Catherine the news of his death and Frances allowed their correspondence to peter out. Catherine consequently took a dislike to Mrs Leigh and was very annoyed when Augusta later became engaged to Fanny's son, George.

Young Byron's schooldays in Aberdeen were broken by his prolonged stay at a farm on Deeside during the summer of 1796 and perhaps again in 1797, where he was sent to recover from scarlet fever. He scrambled happily about the hills; the beauty of the highlands sank into his memory and coloured his imagination as deeply as the mountains of Greece did afterwards. At nine years old he fell in love for the first time, with Mary Duff, and the only remarkable thing about that is the importance he later attached to it.

In May of 1798 John Hanson, the family lawyer, informed Mrs Byron that the legendary recluse at Newstead was dead at last, and the summer passed in a bustle of preparation for the long journey south. Mrs Byron sold her furniture for only £74 17s. 7d., from which she paid £35 in travelling expenses and £25 for mourning clothes: she felt obliged to make this gesture for the eccentric Baron who had ignored their existence and despoiled the estate in anger when his son married Juliana Byron (Fanny's sister). His destructive fury had increased when he learned that he would be succeeded by the grandson of his hated brother, the Admiral.

Mrs Byron, her son, and the nurse (May Gray) arrived under the Pilgrim Oak at the plain wooden gate of Newstead Abbey in the autumn. The sandy drive wound through the heath and bracken until a final curve brought the gleaming lake and the grey stone walls into view. Byron never described his feelings at that moment: perhaps he was too deeply moved to reveal them; but his famous description of the 'old, old Monastery' in *Don Juan* (Canto XIII) demonstrates his extraordinary memory for detail, his genius for graphic description and contrast, and his lasting, poignant love. His portrait of the Abbey explains why his memory pervades it today; he actually spent little time there.

For a few happy weeks the boy explored every corner of the old house and rambled over the estate, making friends with his tenants at the farms and planting a tree on the south lawn. Mrs Byron, occupied with business and planning for the future, pressed her son to serve as secretary at least once: his first letter, as he proudly pointed out, informed his great aunt, Frances, the Hon. Mrs George Byron, that 'the potatoes are now ready and you are welcome to them whenever you please' and requested her to ask Mrs Parkyns if she wished the 'poney' to go round by Nottingham or to go home the nearest way, 'as it is now quite well but too small to carry me'.[8]

Despite straitened means, Frances Byron still maintained the house in Gridlesmith Gate (now Pelham Street), which must have been too large for her since Isabella's marriage because John was rarely at home. Possibly her sister, Ann Parkyns, also a widow, lived with her, as both are described as of Gridlesmith Gate in the Nottingham Directory for 1799. The new Lord Byron and his mother gratefully accepted her hospitality, but their visit was not an unqualified success. Frances was becoming highly eccentric in her old age and George's dislike unfortunately found expression in well-known, uncomplimentary lines:

> In Nottingham county there lives at Swine Green[9]
> As curst an old Lady as ever was seen;
> And when she does die, which I hope will be soon,
> She firmly believes she will go to the Moon!

This was a distressing time for Byron. His mother wanted him to stay in Nottingham to continue his education and to receive medical treatment for his lame leg. She took lodgings for him and for May Gray in the house (still standing) of a Mr Gill, at the top of St James's Street. Then she returned to Newstead. Byron doubtless felt homesick and unhappy when he wrote to ask her when she would send the horses to go to Newstead, but he made no direct complaint and sought distraction in exploring the interesting old town with its great Market Place. He liked his tutor, Jeremiah Dummer Rogers, an American loyalist who also taught the Parkyns girls. But the so-called surgeon, Lavender, was an ignorant quack who tortured him without benefit. May Gray, despite her apparent piety, was irresponsible and corrupt. His leg had showed no improvement by July of 1799 and therefore Mrs Byron sent him to London, where John Hanson put him under the care of Dr Matthew Baillie and Dr Laurie, whose treatment continued for three years with better results and less pain. Byron unburdened himself to the family lawyer, confessing that his nurse had been coming to bed and playing sexually with him. Without specifying this episode, which he revealed to Hobhouse only after Byron's death, Hanson bluntly informed Mrs Byron that May Gray was bad for her charge and the nurse was dismissed. Byron's inevitable guilt and contempt had lingering consequences.

Hanson entered Byron at Dr Glennie's school in Dulwich, where he began studies in August. Henceforth he spent most of his holidays at the Hansons' house in Earl's Court, where he could share the rough-and-tumble life of other children. His cousin, Lord Carlisle, was persuaded to become his nominal guardian, but when Hanson took Byron to the Carlisle's house in Grosvenor Place, the painfully shy boy, acutely conscious of his lameness, seemed anxious to get away. Byron met younger cousins, too, and fell in love with one of them, Margaret Parker, a beautiful girl of about thirteen whose mother had been his father's youngest sister, Augusta.

During her son's minority Mrs Byron had received £500 a year from the Court of Chancery for his education; she also kept up a home for him, which left little for herself, and she had undertaken to put Newstead in order. She strove with great tenacity if not always with great patience to remedy the inefficient management at the Abbey, where the rents were often unpaid and the steward lax and uncooperative. In July of 1799 she had to petition the Duke of Portland, Tory leader of the House of Lords,[10] for a pension, which he obtained for her on 24 August. She received £300, which was irregularly paid, and had to practise careful economy. She persuaded Lord Carlisle to send Byron to Harrow in April of 1801, but her further importunities exasperated that touchy nobleman, who declined to take further interest in his ward.

Frances Byron, too, was in trouble. In 1800 she and her sister, Mrs Parkyns, had each received a legacy of £50 a year for life under the will of a cousin, John Levett of Lichfield; but in August of 1801 she was sued in the Borough Court of Nottingham by John Renshaw, an attorney in St Mary's Gate, for a debt of £140.

Poor Mrs Byron's efforts to establish good relations with her husband's family were still largely ignored; but when Lady Holdernesse died in 1801 Catherine wrote with affectionate sympathy to her step-daughter. Byron still knew little of this half-sister, Augusta, who was now free to show as much interest as she pleased in her young brother, and from 1804 they corresponded regularly.

Mrs Byron and her son spent Christmas of 1802 at Bath. Newstead was let while Byron was at school, to give the property time to recover before he reached his majority. The family showered unwanted advice on Mrs Byron: Captain John came over from Nottingham and fussed about the felling of a few trees in the garden, which he declared he would discuss with Hanson. The previous October Hanson had told Owen Mealey, the steward, that the two Miss Launders of Basford (impeccably recommended by Lord Grantham) would live in the Abbey until a proper tenant was found and now a tenant was nibbling—Lord Grey de Ruthyn. The lease was to run for 5½ years from Christmas of 1802, reserving to Lord Byron the liberty of hunting, fishing, coursing and shooting; the tenant to purchase the furniture and things in the house, giving the landlord the option of buying them back, and to pay £50 a year, plus taxes and repairs. Lord Grey accepted immediately and after signing the lease he wrote to Hanson (8 April): 'If Lord Byron can make it convenient & agreeable to pass any of his time at Newstead I shall be most happy to receive him & to contribute to his amusements as far as lays in my power'.[11] The Misses Launder proved difficult to dislodge, however, and Catherine was obliged to be aggressive with them.

She had rented Burgage Manor, a pleasant house in Southwell, which became her home for the next six years. The quiet little town clustered around the Minster had few attractions for a schoolboy and when Byron came home from Harrow for the summer holidays he gladly availed himself of Lord Grey's invitation to ride over to the Abbey, where he lodged with the steward and fell madly in love with Mary Chaworth of neighbouring Annesley Park. She was seventeen, two years older than Byron, and engaged to John Musters of Colwick Hall, the former home of the Byrons. Nevertheless, Byron dreamed of marrying her and thus ending the feud dating from the celebrated duel of their respective great-uncles. He rode over to Annesley day after day, sometimes staying the night; and he shot at a door on the terrace for pistol practice. For two months he remained deaf to his mother's commands and appeals, refusing to return either to Harrow or to Southwell. Catherine drove out to Newstead at the end of October, determined to remove him; but perceiving that he was bitterly unhappy she agreed to let him stay until after the next holidays. She was as indulgent to him as she had been to her fascinating husband.

Early in October Mrs Byron sent for all the pictures in Mealey's keeping: 'She has got every one away from Newstead' he wrote to Hanson.[12] Catherine wrote: 'The House . . . will soon be in ruins, and the Park is in a deplorable state'.[13] She had taken a great liking to Lord Grey and was very angry with her son for quarrelling with him.

It is now known that Grey had made some sexual advance which had repelled Byron, but which he could no more explain to his mother or his sister than May Gray's perversion. His disillusionment was deepened by a contemptuous rebuff from Mary Chaworth. One night he over-heard her declare that she could never love 'that lame boy'. It struck him 'like a shot through his heart', and he ran wildly from her house, he hardly knew where, until he reached Newstead.[14] Early disappoint-ment, isolation, loss of sexual innocence, coupled with his distressing lameness and his very good looks, caused Byron to develop a self-defensive carelessness with women. From his mother he inherited a saving sense of humour and a strong need and desire to love and be loved, which meant that he was frequently ambivalent in his amours, fearing loss but seldom finding satisfaction. Mary Chaworth had intensified his temperamental conflict.

Barred from Newstead by his quarrel with Lord Grey, Byron spent the Easter vacation of 1804 at Southwell and turned to his sister. They began to correspond regularly. Augusta was already engaged to her cousin, George Leigh, a Lt Colonel of the 10th Light Dragoons and former friend of the Prince Regent. He was twelve years older than Augusta and his father, General Charles Leigh, opposed their marriage, principally because she had only £350 a year from her grandmother, Lady Holdernesse. Augusta, who spent the autumn with the Carlisles at Castle Howard, spoke to Lord Carlisle about her brother and he agreed to see more of his ward without Mrs Byron. Temporarily at least Byron felt friendly towards his relatives and resumed better relations with his guardian's family.

Mrs Byron had invited Augusta to visit her, but as she disapproved of her step-daughter's engagement, Byron advised his sister to avoid Southwell. He had begun to quarrel with his mother, but he had a happy last term at Harrow, carving his name twice in the old school room and distinguishing himself in the cricket match against Eton. Afterwards the teams dined together and went to the Haymarket Theatre, where they 'kicked up a row'. Byron dreaded leaving school, but he had made friends at Southwell, where he shared his literary interests with John and Elizabeth Pigot, who lived across the green, and played in amateur theatricals.

He had hoped to go to Oxford because several of his Harrow favourites, boys with whom he struck up warm, sentimental and protective friendship, had gone there, but no place was available and in October of 1805 he went up to Trinity College, Cambridge. Mrs Byron had unwisely given him the allowance of £500 a year that she received for his education, leaving herself with only her pension and the tiny income from her remaining Scottish capital; but Byron convinced himself that he was not depriving her of sixpence and wrote thoughtlessly to her that he found it inconvenient to remain at college and that he had a few hundred in ready cash by him.[15] He was already deeply in debt. He talked of going abroad. Catherine was in agony over his recklessness and his extravagance and even Augusta was annoyed when she saw him in a London theatre, because he should have been at Cambridge. But he did not return to Trinity that term. Nevertheless, his mother managed to raise a loan of £1,000 for him, largely from the Hon. Mrs George Byron, widow of the Admiral's brother; her nieces, the Misses Parkyns; and with some assistance from Mrs George Byron's son, Captain John Byron, who could not get the dilatory Hanson to answer his letters.[16]

Despite vows to the contrary, the thoughtless son returned to Southwell in the summer of 1806, but he quarrelled with his mother again and escaped to London in the middle of the night, aided by the Pigots. 'Mrs Byron furiosa' pursued him to the lodgings hired from Mrs Massingberd, who had already lent him money on complicated and extortionate terms. She saw the extravagance of her charming husband repeated in her son, but was unable to move him and retreated. Byron went triumphantly to Worthing and Littlehampton to stay with Edward Noel Long, a Harrow and Cambridge crony. He visited Harrogate in September, accompanied by John Pigot, a valet, groom, horses, Boatswain (the Newfoundland dog) and Nelson (a bull-mastiff), the first of several such menageries. He did not return to Cambridge until the summer term of 1807.

Meanwhile, he had begun to publish poetry. *Fugitive Pieces* was prepared for private publication in 1806, but when a clergyman, John Thomas Becher, who had been acting as Byron's literary adviser, protested against the eroticism of some verses Byron called in the edition and all but four copies were destroyed. In January of 1807 his private publication of a new, revised and enlarged edition, *Poems on Various Occasions*, had been so favourably received that he issued another, further enlarged and revised, 'for the public at large'. Published in June as *Hours of Idleness* by 'George Gordon, Lord Byron, a minor', it brought him many compliments, but was eventually attacked with devastating irony by the *Edinburgh Review*:

> His effusions are spread over a dead flat, and can no more get above or below the level, than if they were so much stagnant water. As an extenuation of this offence, the noble author is peculiarly forward in pleading minority. We have it in the title-page, and on the very back of the volume; it follows his name like a favourite part of his *style*. . . . His other plea of privilege, our author rather brings forward in order to waive it. He certainly, however, does allude frequently to his family and ancestors—sometimes in poetry, sometimes in notes; and while giving up his claim on the score of rank, he takes care to remember us [*sic*] of Dr Johnson's saying, that when a nobleman appears as an author, his merit should be handsomely acknowledged.

The review ridiculed Byron's pedestrian verses—'viewing them as school exercises, they may pass'—and cut at him personally. Byron had said that he did not expect to become an author again:

> Therefore, let us take what we get and be thankful. What right have we poor devils to be nice? We are well off to have got so much from a man of this Lord's station, who does not live in a garret, but 'has the sway' of Newstead Abbey.[17]

Although Byron later made light of it, he was bitterly hurt. He felt all a new author's sensitivity to adverse criticism and his personal pride was wounded by the hits at his family and title. The assault by a powerful Whig journal, with whose politics he sympathised, set him thinking about another work in which he could satirise everyone, regardless of party. The new satire was to establish him as a notable poet.

But meanwhile he had returned to Cambridge, where he formed the close relationship with John Cam Hobhouse which was to endure for the rest of his life; and by the following spring he was again bored and again in London, even more deeply in debt.

> I have been introduced to Julia Byron [George Anson Byron's daughter] by Trevannion [*sic*] at the Opera [he wrote to Augusta], she is pretty, but I do not admire her, there is too much Byron in her countenance, I hear she is clever, a very great defect in a woman, who becomes conceited in course; altogether I have not much inclination to improve the acquaintance, I have

seen my old Friend George [her brother], who will prove the best of the family, and will one day be Lord B.—I do not much care how soon.—Pray name my nephew after his uncle, it must be a nephew (I *wont* have a *niece*) I will make him my *heir*, for I shall never marry, unless I am ruined, and then his *inheritance* would not be great. George will have the title and his *laurels*, my property (if any is left in five years time) I can leave to whom I please, and your son shall be the legatee.[18]

Despite frequent absences, Byron received his M.A. at Cambridge, where peers were still privileged beings, early in July of 1808 and then he visited Brighton, where he saw Augusta's husband, Colonel George Leigh, whom as yet he knew only by sight: 'Indeed my relations are those whom I know the least, and in most instances, I am not very anxious to improve the acquaintance.'[19]

He was particularly glad to be free of his mother, complaining in the same letter that he could not breathe under the same roof with her. Catherine was already ill and still distressed by financial entanglements from which she had vainly tried to extricate him, but her natural irritation only drove him to a greater distance. Nevertheless, he arranged to meet her at the Infirmary Ball in Nottingham on 12 October and took a friend there after drinking tea with his great-aunt, Frances Byron.

Byron was confused amid his self-imposed difficulties and his uncertain fortunes. He dined with Mary Chaworth-Musters, feeling only bashful and tongue-tied with her, and then in November Boatswain went mad and died, a great grief to Byron, who erected an imposing monument to the dog's memory on the supposed site of the high altar of the priory church at Newstead. (His love for animals, one of the few positive qualities inherited from his father, remained one of his marked characteristics.) At his coming of age in 1809 Byron asked John Hanson to attend the festivities at Newstead on 22 January, where oxen were roasted and sheep boiled and an ode composed by a country schoolmaster in his honour. Mrs Byron had to remain at Southwell while her son absconded to London to dine on eggs and bacon and a bottle of ale. The birthday celebrations solved none of the young Lord's difficulties, of course. He was in debt for £12,000, which may explain his frantic determination to leave England, come what may.

On 13 March, Byron had another experience in which triumph was seasoned with humiliation. He took his seat in the House of Lords unsupported by the customary friend or relative: Lord Carlisle, who should have introduced him, failed to supply details of his parentage, the proofs of which (particularly of the Admiral's marriage) the procrastinating Hanson was obliged, with some difficulty, to obtain. Byron must have been doubly satisfied with the success of his new publication, however. *English Bards and Scotch Reviewers*, which he had written at Newstead in retaliation for the onslaught of the *Edinburgh Review*, attacked writers, poets, critics and the fashionable world in general. The first anonymous edition, published on 1 March, had been so enthusiastically received that he immediately prepared a new edition under his own name.

Byron's preparations for travel went forward apace, despite Hanson's dilatoriness and the lack of funds. His brilliant Cambridge friend, Charles Skinner Matthews, has left a lively description of the farewell house-party at Newstead in May, where the days were spent in reading, fencing, singlestick or shuttlecock in the great hall; walking, riding, and cricket, playing with the bear, and teasing the wolfhound; dressing up as monks in the evening, the 'Abbot' and his guests went buffooning around the house. Byron had miniature portraits of his favourite school-fellows painted by George Sanders, to whom he sat for his own likeness at a charge far beyond his means. He set sail at last on 2 July, accompanied by John Cam Hobhouse, William Fletcher, and Robert Rushton (son of one of the tenants), the 'page' in *Childe Harold* who, with Joe Murray, accompanied them only as far as Gibraltar. Their delayed departure was made possible by Scrope Berdmore Davies, the gifted, witty Fellow of King's College, Cambridge, who loaned Byron more than £4,600 by signing a bond to money-lenders.

Byron's volatile spirits soared upon leaving England. The details of his travels during the next two years through Portugal, Spain, Albania, Greece and Turkey (where he swam the Hellespont and told the world about it) were poured out in a stream of letters to friends and to his mother, whom he had installed at Newstead and who was left to cope with his financial entanglements and the innumerable petty difficulties of running the estate.

By the time Byron had been away from England for four months he had started work on the autobiographical poem which was to make him famous, 'Childe Burun', a name he later changed to 'Childe Harold'. But his was not the 'weary pilgrimage' of his alter ego, and he responded to the experiences of his travels with exuberance: the village of Cintra in Portugal he found 'perhaps in every respect the most delightful in Europe',[20] and Cadiz 'the most delightful town I ever beheld . . . full of the finest women in Spain'.[21] From Gibraltar Murray and Rushton were sent home; Murray as being unfit for the anticipated fatigues ahead and Rushton because 'boys are not safe among the Turks'. By the end of September the travellers had arrived in Greece and Byron had already seen a glimpse of the marshy town of Missolonghi where 15 years later he was to die. On 12 November Byron wrote at length to his Mother, telling her of his famous visit to Ali Pasha, who had admired his birth (and beauty), how he had come close to being ship-wrecked, how he travelled with 16 horses and six or seven men and how he had purchased three Albanian dresses for 50 guineas each which 'have so much gold they would cost in England two hundred'.[22] This letter did not reach his mother till late in April 1811, but she responded with enthusiasm:

'A thousand thanks my *Dearest Dear* son for your *long kind* and *entertaining* letter . . .'.[23]

As he travelled through Greece and Turkey Byron's ideas of the East began to crystalise: a delight in the climate and beauty of the country and enthusiasm for the spirit of the people was coupled with a sadness that Greece had fallen so far from its golden age and a growing dislike of the arbitrary government of the Turks. Returning to Athens from Constantinople he wrote to his mother:

'I have arrived here in four days from Constantinople which is considered as singularly quick particularly for the season of the year; *you Northern Gentry* can have no conception of a Greek Summer, which however is a perfect Frost compared with Malta, and Gibraltar, where I reposed myself in the *shade* last year after a gentle Gallop of four hundred miles without intermission through Portugal & Spain.—You see by my date that I am at Athens again, a place which I prefer upon the whole to any I have seen. . . . I am already woefully sick of travelling companions after a years experience of Mr. Hobhouse who is on his way to Great Britain . . .'[24]

In fact after Hobhouse had returned to England Byron settled to a period of dissolute living, his letters to his friends in England suggesting both male and female liaisons. As always his moods at this time were mercurial, sometimes light-hearted but other times gloomy and disillusioned. There were also financial worries to cloud the scene: 'It is in the power of God, the Devil, and Man, to make me poor and miserable', he wrote to Hanson, 'but neither the *second* nor *third* shall make me sell Newstead . . .'.[25] Sadly this was not a resolution he was able to keep.

By the spring of 1811 Byron began with some reluctance to retrace his footsteps towards England. 'If I am a poet,' he said later, '. . . the air of Greece has made me one.' It is hard to overestimate the effect that two years travelling had had on Byron. Apart from being a perpetual source for literary inspiration the climate of Greece and the cosmopolitan way of life had become deeply instilled in him; the shores of the

Mediterranean were seldom far from his imagination during his remaining five years in England.

While her son enjoyed the expansive climate of the east, Mrs Byron in the wintry old Abbey strove to prevent the sale of his personal effects. She conscientiously took charge of his menagerie, including the bear, which died while Byron was abroad. She increased the livestock by begging fish from the Hardwick estate of the Duke of Devonshire. She insisted that the rents be raised from the pre-war rates and was for ever prodding the apathetic Hanson. Brothers, the upholsterer who had supplied many of the expensive furnishings, faced bankruptcy through Byron's failure to pay his bill for £1,512 2s. 0d. Yet despite these worries and increasing ill-health she replied cheerfully and without complaint to her son's letters from abroad. Her illness was long-standing and we now know that anger about the upholsterer's bill was not the cause of her death, as represented by Thomas Moore and many subsequent biographers. Brothers' execution had been pending for months and so far from raging she pitied his own difficulties and urged Hanson to pay the bill by securing a mortgage on Newstead.[26]

She had a presentiment that she would never see her son again. He returned to England in the middle of July 1811, but stayed in London to sign papers and settle outstanding business. On 31 July the apothecary who attended Mrs Byron wrote to Byron to say that his mother was dangerously ill and asking for him. Dr Marsden had been summoned from Nottingham. Byron hurried from London, but she died before he could reach her.

His grief was deep and sincere. He refused to attend the funeral at Hucknall but watched the procession leave the Abbey and then began boxing with Rushton as if to get the better of his feelings. He insisted that his mother's death should make no difference to an action for libel on himself and her which he was bringing against the editor of *The Scourge*, who had declared her 'days and nights are spent in the delirium of drunkenness'. And he wrote to Hanson that he would have no stain on her memory, for with all her 'foibles & irritability, she was without a *Vice* (& in these days that is much)'.

Byron's mood darkened when he learned a few days later that the brilliant, sardonic Charles Matthews had been drowned while bathing in the River Cam; more bad news followed: Edward Long and John Wingfield (one of his Harrow favourites) were likewise dead and so was John Edleston, the Cambridge chorister so sentimentally loved. Feeling miserable and lonely, Byron invited Scrope Davies to Newstead and busied himself with his mother's bequests. She had left some jewels, which must have been a family bequest, wondrously kept from the pawnbrokers—possibly they came from Catherine's paternal grand-mother, born Margaret Duff, who had died in 1801. Rundell & Bridge paid £1,130 for them. The money settled some debts.[27] Byron kept his mother's ring containing the hair of King James II of Scotland. He altered his own will, entailing Newstead on his cousin, George Anson Byron, or whoever might be his heir. He made legacies to friends and servants and directed that he should be buried in the garden vault beside his dog, without any ceremony or inscription. If his successors removed his body, they would forfeit the estate to Augusta and her heirs.

He invited other friends to visit him, as well as Augusta, whose family and financial entanglements prevented her from accepting. His Cambridge friend Francis Hodgson was tempted by the beef, sea-coal fires and wine. Byron considered asking George Anson Byron and his sister Julia, who were staying with Robert Dallas (a distant kinsman by marriage), until he reflected that there was nothing to amuse his cousin. The horses were sold and the Captain, he suspected, would be 'meddling with the wenches'.[28] He had been meddling with the wenches himself, getting one of them with child. The faithlessness of the other, Susan Vaughan, hurt him deeply, confirming his capriciousness and defensiveness with women.

At the end of 1811 Byron visited Rochdale, his estate in Lancashire, but he took a very perfunctory interest in the collieries and soon returned by way of Cambridge to London, where he won the friendship of Thomas Moore, who had figured so ludicrously in *English Bards and Scotch Reviewers* that he wanted to fight a duel with him. It was the first of his many friendships with literary men, including Samuel Rogers, the banker and fashionable poet, Percy Shelley, and Walter Scott.

Byron was already a figure of considerable interest, but within a few weeks his fame had sprung up full-fledged. *Childe Harold's Pilgrimage*, the romantic Spenserian poem based on his travel experiences, was published by John Murray on 10 March 1812[29] and it immediately made Byron the most sought-after man in fashionable London. The lame nobleman who was as handsome as Apollo and who bit his nails nervously met the first celebrities of the day and moved henceforth in exclusive circles. His literary success was preceded by a memorable speech in the House of Lords on 27 February, when he castigated the inhumanity of the frame-breaking bill, which condemned the 'Luddite' rioters to death for smashing the new stocking frames which threatened their living. But it was as a poet and a peer and not as a politician that he conquered society. He soon became familiar at Holland House, where Lord and Lady Holland presided over a prestigious Whig circle and which was the meeting place of all who shared its kindly owner's interest in politics and literature. He was taken up, too, by the more frivolously fashionable Devonshire House set and welcomed at Melbourne House in Whitehall, where Lady Melbourne's daughter-in-law, the nympho-maniac Lady Caroline Lamb, became the most spectacular, the most embarrassing, but not the most important of Byron's society amours. He was presented to the Prince Regent and (through Lord Holland) became involved in the affairs of the Drury Lane Theatre. A round of visits to country houses and a much-needed 'cure' at Cheltenham completed his first year in the world of fashion.

Despite the expenses of fashionable life, Byron continued to spend lavishly during his next four years in England; although already deeply in debt he gave the copyright of *Childe Harold* to his rather officious kinsman, Robert Dallas, because he thought it beneath the dignity of a peer to earn money! Dallas had assisted Byron in publishing the poem, but the gesture was typical of an exotic extravagance which forced Byron to consider selling Newstead, which he had once vowed he would never abandon. The estate was put up for sale at Garroway's Coffee House in August but failed to reach the reserve price (£120,000). In September, however, Byron accepted a private offer of £140,000 from one Thomas Claughton, a transaction which led to many difficulties. By March of 1813 Byron suspected that Claughton could not pay. He was himself too short of money to help his hard-pressed sister. In June he considered selling his books, plate, linen, silver and pictures, but this was never done, although negotiations with Claughton dragged on unresolved for another twelve months.

The fashionable woman who most decisively influenced Byron was not one of his loves but the elderly Lady Melbourne who, despite his hectic and scandalous affair with her daughter-in-law, remained his staunch and affectionate friend, giving him worldly advice and motherly understanding. Lady Caroline, on the other hand, pursued him relent-lessly after their brief liaison, made fearful public scenes, which he most loathed, and in July of 1813 finally exasperated her intensely self-conscious lover by melodramatically slashing herself with a piece of glass at Lady Heathcote's ball because Byron had told her that she might waltz or not, as she pleased. (He disliked that fashionable dance and satirised it.) Meanwhile, he had become involved with Lady Oxford, a mature autumnal beauty with whom he spent most of the winter of 1812–13 at Eywood, the Oxfords' country house in Hereford-shire. He always remembered Lady Oxford with affection and Lady Caroline with fury: she was a fiend, and, as he very well knew, an inveterate enemy and mischief-maker.

A new distraction presented itself in the autumn of 1813. In an effort to find good situations for his domestic staff, Byron resumed his acquaintance with the foolish James Wedderburn Webster of Ashton Hall, near Rotherham. On 27 September he wrote to Thomas Moore:

> I have been in the country, and ran away from the Doncaster races. It is odd,—I was a visitor in the same house which came to my sire as a residence with Lady Carmarthen (with whom he adulterated before his majority—by the by, remember, *she* was not my mamma)—and they thrust me into an old room, with a nauseous picture over the chimney, which I should suppose my papa regarded with due respect, and which, inheriting the family taste, I looked upon with great satisfaction.

In this, and in the tenor of his fashionable life in general, we may detect a desire to resemble the father he had never known, and whom he imagined to have been a dashing, careless, enviable Lothario. Perhaps some such desire prompted him in part in his flirtation with Webster's wife, Lady Frances, when 'Platonism' seemed in some peril; but he was soon bored by her evasions and glad enough to resume his London life. However he had extended his vast debts even further by lending Webster £1,000. He made another loan of £100 to Francis Hodgson, who wanted to marry.

In November the younger son of the Reverend and Honourable Richard Byron, the Reverend Henry Byron, who had just lost his wife,[30] brought his little daughter, Eliza, to call on her famous cousin. Byron was captivated by her:

> She will grow up a beauty and a plague; but, in the mean time, it is the prettiest child! dark eyes and eyelashes, black and long as the wing of a raven. I think she is prettier even than my niece, Georgina,—yet I don't like to think so neither; and, though older, she is not so clever.

Despite many distractions, Byron was writing, always a necessity for him. He poured out his perplexities and inner turbulence in more verse tales: *The Giaour* and *The Bride of Abydos* appeared in 1813 and during December he wrote *The Corsair* while staying with his sister at Six Mile Bottom, her home near Newmarket, among all the screaming confusion of her family. In January he took Augusta to Newstead, where they remained snow-bound very comfortably for three weeks with Claughton, the defaulting purchaser, who was accommodated in a separate wing. Claughton's offer for the Abbey must have been a speculation, because he (or the mysterious Mr Leigh supposed to be behind him) thought there were coal mines under the estate.[31] By August of 1814 Byron had agreed to accept Claughton's forfeit of £25,000 from the £28,000 deposit. A proposed sale in 1815 was cancelled and thus Newstead remained unsold until 1817.

In the spring of 1814 Byron left his rooms in Bennet Street and moved to Viscount Althorpe's spacious apartment in the Albany. He sub-leased it for seven years, retrieved his books from Murray and settled down there with a macaw and a parrot. He boxed with 'Gentleman' Jackson the pugilist and fenced daily. Wedderburn Webster came to London to seek another loan from Byron, whom he took to a party given by Lady Sitwell; there Byron saw his beautiful cousin, Mrs Wilmot, wearing a black spangled dress.[32] He drank a tumbler of brandy to her health and the next day wrote his famous lines upon her:

> She walks in Beauty, like the night
> Of cloudless climes and starry skies;
> And all that's best of dark and bright
> Meet in her aspect and her eyes. . . .

Later that year another cousin was the subject of 'Elegiac stanzas on the death of Sir Peter Parker, Bart.'. Son of Admiral John Byron's daughter Charlotte Augusta, Parker was a naval officer who was killed in August at the age of 28 while leading a party from his ship, the *Menelaus*, to attack an American camp near Baltimore. Byron scarcely knew him: there is less feeling in these verses than in those written to the memory of Parker's sister, Margaret.

Meanwhile Augusta remained pre-occupied with her growing family, harassed by financial troubles and unaided by her husband, whom Byron considered a helpless drone and who spent his days at the race track. But by the summer of 1813 Augusta paid two short visits to London, where her brother escorted her to a party at Lady Davy's and to a masque at Almack's. Byron liked his sister so much that he wished she were not married. They were Byrons; they laughed together.

Books and articles by the dozen have speculated about Byron's relationship with his sister. Their 'crime' later gave his implacable wife a hold over her sister-in-law. But even if they were lovers in the full sense, neither he nor Augusta had any idea they were repeating their father's relationship with *his* sister, Fanny (who lived until 1823). Augusta's fourth child, Elizabeth Medora, born 15 April 1814, came to believe she was Byron's daughter. A biography of Medora assumes as much in its title.[33] It may never be possible to settle the question, but the available evidence suggests that Medora was not Byron's child. She closely resembled her father, Colonel Leigh, who never differentiated between her and his other children and who, at a later family crisis, intervened in Medora's affairs exactly as if she had been his own daughter. Byron himself never singled out Medora for any special interest or affection, never alluded to her in any way as his child, and provided for Augusta's children equally in his will. If anything, he favoured Georgiana, Augusta's eldest daughter, and when he presented Augusta with £3,000 and advised her husband to find some way of regulating his expenditure, Byron brushed her scruples aside by saying, 'consider the *children*—& my Georgiana in particular'.[34]

Despite his literary and social success, Byron was insecure and uncertain. He longed for action and considered going abroad. Augusta wanted to see him established and suggested a wife for him—Lady Charlotte Leveson-Gower, who was as shy as the poet himself. Byron's letter to his sister about his encounter with Lady Charlotte at a party given by Earl Grey, the Whig statesman, exemplifies the happy, unself-conscious understanding he enjoyed with Augusta at this time. He recounted the incoherent dialogue, which 'I endeavoured to improve . . . into something like sense—still taking you and people she knew— (and the dead Marquis of Granby I believe) for the topics—in this interval she lost her party and seemed in an agony'. He remarked that she was as shy as an Antelope, but as pretty, and that she had soon escaped from him:

> By the bye—I must say—that it looked more like *dislike* than shyness— and I do not much wonder—for her first confusion in calling you a *friend*—forgetting the relationship set me off—not laughing—but in one of our *glows*—and stammers—and then all I had heard from you and others of *her* diffidence—brought our own similar malady upon me in a double degree. . . . The Duchess of Somerset also to mend matters insisted on presenting me to a Princess *Biron* Duchess of Hohen—God knows— what—and another person to her two sisters—Birons too—but I flew off—& *would* not—

They had continued this very awkward courtship a few days later:

> Last night at Lady Jersey's—after as many movements as ever were upon a Chess-board—your friend & I got fairly checkmated in a corner—& talked a very good half-hour—& by persuading her that I was in a greater fright than herself she got over much of her shyness—and we prated something like you & me at our second or third interview—I only heard her say one disagreeable thing—& that is that Lady S. [Lady Stafford, mother of Lady Charlotte] & the whole family leave town very soon for Scotland.

Augusta had been more active in pursuit than he; but the Antelope dashed off in a fright and nothing came of the projected romance. This incident left Byron more uncertain than ever, but still willing to consider marriage. The possibility teased him during the next two months. He noted in his Journal:

> George [Anson Byron, who had been promoted to Commander, R.N. in 1812] is returned from afloat to get a new ship. He looks thin, but better than I expected. I like George much more than most people like their heirs. He is a fine fellow, and every inch a sailor. I would do any thing, *but apostatize*, to get him on in his profession. . . . I hope he will be an admiral, and, perhaps, Lord Byron into the bargain. If he would but marry, I would engage never to marry myself, or cut him out of the heirship. He would be happier, and I should like nephews better than sons.

In the same place he observed:

> Yesterday, a very pretty letter from Annabella [Milbanke], which I answered. What an odd situation and friendship is ours!—without one spark of love on either side, and produced by circumstances which in general lead to coldness on one side, and aversion on the other. She is a very superior woman, and very little spoiled, which is strange in an heiress—a girl of twenty—a peeress that is to be, in her own right—an only child, and a *savante*, who has always had her own way. She is a poetess—a mathematician—a metaphysician, and yet, withal, very kind, generous, and gentle, with very little pretension.[35]

Although Byron disliked intellectual women, the conventional in his varied temperament inclined him to admire this strait-laced, self-righteous girl who had already refused him, but whose convoluted letters held out some hope, and he continued to correspond with her. By September of 1814 he was back at Newstead with Augusta, full of nostalgia. Encouraged by his sister, he wrote a tentative proposal to Annabella which would nevertheless leave her free. He was so doubtful of success that he was considering an alternative plan of going to Italy with Hobhouse when her answer arrived on 18 September. The icy Miss Milbanke had accepted him.

Anne Isabella, only child of Sir Ralph Milbanke (Lady Melbourne's brother) and Judith Milbanke (formerly Noel, daughter of Lord Wentworth) of Seaham, Durham, was four years younger than Byron. She was born 17 May 1792 to parents who had been childless for fifteen years and she was consequently spoilt and thought much of her own judgments and opinions. Annabella (as she was always called) spent her sheltered early years almost entirely at Seaham under the care of parents who thought her perfect and a governess who encouraged her undoubtedly good intellect; but the self-confidence that in later years became a fixed belief in her infallibility was allowed to develop unchecked. Literature, chess, and mathematics were her chief interests and when she had her first

London season in 1811 under the chaperonage of Lady Gosford she was more bored than entertained by fashionable amusements, although she was fond of dancing. Years later Byron told Thomas Medwin:

> There was something piquant, and what we term pretty, in Miss Milbanke. Her features were small and feminine, though not regular. She had the fairest skin imaginable. Her figure was perfect for her height.[36]

She was socially successful and refused two offers of marriage, suspecting that they were inspired by her prospects as heiress, through her mother, to the Wentworth fortune.

Miss Milbanke's second season was even better: her numerous suitors included men of high rank and wealth, yet they all fell below her exacting standards. 'Good, amiable, and sensible, but cold, prudent and reflecting . . . she is really an icicle', was the shrewd verdict of Lady Elizabeth Foster (afterwards Duchess of Devonshire) whose son, Augustus, was one of Annabella's rejections.

But when Annabella first saw Byron at a waltzing party at Melbourne House she wrote long diary entries which reveal her interest. Characteristically, she could not admit this to herself. A few more meetings with him convinced her 'that he is sincerely repentant for the evil he has done, though he has not resolution (without aid) to adopt a new course of conduct and feelings'. Already she was wondering if she could supply that aid. Byron, for his part, was interested in this quiet, self-possessed, intellectual girl whom he dubbed the 'Princess of Parallelograms' but was later to call his 'Mathematical Medea'.

On refusing Byron's first proposal in 1812, conveyed through her aunt, Lady Melbourne, Annabella drew up a 'character' of her future husband (she was given to writing such 'characters' and passing judgments on people) which accompanied her answer. She required 'consistent principles of Duty governing strong & *generous* feelings', and freedom from suspicion and habitual ill-humour. She expected her husband's feelings to be commanded by reason and would not marry into a family in which there was a tendency to Insanity.[37] She noted that Byron's passions had guided him from childhood and that he was chivalrous, generous, unselfish, but with a perverse desire to conceal his best qualities: 'He is extremely humble towards persons whose character he respects, and to them he would probably confess his errors'.[38]

Annabella deceived herself when she said that she refused Byron because she did not have strong affection for him; and she soon demonstrated this by re-opening a correspondence the following August, when she wrote him a long letter hinting that her affections were already engaged. She thus drew Byron into an exchange of letters which

[199]

led to his second proposal, but she had to write some tortuous explanations to extricate herself from the lie that she was otherwise attached.

His witty, humorous, refreshingly honest responses to her stilted and pedantic style are perfect illustrations of Byron's genius for pleasing. He instinctively told her what she wanted to hear, patiently and politely expounding his philosophy and his religious views to this serious girl who wanted to reform him. In the end she hinted she was free. He was anxious to settle; the Antelope had escaped; Augusta was encouraging—and so he proposed again. Annabella's joyful reply arrived at Newstead just after the gardener had brought Byron his mother's lost wedding ring, dug up under her bedroom window, and Byron exclaimed that he would be married with it. He did not consider it an ill omen.

He was in no hurry to see his bride. There were many business arrangements to make with Hanson and he had misgivings because Annabella was so good. She had no misgivings. The Milbankes announced the engagement, to the relief of Byron's Aunt Sophia and Annabella's uncle, Lord Wentworth, who met at Lord Scarsdale's, when neither dared to mention the news for fear the other had not been told. Society at large was soon discussing it. Mrs Piozzi recalled her friendship with Byron's grandmother, 'a favourite of Dr Johnson, [who] would have been glad that her grandson was a poet, and a poet he is, in every sense of the word . . .'. She knew he was a favourite with women: 'We all agreed that he might throw his handkerchief; and I rejoyce so pretty and pleasing a lady picks it up'.[39]

Byron was now forced to sell Newstead to pay the marriage settlement. John Murray, who had visited the Abbey earlier that year, told his wife it would cost about £100,000 to put into good repair and the wonder was that Byron had ever lived there at all. Byron's debts made such an expenditure impossible; he had to settle £60,000 on Miss Milbanke, at her family's insistence. (His friend Francis Hodgson thought these terms exorbitant.)

Therefore Byron lingered long in London, annoying the Milbankes very much. He finally arrived at Seaham, the family estate in County Durham, on 2 November for an inauspicious visit. Troubled by his unaccountable moods, Annabella offered to break off the engagement, whereupon he fainted (or so she later declared), convincing her of his love. For his part, Byron was troubled by Annabella's scruples, fine feelings and frequent illnesses. He described her scene with him as in Lady Caroline Lamb's style and wrote Lady Melbourne a prophetic letter:

> I hear of nothing but 'feeling' from morning till night . . . . but I am never sure of A[nnabella]—for a moment—the least word—and you know I

rattle on through thick & thin ... or alteration of tone—has some inference drawn from it. . . . I don't think her temper *bad* at any time— but very *self*-tormenting—and anxious—and romantic. . . . In short—it is impossible to foresee how this will end *now*—anymore than 2 years ago—if there is a break—it shall be *her* doing not mine.—

But he found her quite '*caressable* into kindness and good humour'.[40]

Byron had shrewdly discerned Annabella's self-destructive tendencies, which contributed to the swift ruin of their marriage. Their mutual misunderstandings on this visit foreshadowed the domestic drama to come. Each felt an unease that resulted in Byron's departure for London on 16 November. He stopped at Six Mile Bottom to see Augusta and visited Cambridge, where the students burst into spontaneous applause as he walked into the Senate House to vote for his friend Dr William Clarke, a candidate for a medical professorship. The unprecedented acclamation made him blush furiously. Back in London he was visited by Henry Byron, eager to remind his cousin that he was first to mention Annabella's name to him years before and that their grandfathers were all in the same house at Westminster School, and by George Byron, with 'his tongue running nine knots an hour'.[41]

Accompanied by Hobhouse, Byron left London to spend Christmas with the Leighs before proceeding to Seaham, where they arrived late on 30 December, to be received by the servants, a tacit rebuke. He was married on 2 January 1815 in a private ceremony conducted by the Reverend Thomas Noel, one of Lord Wentworth's illegitimate sons. Byron was shy about facing the publicity of a large Church wedding. He and Lady Byron left immediately for Halnaby Hall in Yorkshire. Hobhouse, deeply moved, put a copy of his friend's works into the carriage as a present for the bride and the two men held hands until it slowly moved off.

We can never be sure just what happened after that, because Byron's own detailed account of his marriage and its consequences was lost when his memoirs were burned, leaving Annabella to make *ex parte* and retrospective statements throughout her long life. Her tendency to draw inferences from every careless word and her serious desire to reform a sinful husband could only exacerbate a sardonic and humorous man like Byron, who played on her shuddering credulity and her readiness to be shocked. They had returned from what Byron called the 'treacle-moon' to spend two very boring months at Seaham before visiting Augusta at Six Mile Bottom in the middle of March. They already felt the strain of married life, but the children were delighted to see their uncle, delighted with their aunt and, since Aunt Sophia had postponed a visit and the Colonel was away shooting, there was plenty of room for the visitors. Afterwards the Byrons settled down in apparent amity at 13 Piccadilly Terrace, an expensive London house rented from the Duchess of Devonshire. Byron was now much troubled by creditors, particularly after Lord Wentworth's death in April. He had left his property to Lady Milbanke, however, and not directly to his niece, so that the debts remained unpaid, like the Milbanke share of the marriage settlement which had proved so expensive for Byron.

Mourning and pregnancy kept Annabella indoors. Byron thought she should be quiet in her condition and he resumed some of his bachelor amusements, joining the Drury Lane management sub-committee and writing the *Hebrew Melodies*, published in the spring. His lack of literary creativity probably reflected a deep disquiet and confusion; even at the most hectic moments, writing was usually essential to him. Annabella, for her part, may well have been disappointed that her marriage to the celebrated poet meant living a secluded life with an alarmingly temperamental husband. Nevertheless, people who saw the Byrons together thought them devoted to each other and when he went to Six Mile Bottom at the end of August they exchanged affectionate letters which indicate no strain. Mrs Leigh had never seen her brother looking better, but on his return to London further difficulties encompassed him. When Augusta arrived at Piccadilly Terrace in the middle of November to see Annabella through her confinement, bailiffs were in the house. Oppressed by his financial difficulties and sexually frustrated, Byron understandably gave in to an attractive actress, Susan Boyce, whom he later recalled as 'a transient piece of mine'.[42] His behaviour at home became more reckless and desperate. In her distress, Annabella turned for help to her sister-in-law. Both women questioned Byron's sanity.

A daughter was born into this tense atmosphere on 10 December 1815 and was given the names Augusta Ada, 'the second a very antique family name,—I believe not used since the reign of King John'.[43] The name does not appear in the pedigree of the Byrons; but an Adam de Byron occurs once or twice in the Middle Ages. Perhaps the poet saw it Latinised as 'Ada' and mistook it for a woman's name. He expressed no disappointment at the birth of a daughter; on the contrary, he was delighted and very solicitous about her. Despite difficulties, he thought his marriage secure and had every reason to expect a future heir. But he was so financially pinched that the rent on their London house remained unpaid and accordingly he wrote his wife a rather cool note on 6 January 1816, asking her to arrange her departure for Kirkby Mallory, in Leicestershire, where she would rejoin her parents. The London establishment was to be broken up and Byron was to join the family gathering there later. He and his wife seemed on good terms and slept together before she left on the 15th with the child. Augusta remained to look after him. George Anson Byron, who had arrived by the new year, was also living in the house. On 2 February Byron received a letter from Sir Ralph, proposing a legal separation.

Numerous books have been written about subsequent events, which ended with Byron signing a deed of separation on 21 April. Lady Byron's many retrospective statements must be read with caution, because they became increasingly coloured by her obsessive need for justification, which became more compelling as the years went by. She had always been ambivalent about Byron and her contradictions became ever more complex, her self-torment more agonising. She had written affectionately to him on the journey to Kirkby and after her arrival there; later she justified those letters on the grounds that Dr Baillie, whom she had consulted about Byron's state of mind, had advised her not to agitate him. She declared Byron's behaviour was so brutal she could no longer live with him; but she remained tender towards him and actually rolled on the ground in agony after deciding to separate from him. Despite her later statements, she had no suspicions of Byron's and Augusta's 'crime' when she invited her sister-in-law to Piccadilly Terrace in November of 1815. Her later guesswork about that was not confirmed until the perfidious Lady Caroline Lamb forced herself back into Byron's drama by revealing his incest and 'worse crimes', such as the corruption of young boys, in a secret interview with Lady Byron at the house of Mrs George Lamb. Although Lady Caroline's revelations were a malicious blend of truth, exaggeration and mendacity, they served Lady Byron as evidence to be reserved for use against Augusta and against Byron himself, should he prove recalcitrant when his daughter was made a Ward in Chancery, as Annabella planned.[44]

Before Byron left England two of his poems, 'A Sketch from Private Life' and 'Fare Thee Well' were published without authority in *The Champion*. The first bitterly satirised Annabella's confidential servant, Mrs Clermont, whom he supposed a mischief-making spy; the second reproached his wife for heartlessness. Annabella felt fresh resentment and jealousy of Augusta when she read his 'Stanzas to Augusta' and his letters from abroad to his sister (which Augusta forwarded, unknown to Byron). They revealed a deep emotional response Annabella had never evoked from him.

Byron truthfully protested that his wife never gave her reasons for leaving him. She was a past mistress in the arts of obliquity and innuendo. At first he blamed her parents and defended his wife to Thomas Moore, who suggested his choice was unfortunate; but later her implacability aroused his scorn and his bitter resentment. He remained grateful to Augusta for a generous love which bore with all his weaknesses and he fortunately never discovered that she, too, had betrayed him.

Never was woman so obsessed with being right and so ignorant of her own motives. Annabella had refused to acknowledge she was in love when she first pursued the famous poet and she was unable to admit even to herself that she was still in love when she left him. Both Captain George Byron, who had received nothing but kindness from his cousin, and Mrs George Villiers, ostensibly Augusta's friend, sided with Annabella, whose grievances deepened over years of brooding. She cultivated Byron's family, particularly George Anson Byron, his wife, Mary Chandos-Pole; and their aunt, Sophia Byron; and she endeavoured to win as many other adherents as possible. She thought of herself as having a righteous cause and was profoundly aggrieved with anyone who sided with the 'enemy'.

In June of 1816 she wrote to Augusta that circumstances compelled her to limit their intercourse and poor Mrs Leigh, beset by creditors and obliged to provide for an increasing family on her small income and her remuneration from her place at Queen Charlotte's court, accepted this cold condescension. She had stood bravely by her brother during the separation, when nearly everyone had deserted him; and despite the rumours rapidly gaining currency about the cause of the separation she had remained with him at Piccadilly Terrace, ordering his meals and generally filling the role of his absconding wife. Hobhouse had called one day to find her in tears, but somewhat comforted by her husband's public denial of the rumours. Then and later, Byron assured his wife, Augusta had been her friend, but Annabella eventually persuaded herself that Augusta had separated them and she strove to extort a confession to that effect from her.

> 'More last words' [Byron had written to his wife, expecting no reply] . . . I have just parted from Augusta— almost the last being you had left me to part with—& the only unshattered tie of my existence—wherever I may go—& I am going far—you & I can never meet again in this world—nor in the next—let this content or atone. If any accident occurs to me—be kind to her——if she is then nothing—to her children. . . . She has ever been your friend.

He asked for occasional news of his child through Augusta and referred to the ring containing 'the hair of a king and an ancestor' which he had sent for Ada.[45] He left England on 25 April 1816. He never came back, and he never saw his wife and child again.

Accompanied by John William Polidori, a young physician who spoke three languages, and by the faithful William Fletcher, Byron travelled through Belgium, where he visited the Field of Waterloo and then drove by way of the Rhine into Switzerland. On 25 May they reached Secheron, near Geneva, where Byron first met Shelley, who had arrived a week or two earlier with his wife, Mary, their baby son, and Mary Shelley's step-sister, Claire Clairmont. After the Shelleys moved to a house on the south side of the lake Byron took the Villa Diodati, within a few minutes walk. He was not anxious to renew his relationship with Claire, however. This uncouth, impetuous girl with intellectual pretensions, who had forced herself on Byron in London when he was still numb from the shock of the separation, was pregnant by him. He was relieved when she left with the Shelleys for Chamounix on 20 July.

In August Scrope Davies and Hobhouse arrived from England and at Coppet Byron found a kind neighbour in Madame de Staël, whom he had met in London. She lent him *Glenarvon*, the sensational novel in which Caroline Lamb avenged herself; he commented that her portrait of him could not be good because he did not sit long enough. England was receding from him, although he had many English visitors. Matthew 'Monk' Lewis, author of a sensationally popular Gothic romance, came to stay at the Villa Diodati. Byron found him a bore, which may be why his guest wrote to Madame de Staël asking for a copy of Byron's poems: '[I]t would probably prevent him and myself from knocking out each other's brains in the course of the day. But *with* Brains or without, we shall certainly pay our respects to you at Coppet on Thursday'.[46]

On 8 October, Byron and Hobhouse left for Italy without Dr Polidori, who had become a nuisance.[47] Byron was keeping a Journal for Augusta and he promised to send souvenirs to Georgiana, his favourite niece. From Venice Byron wrote to Hanson that Ada must not leave England without her father's consent: a rumour had reached him that Lady Byron planned to go abroad. When he learned in the spring of 1817 that his daughter had been made a Ward in Chancery he decided, in a fury, to return to England; but a slow fever prevented him. In Venice he assuaged grief with numerous women, 'all whores'. He established a longer liaison with Marianna Segati and reported a battle between this mistress and her sister-in-law to Augusta for the amusement of their Aunt Sophy, who despite Annabella's efforts, took a lively interest:

I know nothing which would make you laugh much—except a battle some weeks ago—in my apartment—between two of the fair '*sect*' (sisters in law) which ended in the flight of one & the fits of the other—and a

great deal of confusion and eau de Cologne—and asterisks—& all that.—
The cause was—one paying me an evening visit. . . . The other one gone
out to a Conversazione—as was supposed for the evening. . . . but lo &
behold—in about half an hour—she returned & entering my room—
without a word—administered (before I could prevent her) about sixteen
such slaps to her relation—as would have made your ear ache only to
hear them. . . . You may tell this to Sophy if she wants amusement.

He repeated this story to Kinnaird and Moore and regaled them with
other exploits. He was amused by a society which went to *conversazione*
to keep silent and in which a married woman took a lover as a matter of
course, marriages generally being arranged. But he was not like his
father and needed something to break his mind upon, visiting an
Armenian monastery every day to study the language and to help one of
the monks with English in the compilation of an Armenian grammar.
In May of 1817 he joined Hobhouse in Rome for three weeks and sat for
the Danish sculptor, Thorwaldsen, for his bust. While there he heard
that George Anson Byron had a daughter.[48] He still felt kindly to the
cousin who had betrayed him: '[T]he father is a good man—an
excellent officer—& has married a very nice little woman—who will
bring him more babes than income—howbeit she had a handsome
dowry—& is a very charming girl—but he may as well get a ship'.[49]

On his way back to Venice, Byron wrote to Augusta from Florence
announcing the birth of his daughter by Claire Clairmont.[50] Despite his
aversion to the mother, he thought of sending for this child and
educating her in a convent because Ada seemed lost to him and he had
to love something. Perhaps reflections on this gloomy theme caused his
access of bitterness about his cousin and heir's defection: 'that other
poor creature George Byron' he called him.[51] His correspondence was
punctuated with fretful demands for toothpowder and magnesia.
Abandoning his indifference to money, he demanded 2,500 guineas for
the fourth Canto of *Childe Harold*, rather than the 1,500 Murray offered.
His creativity had reawakened since his exile and he was again writing
busily—*Manfred, The Prisoner of Chillon, The Lament of Tasso*, two cantos
of *Childe Harold*, and *Beppo*, all written by the end of 1817—and now he
appreciated the financial rewards.

He continued to prod his slow, inefficient lawyer about selling
Newstead and finally he learned in December of 1817 that his old
Harrow schoolfellow, Colonel Thomas Wildman, had bought the Abbey
for £94,500, more than Byron had hoped. The poet's grief in parting
with the family estate must be guessed: it was one of the rare subjects he
did not talk about, concentrating on the financial advantages in writing
to his lawyer and his friends.

Thus Newstead Abbey passed away from the Byrons. The new owner, who was rich, made some tactful and imaginative changes, restoring and remodelling parts of the house and carrying out improvements in the park. After his death in 1860 the Abbey was sold to William Frederick Webb, who redecorated the chapel and built a stable block and spire alongside the fifth Lord's 'castle' kennels. Mrs Webb had extensive landscaping carried out in the grounds. The Byrons and all posterity can only be grateful for the affectionate care with which the Wildmans and the Webbs preserved Newstead's past. In 1931 Charles Ian Fraser, the Webb's grandson, sold the Abbey and most of the park to Sir Julien Cahn, a Nottingham businessman, who presented it to the City. Now owned by the Nottingham Corporation, Newstead still dreams by the lake so many Byrons loved. The poet seems to linger there yet. His rooms house his bed and many personal memorabilia.

Early in 1818 Byron rented the Palazzo Mocenigo, on the Grand Canal. Marianna Segati was superseded by Margarita Cogni, 'La Fornarina' or baker's wife, with tempestuous ways. He kept a large menagerie—two monkeys, a fox, a wolf, cats, a hawk, a crow, and later a bulldog and Newfoundland dogs. In April his little daughter Allegra arrived from England, escorted by the Shelleys. In the summer he wrote his *Ode on Venice* and *Mazeppa* and by the middle of September he had completed the first canto of a new comic work, *Don Juan*, which was to be 'quietly facetious upon every thing.'

In April of 1819 Byron met the Countess Teresa Guiccioli at the Countess Benzoni's *conversazione*. Teresa was plump and petite, with a well shaped bust and shoulders, a handsome face, large melting eyes, and rich auburn curls. Neither remembered that they had first met a year before, when Byron escorted her to see the sculptor Canova's 'Helen' at the Countess Albrizzi's, but they soon conversed readily about the great Italian poets, on whom Teresa was well informed. Before they parted that night, Byron asked to see her again. Ten days later, the Guicciolis departed for Ravenna, but not before 'we had consummated our unlawful union with all the proper rites four days and daily—previously to *her* leaving Venice', he told Hobhouse.[52] After some initial resistance, he settled down as her *cavalier servente* or *amico*, an Italian role which enabled a wife's lover to be accepted by her husband and by polite society.

For all his incisive insight, Byron never understood Teresa's elderly husband, Count Alessandro Guiccioli, an enigmatic nobleman of fifty-eight. His first wife had brought him a huge dowry, but he had banished her to the country when she objected to his liaison with a housemaid who bore him six children and whom he subsequently married. When his second wife died he had gone out to the theatre that night as usual. Calculating in political matters, he sided with the people during the French occupation of the Romagna, but after Napoleon's defeat made himself agreeable to the Papal Court. Rumour accused him of murdering two political rivals. He was subsequently suspected for his third marriage to Teresa Gamba, whose aristocratic family were all devoted patriots. This may explain his continued friendliness to his wife's cavalier, whom he asked to obtain a post for him as British Consul or Vice-Consul in Ravenna. He also tried to borrow money from Byron.

Despite the Count and many other difficulties, Teresa won and held Byron, who became absorbed in his passion for her. Ever vacillating in mood, however, he pursued a certain Angelica after Teresa had left Venice, and he wrote to Augusta as well, declaring, 'I have never ceased nor can cease to feel for a moment that perfect & boundless attachment which bound & binds me to you— which renders me utterly incapable of *real* love for any other human being'.[53] The intimidated Augusta passed this letter to her tormenting mentor, Lady Byron, with the comment that he must be a maniac.

But Teresa was to dispel Byron's dissatisfaction and his defensive cruelty. With her he enjoyed the best and the most conjugal relationship of his life and his last deep passion. He followed her to Ravenna and then to Bologna in his big Napoleonic carriage (built by Baxter of London three years before and still unpaid for). When Teresa miscarried, he felt the deepest anxiety and fretted that she might be snatched from him, after all. He wrote passionate letters from the stuffy little inn at Ravenna. When she felt better they went for drives in her carriage.

He followed his *amica* dutifully after that, submitting to the restrictions of her customs and her world. Count Guiccioli remained complacent and friendly for a while, inviting his wife's lover to occupy the ground floor of his palace in Bologna. One day (23 August) Byron found Teresa's purple-bound copy of Madame de Staël's sentimental novel *Corinne*, which he teased her for liking, and he wrote in it:

> My dearest Teresa—I have read this book in your garden;—my Love— you were absent—or I could not have read it.—It is a favourite book of yours—and the writer was a friend of mine.—You will not understand these English words—and *others* will not understand them—which is the reason I have not scribbled them in Italian—but you will recognize the hand-writing of him who passionately loved you—and you will divine that over a book which was yours—he could only think of love. In *that word* beautiful in all languages—but most so in yours—*Amor* mio—is comprized my existence here and hereafter. . . .

At the end of August, Allegra joined her father in Bologna and he wrote to Augusta:

> Allegra is here with me—in good health—& very amiable and pretty at least thought so.—She is English—but speaks nothing but Venetian— 'Bon *di* papa' &c. &c. she is very droll—and has a good deal of the Byron—can't articulate the letter *r* at all—frowns and pouts quite in our way—blue eyes—light hair growing *darker* daily—and a dimple in the chin—a scowl on the brow—white skin—sweet voice—and a particular liking of Music—and of her own way in every thing—is not that B. all over?[54]

In September the imponderable Count allowed Byron to escort Teresa to Venice to consult Dr Aglietti, professor and head of the medical school. There Teresa lived with Byron in his Palazzo Mocenigo, before accompanying him to La Mira, his villa near Venice. When Thomas Moore arrived at La Mira on 7 October for a long-promised visit, he found Byron's spirits revived. Byron recalled his happy bachelor days in London. He had thought of returning to England, until he realised that he had no one but his sister to receive him and that the income which allowed him a magnificent life in Italy would mean a meagre existence in London.

Later that month Byron returned to his Venetian palace, where he was seized with one of his recurring bouts of fever. Teresa went in to nurse him and they were joined there by the Count, whose reserve had finally broken and who was determined to allay the gossip about his wife's lover. There were terrible scenes and quarrels between Teresa and her husband. Once the Count came crying to Byron to make it up and eventually the harassed lover persuaded Teresa to return to Ravenna with her husband. In his emotional distress, Byron seriously considered returning to England. He was actually on the point of departure when a letter from Teresa's father with news of his daughter's illness recalled Byron to Ravenna, where he arrived on Christmas Eve. Teresa eventually persuaded her husband to rent the upper floor of the Palazzo Guiccioli in Ravenna to Byron and there Luigi Morelli (a servant) and a Negro page employed by Count Guiccioli watched the stairs during Byron's clandestine visits. They managed their love-making while the Count took his siesta; it was all in the style of a grand opera.

Byron secured the friendship of Teresa's brother, Pietro, as well as her father, Count Gamba, who applied to the Pope for a separation for his daughter. When the Pope granted this by a decree on 6 July 1820, Teresa escaped her husband's wrath by absconding with the help of servants and joining her father at Filetto, his country house near Ravenna.

Through the Gambas, Byron had joined the *carbonari*, an organisation of patriots who planned to overthrow the occupying Austrians. His house became a cache for their weapons and he thoroughly enjoyed the danger and the possibility of political action. But the Neopolitan campaign collapsed and the authorities sought to rid themselves of the troublesome English peer by banishing the Gambas in July of 1821, expecting Byron to follow his friends. The Gambas sought refuge in Florence, but Byron stayed on in the great Palazzo Guiccioli, writing. He was continuing *Don Juan*, making some translations, and writing his memoirs; these last he sent to Thomas Moore, who was living in Paris to dodge his creditors. It was understood between them that Moore would publish the memoirs only after Byron's death. Byron had completed two historical tragedies: *Marino Faliero, Doge of Venice*, and *Sardanapalus*, about an indolent but benevolent Assyrian monarch forced into a life of action and obliged to confront the difficult realities of power. He began to write *Cain*, a choral drama in the earlier style of *Manfred*, in which he further explored the problem of man's existence, returning to the bitter conclusion that knowledge brings sorrow rather than happiness or life.

When Percy Shelley called on Byron in August to enquire about Allegra, the two poets talked all night. Shelley stayed several days, sight-seeing in Ravenna and visiting Allegra at the Convent of Bagnacavallo, twelve miles away on the Bologna road, where she had been since 1 March. Then he returned to Pisa to find a house for the exiled Gambas and a palace for Byron on the Lungarno (the Casa Lanfranchi). Byron left Ravenna to live in Pisa, travelling through the Appenines with the London banker-poet Samuel Rogers, whom he met by pre-arrangement at Bologna. A chance encounter with Lord Clare, his old Harrow friend, stirred him deeply:

> We were but five minutes together, and in the public road; but I hardly recollect an hour of my existence which could be weighed against them.

Upon taking possession of the airy palace Shelley had found for him, Byron became the leading figure in that famous 'Pisan Circle' to which so much literature has been devoted. Other members of that circle had compelling reasons for living abroad. Shelley, who had abandoned his first wife to elope with Mary Godwin, had understandably been denied custody of his children by Lord Chancellor Eldon, a decision which caused him much bitterness, and he had a dubious reputation in England. Edward and Jane Williams were actually an eloping half-pay lieutenant and an officer's wife. John Taafe, a literary Irishman, was escaping the consequences of an unfortunate affair with a woman in Edinburgh. Thomas Medwin, who had served with Williams in the 8th Dragoons in India, turned out to be a bore and Byron was not sorry to see him leave on 11 March 1822. Edward John Trelawny, an insecure braggart, joined the circle on 14 January.

When Byron's mother-in-law, Lady Noel, died in January of 1822, Lord Wentworth's property legally passed to Byron, by right of his wife; under the terms of the separation it was divided by arbitrators. On receiving half of this bequest, Byron was obliged to assume the name of Noel. The law's inevitable delay, however, meant that he did not receive the income for some time. Although he felt sympathy for his wife, who adored her mother (as he told Medwin), he had disliked Lady Noel and felt no sorrow at her passing.

But the death of his illegitimate daughter, Allegra, in April was such a bitter grief that he never spoke of it, even to the devoted Teresa. His distress was complicated by anger over the preposterous fees the embalmer tried to charge. Byron wanted to have the child buried in Harrow Church, but eventually he learned that the churchwardens would not even allow a memorial tablet to be erected inside it. Allegra was eventually buried in the churchyard, with neither tablet nor memorial stone.

This shock was swiftly followed by another. In July Shelley, Captain Williams and a sailor boy, Charles Vivian, were drowned when their boat, the *Don Juan*, capsized en route from Leghorn to Lerici, Shelley's temporary summer home. After a long search, which Byron financed, their bodies were recovered, in an appalling condition, and Byron was disturbed by the theatrical and unnecessary cremations on the beach which the histrionic Trelawny insisted on performing. Charles Vivian was fortunate in having none to mourn him; his body remained where it was interred after the waves had washed it ashore.

Shelley had just welcomed Leigh Hunt and his family, who had come to Italy so that Hunt could collaborate on a new projected publication, *The Liberal*; but this catastrophe threw them entirely on Byron's generosity. Hunt, the model for Harold Skimpole in *Bleak House*, always needed help, but the very generous treatment he received from Byron did not prevent him from writing very meanly about Byron after his death.

In September Byron moved to Genoa, where he lived with Teresa in the Gamba's villa, the Casa Saluzzo. Shelley's death broke up the Pisan Circle. In addition to his annoyance about the helpless Hunts and their dirty, undisciplined children, who ran about like Yahoos, Byron had to provide for Mary Shelley, who was miserable and full of grievances.

The planned publication failed eventually, despite Byron's contribution of *The Vision of Judgment*, his brilliant satire on Robert Southey's dismal eulogy of King George III. But amid grief and confusion Byron went on writing: he had finished another historical tragedy, *The Two Foscari*; the fragment of another choral drama, *The Deformed Transformed*; a melodramatic tragedy, *Werner*; and more cantos of *Don Juan*. Another choral drama, *Heaven and Earth*, on the theme of the marriage of the sons of God with the daughters of men, brought charges of atheism and sedition against him, as *Cain* had done. The conservative John Murray was reluctant to publish such provocative works. Consequently Byron withdrew from Murray as publisher and gave his work to Leigh Hunt's brother, John, in London. He began the seventeenth canto of *Don Juan*, but completed only fourteen stanzas. He wrote little more, because he was embarked on a decisive adventure.

The dream of freeing Greece from Ottoman domination had finally resulted in an uprising there in 1821. Afterwards a Greek Committee, which included John Cam Hobhouse, had been formed in England. In March of 1823 it unanimously elected Byron a member. At first he took no active part because he did not want to distress Teresa with the possibility of leaving her, but he sent sound advice to John Bowring, the Honorary Secretary, about equipment the Greeks most needed. He resisted the call to action a long time, but it eventually became too strong for him. By June of 1823 he had decided to leave his comfortable life in Italy and to go to Greece himself. After months of elaborate preparation, he hired a schooner, the *Hercules*, which sailed from Genoa on 17 July. In Byron's party were Dr Bruno, an Italian physician; Teresa's brave and loyal brother, Count Pietro Gamba; and William Fletcher—still wrapped in gloomy memories of earlier discomforts in Greece—as well as the ubiquitous Trelawny, who planned to further his own ends by joining the expedition of so bold and charismatic a leader.

On reaching the island of Cephalonia early in August they discovered that Captain Blaquiere, whom they had expected to meet, had left for home, and that political dissension was rife among the Greeks, an inevitable result of the tribal loyalties so exasperating to Europeans. Byron was friendly with Colonel Napier, the Governor, whose neutrality (at least) was essential because Cephalonia was a British protectorate. Byron decided not to commit himself at once to any party and he remained for several months on Cephalonia to determine the best course of action. The shifty and indiscreet Trelawny, unable to shine as he had hoped, departed for the mainland to join Odysseus, the treacherous leader of another faction.

At the end of September Augusta reported that Ada was ill, news which so distressed Byron that he suspended the Journal he had resumed and begged his sister for more information. He wanted to know about Ada's habits and temper, hoping that the gods had made her anything but poetical: 'it is enough to have one such fool in a family'.

He finally decided to cooperate with Prince Mavrocordatos and the whole party sailed for the mainland on 28 December 1823. Byron's boat narrowly escaped the Turks, who actually captured his companion vessel with Count Gamba, but they all arrived safely at last in Missolonghi, a dismal, wet, fever-ridden town infested with mosquitoes, to a rapturous welcome from the Prince, the Greeks, and the English Colonel Leicester Stanhope.

Despite his determination and cheerfulness, Byron was very ill. He had suffered a kind of fit at the Monastery on Samos in Cephalonia early in August, tearing his clothes, breaking furniture, and cursing the Abbot. He had lost much weight and seemed pale and listless, but he gathered his waning energies to face the difficulties which crowded upon him in that dark, rain-lashed town. He had to be Commander-in-Chief, to discipline and to pay troops, to assemble military and medical stores, to compose the numberless differences between the factions and to arbitrate quarrels between Colonel Stanhope and William Parry, a Naval Firemaster who joined them at the end of January. Byron nick-named Stanhope 'the typographical Colonel' because he wanted to establish a free press in a largely illiterate country torn by war and rebellion; he found the practical Parry a more helpful and even a comforting comrade.

Then, in the middle of February, Byron endured a severe convulsive attack, but he apparently recovered in a few days. He refused to return to the Ionian Islands and continued his duties with clear-headed courage, gaiety, and determination. He was an effective mediator between the Greeks and a generous enemy to the Turks, helping refugees from both sides in the hope of mitigating the horrible cruelties of the war. A letter from Augusta enclosing a long report on Ada from Lady Byron cheered him immensely and he wondered whether to send home a little Turkish girl, one of his protégées, as a companion for his daughter. Although he was obviously unwell he remained very active and went riding with Gamba in the incessant spring rains. By 15 April he was unable to leave his bed. The three doctors summoned to aid the inexperienced young Bruno quarrelled loudly about the appropriate treatment, arguing in different languages and unable to understand each other. Byron was bled copiously, over his protests and the

[213]

opposition of William Parry, but bleeding was still recognised practice and no one listened to them. The patient's constitution was further undermined by their treatment and he grew weaker. On 18 April Byron tried to give Fletcher a long message, most of it inaudible, and after mumbling, 'My sister, my child,' he lapsed into a coma from which he never emerged. He died at six o'clock on the evening of 19 April 1824.

The Greeks were stunned by the national catastrophe of Byron's death. Prince Mavrocordatos, who had counted on his unifying leadership, ordered general mourning for 21 days, cancelled the Easter festivities, and directed that all shops and offices close for three days. On 20 April the grieving young Count Gamba began to arrange Byron's papers and to prepare for the long voyage to England. The heartbroken Fletcher composed a long, pathetic letter to Augusta Leigh, describing his beloved master's illness and death and repeating the few last words he had been able to catch:

> I must conclude By my Prayers for you to receive this fatal news with the consolation of being serting My Lord his happier than any of us. I remain Hond Madam Your most obt verry miserable and verry Humble Servant, W. Fletcher.[55]

After a crude autopsy and embalming, Byron's body lay in state before being taken to the Island of Zante, where his rough wooden coffin was placed in a large cask full of spirits and then carried on board the *Florida*, accompanied by Byron's servants and his dogs. Colonel Stanhope took charge of the party. They sailed on 24 May and reached the Downs in the Thames estuary on 29 June, well behind the news of his death, which had reached England on 14 May.

Byron's activities in Greece were the final efforts of a dying man, but to Englishmen his death was as unexpected as it had been to the Greeks. The praise bestowed on his endeavours by the formerly hostile English press would have moved Byron to sardonic laughter. Lady Byron, who had a premonition about her husband's death, was at Beckenham when Captain George Byron (now seventh Baron) came to break the news. She knew at once what he intended to say. She asked to see the accounts of her husband's death, which were supplied by Hobhouse and the grief-stricken Augusta, who forwarded Fletcher's letter. Yet Lady Byron's feelings were as painfully ambivalent as they remained for the rest of her life. Despite her grief, she was subsequently angry with Mrs George Lamb for sending a carriage to Byron's funeral! Lady Byron was able to keep her version of events before the world because Hobhouse, motivated largely by his jealousy of Moore's friendship with Byron, took immediate action to destroy his friend's memoirs, which contained a full account of the marriage and its consequences. Moore, with Byron's approval, had sold them to Murray for 2,000 guineas, with the option of redemption any time before the poet's death. Hobhouse worked on Augusta and easily secured her consent to the destruction of the provocative document, which he had never read. Hobhouse and Douglas Kinnaird offered Moore the price of redemption if he would put the memoirs at Mrs Leigh's disposal, but Moore, believing that his option extended for three months after Byron's death, declared he would redeem the MS himself (with money from Longman's) and gave it to Mrs Leigh. A meeting had been arranged at Augusta Leigh's home when Moore changed his mind and decided to redeem the memoirs and publish extracts from them. During a meeting at 50, Albemarle Street, Murray (who had not read them) insisted that they be destroyed and after much argument they were torn up and burnt by Colonel Doyle (Lady Byron's representative) and Wilmot Horton (acting for Mrs Leigh). Moore, who *had* read the memoirs, protested against their destruction, but he was overruled: Byron's original manuscript and one copy made by Moore were reduced to ashes in John Murray's fireplace. Subsequently it was discovered that Moore's memory was at fault: the option expired at Byron's death and the manuscript was therefore the property of John Murray. Consequently, Moore paid over the money he had received from Longman's and was unnecessarily the loser.

Thus one of the world's great autobiographies was lost and the field left clear for malice and speculation. Lady Byron had characteristically refused her husband's offer to read and comment upon his memoirs and she as typically denied that she desired their destruction, which actually 'relieved [her] anxiety'.[56]

Hobhouse went aboard the *Florida* on 1 July. He was stabbed by the sight of his friend's three dogs playing on deck and then he heard the sordid details of his death from the doctors and the sobbing Fletcher. Westminster Abbey had refused burial to the reprobate and it was accordingly decided to bury Byron at Hucknall Torkard.

The long funeral procession reached Nottingham early on Friday morning, 16 July. The coffin remained for several hours at the Blackmoor's Head in Pelham Street, where the public were admitted in groups of twenty to see it. A vast and silent crowd assembled in the big Market Place to watch the departure for Hucknall Church at 11:45 a.m. Hobhouse, Hanson, George Leigh, Colonel Thomas Wildman from Newstead, Colonel Leicester Stanhope and others from Missolonghi were the chief mourners; the Nottingham Corporation was represented by the Mayor and other local officials in two coaches and six. The procession, a quarter of a mile long, included Lord Rancliffe's tenants from Bunny (home of Byron's cousins, the Parkyns family) and forty gentlemen on horseback, riding two by two. At 3:30 p.m. the cortege reached the little Church where, after a short service at which Fletcher broke down completely, the poet was lowered into the vault that held so many of his ancestors.

Byron once told Lord Blessington that he would prefer a Greek stone over him to Westminster Abbey, a wish which was fulfilled in a different form in 1881, when the King of Greece sent a memorial slab of Greek marble which was inserted in the chancel floor over his burial place. A century after his death the Prime Minister of Greece took the chief part in a ceremony presenting Byron's ancestral home to the Corporation of Nottingham. But another forty-five years passed before Westminster Abbey acknowledged Byron.

In 1826 Hobhouse had inaugurated a monument committee which raised funds for a large statue by Bertel Thorwaldsen, who had made a bust of Byron from life, but the Abbey had refused it and after many years delay the white marble figure was presented to Cambridge University, where it may be seen in Wren's Trinity College Library. 'I am so glad you like the head—it pleased me more than anything I have seen since the Original because one can see it in *every* point of view,' Augusta Leigh wrote to Henry Porter Smith. 'Did you ever hear of the *enthusiastic* reception given him . . . in Trinity College.'[57]

Eventually the Abbey accepted a white marble floor tablet. On 8 May 1969, the Queen's Poet Laureate, C. Day-Lewis, laid a wreath of laurel and red roses. William Plomer, President of the Poetry Society, unveiled the memorial and remarked:

> One can imagine that Byron's shade, if present here today, may be wearing a slightly sardonic smile.[58]

## · 9 ·

# Too Haughty a Name:
# The Successors to the Title

And theirs was the wealth and the fulness of Fame,
And mine to inherit too haughty a name;
And theirs were the times and the triumphs of yore,
And mine to regret, but renew them no more.

*Newstead Abbey*

RICHARD, oldest son of the Reverend Richard Byron and his wife, Margaret Farmer, had entered the Navy and, like his uncle 'Foulweather Jack', he rose to the rank of Admiral. His most famous exploit was an incident during the War of 1812. Ships of the U.S. Navy, commanded by Commodore Rodgers, were trying to capture a fleet of about one hundred sail of homeward-bound Jamaicamen when they fell in with the British 36-gun frigate, the *Belvidera*, commanded by Captain Richard Byron. It had been lying-to, waiting to intercept a French privateer schooner, the *Marengo*. The subsequent exchange of shots broke the *Belvidera*'s longbolts, breeching hooks, and damaged the long guns. Captain Byron received a blow which caused a severe contusion of the inside of his thigh. The *Belvidera* escaped the American squadron only with the loss of 2 killed and 22 wounded from the crew of 230 men and boys.[1]

The following year (8 February 1813) boats from the *Belvidera* and another ship chased a schooner from Baltimore in Chesapeake Bay and captured her. Byron behaved most generously to the injured enemy Captain Southcomb, took him on board the frigate until he died, and then had his body sent ashore with every mark of the respect due to a brave officer. He subsequently received a letter of thanks from Captain Charles Stewart of the American frigate *Constellation*.

That his gallant and chivalrous gesture was characteristic is confirmed by his later courtesy to Edward Varney, who wrote from Trinidad to the Earl of Verulam on 16 September 1819:

[217]

After a most terrible passage from Dominica to this island, in which I was near starved to death and left nearly without water, having been out to sea 14 days instead of 3 or 4, I arrived at Margarita, where I found Admiral Biron and General English, of the patriot service. Their attentions to me were very great; the admiral most kindly and handsomely lent me one of his armed sloops to convey me hither.[2]

Apart from his distinguished naval career Admiral Byron lived quietly, like his father, far from the strident publicity that attended so many of the Byrons. He died as unobtrusively as he had lived, at his London house, on 2 September 1837, and he was survived by his wife, Sarah, daughter of James Sykes, whom he had married 23 September 1801, and who lived until 11 August 1861.[3]

He left four children. Richard, born in 1802, became a Commander in the navy and died at sea in command of the sloop *Champion* on 23 February 1843. James, born 1803, was an army captain who died in May 1858. John Byron, born 21 September 1804, emerges more clearly. He married (8 December 1830) Mary, daughter of William Richardson, and they had a family of seven children. John took Holy Orders, like his grandfather, and became Vicar of Elmstone-Hardwick, Gloucester, and Chaplain to the Duke of Sutherland. He died 6 December 1878. From his oldest son, Major-General John Byron, the twelfth[4] Lord Byron was descended.

Although Admiral Richard Byron's youngest son, William, born 13 November 1805, seemed to lead an unobtrusive and undistinguished existence, he presents the great mystery of the family. His career was outwardly conventional: he was educated by the Reverend William Greenlaw at Blackheath School, admitted to Emmanuel College (Cambridge) where he matriculated at Michaelmas, 1823 and received his B.A. in 1827. In November of 1825 he was admitted to Lincoln's Inn, when he was described as the fourth son of Richard, R.N., of Leatherhead, Surrey. Afterwards, however, he disappeared into the service of the East India Company, where he seems to have drudged for years as a lowly clerk in the Marine Branch, never even rising to an 'Assistant'. His career appears to be mediocrity unrelieved, but he enjoyed his creature comforts: he was a member of the Surrey County Cricket Club and lived at 6, Kennington Terrace, Surrey, where he died on 3 January 1901 at the advanced age of 95. Although his expectations as a clergyman's grandson and a youngest son must have been meagre, his will was proved for the astonishing sum of £71,115 (later revised to £71,245). One can only conjecture that he may have used his position with the East India Company to make less than scrupulous but profitable arrangements, possibly involving cargoes. If so, he would naturally have to conceal the fruits of such activities by maintaining an unsuspiciously modest standard of living. Since he was a bachelor with few responsibilities or expenses he left a considerable estate to his nephews and nieces as his will (dated 28 August 1895) indicates:

> . . . I give all my real estate (including chattels real) situate in the county of Lincoln to my niece Ada Blanche Byron. . . . I also give to my said niece . . . all my silver and plated articles my wines pictures furniture and jewellery and domestic goods. . . . I give the following legacies namely to the said Ada Blanche Byron ten thousand pounds to my niece Fanny Lucy Byron ten thousand pounds to each of them Richard Byron and Ada Mary Dicken (wife of Captain Charles Gauntlett Dicken R.N.)—Son and daughter of my late nephew John Byron—deceased one thousand pounds.

He left two servants three years wages in addition to any wages due and divided the residue of his estate between his two unmarried nieces, who did not long survive him.[5]

*

The newspapers had reported that the other seaman of the family, Captain George Anson Byron, the new (seventh) Baron, was ill at Bath when the poet's coffin was lowered into the vault at Hucknall Torkard. Ostensibly he was too ill to attend the funeral. Actually he was sulking and bitterly hurt because he had just discovered that he had inherited the family title with neither lands nor money to maintain it.

Although he had formerly been on friendly, but never close, terms with his cousin and before the poet's marriage may well have had good reason to suppose that either land or money would come to him as heir-at-law, their relationship had been permanently ruptured after the separation, when he had sided with Lady Byron's faction. The poet had made his last will, which excluded his cousin, in 1815, with Lady Byron's full knowledge and consent, but she had never told Captain Byron of its contents. His behaviour during the separation, when he had gratuitously volunteered to testify about the sixth Baron's impossible conduct as a husband, had elicited some scathing comments from the late Lord Byron, once he understood his cousin's role in the affair. But if the poet had no sons, then of course George Anson Byron would inherit his title and accordingly he did all he could to prevent a reconciliation. Nevertheless, his resentment at being cut out was extreme, and he and his wife lost no time in conveying their feelings to their dear friend:

> My dearest Annabella:
> The more we consider the most prominent subject in your letter the more we are convinced of the truth of that dreadful history connected

[219]

with it. It was a fact unknown to George that the will was made at so early a period after the marriage, which disproves most effectually the possibility of the disposition of the property being made under feelings of resentment towards him—Though he was ignorant of this circumstance, I can confidently assure you he has always expressed his belief, that Ld B. was entirely influenced by the power of a stronger tie than that of animosity towards him.... He cannot see without pain the various newspaper paragraphs though they are so little worthy of attention, and he did notice the one to which you allude.... He is anxious to add a few lines himself....

My Dearest Lady N B
   I have just come in from my ride which I intend to take daily and I hope will do me good, respecting the will the very thought of it is painful[.] What Mary has said about it is too true, but I will leave the subject till we meet which I think will be in a fortnight from this time....

He added that they were letting their house unfurnished and therefore 'our packing troubles commence from this day' and he mentioned insurance matters he had been discussing with the ubiquitous Dr Lushington.[6]

When Lady Byron allowed them the income from her marriage jointure their gratitude and affection naturally increased. They supported her in everything, including her persecution of Augusta Leigh, and Captain Byron carried his appreciation to vigorous lengths.

The new Baron was a year younger than his predecessor; he was born at Bath on 8 March 1789, only son of Captain George Anson Byron (grandson of the fourth Lord) and Charlotte Henrietta, daughter of Robert Dallas of Jamaica. He was therefore the grandson of Admiral John Byron and cousin to the other Admiral, Richard Byron. His early life had been difficult and lonely since the premature death of his parents: his mother had died in Bath on 26 February 1793, at the early age of 29, and his father had then taken the two children—the youngest, Julia, was one or two—to Dawlish, where he died shortly thereafter. A stone at the entrance to Dawlish church recorded the dates of their birth and death.[7] Consequently he and his sister were brought up by relations, including their dissolute Aunt Fanny, and if in his insecurity he developed an inordinate need for family support and affection, then his profound chagrin on discovering that he had inherited only a title from the cousin who failed to be 'influenced by the power of a stronger tie than that of animosity' becomes more comprehensible. He had become a midshipman when only 11 years old, joining the *Hindostan* as a volunteer in December, 1800. Thereafter he sailed as a midshipman aboard the *Tremendous* (74 guns) in March of 1801, under the command of Captain John Osborn and bound for the East Indies. He served thereafter on a succession of ships and enjoyed sea life, writing to James Sykes from Madras some time in 1803 that having lately been very unfortunate in a gale of wind and having lost most of his 'cloaths' he had been obliged 'to draw on you for £15' and adding, 'Capt Francis shows me a great deal of attention and I am very happy.'[8] He returned to England in the frigate *Concorde* and obtained his first commission 24 August 1807. In January of 1808 he joined the *Tartar* (32 guns). His cousin, Captain George Byron Bettesworth, was in joint command. On the following 15 May a Norwegian armed schooner and five gunboats attacked, killed Bettesworth and severely damaged the ship. After this exciting action, Byron served in the flagship *Barfleur* (98 guns) on the Lisbon station before being appointed in 1813 as Commander of the *Woodlark* and the *Penguin* on the Baltic and Channel stations.

He became a Captain 7 June 1814 and in that same year stayed with his cousins the poet and Augusta Leigh at Hastings, when they discussed whether Lord Byron should renew his proposal of marriage to Annabella Milbanke. Much later he told Annabella that Augusta had persuaded her brother to do so.[9] He had borrowed money from his cousin, as we have seen, and he stayed with him again in 1816 during the separation, when he courted Elizabeth Mary, daughter of Sacheverell Chandos-Pole, of Radborne, Derby. The nerve-wracked Augusta tried to distract her brother from drinking by getting him interested in George Byron's court-ship; but the poet was so drunk that he fell on his face and could be heard talking loudly from the very top of the house when Captain Byron went to 'pop' the question to Miss Chandos-Pole. He was very nervous, but to his joy she accepted him. His prospective mother-in-law's rigorous opposition dejected him, as Augusta wrote to Annabella:

> Poor G.B. is in sad consternation, tribulation, &c at Mrs. *Fool's* objections, which only regard his want of *monies*. She wants them to have £600 a yr. more! & to wait a year or 3 years in hopes I suppose of finding a *mine*—& he swears he won't wait—& the young lady that she will never marry another—& so on, quite en regle—but worst of all they want to see ME! to talk it over. . . . GB. still wishes to know if *Bosworth House* [in Leicester] is vacant—will you enquire for him without saying exactly *why*. B. is in a fuss about it all & I rather like his having such a subject to fuss upon.[10]

That evening she added that Byron and George Byron had gone to the play. Lord Byron was behaving erratically and Augusta reported that on his birthday he had been 'savage' (22 January). Three nights later Lord Byron and John Hobhouse went to the Royal Society and Annabella had an evening with George Byron and the Poles, when they discussed the various marital problems assailing the family. On 24 January George spoke to his cousin 'very sensibly & seriously' about what he was bringing on himself; and on 31 January he reported to Annabella that Byron was disposed to a separation. Later he informed Mrs Clermont, Annabella's messenger, that had he known Annabella before her marriage he would have tried to save her from it, knowing his cousin unfit for domestic life.[11] He was, in short, as obstructive, unhelpful and treacherous as possible and, his own approaching marriage being temporarily obstructed by financial difficulties, tried hard to prevent any reconciliation so much at variance with his own interests. Although he had allied himself with Lady Byron, his cousin still wrote genially about him on 1 March 1816:

> G[eorge] Byron is about to be married—I wish him as much luck & as little law as possible—the Lady is said to be a distant relative of the Noels—she is pretty—& agreeable—& I think they have a very good chance of going on very well.

Despite the tension and misery of the separation and the upheaval in the Piccadilly household George Byron persevered: he and Elizabeth Mary were married in St George's, Hanover Square, on 18 March 1816. They were to enjoy a very long and happy married life and had nine children. Their first, Mary Anne, born 20 March 1817 and baptised at Marylebone Parish Church, was married while still a minor to John Blenkinsopp Coulson, of Northumberland, on 4 June 1834, in the same church as her parents. Her father gave his consent and among the witnesses was his sister Julia, aunt of the bride, who had married the Reverend Robert Heath. Mary Anne herself became the mother of five sons, the youngest of whom became a distinguished actor.

George and Elizabeth Mary's second child, born the following year (30 June 1818) in Cheltenham, was George Anson Byron, who eventually inherited the title. Their second son, Francis, born 30 March 1820 and baptised at Botley, Hampshire, died the following October and was buried at Bishopstoke on the 31st. They were more fortunate in their third son, Frederick, born 3 February 1822, baptised at St James's Church, Bath, on 6 March. He eventually became a barrister. Their second daughter, Georgiana, was born 27 April 1824 at Bath, and baptised at Walcot Church.

By that time George had not had any active command for years, but he was still interested in the navy and on 1 May 1824 had been looking at the North Pole ships with his friend Captain Parry, who was preparing a Polar expedition.[12] News of the poet's death at Missolonghi on 19 April reached England on 14 May, and on 5 June the new Lord

Byron learned that he had been appointed to the command of the *Blonde* (42 guns). Four days later he was drafting a letter to the Lord Chancellor, claiming his title with accompanying documents and pedigree; he explained that he could not come in person because his frigate was sailing 'long before the next session of Parliament. I am therefore anxious to take my seat before the present session expires'.[13]

The news of his cousin's will caused him to take a strong turn against Augusta Leigh and on the day of his cousin's funeral he wrote bitterly to Annabella, 'our feelings cannot allow us to receive anything from Augusta'.[14]

Robert Charles Dallas, whose sister had been married to the sixth Lord Byron's uncle (the seventh Baron's father), intended to publish a volume of the late Lord Byron's correspondence with his mother, but John Hobhouse, the executor, encouraged and supported by Augusta Leigh, had successfully obtained an injunction on 7 July to prevent its publication. Thereupon the author's son, the Reverend Alexander Dallas, successfully persuaded Captain Lord Byron to write an affidavit stating that although he had formerly been reluctant to approve the publication without previous examination by relatives and friends, he had now read the book and was content for it to be issued without that precaution. According to Doris Langley Moore,

> There were few things in Augusta's whole life, full of calamities though it was, that hurt her more than this contemptuous slight from George Anson Byron, whom she had loved with an unswerving loyalty, and had looked on as her intimate friend. Moreover, he was without the right to make such pronouncements: he had inherited nothing from her brother but his title, whereas she was not only of nearer consanguinity but the chosen recipient of his property.
>
> These, if she had only known it, were precisely the reasons why her cousin took pleasure in the opportunity of annoying her. Lady Byron did not like Augusta to have intimate friends, and in every instance where the occasion was granted her, she managed to find some excuse for bestowing, in whole or in part, those confidences which never failed to leave her audience agape with wonder at her magnanimity and Augusta's wickedness.[15]

Barred from publishing in England, Dallas brought his book out in Paris, first in French and then an English translation. The letters included some slighting references to Hobhouse that Byron had made many years before. Its publication effectively ended the friendship between George Anson Byron and Augusta Leigh, who wrote angrily to Annabella:

> What business had Mr Dallas to publish letters of the *late* Lord Byron's? (omitting all that relates to the *Manner* in which he wd have done it)—and

what right had the *present* Lord Byron to Sanction such a publication which he did in the original Book—which original Book I have read, NOW published in French. . . . The *least* that can be said of G B's upholding his Uncle in such a measure was that he was weak & good natured enough to wish to put a little Money in his pocket—& considering that Uncle's past obligations to my Brother, I think he might have had the *delicacy* to have *tried* at least to have prevented his adding to those obligations by such VERY *indelicate* & improper means—to have *protested against* it, if he could have done nothing more effective.[16]

George Anson Byron could not carry on the argument with Augusta because he had gone to sea again. The King and Queen of the Sandwich Islands (Hawaii), who had created something of a social sensation on their London visit to their 'great and good friend' King George IV, were unfortunately not immune from European disease and they had both died of measles. The British government ordered that their bodies be returned in the frigate *Blonde*, which lay at Woolwich on 8 September. On 28 September the King's native suite went aboard at Spithead and they sailed the following day. The ship's company included James Macrae, a young botanist sent by the British Horticultural Society, who kept a useful diary of the voyage; two nephews of Sir Thomas Lawrence, the painter—Andrew Bloxham, who also kept a diary, and his brother, a clergyman; Robert Dampier, an artist and craftsman whose journal was illustrated with many sketches. Lord Byron was charged to establish friendly relations with the Sandwich Islands and to investigate any foreign influences. As Lord Colchester wrote to Lord Amherst:

> . . . Captain Lord Byron has sailed in the 'Blonde' with the mortal remains of their Majesties the King and Queen of the Sandwich Islands, to be deposited in their native country. From the learned I have heard that a considerable trade is carrying on, and may be increased in British Ships from Europe to the Pacific, where our Sandwich friends may do us much service, and save the Americans the trouble of selling them their wares at higher prices.[17]

The *Blonde* touched at Madeira, which they left on 23 October. The ship's band, officers and crew, put on a show, parading about as gods and goddesses of the sea, and addressing the Captain:

> Neptune's brave sons shall never fear,
> Shall never shed a coward's tear,
> But pass their days, most noble Byron,
> In ships of oak with hearts of Iron.
> Then shall old England's fame be spread
> And Neptune's sons from shore to shore
> Shall raise an universal dread
> Till time and England be no more.[18]

Byron showed his 'phantasmagoria' or magic lantern to the Islanders, who were excited about the special effect and 'could not imagine how the figures moved and increased and decreased in size so suddenly'.

On 4 February 1825 they anchored in Valparaiso Bay, where one of the King's suite and also a member of the crew, a carpenter, died. Smallpox had developed among the crew and the ship was quarantined and did not leave Valparaiso until 5 March. Weather was fair and on the warm nights, with the moon near full, Byron and several of the officers talked with the Sandwichers at the stern. They discussed the Islands and wondered what their reception there would be.

They had their first sight of them on 3 May and saw surf breaking violently on shore and straw huts looking like haystacks. When they dropped anchor in Hilo Bay they met canoes bearing news of a war at Kauai, where the chiefs refused to accept a governor appointed by the victor. Three days later they landed at Oahu, described by Andrew Bloxham:

> The situation of the town of Honoruru [Honolulu] is pleasant, being built on a low plain at the foot of lofty abrupt hills intersected with numerous dark valleys running across the island in a northeast and southwest direction. The ground is covered with vegetation and the upper parts of the hills abound with trees and shrubs. A large, square, mud-built fort stands at the landing place.[19]

Byron, the natives and the chaplain went ashore to be greeted by Islanders wailing for the dead. The following day James Macrae and most of the principal officers of the ship went ashore as well. They were met by the British Consul and a number of chiefs who escorted them to the house of Kramaku or Kalaimoku, the Regent, also known to the Europeans as 'Billy Pitt'. He was thin, courteous, and lacked one eye. The new young King, aged only 11, sat with his sister on a shabby sofa with large handsome feather plumes behind it. Byron presented him with a complete set of Windsor uniform with solid gold buttons, which the boy tried on at once. Byron then led him to Billy Pitt and, putting his hand on the boy's head, told him to be good, attend well to his studies, and mind all his kind friends the missionaries.

The American mission was staffed by particularly sanctimonious puritans from Boston, among the first of a long line of evangelical zealots who did much to wreck the culture of the natives they were supposed to serve and convert. One of them, the Reverend Charles Samuel Stewart, whose journal abounds in self-conscious pieties, was well-pleased with Lord Byron's condescending gesture and hastened to improve their acquaintance:

[ 225 ]

The easy and unaffected familiarity of Lord Byron, and the interest he manifested in the welfare of our mission, were gratifying beyond expression. I accepted his polite invitation to dine on board the Blonde, and spent several hours in answering his lordship's numerous inquiries respecting our Mission, the former state of the Islands, and their recent improvements. I have rarely spent a few hours more pleasantly in the society of any man. . . . In his person he is tall and slender, fine dark eyes and hair, with strongly marked but open and interesting features, no particular resemblance to his cousin, except in what is usually called a family likeness, unless it may be in the nose, which is of the same style, but not so finely formed as that in engravings of the poet. His eye is inquisitive and penetrating, and shews him to be a man of a decisive and energetic character. In manners he is plain, frank, and cordial; and in conversation perfectly affable and familiar; no affectation of dignity, no hauteur, nothing in looks or expression of countenance, indicative of a trait of character, which, ever since I saw the likeness of the poet, I have best understood by the term, 'Byronic curve of the upper lip'.[20]

Macrae, bored with the preliminary ceremonies, had slipped away to look for plants, but was recalled by Lord Byron and presented to the Regent as the man who had brought plants from the London Horticultural Society. Pitt thanked him and in return gave him permission to collect what native plants he wished, but Byron asked Macrae not to do so until after the funeral.

On 11 May the coffins of the King and Queen were lowered into a launch and 26 minute guns were fired from the ship to be answered by the same number on shore and by a few from an American ship anchored in the harbour. They were taken ashore and placed on two carts covered with tapa (native cloth). Their favourite servants followed in procession and then the marines, with the band playing slow marches. The young King, with Lord Byron on his right, the British Consul on the left, all in full uniform, followed. Next came the lieutenant, gunroom messmates, the king's surviving queens, all in black. Macrae, the botanist, followed with the passengers from the ship. The lower rank natives, sailors and midshipmen brought up the rear.

Byron, who was utterly unlike his predecessor in claiming his prerogatives and his creature comforts, had a handsome wooden house assigned to him, at which the officers refreshed themselves afterwards; the men returned to the harbour. Charles Stewart, the missionary, described the accommodation on the ship:

> The Blonde is a forty-six gun ship, of fine model, and perfectly new, this being her first voyage. Lord Byron's accommodations consist of an after-cabin, fitted up as a reading and sitting room, in which tea is served; a

[ 226 ]

forward or large cabin, used as a breakfast and dining room; and a sleeping and dressing cabin. The whole are substantially and handsomely finished and furnished, particularly the after-cabin. In this there is a beautifully engraved likeness of his majesty George IV from a full-length portrait by Sir Thomas Lawrence; a half-length portrait of the present Lady Byron; and one of the same size of Moore, the poet, who is an intimate friend of the Byron family.

He had the gratification of taking breakfast with Lord Byron, who spoke of his predecessor's latest publications in terms of 'unqualified reprehension'; he also talked of Newstead:

> The extraordinary genius, popularity, and whole character of its late proprietor, has thrown an interest around it that few private mansions can boast; and it will, ever hereafter, be an object of curiosity to the scholar and traveller, if to no others . . . [But Byron's suggestion that he visit the Abbey had little charm because] I am sure the gratification I might receive from treading the halls and cloisters of Newstead would not arise from any feelings of veneration or respect for its former master. I admire the powers and brilliancy of his genius, less than I abhor their later monstrous perversion and prostitution.[21]

After this mutually complacent exchange Byron went riding with Bloxham's brother and got kicked by the horse, an injury which troubled him so much that he later demanded at least 30 natives should carry him in a hammock! But he was well enough on 27 May to present his magic lantern show at the King's hut, when Macrae entered a well deserved rebuke in his journal:

> Lord Byron had a magic lantern show at the king's hut, but owing to the religious fanaticism of the American Methodists, the king was prevented from being present. These missionaries, many of them being but illiterate mechanics, possess what power they please over the credulity of the natives, and have already carried their system of religion too far to be upheld.[22]

On 6 June the marines who had gone ashore to perform exercises for Billy Pitt became too drunk en route through the town to do so, to Byron's disappointment. However, he met with Charlton (the British Consul), two missionaries, and others, to discuss politics. The following day the *Blonde* sailed for Hilo, which they reached on Sunday, 12 June. The botanists were exploring and collecting constantly. Macrae and one party reached the summit of Mauna Kea, which they calculated was 70 miles from Byron's (Heddo) Bay, on 17 June. They estimated its height as about 18,000 feet above sea level (a good guess; it is 13,825 feet). On 27 June, Macrae and a party reached Kilauea Volcano, where

they watched terrific smoke and listened to noise among burning craters
and actually managed to go down among smoking pillars. The next day
they set out at daylight and met on their return journey Lord Byron
with 30 natives, who carried his hammock. Byron, 'in his usual pleasant
manner', told Macrae's group, who were short of provisions, to take
anything they wanted from his carriers as he had plenty.

Byron's party 'camped out' quite comfortably that night: the natives
squatted in groups about the fire and Byron poured tea. They walked
36 miles to the Volcano, which they reached the second day. There they
looked into an immense black gulf at least 8 miles in circumference; a
ledge of lava extended around it. As night came down on them they saw
fires caused by the smaller craters nearby casting out ashes and lava.
Most of the party went down into the main crater with long canes and
poles to test the ground. The black, glossy surface seemed likely to crack
under foot and they could thrust their sticks through apparently
bottomless holes and fissures in this brittle surface. White curling
vapours issued from the summit, but Byron was determined to descend
and the rest of the party followed in some trepidation. Stewart, the
missionary, was deterred from praying to 'Jehovah' in the midst of such
wonderful works by the rising of fumes which drove them all back to the
top. Byron broke off some lava and took it with him. Shortly after their
hasty ascent the whole chasm filled with thick, sulphurous smoke. They
got well clear and went looking for wild strawberries to eat with dinner.

After dinner Bloxham and a colleague walked along the ledge of the
main crater on the north side for more than a mile, picking up various
specimens of sulphur, lava and rock, which Bloxham noted carefully in
his diary. When they regained the brink, loaded with specimens, they
found a comfortable cup of tea awaiting them. The night was particularly clear and beautiful, with a full moon, and Bloxham sat up for
nearly two hours watching the ejection of stones and lava from various
craters through his spy glass. A party of midshipmen arrived the next
day and went into the crater with much excitement and enthusiasm.
Byron's party returned to the *Blonde* on 1 July, some of them very lame.

On 7 July the *Blonde* put off again and sailed back to Honolulu, where
they anchored on the 9th to discover that Billy Pitt had just married a
young woman of 19. He came aboard on 12 July and was shown all over
the ship. Byron humoured him in his request that they make sail and
get out to sea by mustering the hands. They put off and when they
made for land again at 3 p.m. the chiefs went ashore to a salute of 13
guns from the *Blonde*.

After this farewell they weighed anchor and sailed for the western
side of Hawaii, Karakakooa Bay, where James Cook had met his death

on 19 February 1779. They picked up Mr Malden, the surveyor, who had been making observations there, but they stayed to investigate the spot where Cook fell. Byron talked to a chief, Naihe, who as a boy had seen Cook killed. He explained that three boats had been stationed a little way off; they kept firing and 80 natives were killed. Cook's body had been taken into a morai (native hut) where the flesh was cut from the bones and burned. The bones themselves were kept as relics.

The following day (15 July) Byron visited a morai filled with crudely carved wood idols. The late King had been credited with abolishing idol worship and thus most of them were rapidly decaying. Before taking his leave of the place, Byron had a simple monument to Captain Cook erected at the top of the black lava hill where his body had been divided among the chiefs: it was a simple capstan bar from the ship, painted white and fixed on a heap of lava raised by the natives. A small copper plate at the top was inscribed:

IN MEMORY OF CAPTAIN JAMES COOK, R.N.
WHO DISCOVERED THESE ISLANDS
IN THE YEAR OF OUR LORD 1778
THIS HUMBLE MONUMENT IS ERECTED BY HIS FELLOW COUNTRYMEN
IN THE YEAR OF OUR LORD 1825

On 16 July Byron wrote a letter of thanks to the Regent for his courtesies. Two days later the *Blonde* set sail for Tahiti. On the 30th they sighted a long, flat island inhabited only by sea birds and a species of brown, short-tailed rat, but the remains of huts built from coral slabs persuaded them that shipwrecked sailors must once have lived there. They named the place Malden Island, after the ship's surveyor. On 1 August they sighted Starbuck Island and then on 8 August unknown land which Byron decided to investigate. It turned out to be Mauiki (or Mauke), one of the Cook Islands. There friendly natives received their gifts and were shown over the *Blonde*. Bloxham admired the well built houses, including a handsome church, and the cheerful Spanish garb worn by some of the Islanders.

After leaving Mauke they faced unfavourable winds and decided to give up Tahiti and make for Valparaiso instead, which they reached on 6 September and stayed for two weeks. Afterwards they put in at Concepçion, where Bloxham observed that the Araucarian Indians, unconquered by the Spanish, still plundered the seaport and had even carried off nuns from the convent only two years before. The *Blonde* returned to Valparaiso on 14 October and did not put off again until 3 December, when they sailed for Coquimbo; there they stayed until the 12th and then began the homeward voyage. They doubled Cape

Horn on 29 December and rescued survivors of a wrecked ship, the *Frances Mary*, bound for Liverpool from New Brunswick (7 March), before dropping anchor again at Spithead on 15 March 1826.

Byron soon received an angry letter from Augusta Leigh, adjuring him 'for the credit & honour of the name you bear, & the title to which you have succeeded' to remove the stigma cast upon both by the publication of Dallas's book:

> It is almost unnecessary for me to condescend to add that both Mr Alexander Dallas & his Work (including his *amiable* opinions of myself) would have passed unheeded and *unfelt*, but for his so cruelly placing on record, & so artfully endeavouring to incorporate with his own malignant insinuations the approval & sanction of that person, for whom I entertained, and would have wished to continue to entertain, so sincere an affection.[23]

Augusta had no notion, of course, that George Byron knew from Annabella all about the 'malignant insinuations', nor that 'Dearest A.'—so they still addressed each other—was in confidential communication with him. He wrote to Annabella at once, enclosing a copy of Augusta's letter made by his wife. They were soon in perfect accord and he sent Augusta a most contemptuous reply:

> The 'open' & 'honourable' measure which you acknowledge you have taken in the disclosure of your 'altered feelings' towards me which awaited my arrival in Bath, would have met with the indifference your letter deserved but that I consider it right to inform you that I hold myself in no manner responsible for any misunderstanding which may exist between you and an author for whose publications & sentiments I can in nowise be accountable.

Adding that he detected a desire to 'divide that intercourse which has hitherto subsisted between us', he declared (contrary to his earlier affidavit) that he had neither read Dallas's work nor even talked to him after August 1824. He concluded that her bitter feelings could only arise from her imagination; and he adopted Lady Byron's unpleasant tactic of returning her reply unopened.[24]

The *Blonde* was paid off 15 December 1826 and Byron went on half pay in 1832. He became a Lord-in-Waiting to King William IV and an Extra Lord-in-Waiting to Queen Victoria. He advanced automatically in rank, and became a full Admiral in 1862. Secure in the friendship and the money of the dowager Lady Byron, he settled down again to family life—four more children were born to them—and to a career of interfering with and advising friends and relations that has caused one biographer to denominate him an 'inveterate busybody'.[25]

In 1827 Thomas Moore began collecting materials for his life of Byron, which was published in 1830. It remains a standard work for any student of Byron, but was rigidly opposed by the poet's friends and relations, and especially by Augusta and Annabella. Captain Lord Byron certainly did not behave as if he supposed Thomas Moore was the 'intimate family friend'; he called on John Murray to protest against the proposed biography, but that conservative publisher assured him that 'he would have nothing to do with the work if there was one word in it that could give offence or in any way wound the feelings of any individual, more especially yourself',[26] Byron reported to Annabella. To her he stigmatised Moore's book as a 'mass of egotism vanity and vulgarism' and later he went further and wrote to Sir Robert Wilmot Horton: 'I wish Messrs Moore and Murray after all their labour had not been delivered of such a horrible and troublesome monster and that it had been strangled at its birth and I should not have much cared if the parents had not survived their production'.[27]

Obviously his 'usual pleasant manner' was not assumed on all occasions. Queen Victoria herself recalled that

> . . . when she was returning in the State Barge from seeing the Thames Tunnel they were nearly run over by a steamer. What she chiefly remembered about this incident was the curious variety of Lord Byron's oaths as he halloaed from the barge to the steamer.[28]

Towards the end of 1829 George Byron's wife received a call from the Baroness Grey (widow of Lord Grey de Ruthyn who had once leased Newstead Abbey) and her husband, the Reverend and Honourable William Eden, who told her a scandal then rocking Canterbury. Georgiana, oldest daughter of the luckless Augusta Leigh, had been married with her mother's whole-hearted approval to a worthless cousin, Henry Trevanion, and was living with him in Canterbury at Bifrons, a house lent to them by the dowager Lady Byron. In March Augusta sent her second daughter, Elizabeth Medora, to live with the Trevanions and Henry had seduced her (he said they read the Bible together each morning) and she was with child by him. On hearing this Lord Byron consulted with Annabella and they arranged for the Trevanion household to go to Calais, where Medora gave birth to a son in February of the following year. This child was left in the charge of a doctor when they returned to England and apparently died shortly thereafter.

Augusta was told nothing. Medora returned to the flat in St James's Palace, where Trevanion called every day, and predictably became pregnant again in February of 1831. Henry confided the situation to

[ 231 ]

Augusta in a letter which Medora copied out and signed. After fearful scenes between mother and daughter, Augusta agreed (Medora threatening to swallow laudanum) that the three should go to a house they had taken in Colerne, near Bath. Augusta asked Colonel Henry Wyndham, a family friend, to break the news to Colonel Leigh, who had rigorously opposed Georgiana's marriage and refused to attend the wedding. He behaved with rare decision and drove at once down to Colerne, took Medora back to London, and shut her up in a house kept by a Mrs Pullen in Lisson Grove. However Georgiana, who seemed understandably anxious to get rid of her husband, assisted Medora to escape. She eloped with her Henry to Normandy, where they lived together as M. and Mme. Aubin. Their child was born dead. Afterwards Medora tried to enter a Convent, but had to leave it because she was pregnant again. In May of 1834 she gave birth to a daughter, Marie.

Since 1830 Augusta had been estranged from Lady Byron over a dispute about the appointment of a trustee of their joint inheritance from Byron and although in her distress she wrote six times to Annabella in 1835, begging for an interview, she was freezingly rebuffed. The worthless Trevanion had already mortgaged his wife's dowry and now Medora herself tried to raise money by mortgaging a Deed executed by Augusta which appointed £3,000 for Medora and her illegitimate child from the fortune tied up in Byron's marriage settlement. To prevent her daughter from obtaining this deed, Augusta had kept the original and when Medora realised she could not get it from her she turned to Lady Byron, who intervened by taking Medora to live with her and be a 'sister' to Ada. According to Medora:

> At Fontainebleau, where she was detained by illness, she informed me of the cause of the deep interest & affection she felt for me & must ever do for me her husband had been my father. . . .

Medora had hitherto supposed Colonel Leigh was her father, although she says her sister and Trevanion had told her otherwise. Lady Byron discussed the whole matter with George Byron and then wrote to her daughter Ada:

> He told me he had learnt from unquestionable authority that your Cousin Georgiana was most notorious in her proceedings at Bath—not with *one*—but with *any one*—& had a Family of younger years than they ought to be—This will not come as a surprise to those who know her early propensities but think of her having been held up as a Model of Virtue by those who must have had an earlier knowledge of these facts![29]

She referred, of course, to Augusta. It does not speak well for George Anson Byron that he indulged in this scandal-mongering and assisted

Lady Byron so diligently in the subjugation of her sister-in-law.

Annabella involved Medora in litigation against her mother to secure the Deed of Appointment, but Augusta surrendered it just before the hearing in the Court of Chancery. Medora proved such a devious and uncontrollable character that Annabella was only too glad to provide her with an income that would allow her to live in France with two servants. However, her troublesome charge still sent menaces and complaints. Eventually Annabella sent one of her friends, Dr King, to Paris, where Medora was running up bills, to offer her £300 a year on condition that she resign control over herself and her child Marie to Lady Byron. After Medora's refusal the servants went to England to claim overdue wages, followed by Medora herself, who in the end retrieved the deed from the lawyers, Wharton and Ford, borrowed £500 on the security of it, and returned to France. There she subsequently married a French army officer. She died of smallpox in 1849.[30]

Despite George Anson Byron's whole-hearted alliance with Annabella, Augusta, who wrote endless letters on behalf of her impecunious relatives in which she appealed to prospective benefactors by invoking her celebrated brother's name, asked the Prime Minister, Sir Robert Peel, to assist Byron's nephew. Robert Heath, the son of Julia Byron and her husband, the Reverend Robert Heath, held a clerkship in the Customs Office. His father, she explained, had only 'the emolument arising from a small Living' and a pension of £100 from the East India Company, which Mrs Heath received for her father's services. She therefore requested a 'Landing Writership' in the Port of London for Robert, who needed to be near his mother, in delicate health:

> . . . the only possible ground on which I venture to hope you will forgive my presumption & grant my request, is that of the favorable regard, which some circumstances, have led me—(I hope not erroneously) to believe you entertain for the Memory of my Brother, the late Lord Byron.

She received a gratifying reply, dated from Whitehall, 30 October 1842:

> Madam
>
> However numerous and urgent the applications which I have received for appointments to the Offices mentioned in your note—I could not but feel disposed to recognize the claim which you have preferred in favour of a near relation of Lord Byron, in a manner calculated to give additional weight to it.
>
> The only cause of my delay in the acknowledgment of your Letter, has arisen from a wish on my part to make inquiry into the character & qualifications of Mr. Heath.
>
> The satisfaction you will derive from my compliance with your request in favour of Mr. Heath will I am sure be increased by hearing—that the

[ 233 ]

good conduct of Mr. Heath Entirely justifies my preference of him to other competitors for the situation to which he shall be immediately nominated.

In her reply Augusta declared she was deeply gratified by his 'kind recognition of a claim my Brother's Memory gave him to your consideration'.[31]

Augusta herself died 12 October 1851, at St James's Palace. In February of 1853 George Byron told Hobhouse about the dreadful fate of the poet's daughter, who had married Lord King (Earl of Lovelace). A brilliant mathematician, friend of Charles Babbage, she had been drawn into calamitous gambling that obliged her to pawn some family jewels, disasters that George Byron repeated, with advantages:

> Joined by Lord Byron who gave me some lamentable details regarding the last illness & death of Lady Lovelace. She suffered agonies from a cancer & for some time had not been in her right mind—He mentioned what I had heard of her previous folly or rather madness in gambling on the turf—She lost 20000£ & more—and was so much in the power of certain black legs that they use[d] to frequent not only Lord Lovelace's house but his table.
>
> Byron also told me the adventures of Lord Lovelace's eldest son—Lord Ockham who escaped from his ship & went to Liverpool under a feigned name to work his way on board a merchantman to America—The London police were put upon his traces—and, thanks to an honest pot house keeper with whom he lodged at 12 shillings a week he was discovered & taken to his father—a fatality seems to attend the Byron family.[32]

Ada had been buried, at her own request, beside her father in Hucknall Torkard Church. Ockham, her eldest son, who had gone early to sea as a midshipman, eventually achieved his discharge from the navy and ran away to become a labourer. He was very strong and muscular and possessed of radical views about social equality—to the extent of dropping his title and taking up manual labour. But he contracted consumption and died in September 1862.[33] His younger brother, Ralph, who succeeded to the peerage, spent much time and labour vindicating the memory of his grandmother. His sister, Lady Annabella King, likewise brought up to venerate her grandmother, married a handsome flamboyant poet, Wilfrid Scawen Blunt, established a famous Arab stud, and became an accomplished linguist, artist and violinist.[34]

The seventh Baron Byron, always well informed about family affairs, led a more retired life as he aged. Georgiana Sitwell remembered him as a lovable old salt:

Our nearest neighbours and greatest friends were the Byrons, and they were often with us during the twenty-one years of my life spent at Renishaw [near Chesterfield] and in the Highlands. Lord Byron [7th Baron] was the picture of a charming English sailor, his wife a kind, sensible, domestic, motherly woman. She had been as greatly esteemed by Queen Adelaide as he was afterward, when Lord-in-Waiting, by Queen Victoria. At Park Hall they lived a very retired life. She wore printed cotton dresses and close mob-caps, and very neat and fresh she looked in them. Their family were remarkably handsome, and their second son, Frederick, was really beautiful. He had a tall, well-made figure, dark, waving hair, large, blue eyes with black lashes, the bright complexion and open expression of an Englishman with the refined, classical features of a Greek statue.

She adds that Lady Byron's eldest and second daughters both married at 17 and that Lady Byron herself had married at that age, while her mother, Mrs Chandos-Pole, had married at 15 and was a grandmother at 50.[35]

George Byron suffered increasingly from influenza, bronchitis and 'low spirits' as he grew older. He died 2 March 1868 and was buried at Kirkby Mallory. His wife survived him by five years, dying 20 August 1873. Meanwhile the finances of the Byron family which had been so sharply diminished at the poet's death had undergone considerable improvement through the marriage of the seventh Lord's two eldest sons, George and Frederick, to the two eldest daughters of the Rev. William Wescomb of Thrumpton Hall in Nottinghamshire and of Langford Grove in Essex. The third and youngest Miss Wescomb married Lord Frederick FitzRoy. These three young ladies were all the possessors of considerable fortunes inherited from their bachelor uncle Mr John Emerton Wescomb on whose death in 1838 the Thrumpton estate had passed to Miss Lucy Wescomb and the Langford estate to her younger sister, Mary Jane. These marriages reintroduced the Byron family to Nottinghamshire where they had for so long been landowners.

The seventh Lord's eldest son, also called George Anson Byron, succeeded as eighth Lord on the death of his father in 1868. He had been educated at Harrow (1831–34), became an Ensign and subsequently Lieutenant in the Scots Fusiliers (1836), and later a captain in the 19th Foot. He retired from the army in 1843, the year that he was married to Lucy Elizabeth Jane Wescomb at St George's, Hanover Square. There were no children of this marriage and the eighth Lord died at Thrumpton in 1870 after suffering many years of declining health.

The eighth Lord's younger brother, Frederick, who had married the second Wescomb sister, lived for most of his short married life at

Edwinstowe Hall in Nottinghamshire which was leased from Lord Manvers. Frederick, who was as handsome as the poet, was called to and practised at the Bar. His main interest in life was hunting and it was as a result of a fall in the hunting field that he died at the early age of thirty-nine.

Frederick's marriage to Mary Wescomb produced two sons who succeeded in turn as ninth and tenth Lord Byron. George Frederick was only 15 years old when he inherited the title from his uncle, the eighth Lord. He was a notorious spendthrift and was rescued from his many debts by Fanny Lucy Brinckman, a divorcee who married him and paid his expenses until his death on 30 March 1917 (after which she became the wife of Sir Robert Paterson Houston). Like his predecessor he had been educated at Harrow (1870–72) and then gone into the army, becoming a Lieutenant in the 4th Battalion Essex Regiment (Militia), 1881–84. Eveleigh Nash gives us this glimpse of him:

> Byron was very careless about his clothes. He once arranged to dine with me at my club, and did not make his appearance until nearly 9 o'clock. He explained that when he started to dress for dinner he could not find a clean shirt, so he dashed out to see whether any shops were open where he could buy one. They were all closed for the day, but after a long search he found a small haberdasher, who lived over his establishment, and succeeded in attracting his attention by flinging gravel at his sitting-room window. The man was not too pleased at the manner in which he was invited to come down and open his shop, but at last he was persuaded to do so, and Byron turned up in a very stiff shirt that seemed to creak every time he moved.

And an anecdote about Lady Byron who, although not a Byron by blood, seems to have been possessed of the family drive and determination:

> Some years after [her] divorce [from Colonel Theodore Brinckman], the late Lord Byron, a small undistinguished-looking man in contrast to his brother, the present [tenth] peer, got into serious financial trouble through guaranteeing a loan to a lady who promised to introduce him to an American heiress who was coming over to England in search of a husband with a title. 'She will bring you enough money to buy back Newstead Abbey, which should never have gone out of the Byron family,' said the lady, who was the daughter of a well-known diplomatist and politician. The idea appealed to George Byron, and for a time he spent more money than he could afford in taking the lady about. At last, she said to him one day, 'Bankers are very tiresome people, George: I want to raise thirty thousand pounds and they won't let me have it unless I can get someone of good standing to guarantee the amount.' Byron consented to do so and later found himself liable to pay the whole amount. Needless to say the

American heiress was a myth, and the unfortunate man was threatened with bankruptcy proceedings. Lucy Brinckman heard of his trouble, and through a friend suggested that she would marry him, pay his debts, and allow him £300 a year. The marriage took place, and she scrupulously carried out her promises. All this and many other things about herself she told me one day with amazing and uninvited candour, when we were lunching at the Berkeley.[36]

This redoubtable and frank lady, so well suited to be the wife of a Byron, was a keen suffragist, deeply interested in the welfare of women, the author of numerous articles on that and other subjects. During the First World War she was donor and administratrix of a Rest Home for tired nurses. Her recreation was yachting and in 1931 she gave $100,000 for the Schneider Trophy Contest. In 1917 she became a D.B.E., among the first five Dame Commanders.

Her second husband's title passed to his brother, the Reverend Frederick Ernest Charles, tenth Baron. He, like his youngest Wescomb aunt married a FitzRoy, Anna Ismay Ethel, the grand-daughter of the Duke of Grafton. On the death of his mother he had succeeded to the Langford estate, and on the death of his Aunt Lucy, the widow of the eighth Lord, in 1912, he inherited the Thrumpton Estate—his elder brother having been excluded from his Aunt's will due to his financial difficulties. The tenth Lord, known by his third name Charles, had been curate at Royston in Hertfordshire in 1888–89 and was subsequently Rector of his own living at Langford from 1891 until 1914 when he transferred to being Vicar of Thrumpton, also his own living, which he continued to be until 1942. He was much loved and respected by his parishioners who were also his tenants and was long remembered by some of them. Although he took his duties as a clergyman seriously he was also sufficiently worldly to respond sometimes to calls which were not of an ecclesiastical nature. For example, he was particularly fond of taking his guests for picnics in the Peak District of Derbyshire and when on one occasion a Red Letter Saint's Day coincided with a desire for one of these expeditions he gave instructions to the chauffeur to stop at the church on the way through the village, where he alighted and fixed to the door a postcard on which he had written: 'NO CHURCH TODAY – BYRON'.

The tenth Lord had literary aspirations and he counted among his friends who used to visit Thrumpton Sir John Murray, the descendant of the poet's publisher. He was sure that the combination of the names Byron and Murray would prove attractive and he persuaded Murray to publish albeit, at his own expense, a slim allegorical volume entitled 'The Gorge'. In this book the author castigated the deformities of much modern art and took up themes which had been treated very differently by his predecessor the poet in *Heaven and Hell* and *Cain*. He argued that two races, the human and 'soul men' could be identified in the book of Genesis:

> Evidently there are two species, Adamites and sons of God or soul men, living together, intermingling and contracting mixed marriages, just as the Israelites, later on, intermarried with the surrounding heathen; or as Christians and non-Christians, at the present day, live intermingled and are yet spiritually apart; the Christian having eternal life and the non-Christian being simply a human animal without immortality or the life soul

For this book there arose little or no demand and a subsequent novel about Joseph and Potiphar's wife was turned down by John Murray. It was during the tenth Lord's tenure of the title that there fell the centenary of the poet's death. Pressure was brought to bear upon him to visit Greece during the centenary year. He refused to do so. To understand this it has to be remembered that in 1924 the poet's life was not so distant, and to many people still seemed quite scandalous, especially to a clergyman of the Church of England who bore the same name. For the same reason he refused to attend the opening of the Byron family vault at Hucknall on 15 June 1938, although he gave his consent.

The tenth Lord Byron was a man who preferred to live a quiet life in the beautiful houses he had inherited from the Wescomb side of the family and surrounded by the possessions which had come with them. He was sometimes described as a collector, but in fact he bought nothing. However, he also sold almost nothing so that the contents of the houses remained intact until his death in 1949.

The tenth Lord died without children and in his will he left the Thrumpton Estate to his widow, Anna, Lady Byron, for the remainder of her life, with a subsequent life interest to her nephew, George Fitzroy Seymour, and thereafter to the sons of Lt Colonel Richard Geoffrey Byron, now the twelfth Lord. However, heavy death duties had to be paid on both the Thrumpton and Langford Estates, and as a result the trustees sold the Thrumpton Estate which was bought outright by George Seymour, so severing again the link between the Byron family and Nottinghamshire. On the death of her husband Lady Byron went to live at Langford and on her death in 1966 that property passed to Richard Geoffrey Byron.

Meanwhile, on the tenth Lord's death the title had passed to his cousin, Rupert Frederick George Byron, elder son of Wilfred Byron (fourth and youngest son of the seventh Baron) and his wife, Sylvia

Mary, daughter of the Reverend Charles Thomas Moore. The new peer was working on his 1,300-acre sheep farm at Dinninup, 200 miles from Perth, Australia, when he heard the news. A former second-lieutenant in the Leicestershire Yeomanry, he had served as a lieutenant in the Royal Australian Navy corvettes during the Second World War. The *Guardian* reported (9 June) that the new Lady Byron (Pauline, Daughter of T. J. Cornwall) received so many congratulatory messages that she burned the cake and forgot to do the family ironing. He announced that he intended to continue his farming. They had one daughter, Isobel Anne, born 23 May 1932, who married 22 September 1951 Robert Reford Corr; they have three sons.

The new peer's cousin— grand-daughter of the seventh Baron's son, the Reverend Augustus Byron, and his wife, Frederica McMahon— had in the meantime become a Dame at Eton. She captured her experiences there with sparkling Byronic humour in a charming illustrated book, published in 1965. She wrote because no Dame had ever done so and explained that the domestic predominated because 'at the time of writing the providing of an adequate service for the Houses has become something of a nightmare for all Dames'.

The Dames at Eton had evolved from the old landladies who previously provided accommodation for boys. The Misses Angelo (daughters of the poet's fencing master) had undertaken such service and gave their names to a house. They were doubtless better than their predecessors, wicked old women who kept boys short of food and warmth and charged them highly. Since then the responsibilities of Dames had multiplied until they took for their motto: 'There is no accident that a boy cannot have'.

> Today's domestic staff do not take any responsibility that they can possibly shove on to M'Dame, nor do they do any work that they can avoid.

Consequently, the Dame now has to oversee the domestic staff, give out medicines, and organise the catering.

Dame Nora Byron inherited the Byron love for animals, writing very affectionately about Juniper, a large beagle, who became something of a local character. He liked the bookshop, where he studied the backs of books on the lower shelves, attended services in both chapels, and once was just prevented from ascending the pulpit.

She runs through a litany of school life that will go to the heart of any teacher—the epidemics, the occasional floods, the ritual of the house photograph, the new buildings, and the being 'on duty' fourteen hours a day, seven days a week, thirty-nine weeks a year, with thirteen weeks of holiday. She includes the special crises of her time at Eton—the war, hospitals, rationing. And she records some inimitable discussions that can only take place among schoolchildren, such as the following:

> 'What sort of a holiday is it?'
>
> Answer: 'Oh, just a holiday, I don't know why. I expect it is for some saint or other, but I don't know which.'
>
> Question: 'Do we have a holiday for all the saints? Because if so, I must try to learn up something about them, and dig out a few more. It would come in handy if they tried to do us out of a saint in order to give us some more work.'
>
> 'Oh, I shouldn't think they would do that. They'd probably clap two or three saints on to one day, and then have them all on Sundays.'
>
> 'That would be too mean—they wouldn't really do that, would they?'
>
> 'I don't know. You might ask M'Dame.'
>
> 'Yes, she does know about saints. Some are more important than others; I expect we only have a holiday for the important ones. Do we have a holiday for St. Vitus?'
>
> 'Yes, I should think we do. After all, he was made a saint for going to a dance, wasn't he?'
>
> 'No, I don't think that can be right—I mean, why should anyone be made a saint for going to a dance? I think I had better ask M'Tutor.'
>
> 'Oh, no, don't do that, or he'll say that tomorrow, being a holiday, would be a splendid opportunity to get on with our work, or else do a bit of research about saints.'[38]

Dame Nora was indeed a Byron, the inheritor of family traits described many years before by the poet's daughter:

> You know I believe no creature ever could WILL things like a *Byron*. And perhaps that is at the bottom of the genius-like tendencies in my family. We can throw our *whole life* and *existence* for the time being into whatever we *will* to do and accomplish. You know perhaps the family motto, '*Crede Byron*'. I think it is not inappropriate. . . .

# First Nights:
# The Byrons on Stage

I could not resist the *first* night of any thing.'

—Letter to Thomas Moore, 23 April 1815

'I HAVE long stood alone in life,' the poet wrote to Annabella Milbanke (19 September 1814). Despite his strong attachment to Augusta Leigh and his later longing for settled domestic life, the sixth Lord Byron had scant interest in presiding over a family which had showed little consideration for him, and by selling the ancestral lands, despoiled though they were, he presaged the scattering of that family. Obliged to find their own way in the world, the Byrons continued to follow traditional careers and to enter new professions; and the gifts and qualities given in fullest measure to the poet soon reappeared in other branches of the family.

Little is known of Henry Byron, the third and youngest son of the Reverend Richard Byron and Mary Farmer, who was probably born at Ryton in 1775 and matriculated at Emmanuel College (Cambridge) in 1793, when his father was Rector of Haughton-le-Skerne, Durham. After receiving his B.A. (1797) and M.A. (1800), he was ordained a priest at York on 5 July 1801 and then became Vicar of Granby and Sutton (Nottinghamshire) until 1814. He was afterwards Rector of Muston (Leicestershire), but went mad and died in confinement in 1821. By his wife, Margaret, daughter of Thomas Powditch, whom he married 18 June 1803, Henry had five children: Henry (b. 17 April 1804; George (b. 12 August 1805), Elizabeth (b. 1806); Francis (b.1810) and Frances (b. *circa* 1811).

George, who joined the army, was (according to his great-nephew) 'a reckless individual and was killed by being thrown from his buggy or dogcart when driving after a convivial party'.[1] This irresponsible adventurer was survived by one son, George Rochfort Byron, from whom the Rochfort Byrons descended.[2] Elizabeth married George

Rochfort Clarke in 1830 and died 21 March 1852. Frances died unmarried 28 June 1878.

In his unpublished autobiography Henry's grandson, George Frederick Byron, recalled them well, particularly Francis (Uncle Frank) who worked for the Government Treasury Department and frequently stayed at their house at 27, Doughty Street. Frank lived to be 86, dying in 1896. He was a naval artist who lost much of his vision early in life and peered through a magnifying glass to read or to distinguish people's faces:

> He was a beautiful character, and I have always regarded him as the best—in the highest sense—man I have ever known. He was queerish, eccentric and could be easily upset or annoyed, but he never nursed grievances or retained ill temper—was generous, forgiving and full of Christian virtues. . . .
>
> My grandfather's sister Elizabeth . . . was the niece to whom the poet Byron refers in his journal as 'my little cousin E – – –. She will grow up a beauty and a plague; and is in the meantime the prettiest child, dark hair and eyelashes, black and long as the wing of a raven.' She fulfilled his expectations as far as beauty was concerned, creating a great sensation when she appeared at a Court Ball.

George Frederick thought Elizabeth's husband 'tyrannical, domineering, ostentatiously pious, crafty and mean' and a complete ogre to his poor sister-in-law, Frances, who kept house for him after his wife died:

> When his wife was alive, she as his wife was to be bowed down to and her judgements and actions (when the poor woman was allowed to express opinions or act on her own initiative) were to be accepted without question. This naturally restricted the circle of her friends. During those years the younger sister Frances was of no account and not considered in any way, but upon her sister's death she was promoted to the vacant throne and all deference was to be shown her. It was understood, but for the illegality—at that time—G. R. C. would have married her. I believe she became a victim to the taint of insanity which now and again manifests itself in this branch of the family.

Frances, 'a kindly soul whose character had been stunted by the long domination of G. R. C.' loved to distribute dainties to her great-nephews, but her formidable brother-in-law, 'talkative, self-satisfied, narrow-viewed', striding about in black, 'upright, tall, spare, and active in mind and body'—outlived her to be married again to a young servant and left no children.

According to W. Carew Hazlitt's malicious recollections, Henry, the oldest of the five children, became a college man who squandered a fortune; but he remained genial if insincere, his disingenuousness somehow exacerbated by straitened circumstances and a fondness for little dinners 'and other sweet impoverishments'.[3] George Frederick Byron probably had that story from Hazlitt, because he says:

> I have always understood that as a young man Henry Byron was wild and extravagant—ran through several fortunes—though where or how he got them I can't conceive, but as an elder brother and watcher over his younger brothers and sisters—he was everything most desirable—and unexpected.

We may infer from this that Henry, who attained a most respectable career, pursued the usual course of a high spirited and rather thoughtless undergraduate and, that like many Byrons before him, he had got into debt. He certainly inherited much of the family talent and charm: H. P. Grattan remembered him with respect and affection, recalling after nearly fifty years his splendid readings from Shakespeare and other loved poets. As young men in London they had shared the same interests and were so thoroughly stagestruck that they volunteered their histrionic services to the Milton Street Theatre in former Grub Street, which was opening without a full company:

> Our offer was graciously accepted on the Pickwickian terms, that we were to do our level best for the management; with full liberty to find our own dresses and pay our own expenses.
>
> I am free to confess that I felt certain the acceptance of my services was owing to the fact that they were offered conjointly with Byron's, whose address, style, and appearance (he was a tall, well-made, thorough-bred-looking, and very handsome man) at once impressed the management with the conviction, that for the line of business he had selected (light comedy) he would be a really valuable addition to their company.

Grattan envied Byron's self-possession, being himself in a state of fear as he picked his way through the muddy streets to the dirty stage door:

> I had seldom been in front, and never behind the scenes of a theatre before; and they—the scenes—seemed the most execrable daubs that ever not only spoiled, but disgraced canvas; while the well-worn and badly patched green baize and stage-carpet, the tarnished dutch-metalled, faded, red serge-covered, rickety regal chairs, the battered and chipped wooden and tin-gilt flagons and goblets, that adorned the royal tables on the high and festive occasions when honoured courtiers joined in a convivial carouse with their condescending sovereign, looked to me like a collection of rubbish, only fit to be carted without loss of time to the nearest dust-heap.

Byron, taking the stage name of 'Mr. Berkely', assumed the leading rôle in a farce, *Damp Beds*, opposite a Mr Hooper, a typically loud and outré stage-gentleman of the time, who tried 'to ride over the real gentleman, as presented by Mr Byron', whose quiet and unstagey style was admirable to all but the general audience, who thought it too tame. When Hooper stopped at last, complaining that he had not received his proper cue, the curtain fell amid hisses on the unfinished farce. Going behind stage, Grattan found Lyman Rede, one of the joint managers, remonstrating with Hooper and congratulating Byron, whom he shook warmly by the hand, prophesying a stage career for him.[4]

At Rede's request Byron assumed the part of Rakewell, which he played to enthusiastic applause; but his promising theatrical career ended when he married Elizabeth Josephine Bradley, a very attractive woman whose father, Dr James Byron Bradley, had served with distinction in the Peninsular War. Her mother was a daughter of Dr Solomon, once well known for a patent remedy, 'Balm of Gilead'. They were married in St Paul's, Covent Garden, and lived for a while in London, where Henry had secured a position on *The Morning Post* and was secretary to the Conservative Association. Afterwards, however, he obtained a lucrative government post as British Consul in Haiti, where he lived for much of his life.

Henry and Elizabeth's son and only child, Henry James Byron, born 8 January 1835 in Manchester, was sent to school in Essex and then went to St Peter's Collegiate School in Eaton Square, London. When he saw his first pantomime, *The Castle of Otranto*, at Covent Garden, he never forgot the comic effect of a big head—not a mere helmet, but an actual face in profile—which rose slowly, a hand with fingers extended and the thumb placed at the end of the nose—the picture of terror and contempt.[5]

Byron soon began writing. At fourteen he spent two days composing a three-act drama, *The Pride of the Village; or, The Convict's Bride*, which he solemnly offered to a West End theatre and then dreamed for days about the unlimited cheque it might bring him. Eighteen years later he spoke to the manager of that theatre, who produced the very manuscript, thick with dust:

> As I read on every speech brought back the memory of the time I wrote it, and on reading the climax to the second act I experienced the old glow I had felt when putting the 'sensation' upon paper. What trash it all was to be sure![6]

His ardent love for the theatre obviously demanded expression, but respectable parents rarely favour the stage for their sons and Byron's were considering the Navy. However, although Augusta Leigh obligingly offered to get him a cadetship, they refused at the last moment—

George Gordon, 6th Lord Byron, the poet, by Thomas Phillips, 1813.

George Gordon, 6th Lord Byron. Statue in Trinity College Library, Cambridge.
'I twine my hopes of being remembered in my line with my land's language'.

George Anson, 7th Lord Byron. A sailor, like his father, he served under Captain Bettesworth and later escorted the bodies of the King and Queen of Hawaii to their kingdom.

Elizabeth Mary, wife of 7th Lord Byron. 'A kind, sensible, domestic, motherly woman'.

Admiral Richard Byron.

The Rev. Frederick Ernest Charles, 10th Lord Byron.

'Inn Yard at Calais', by Frederick Byron. Reproduced by permission of the British Museum from a fine series of coloured aquatints rich in the humour of travel.

Henry James Byron, dramatist and actor. Reproduced from *The Theatre*,
1 October, 1878 by permission of The British Library.

Cartoon of Henry James Byron, *The Entr'acte*, 9 September, 1876. Reproduced by courtesy of the New York Public Library Theatre Collection. A prolific author, Byron wrote many burlesques and farces.

Harry Conway (H. Blenkinsopp Coulson), actor. Reproduced from *The Theatre*, 1 March, 1884 by permission of The British Library. 'Conway created a sensation in the 'eighties almost equal to that made by the more famous beauty, Lillie Langtry.'

George Frederick Byron, youngest son of the dramatist. He wrote an autobiography in his old age which evokes his father and their family life.

*Photograph courtesy Mrs Joy E. Byron*

Charles Hubert Byron, grandson of the dramatist. A charming, commanding personality with the family talent for conversation and letter-writing.

*Photograph courtesy of Mrs Joy E. Byron*

Mrs Joy E. Byron, wife of Charles Hubert Byron. A journalist and author.

*Photograph courtesy Lady Byron*

Rupert Frederick George, 11th Lord Byron.

Major General John Byron, by S. Hodges, RA.

Richard Geoffrey Gordon, 12th Lord Byron, outside Newstead Abbey.

*Photograph courtesy 12th Lord Byron*

The Hon. Richard Byron.

Colonel Richard Byron.

Lt-Colonel Richard Geoffrey Gordon Byron, DSO (later 12th Lord Byron).

The Hon. Robin Byron, and family.

understandably, since he was their only son and a sailor's life rough and dangerous—and sent him to a tutor in the country, instead. Subsequently he was articled to Miles Marley, a surgeon living in Cork Street, Burlington Gardens. Later he studied in Buxton with his grandfather, Dr Bradley, and at some unspecified time he had his first play, *The Boots at the George*, brought out at the Little Buxton Theatre. He so loathed surgery and post-mortem examinations that he decided to become an actor and embarked on a tour.

Any illusions the eighteen-year-old novice entertained were rapidly dissipated in the provinces. The life was neither glamorous nor easy. Byron always remembered the ugly front of Covent Garden Theatre and the Garrick's Head, where John Lee, Edmund Kean's secretary, had started a theatrical agency. Hiring was frequently done through such agents, who demanded a fee. To find engagements, leading ladies walked through dingy coffee rooms of public houses to see the 'agent'— usually in the public bar—but, disagreeable as this was, the novice at least gained experience.

Byron was engaged to play first at Colchester and then travelled with a touring company, often playing eighteen parts a week, singing songs between the acts, sometimes unsure of even half his salary. He recalled those provincial hardships with a shudder. But although he had gained essential experience by the time he returned to London, his first venture there, a 'monologue' at a vacant Marionette theatre, announced as *A Bottle of Champagne, Uncorked by Horace Plastic*, was absurdly unrealistic.[7]

The discouraged playwright entered the Middle Temple to become a barrister, but his original interest never flagged. In 1857 his burlesque *Richard Coeur de Lion*, was produced at the Strand Theatre, then under J. H. Payne's management:

> I wrote an exceedingly bad burlesque, which was abominably performed to small but discriminating audiences at a London theatre, which was then under a cloud. The piece was written for a joke, and sent in to the theatre as a joke, and it was not until the manager produced it, and it was performed, that the seriousness of the joke was made manifest. . . . Someone, however, said it showed symptoms of a latent dramatic something or other, and before I was well aware of what I was about, I found myself writing pieces for two or three theatres at once.[8]

When Ada Swanborough, well known in the theatre, leased the Strand, he offered her another piece, *Fra Diavolo*, produced in 1858. Its success established his reputation. Later that year Charles Dickens saw Byron's Christmas burlesque and wrote to John Forster about it on 17 December:

> There is the strangest thing in it that ever I have seen on the stage. The boy, Pippo, by Miss Wilton. While it is astonishingly impudent (must be,

or it couldn't be done at all), it is so stupendously like a boy, and unlike a woman, that it is perfectly free from offence.⁹

Byron's career was now well launched and he went on to write a burlesque of his famous kinsman's poem, *Mazeppa*, and 'A New and Original Burlesque Extravaganza', *Babes in the Wood*, first performed at the New Adelphi on 18 July 1859. He became a prolific but hard-pressed hack writer, too busy and too dependent on his pen to make innovations, relying on stock plots, stylised characters, and intricate, even tortuous, verbal pleasantries. He so thoroughly understood the theatre of his day that he made a good living in it for twenty-five years, only to be forgotten when that dramatic world passed away.

At his death Byron left more than a hundred dramatic works, published and unpublished, an extraordinary achievement, considering that he sometimes collaborated with other writers, that he acted frequently himself, undertook several risky managements, and wrote numerous articles and two novels. Perhaps family responsibilities and troubles spurred this amazing activity and kept him on the move in every way. Byron was so restless that he walked up and down a room in conversation. He went from house to house, from town to town, often working on three commissions at once during his ephemerally successful career. Yet despite all this activity he was, in his own words, 'a terrible home-bird and a horrible sailor' and refused all offers to go to America.¹⁰

His family moved frequently, accommodating itself to the vagaries of Byron's Bohemian life. He met his wife, Martha Foulkes, daughter of John Foulkes, of Ashfield, at Buxton, and they were probably married in 1857, on his return from the provinces. By 1860 they already had two children—Alfred, born in 1858, and John, who arrived the following year. Inevitably the family faced frequent financial difficulties and although Mrs Byron, a warm, affectionate, shy woman, was deeply in love with her handsome, energetic husband, his unsettled habits and, inevitably, his involvement with women of the theatre, strained their marriage.

Byron was now much in demand for dramatic pieces and had been invited to collaborate with James R. Planché, a popular writer of burlesque. He worked ceaselessly and zealously from this time, increasing his output every year until illness weakened and overcame him. His occasional sketch, *The Garibaldi Excursionists*, featuring a ballet company at the Princess's Theatre in November of 1860, was immediately followed by another Christmas pantomime, *Blue Beard from a New Point of Hue*, at the Adelphi, starring a rising comedian, J. L. Toole, for whom Byron later wrote comedy parts: he looked 'half modern swell, half oriental tyrant' in wiry military whiskers rather than the conventional blue beard. A transformation scene of gorgeous lights and transparencies concluded the extravaganza.[11] One of Byron's best pieces, which has enjoyed a long life, was his pantomime version of *Aladdin*, for which he created Widow Twankay-Jones. James Rogers took this rôle and Marie Wilton was Aladdin in its first performance at the Strand on Easter Monday (1 April) 1861. On 3 January 1970 *The Spectator*'s Hilary Spurling reviewed a revival at the Players' Theatre (under the arches in Victoria) thus:

> This year the pantomine is *Aladdin* by Henry James Byron, wit, punster and descendant of the poet with, according to Marie Wilton, 'a marked inheritance of the beauty of his gifted kinsman'. Miss Wilton—who was the admired of all beholders, from Charles Dickens to the future laureate (While Saucy Wilton winks her wicked way/ And says the more, the less she has to say'), Alfred Austen, or W. S. Gilbert—created the part of Aladdin Twankey-Jones at the Strand around a hundred years ago; and the play, with its curious scenes in Pekin and Egypt or down a Welsh pitshaft, is as captivating today as it must have been when its genies first amazed the town by travelling 'At a hundred miles or over/ Or faster than the London-Chatham-Dover'.

1861 indeed proved fertile for Byron: he edited *Fun*, a comic newspaper he founded with F. C. Burnand, another celebrated and prolific writer of burlesque; and he encouraged the hopeful W. S. Gilbert, whose 'Bab Ballads' first appeared in that paper. Gilbert remembered turning out an article and a half-page drawing with incredible labour, only to be staggered by a message from the printer, who presented Byron's compliments and asked Gilbert for a column of copy and a half-page drawing every week. Convinced that he had exhausted himself, Gilbert nevertheless responded. He was 'paid, and paid well' for every verse and he preserved a grateful, uncritical admiration for Byron's works. The 'Bab Ballads', issued as a book in 1869, established Gilbert's literary reputation, while his connection with *Fun* led directly to his appointment as critic for *The Illustrated Times*.[12]

Byron and his friend Tom Robertson joined 'The Serious Family', a Bohemian group of dramatic critics and journalists who met weekly at his chambers in Gray's Inn. Gilbert was excused the two-guinea subscription in return for supplying pie, beef, Stilton cheese, whisky-and-soda and bottled ale every Saturday night. These enchanted evenings owed much to Byron's charm.[13] Byron likewise belonged to the Savage Club, an organisation of writers and actors who frequently raised funds for charity, and to its offshoot, the Arundel Club, a delightfully

Bohemian institution which he thoroughly loved, resisting efforts to turn it into a dignified London club. He was often at the house of the comedian Charles Mathews in Pelham Crescent, where James R. Planché, a little old man with simian countenance, still cracked jokes; and there the delivery of Byron's pleasantries and puns gained a charm from his tone and manner which evaporates in print.

1861 also saw the development of Byron's talent in another direction: he wrote a novel for *Temple Bar* magazine, *Paid in Full*, which eventually went through three editions, published in three volumes by Maxwell. Based on his experiences as a medical student it retains some interest, but Byron's style was laboured and his greatest defects—structural faults, reliance on incident and stock characters—marred his prose as well as his drama. He wrote another novel, *A Bad Debt*, apparently unpublished.

Continuously writing burlesques and extravaganzas, mostly for the Strand, Byron nevertheless found time to start his own newspaper in 1863, *The Comic News*, which he launched with an optimistic editorial on 18 July:

> We think there is an opening for us, and we have commenced by getting together the best band of literary and artistic humourists procurable for love or money. We have thought it better to give our purchasers a few good pictures rather than a quantity of hastily drawn and poorly-engraved blocks, or worse still those cheaply obtained amateur productions which are certain to turn out very dear in the end, and while the barb of humour will never be tinctured with the poison of personal abuse, we shall not shrink from exposing shams or from levelling well-directed darts at the follies and humbugs of the age.

In its issue for 24 October *The Comic News* castigated an elaborate production of Lord Byron's *Manfred* at Drury Lane Theatre, starring the respected Shakespearean actor, Samuel Phelps:

> Really, to produce a dramatic poem, written expressly *not* to be performed, appears a strange, not to say an obstinate, act on the part of a manager. No one would deny the wild intense beauty of the dialogue of *Manfred*, in which the 'earthiness' of the poet's stock misanthrope is less evident than in any other of his works, but the very absence of that mundane interest surrounding the broken-hearted heroes in which Byron delighted, renders *Manfred* unfit for the stage. Those critics who prate about the legitimate drama being upheld by the production of an undramatic poem—undramatic in the stage sense—talk nonsense.
>
> *Manfred* does not belong to the legitimate acting drama of England. To attempt to bolster it up by fine scenery, singing, and ballet dancing, is an insult to the poet's memory. . . . With so popular an actor as Mr. Phelps

at the head of an excellent working company, surely the managers can give us some plays written to be acted, and avoid those which were written *not* to be so.[14]

In December the *News* reported that Richard Sothern (Lord Dundreary) was about to appear at Liverpool in a new one-act drama written for him by Mr Byron, and this Christmas Box double number ran several special features by other well-known writers, including verses from Charles Mathews, the comedian, and from Thomas Hood. Byron himself contributed a rather melancholy little piece, 'Christmas Day in a Chop House'; but despite its distinguished contributors *The Comic News* was unable to compete with *Punch* (started by Mark Lemon in 1841) and it folded the following year.

In 1865 Byron went into partnership with the charming Marie Wilton. A leading attraction at the Haymarket, Adelphi and St James's theatres, she was largely responsible for the success of the little Strand and she displayed characteristic acumen and confidence in borrowing a thousand pounds and assuming management, with Byron, of the Queen's, a small, deteriorated theatre in Tottenham Court Road, known with more candour than charity as the 'dramatic dusthole'. They made it the 'Gold-dust hole'. She took the financial risk while Byron, always impecunious, agreed to write exclusively for her. Marie Wilton saw her re-named Prince of Wales Theatre enjoy many successes. Tom Robertson, the playwright, and John Hare, the comedian, were two of Byron and Marie Wilton's discoveries.

A number of Byron burlesques had been performed in Liverpool and by the end of 1866 he had assumed management of the Theatre Royal there. Barry Sullivan was the leading tragic actor; his Christmas pantomime was *Little Dick Whittington, Thrice Lord Mayor of London; or, Harlequin Hot Pot and the Fairies of the Elfin Grot.* Soon afterwards Byron leased the Royal Alexandra Theatre, where the acting managers staged spectacular Shakespearean revivals and opulent productions of two poetic dramas by Lord Byron which, although attractive, cannot have pleased the aesthetic sensibilities of the official lessee![15]

Byron took a house at 21 Huskisson Street in Liverpool, leaving his family and his theatrical obligations in London for much of the time; but he was still bound to write for Marie Wilton, who had given up playing burlesque, and on 5 May 1866 his original comedy, *A Hundred Thousand Pounds*, was first acted at the Prince of Wales. His co-manager was less than pleased with it, aptly criticising its construction; she thought the first act so complete and clever that the rest seemed weak. The burlesque he wrote for her theatre, *Der Freischütz* (10 October

1866), ridiculing Weber's famous musical melodrama, was likewise unsatisfactory. As for *Pandora's Box; or, the Young Spark and the Old Flame, a Mythological Extravaganza* (26 December 1866), it never, she said, burned brightly, and she told him so with characteristic frankness. Byron, for his part, considered she wronged him by refusing to play in burlesque—he was best when writing for a particular performer—but after a candid correspondence they parted amicably and remained good friends. Byron was soon to abandon burlesque himself. In 1872 he wrote:

> I never intend doing another Burlesque—the game doesn't pay for the candle. With the [exception] of some four five or six the burlesque artistes are mere gabblers or can do nothing but dance themselves breathless. This is altogether different to the old days and the public are finding it out.[16]

In Liverpool his professional life began to go very wrong. He was lessee of the Theatre Royal and then took over the Royal Alexandra Theatre from Alexander Henderson, to which he added the Royal Ampitheatre (later the Court) in May of 1867 on the death of its manager, W. R. Copeland. Theatrically, this period proved significant for him, especially his sensational but realistic drama, *The Lancashire Lass*, which depicted a real ferry steamer, one of those numberless special effects so dear to Victorian theatregoers. Henry Irving as Robert Redburn, the conventional adventurer, caught the attention of Charles Dickens in the London performance: 'and if that young man does not one day come out as a great actor, I know nothing of art,' Dickens declared. But financially the Liverpool venture ruined Byron and he went bankrupt, losing approximately £120,000. After relinquishing management of the Ampitheatre to one of Copeland's daughters, he announced from its stage that he would repay everything he owed their family, a promise he faithfully kept, at great sacrifice.

Byron's personal life, too, was going wrong. His daughter, Elizabeth, was born in 1861 and his youngest son, George Frederick, in 1862. A family of four was considered small, but no more followed. After Byron went to live in Liverpool he and his wife agreed, despite their happy years together, to live apart. He was often and inevitably absent and had other women in his life; but Mrs Byron refused all advice to divorce him, hoping he would return to her. He never did.

The Liverpool débâcle meant a straitning of the family finances. The children grew up in the London Doughty Street house until 1868, largely under the care of servants, some of them remarkably slatternly. Most vivid in George Frederick Byron's memory were the cook, a full bodied woman of 40, greasy faced, untidy, always at work at high speed, almost unintelligible in her low-class cockney speech, unable to read or write or I suspect count above her ten fingers, but I believe she was a splendid cook and adored in a dumb almost animal manner her master and mistress, and in a decidedly lesser degree their troublesome children,

and Maria, the nurse, a thin woman whose expressionless face was marked with smallpox. She had a 'bilious temper' and instilled into the children respect for herself, for parents, and (in a lesser degree) God,

who had a rather spiteful eye on erring children, and whose decisions, rebukes and punishments were administered by his officers, the Sweep and the bogeyman who lived in a nursery cupboard, and with whom Maria had peculiar influence. Maria had the help of an under nurse Sarah, a young girl either from the workhouse or the adjacent Foundling Hospital, a kindly savage, quite ignorant, but clean, honest, loutish and quite incompetent.

Sundays were 'horribly sacred': no toys, and no amusing books; but whenever a gory crime was reported, Maria read the newspaper or the kitchen copy of the *Police News* to the other servants. George Frederick sat in a corner pretending to read a picture book showing Christ in the middle of little children, but really straining to hear the details of a choice throat-cutting read with excruciating mis-pronunciation, since Maria understood only half the words. When she caught him listening she swiftly warned the small child that 'God would be very angry with little boys who listened when they ought not'.

It was not a religious household, but the servants went regularly to gloomy church services—probably to escape domestic drudgery for a time—and sometimes the children attended them too at the Children's Hospital and afterwards watched the occupants eating their Sunday dinner—

which was a very usual procedure of the congregation who bathed a while in self-satisfaction at the evidence of their vicarious charity in feeding the hungry and were able to go empty away with an appetite nicely tuned up for over-feeding at their home tables.

His parents were irregular in church attendance; and he remembered church as 'dismal, ugly, stuffy' and preachers as 'ugly and frightening'.

To the pale, sensitive boy Doughty Street itself seemed gloomy and despondent. The typical Victorian town house was crammed with heavy furniture, flocked (velvety) wallpaper, and thick carpets; its dismal atmosphere was deepened by the heavy curtains and the wire screens covering the lower windows to obstruct the gaze of curious passers-by. George Frederick particularly remembered the dining room, with its huge sideboard and heavy mahogany furniture, because brighter scenes were enjoyed there.

Henry J. Byron inherited all the family charm and good looks. He was an excellent host and sometimes his children joined the adults at his convivial parties. His young son always remembered how, hastily tidied up by the nurse Maria, he was propelled into the dining room:

> A table crowded with glasses, decanters, and dishes filled with bright coloured fruits and ornamented with silver bowls containing flowers, and surrounded by smiling ladies and nut and joke-cracking gentlemen. A rich aroma of food pervaded the room and the meal had reached that stage when orange peel, grape skins, and nutshells overspilled the plates, the wine circulated freely, and far from silent gentlemen dallied with the cruet. Laughter rippled or roared, talk was loud, chairs were irregular, the men's shirt fronts had lost their stiffness and bulged comfortably with food and satisfaction.

Such recollections brought his father back vividly:

> My father was a tall and well built man, with dark hair and eyes and wore a full moustache and sometimes an eyeglass. He was a brilliant talker and was known as one of the wittiest men of his time as well as one of the handsomest. His eyes sparkled with mirth and his laughter was hearty and infectious. . . . He had the kindest of eyes and long beautifully shaped hands and a voice of great charm and expression. I have been told that he would have made an admirable doctor, but he admitted that he could not stomach the anatomical & post mortem studies and surgery did not attract him.
>
> He was a delightful host, I have heard, from those who recalled the happy times they had enjoyed at my father and mother's hospitable board in the old Doughty Street days. My mother, who was then in the early thirties, was of medium height but inclined to stoutness, with a fair round face and hair of a brown-gold colour which she wore in the fashion of those times parted in the middle and rippling to the sides very prettily. She had large blue eyes suggesting not too strong a heart (she died of heart disease in 1875) [actually 1876]. She was bright and amusing and much loved by all who knew her, was rather superstitious, very affectionate and absurdly in love with her brilliant husband.

Guests at these cosy gatherings were government officials from the Treasury, War and Foreign offices (those holders of sinecures for younger sons of influential families), as well as *literati*, artists, actors and theatrical people. The dinners were relatively informal (evening dress not required) and were often served as early as four o'clock to let actors get to the theatre. The food was good and simply placed on the table, the guests serving themselves and the maids merely removing plates and bringing in new dishes. All men could carve well. The guests helped themselves to cheese and fruit from the big sideboard. After dinner everyone went to the drawing room, the men following the ladies and sometimes smoking cigars (never pipes; cigarettes were almost unknown), to sing sentimental and comic songs. Vast piles of sheet music seemed to be available, as well as volumes of classic works.

Adults, particularly men with their big beards and whiskers, seemed tremendously old to the children, who lived their own life. George Frederick felt most like an outsider: he regarded himself as 'very plain, unattractive . . . pasty faced'; he frequently needed the doctor, became frightened at night and was prone to sleep walking. At least once he woke in the dining room—a startled boy in nightshirt amid the guests:

> I would be gathered into my mother's arms, reassured and safe, and then carried up to my bed where she would sit with me, humming a soothing melody until I was asleep again. My most lasting memory of Doughty St. is of the impression fixed in my mind of the sudden waking up in the doorway of a brilliantly lighted room reeking of rich food and warm humanity.

The lonely boy also sought the companionship of his brilliant, busy, hard-pressed but affectionate father, who sometimes found time to play with his children, even after the Liverpool disaster, when he was trying to pay his debts:

> My father must have been working very hard during those times for it was a very busy period of his life and I can never understand how he managed to do so much writing and at the same time be so much engaged in the management of the Prince of Wales's and of the Theatres in Liverpool. . . . He was, however, able to write under almost any conditions, & I remember playing noisily with bricks and tin railway trains on the floor, as he wrote at the table quite undisturbed by my prattle and of others conversing in the room. There were two things he objected to when writing— whistling and whispering. He did a lot of writing at night and in early years kept very late hours, a system he entirely abandoned later in life when he took to early hours and wrote almost exclusively in the morning. . . . There were happy mornings when I was admitted to my parents' bedroom and played tigers with my father while he was still in bed, and was allowed to watch him shave when he rose. He was a delightful play-fellow on those occasions and would dab his lathered brush on my nose to our mutual delight—and would roar with jolly laughter at my antics and contortions.

Sometimes Byron joined a game of cricket or let off fireworks with his children:

[ 253 ]

My father was amusing and kind and full of fun and interested in all we children. Alfred was a handsome boy with what Papa (by the way it was always Papa & Mama) called a face like a 'button'; my face was like 'a suet pudding,' my mouth like 'a letter box,' & John escaped such labelling—or I cannot remember what his was.

George Frederick's sister Elizabeth, known as 'Creedy', was very pretty, with golden hair and 'wondrous dark eyes'. A general favourite, she made amusing remarks; but he felt very pale and indefinite and was indulged because everyone thought him destined to an early death, although he outlived them all. He evidently had something of an 'inferiority complex', feeling himself plain in comparison with Elizabeth, and dull-witted as opposed to the intelligent John, whom he adored:

> He was short for his age but strongly built with what barbers called 'obstinate' hair of dark brown to black colour, brown eyes, small features, nose slightly snub or turned up: not good looking in the ordinary sense as was Alfred, who was decidedly handsome, but he had an extraordinary attraction for most men and women, but chiefly the discerning, and people of mental qualifications.

At school John was feared by the other boys as a courageous fighter and so was left alone. George Frederick saw little of the handsome Alfred ('who mixed with bigger and less orderly boys') and always disliked him. Alfred and John quarrelled frequently. Alfred's moods were uncertain and sometimes 'queer'. He later became something of a libertine and seems to have pursued an erratic and disappointing career. He died young in 1891.

Naturally the children developed their own imaginative life, living as they did in gloomy houses among disagreeable servants. One of their passions was the toy theatre, for which their productions were almost professional. They frequently acted plays:

> At one period we were all together when H. J. B. was running the theatres in Liverpool in 67/68 & living at Huskisson Street. We were noisy children, often getting up Parlour theatricals in which we all had 'shouting' parts in plays concocted by John, the clever one of the family, with Alfred, who insisted always on being the hero and rescuing Lizzie, the heroine, from the clutches of the villain, John—generally by her hair—and I was the agitated father, comic country man, village idiot, or occasionally an army, a fairly extensive repertoire. Think of it, a distraught parent aged 6. The performance generally ended up in a real fight between Alfred and John, who never got on well together, my sister viciously attacking the party that happened to be on top at the time, and I, dancing round the heaped contestants on the floor, shrieking encouragement and hitting at any stray anatomy within reach, as an army should. The grownups did

much the same in their hours of relaxation. At Waterloo or New Brighton
. . . on the coast near Liverpool, where we all spent some summer weeks,
the visiting companies acting at one or other of the theatres would engage
lodgings and attend the performances by train or ferry, but in their
improvised plays, mock trials and variety rompings they stopped short by
a great deal of the frenzied mêlée which brought down the curtain—*and
Maria*—on our entertainment.

The Bancrofts played for a month at Liverpool and joined the weekend productions for the 'Theatre Royal Back Drawing Room' with
W. S. Gilbert, still a briefless barrister. George Frederick vaguely
remembered visiting Buxton and his father's mother (probably staying
with her father, Dr James Byron Bradley) and a balloon ascent from the
public gardens. The little boy overstuffed on cherries, which made him
violently sick, and his grandmother was inevitably blamed for over-
indulgence.

Meanwhile the Doughty Street house was occupied by Uncle Frank,
the Clerk in the Treasury office, and by George's grandfather, Henry
Byron, on leave from Haiti, where he was still Vice-Consul. Once,
young George was put to bed in the London house when Uncle Frank
came up late:

> I watched him undress and before blowing the candle out, kneel down at
> his bedside and say his prayers and I wondered what a lot of relations he
> must have to take so long praying for them.

The worried, overworked father tried to provide a stable atmosphere,
despite the endless travel and the heavy work that the Liverpool disaster
entailed. On tour he always remembered his children and sent them
great boxes of sweets, 'wonderful cakes from Edinburgh, candies from
Glasgow, all on the most lavish scale'. Cheerful as he always seemed, he
may well have been inwardly unhappy. George Frederick mentions the
'unhappy condition of affairs matrimonial' and Carew Hazlitt declares
that Byron was corrupted by the Green Room.[23] Byron was resolutely
tactful about his private life. His few surviving letters, concise, direct,
businesslike, often composed in haste, reveal nothing of the private
man. He was openly convivial, witty, with a capacity for anecdote and
repartee unsurpassed even in circles famous for 'smart' conversation;
and he had the Byrons' love for animals:

> It was from the first floor windows of this [Doughty Street] house that my
> father and Captain Wombwell saw a cabman brutally illtreating his
> horse. They ran out immediately, took the cab and directed the driver to
> go to Bow St. (?) police station and there gave the man in charge. I
> believe the magistrate was sitting . . . and the matter gone into at once

and finished to the dissatisfaction of the cabby. My father confessed to some apprehension as he had to give his evidence within kicking range of the accused whose disgust and indignation were almost beyond control.

Byron was cheerful and humane, if troubled in spirit, and he flung himself more furiously into work, essaying the hopeless task of repaying his creditors by writing two or three pieces at once and reappearing on stage. He played Sir Simon Simple in his own drama, *Not Such a Fool as He Looks*, a part originally written for Richard Sothern ('Lord Dundreary'), which had opened at the Theatre Royal, Manchester, 4 December 1868; Byron played the part himself on 23 December 1869 at the Globe. His quiet, unconcerned style when telling a joke became famous. He looked as if he had just stepped from a Hackney coach onto the stage, and while he was criticised for playing himself as an actor, many found his quiet, unstagey style pleasing. W. Davenport Adams 'liked to hear Byron slowly rapping out his own clever lines: they seemed to come from his lips with added point'.[18]

When Byron acted Fitzaltamont in his own play, *The Prompter's Box*, at the Adelphi on 23 March 1870, the eight-year-old George Frederick was taken there and deposited in the dressing room of Sarah Woolgar, his father's old flame. Young Henry James Byron had been madly in love with her until he made the mortifying discovery that she was married to Alfred Mellon; but to his son—

> she had been a beauty in her time but I only remember her as a motherly demonstrative woman who warmly took me in her arms and embraced me vigorously and stuffed me with sweets, and was overwhelming in her affectionate attentions. I was taken to the wings when the play was in progress but was not permitted to stay there long as I could not be relied on to keep silence in spite of the SILENCE notices painted on the walls about. My brother John had even better luck for he was taken by my father on one of his tours, but he was 12 or so and very intelligent and even at that age was quite an appreciated companion by men, having opinions of his own, sometimes startling and quaint, with a power of language and wit by which to express them.

Byron appeared at several theatres thereafter, acting Lionel Leveret in his three-act comic drama, *Old Soldiers*, at the Strand in January 1873; Harold Trivass in his comedy *An American Lady*, on 21 March 1874 (the opening night of the Criterion Theatre, where he had become manager); and Gibson Greene in *Married in Haste* at the Haymarket, 2 October 1875. When this was revived at the Folly Theatre on 3 January 1880, Clement Scott, reviewing it for *The Theatre*, observed that no one spoke Byronisms better than Byron, who was as grave as a judge and apparently unconcerned about his own conceits, although his undefined twinkle showed he relished the humour.

One of the Christmas novelties at the Lyceum in 1876 was Byron's comedy, *Old Chums*, about two schoolboys, Richard Jones and Thomas Smith, both in love with Miss Amaranth Greythorpe. *The Illustrated London News* (23 December) observed: 'The part of Richard Jones was . . . filled by Mr. Byron himself, and caused much laughter'. In the autumn of 1879 he played at the Gaiety in a series of afternoon performances of four of his own plays—*An English Gentleman, Daisy Farm, Not Such a Fool as He Looks,* and *Married in Haste*. He last appeared in November of 1881 at the Court Theatre, as Cheviot Hill in a revival of W. S. Gilbert's comedy, *Engaged*, when he exasperated Gilbert by his vagueness at rehearsals, but was well received and, according to *The Theatre* (30 November 1881), acted 'quite after his own style. He is quiet throughout, and delivers his lines with point and emphasis'.

Byron's greatest financial success and his best known play, *Our Boys*, first produced at the Vaudeville Theatre (16 January 1875) with an experienced comedian, David James, as Perkyn Middlewick, achieved the longest run ever at that time, playing continuously until 18 April 1879. It was acted all through the provinces, revived several times in London, and would have made its author's fortune but for the voracious debts that continued to devour his profits.

Alfred Darbyshire, a perceptive theatregoer, observed that 'in common with other of Mr Byron's works, [it] is unduly leavened with farce, and can boast little correspondence with nature and reality'. He noted the inexplicable friendship of two such disparate characters as Sir Geoffrey Champneys, proud baronet, and Perkyn Middlewick, an ignorant old butterman whose violence in discarding his son for marrying an heiress who scorns the butter trade remains unintelligible. Darbyshire thought Talbot Champneys (the baronet's son) a curious combination of cub and fop (until misfortune develops his real worth), but that the drollery of David James in the rôle of the foolish old butterman who talks constantly of his trade was greeted with incessant laughter: '*Mr. Middlewick*, indeed, will probably take rank among the most popular creations and personages of the modern stage'.[19]

Byron's plays were often written as vehicles for such famous comedians as J. L. Toole, David James, and Richard Sothern. The working out of the story, which gave him such trouble, is usually the most unsatisfactory feature of his dramas, as many reviewers noticed at the time.

Sometimes good acting and dialogue overcame puerilities and absurdities, sometimes not. Byron's work methods suggest he knew his

[ 257 ]

weakness: he gave much time to planning, setting out the action and marking the exits and entrances before writing dialogue, which came easily and which he could do amid much distraction.

Even in his best play, *Cyril's Success* (1868), Byron evaded serious issues, and this is particularly disappointing because the first act promises much: the wife of a successful novelist and dramatist feels neglected and lonely; she broods on her husband's preoccupation with business and writing. Tensions develop; but the rest of the play relapses into the usual formulae of unlikely incident and mistaken identity. Domestic happiness and understanding always win the day. Perhaps this play brought out some of Byron's personal difficulties in marriage; if so, he also avoided dealing with them in other comedies (*Partners for Life, Married in Haste*) which depict unhappy couples.

Byron's conservatism and the speed at which he was forced to work prevented him from developing anything serious which would be acted outside the late Victorian theatre. In an article opposing the creation of a national theatre he stated clearly that for him the theatre was harmless entertainment, morally edifying, and that the playwright must depend on his audience. Two years later he was opposing Bancroft's abolition of the pit at the Haymarket. The perpetual pirating and plagiarising of other authors, particularly in translation, drew the quiet comment that he himself had adapted only three French comic operas whose authors were identified on the bills and in the published books:

> We are too apt in our sweeping assertions as to stealing from abroad to ignore the fact of our own plays being often 'annexed'. *Our Boys* has been played all over the continent. . . . I have not received one penny for this.

He complained about frequent first night criticism, thinking the verdicts often hasty, adverse, and preconcerted. And he considered the causes of failure numerous and not necessarily the author's—wrong location, circumstance, wrong actors, awkward time, overcrowded theatre, long waits between acts, an unfortunate incident or speech— all might damn a play. He thought actors the best judges of a piece, but a sensible author should not moan and bore his friends, but must pocket his feelings and work with a will.[20] This philosophy informed his whole professional life: he was without self-pity or professional jealousy, and so acutely attuned to his audiences that his highly successful reputation did not long survive them.

He was as pragmatic about launching his last comic serial publication, *Mirth*, published by the Tinsley brothers. Byron wrote numerous articles and verses for it; other contributors included Godfrey Turner, W. S. Gilbert, Robert Reece, J. R. Planché, James Albery, William

Archer, E. L.Blanchard and George Augustus Sala. But economic uncertainties doomed *Mirth* to a shorter life than the *Comic News*. Byron had projected *Mirth* for 12 numbers, November 1877 to October 1878 being the first publication year; but by 22 May he wrote to W. Tinsley from Brixton in his usual decisive style:

> The question of the *volume* sale is quite problematical, and what is the use of relying on a possible sale when we are *certain* of a loss up to Xmas that must over balance any profit.
>
> Of course we must stop the magazine after this forthcoming number. It is the only sensible course. I cannot afford to pay such a loss and the longer Mirth lasts the worse it will be for us both.
>
> I will see you in a day or so and pay over my share.
>
> I have sent (on the 20th) a capital number full of copy for next number to Mr. Cunningham.[21]

During the busy and personally troubling time of the Liverpool management, Byron's sons were away at school. In about 1871 Alfred and John went to Germany, to a school run by a Herr Vilmar somewhere in Hanover. They enjoyed their year and a half there: John got on well with both English and German boys. They walked in the Black Forest. John, a born observer and collector, was fascinated by everything, particularly the little villages: he bought coins, stamps, and books. He was interested in everything from European politics to sports and the arts. According to his admiring younger brother, he sent his mother 'capital letters' and photographs of masters and boys. To George Frederick, John's wit, talent, and knowledge seemed boundless. They shared their possessions and pocket money, spending on the pit or gallery of a theatre when they could.

George Frederick was shunted from school to school in England. He had grim experiences at some of them and reported one particularly sadistic episode to the masters. But he enjoyed himself, too, and obviously inherited the family talent, despite his constant self-deprecation, becoming a teller of stories after lights out:

> Someone had told me that Latin was the easiest language to learn, and in a weak moment, I actually asked Mullins [the Headmaster] if I could join his class. He was at first almost dumb with surprise at my temerity, but quickly recovered himself and regarding me as a savage might the appearance of a plump missionary enquiring about lunch menus, mastered his surprise and very seriously and somewhat ominously expressed his willingness and 'hoped I would like it.' That night as I was in the middle of my story-telling, he passed the open door and called to me that he had placed a Latin grammar on my desk, having written my name in it and

left it open to dry. 'Thank you, Sir,' I replied, 'I have no doubt I shall find it dry enough in the morning.' He laughed and so did I.

Byron's troubled marriage ended on 25 September 1876 with the death of his devoted wife at Brighton; and shortly thereafter (17 October) he married a solicitor's daughter, Eleanor Mary Joy, by whom he had two daughters, Margaret Ada (b. 13 January 1878) and May (b. 1880). This remarriage caused a family rift that was never closed. Furthermore, Byron knew that he was dying: on 18 October 1882 he made a will leaving all his assets vested with trustees for the benefit of his second wife and her children, without any reference to his first family—a startling omission.[22]

Whatever the domestic upheavals, Byron was professionally more successful than ever, but he had not cleared his debts and he was very ill. He wrote short but affectionate letters to the absent George Frederick; and perhaps at some time in 1878 he sent ominous news from 1, Eccleston Square, S.W., his London house:

> Dear Georgy:
>     Your money slipped my recollection. I hope it has not put you to inconvenience. I have been very seedy, and Wilkins found a sore spot on my lungs which I fancy is of longer standing then *he* does. This is serious, but can't be helped. I am better these two or three days, having eaten better.
>                         Your affectionate father,
>                         H. J. Byron

When George broached the subject of his career, Byron replied on his personal stationery, headed with the Byron crest—the mermaid carrying a glass and the motto *Crede Byron*—

> My dear Georgy:
>     *I* am very pleased at your sensible letter.
>     Certainly I think an architect's profession would be advisable and when you come home at Christmas we will make full enquiries.
>     We all unite in love to you and I am (in haste)
>                         Your affectionate father
>                         H. J. Byron
> Mrs. Byron has knitted you a comforter which will go with the apples.[23]

After 1880 Byron was known to be in a consumption. He made his last public speech at the Savage Club dinnner in 1879, responding for the Drama and remarking that one always heard of its 'palmy days':

> People are always speaking of the decline of the drama. I verily believe that there never was a time when they did not speak of it. Probably Thespis, when he went about in his cart, if he heard that a circus had

come into the neighbourhood, complained that the drama was going to the dogs while the public were going to the horses.[24]

On 22 March Byron had to write to F. A. Hawkins, publisher of *The Theatre*, that he had been 'exceedingly unwell' for some time and 'that all kind of work has been most irksome and I have had to put it aside'; but he promised the 'little article' and much more, an undertaking he kept.[25] Moreover, he managed to act in his own plays in the autumn at the Gaiety Theatre. His comedy, *Courtship*, was running at the *Court*; and a year later another of his dramas, *Bow Bells*, was acted at the Royalty (4 October 1880). On 14 March 1881 his adaptation of *Michael Strogoff*, a five-act drama by D'Ennery and Jules Verne, was produced at the Adelphi with Byron himself playing John Blunt, an English correspondent. This drama was both melodramatic and spectacular and therefore popular: by September it was playing at the Nottingham Theatre Royal with Charles Dornton, a provincial actor-manager, acting Henry Blunt very much in Byron's manner.

His frenetic activity and striving for solvency were hastening his end. Byron tried to increase his output by relying on adaptations: his farcical comedy, *Fourteen Days*, based on a French play, *Un Voyage d'Agrement*, by Gondinet & Bisson, opened at the Criterion on 4 March 1882 with Charles Wyndham as Peregrine Porter. Its plot is typically convoluted, Byron and its characters unbelievable.

Byron was reported as very ill during the run of his last new play, *Auntie*, 'a new and original farce in 3 acts' which opened on 13 March 1882 at Toole's Theatre. He spent the last winter of his life at Hastings. On 25 November 1883 he wrote to Toole from St Leonard's that he felt 'much better'. But he was now failing rapidly; one of his lungs was destroyed; and the change of air and scene had little effect. He returned to Clapham Park, where he soon became bedridden; but he was characteristically cheerful to the end, writing to Robert Reece, with whom he was unable to collaborate, that he had been sitting in the same chair for two months. However, he concealed his condition from Reece, whom he had helped, and who almost worshipped him:

> It was pitiful to hear his cough, though he never seemed to be affected by its significance. To the last he believed that he had conquered the serious malady. I could not bear to visit him; for I could not trust my capacity to restrain from breaking-down and distressing him. I loved him so dearly . . . that to see him fading, whilst such as I existed, was a torture to me. Then I heard he was very ill. Of course I threw aside compunctions; I would go. It was forbidden. On Good Friday I heard bad tidings from his constant friend (and executor), Mr. A. H. Pearpoint. Attended by his most loving wife, the dear fellow, cheerful to the last, took a little

refreshment, turned his face to the wall, and died without a sound. A perfect ending. Mr. E. W. Garden, his good and assiduous friend and helper, was happily—and naturally—near him, in the house. . . . When I entered that darkened house my heart faded; but when I saw his beautiful face; always beautiful—but now refined to a spiritual loveliness—my sorrow passed into another feeling: it was almost envy.[26]

The Liverpool ventures had overwhelmed Byron financially: his will was eventually proved for only £4,783. *The Theatre*, in an affectionate obituary, said that he fought on bravely after ill fortune and wrote to drive away care.

Byron died on 11 April 1884. It was Good Friday in just such a bleak Easter season as saw the death of the poet at Missolonghi. He was buried in Brompton Cemetery on 17 April, one of the harshest days of a bitter spring. Crowds of theatre people attended the interment at 2 o'clock. A deep grave had been dug, to the left of the path as one comes up from the chapel, and the oak coffin bearing a simple plate with inscription was cautiously lowered to avoid disturbing the many flowers heaped upon it: a cross of primroses came from Sophie Larkin of the Vaudeville Theatre; wreaths from Charles Warner, Henry Irving and Mrs Swanborough. George Loveday, Toole's stage manager, sent a floral cross; J. L. Toole a floral wreath; another large wreath came from the original cast of *Auntie*.

David James was among the guests at the house, together with J. L. Toole, who walked only part way with the procession because he had an engagement:

> Poor Byron! the day he was buried I played 'Chawles' at the Crystal Palace; I could not help it, one is obliged to keep one's engagements; but I felt very sad. It seemed to me once or twice as if I could hear the funeral service while I was speaking the dear fellow's merry lines.[27]

When the procession reached the cemetery showers of sleet were falling and a cutting east wind blew dust into the faces of the mourners, who kept their ground and showed deep emotion as the Chaplain, the Reverend A. Vesey, read the beautiful burial service that speaks of the Resurrection and the Life. A crowd gathered about the open grave for a last look at the coffin, many whose careers and interests had been furthered by his generous interest—Arthur Pinero, W. H. Kendal, John Hare, Robert Reece, Godfrey Turner and W. Tinsley (who published *Mirth*), and Charles Wyndham, just back from America.

The *Era* closed its lengthy obituary with verses by James Albery, concluding:

> The brilliant wit who, had he only said
> One half the jests that did not bring him bread:

But scattering to the winds sent laughter free,
To all glad hearts a lasting legacy,
Leaves to his country to all just intents
More than ten sessions of dull parliaments.
Yet hush your laughter, for our Byron's gone,
And mirth should rest a little time to mourn.

If Byron lacked the brilliance his contemporaries ascribed to him, he imparted much pleasure to theatregoers and to his friends; he showed courage in adversity, great generosity, loyalty and kindness. 'He brought out Mr. T. W. Robertson and discovered Mr. Gilbert, and has never been jealous of anybody'.[28]

*

Among the few relatives assembled at Henry J. Byron's house in Queen's Park on that bleak 17 April was a handsome young matinée idol, known as Harry Conway, who had already established his own spectacularly successful theatre career. According to Ellen Terry, 'his good looks were talked of everywhere':

> He was a descendant of Lord Byron's, and had a look of the *handsomest* portraits of the poet. With his bright hair curling tightly all over his well-shaped head, his beautiful figure, and charming presence, Conway created a sensation in the eighties almost equal to that made by the more famous beauty, Lillie Langtry.[29]

John Forbes-Robertson, who acted with him, said:

> He was rather short, but his head was well set on his straight shoulders and his features were clean cut and regular as an antique cameo.[30]

Conway derived his beauty from the good-looking Anson Byrons and not directly from the poet. He came from the landed gentry of the North Country and was the youngest son of John Blenkinsopp Coulson (1799–1868) and his second wife, Mary Anne Byron, oldest daughter of 'the able bodied seaman George', seventh Baron Byron.[31] They all seemed well settled and conventional and the youngest, Harry Blenkinsopp, born in 1849, was doubtless destined for a similarly predictable career. He was educated at Rossall School where he displayed, like his father and brothers before him, much enthusiasm for sports; but he also loved drama and read every play he could; and when, in 1867, he went to study at the University of Berlin, he neglected scholarship and social life to go to the theatre.

However, his father, a most respected Justice of the Peace, Deputy Lieutenant and High Sheriff, and Captain in the Grenadier Guards, died on 12 June 1868. Harry was therefore obliged to earn his own

[ 263 ]

living, but he astonished his family by announcing that he intended to go on the stage. They warned him, as families usually do, that he would repent such folly; whereupon he went to London and eventually got the tiny part of Bernard in a morbid and disagreeable play by Edmund Yates and A. W. Dubourg, *Without Love*, at the Olympic Theatre (16 December 1872). In view of his family's emphatic opposition he assumed the stage name of Conway. One night the juvenile lead in a commonplace melodrama by Charles Young, *Maggie Dorme*, went missing and the management eagerly accepted Conway's offer to assume the part. His success in the unenviable rôle decided the management to cast him as David Copperfield in *Little Emily*, one of the numberless adaptations that were staples of Victorian Theatre.

This performance launched Conway's career in 1873, which proved a propitious year: Squire Bancroft, recognising Conway's merits, engaged him for a provincial tour with *Man and Wife*, by Wilkie Collins; he married an attractive comedienne, Kate Phillips (née Katharine Barnard Goldney) who pursued her own successful career beside his and sometimes acted with him; and he assumed the rôle of François in a revival of Lord Lytton's *Richelieu* on 27 September 1873 at the Lyceum Theatre, managed by Henry Irving. This last engagement led to a series of parts with that famous actor-manager. At about this time Conway wrote to a friend: 'Both from Mr. Bateman and Mr. Irving I received the greatest kindness and encouragement'.[32]

Conway's rôles at the Lyceum included Christian in *The Bells* by Leopold Lewis, in which, according to the *Athenaeum* (3 October 1874) he 'displayed remarkable freshness as young *Gayfare*'; he was Compte de Flamarens, unrequited lover of the heroine, in *Philip*, an improbable melodrama by Hamilton Aide; Lord Moray in a revival of *Charles the First* by H. G. Wills (with Irving as the King); and Osric through a long, highly acclaimed run of *Hamlet*. Joseph Knight, writing in the *Athenaeum* (4 January 1879), called Irving's *Hamlet* the best in a quarter century. It was unostentatiously acted in an Elizabethan setting, 'and the interpretation has an ensemble rarely found in any performance'. The scene between Hamlet and Osric was staged outside the Castle of Elsinore, giving point to the line, 'Put your bonnet to the right use; 'tis for the head'.

In the spring of 1875 Conway joined a touring company led by the well-known actress Mrs John Wood. He returned to the Haymarket Theatre in August, opening there as Dick Dowlas in a version of George Colman the Younger's *Heir at Law* and in juvenile rôles. He played Dowlas in America later on, appearing at the Park Theatre, New York, 19–21 September 1888, when he was described as a 'handsome London juvenile'.³³ On 17 January 1876 he appeared in an all star production of *Romeo and Juliet* with the celebrated Adelaide Neilson, most brilliant of Victorian Juliets; Charles Harcourt, considered the best Mercutio of the time; Harold Kyrle (later famous as Kyrle Bellew) as Paris; the well-known Haymarket comedian, J. B. Buckstone, as Peter; and Miss Emily Thorne (star of H. J. Byron comedy) as the Nurse. The play was given in six acts—the curtain being dropped on the balcony scene (II, ii), which thus made an act in itself, with very good effect. Conway had been asked to play Romeo ten days in advance, to his consternation, but although he had other pieces in rehearsal he mastered the lines and made an excellent impression. The *Illustrated London News* (22 January) thought his Romeo 'good, though too fast in delivery to permit the poetic imagery and cadence of the dialogue to be perceptible. This is a great fault in the Shakespearean actor; for the mere drawing-room tone is not the only natural one'. The *Daily Telegraph* (19 January) said he gained ground as the play proceeded; the *Athenaeum* (22 January) commented that his qualifications hitherto had been youth and good looks, and praised his intelligence and moderation. Conway himself thought his performance defective in many ways; but he found that the management and Miss Neilson were 'kindness itself'.³⁴ He acted many times with Adelaide Neilson before her untimely death and appeared in numerous Shakespearean revivals.

He was Orlando (*As You Like It*); Sir Thomas Clifford (*The Hunchback*, by Sheridan Knowles); and Sebastian (*Twelfth Night*). The *Daily Telegraph* (3 April 1876) particularly praised his Lucio (*Measure for Measure*):

> There was one performance . . . of marked excellence. This was the *Lucio* of Mr. H. B. Conway, who acted with such spirit and ease that he was enabled to brighten up the very scenes which most require careful handling. The success of *Lucio* was not alone due to a natural buoyancy of temperament, or to the more physical advantage of youth. Mr. Conway understands the value of acting even in repose, as was observed in the scene where Isabella pleads for her brother's life. His anxious face throughout this interview materially assisted the situation and gave life to one of the best acted scenes in the play; and in all the comedy passages with the Duke, Mr. Conway made his points as naturally and so genially that the audience followed the young *Lucio* with laughter and applause.

During that summer of 1876 Conway toured with Adelaide Neilson and in the winter he played Bertie to Sothern's Colonel White in a revival of *Home* (by T. W. Robertston). On 4 November he appeared at the Royal Court Theatre, managed by John Hare from the Prince of Wales company, to play Fred Meredith in a very bad original play by

Charles F. Coghlan, *The Brothers*. Ellen Terry was the unsympathetic flirt Kate Hungerford.

Conway joined the Prince of Wales company as juvenile lead, playing Julian Beauclerk in *Diplomacy* (31 May 1879), an adaptation of Sardou's melodrama *Dora*, by Clement Scott and B. C. Stephenson. Marie Wilton had married Sidney (later Sir Squire) Bancroft and inaugurated a famous joint management there after H. J. Byron's departure for Liverpool. Conway also appeared as Charlie in a revival of *Good for Nothing* at the Haymarket and as Harold Dyecaster in *Heads or Tails*, a short comic piece by Palgrave Simpson. On 11 May and 17 June 1878 he supported Sothern in two plays by H. J. Byron, *The Crushed Tragedian* and *The Hornet's Nest*, both reviewed in no complimentary terms by the *Athenaeum* (18 May and 22 June):

> The thread of connection [*The Crushed Tragedian*, a rewritten version of *The Prompter's Box*] possessed in the shape of a slight but tender love interest, is now so attenuated as scarcely to be recognisable, and farce throughout the entire work holds carnival.

However, Mr Sothern's makeup was very droll, and Conway, Marion Terry and others 'acquitted themselves well'. It was poorly received: 'A feeling nearer weariness than exaltation attends the close of the performance'.

Nevertheless, when Conway played the lead in a revival of *Romeo and Juliet* at the Haymarket the *Graphic* (13 April 1878) remarked that his Romeo 'possesses more vigour than that gentleman usually exhibits'. He acted at the Aquarium, usually an afternoon theatre, in an evening piece, *The Vicar of Wakefield*, revived on 1 June 1878. On 24 March 1879 he appeared at the Olympic as Faust in W. S. Gilbert's *Gretchen*, a blank verse adaptation without Mephistopheles; as Gilbert himself admitted afterwards, 'I called it *Gretchen*, the public called it rot'.[35] The *Athenaeum* (29 March) remarked on its artificiality and the difficulties of the cast in realising their parts. *The Theatre* (1 April 1879) thought that 'Mr. Conway's romance lacks something of the true ring'.

Conway went on to other rôles, notably Philip Dene in James Albery's *Duty* (Prince of Wales, 27 September 1879). The same year he joined Miss Kate Vaughan to form the Vaughan-Conway Touring Company, an arrangement he repeated in 1887 when he founded the Conway-Farren Comedy Company and toured during the summer and autumn with the famous comedian William Farren. He was thus remarkably successful, but he had not been fully challenged as an actor, although from his first enthusiastic days at the Olympic Theatre he had been scarcely three months out of work and had built up an impressive repertoire.

The Bancrofts had followed their triumphs at the Prince of Wales by refurbishing and resuscitating the Haymarket, long fallen into decline from its great comic days. An attractive new drop curtain depicted characters from the Prince of Wales production of *School for Scandal*. The Bancrofts abolished the pit, a move opposed by Henry J. Byron, and this unpopular decision led to disturbances at the first night production of Lord Lytton's classic comedy, *Money* (31 January 1880). The restless audience brought Squire Bancroft, dressed as Sir Frederick Blount, on to the stage before his time to explain that the substitution of plush red chairs (stalls) was a financial necessity. The play then proceeded with moderate success. *The Times* reviewer thought the company 'off balance'. To Clement Scott, writing in *The Theatre*, the scene between Alfred Evelyn and Clara Douglas (Marion Terry) was tame and inanimate: Miss Terry over-accentuated the nervous pathos, was too over-whelmed and sorrow-stricken, while Conway as Evelyn demonstrated his own peculiarities:

> I am quite certain that Mr. Conway cannot possibly know how his strongest efforts are marred by so continually emphasising the unimportant word in a sentence and slurring over the important ones. Dozens of instances could be given, but one occurs to me particularly. He says, 'Go, Clara! AND be happy if you can.' Now why lay a stress upon the word 'and' in this sentence? Of what value is it, and why should it be emphasised at all? I remember that in 'Duty', in one important scene, Mr. Conway, who acted admirably enough, replied to a young lady's inquiry whether he had anything to say: 'Only THAT I love you! only THAT I love you!' thus destroying the intensity of the sentence and losing its point. A very little thought would correct this strange desire to lay stress upon such words as 'and', 'but', 'the', and 'that', seeing that there is scarcely any force to be got out of them.

Conway went on to further rôles at the Haymarket, where he doubtless learned much from the Bancrofts, who insisted on an orchestrated performance. Their son, who often went behind the scenes during his school holidays, recalled that his father furiously reprimanded Conway for being late:

> 'Well, but I've been riding. I've come straight from the Row.'
> 'Mr. Conway, in my theatre the company must be dressed suitably and treat their work seriously. Never let this happen again.'[49]

Conway appeared as Lord Beaufoy in a revival of T. W. Robertson's *School* on 1 May 1880. Bernard Henry Becker, reviewing for *The Theatre* (1 June), pronounced it an impossible play on the Cinderella theme—a pupil-teacher marries a handsome young lord—and found the dialogue 'only remarkable for the closeness with which it approaches the stupidity of modern everyday conversation'. Consequently the whole burden was thrown on the actors, who admirably made the best of the 'milk jug idyll'.

Conway faced as great a challenge in the part of Archibald Meek in Dion Boucicault's three-act comedy, *A Bridal Tour*, produced for the first time at the Haymarket in 2 August 1880. It was neither comedy nor farce. A sentimental couple, Archibald Meek and Fanny Tarbox, threaded their way through a convoluted plot. At the seaside for a day the Meeks fall asleep before dinner, reading poetry, and leaving the audience uncertain whether to laugh or sympathise. Henry Becker, in *The Theatre* (1 September) wondered whether Boucicault had intended to write a fashionable ironical comedy; he praised Conway, who 'played the young husband with his accustomed ease, although he seemed as much puzzled by the sleeping scene as everybody else in the theatre'.

When Conway played Sir Charles Pomander in a revival of Tom Taylor and Charles Reade's *Masks and Faces* at the Haymarket (5 February 1881), *The Theatre* (1 March) declared it well acted and praised Lewis Wingfield's costumes. The *Athenaeum* added (12 February):

> Very pleasant is it to see a picture such as Mr. Conway exhibits when, with his snuff-box in his hand, he stands in his silk coat with its wadded skirts to watch the result of his plots. . . . Mr. Conway's Sir Charles Pomander was admirably insolent.

Of Conway's later appearance in a revival of *Plot and Passion* (Tom Taylor and John Lang), the *Athenaeum* (3 December 1881) said that, although the whole company seemed nervous—even Ada Cavendish as Marie de Fontages was 'artificial and ill at ease'—

> As Henri de Neuville Mr. Conway acted with gallantry and a certain measure of fire. As he gets rid of *mauvaise honte* and lets himself go Mr. Conway commences to render valuable services to the stage.

He appeared in the afterpiece also, a 'mirthful and attractive piece', *Lesson*, by F. C. Burnand.

Conways strengths continued to develop, as we may see from the *Theatre*'s review of Boucicault's *Devotion* at the Court Theatre on 1 May 1884. Marie de Monbazon (Ada Cavendish), the heroine, cannot decide whether she prefers her husband or her lover—indecision which robs the play of interest—

> but for the Comte de Chalais [the lover] of Mr. H. B. Conway, only praise can be accorded. It is a decided advantage to this gentleman that in a 'costume play' like 'Devotion' he can wear his beautiful dresses as though to the manner born, and not as many do, in a painfully 'for this night only' fashion, and it is also an advantage to his audience where he does so,

for when in velvet and ruffles, Mr. Conway is apparently no longer afraid to let himself go, and always plays with far more vigour and boldness than when in every day dress. His de Chalais is a natural and fervent performance, and between his Count and Mr. [John] Clayton's Duke all honours must be divided. . . .

He was weaker in *Peril*, an adaptation of Sardou's *Nos Intimes* revived at the Haymarket 16 February 1884; as Captain Bradford, would-be lover and tempter of Lady Ormond (Mrs Bernard-Beere) he gave, said *The Theatre*, 'too often a singularly lifeless and unimpressive performance. . . . Mr. Conway, however, looked the part to perfection. He was a thorough gentleman.'

Conway showed he was learning his craft and reading the reviews when he appeared at the Vaudeville Theatre in *Saints and Sinners* by Henry A. Jones, yet another improbable melodrama. *The Times* praised the acting as helping to make the piece credible. The *Daily Telegraph* declared:

> [Fanshawe] was played by Mr. Conway in a singularly unconventional and daring fashion. The wicked captain might have made the most stagey of scoundrels, but Mr. Conway took a new view, and a very clever one. He made him a man who conquered his victim by pure force of will, who fascinated her as an eagle might a wren, and who won his prize by sheer determination. The character was consistent and very naturally acted.

The *Athenaeum*, reviewing the piece at length on 4 October, concluded: 'Mr. Conway's disappearance at the close of the third act was regarded by the audience as a misfortune.'

Conway was also appearing in *Evergreen*, a two-act adaptation of a French comedy, by W. H. Pollock (Haymarket, 9 August) and in another three-act comedy, *Bachelors* (1 September 1884). During August Kate Phillips played in *Confusion* at the Vaudeville Theatre. It was thus a busy and fruitful time for them both.

The intelligence, the 'suppressed passion' of Conway's best acting was noted by *The Theatre* (1 December 1884) in its review of *Young Mrs Winthrop*, an original American play by Bronson Howard (Court Theatre, 6 November), a difficult play about quarrelling lovers. Their child dies; they are further estranged; and eventually reconciled. The *Illustrated London News* (15 November) praised the 'manly acting of Mr. H. B. Conway as Mr. Winthrop'; and *The Theatre* (1 December) had this to say:

> . . . No young actor has improved so much of late as Mr. H. B. Conway. His performance in 'Saints and Sinners' of the strong and determined lover was good enough; but this is even better. The character of Douglas Winthrop is one of unusual difficulty, but Mr. Conway has mastered it completely. His suppressed emotion is admirable.

Conway's other rôles included Philip Eden in *Odette* (Haymarket, 25 April 1882); George d'Alroy in Robertson's *Caste* (1883); Fawley Denham in *The Denhams* (1885); *Opal Ring* and *Phyllis* (1885). He sometimes played several parts concurrently. Indeed his future seemed assured until he acted Faust again, in yet another adaptation of Goethe for a spectacular staging during the Lyceum's Christmas season (1885). There disaster overtook him.

The new *Faust* was geared to Henry Irving's terrific histrionic talent, of course. He had gone to enormous trouble and expense over it, even taking his August holiday in Nuremberg with the scene-painter, Hawes Craven (a colourful character who dabbed away at huge canvases with his head bound up in a red bandana). The two took notes and imbibed local colour. Irving frequently consulted H. G. Wills, the adapter, and spent hours working out the mechanisms needed for the special effects. The final Walpurgis-Nacht revels on the Brocken were simply a vehicle for spectacle. The wild craggy rocks bathed in moonlight; thunder and lightning; hags and demons rising from the bowels of the mountain; witches on broomsticks; Mephistopheles with imps crawling over his knees as he sat on a huge flaming, crackling rock; and the concluding scene, an angels' ladder reaching to heaven—achieved with special lighting and cobalt paint—all this series of colourful spectacles was aimed at the contemporary playgoer and made up the lack of dramatic interest. Spectacular even in that theatrically spectacular age, it was to be the first of Irving's really big financial successes; but the first night went badly.

The audience was headed by the Prince and Princess of Wales. Everything was set for a brilliant opening. Conway played Faust to Irving's Mephistopheles, Ellen Terry was Marguerite. However, the beautiful visions Mephistopheles shows Faust never materialised—the transparencies had broken down. Ellen Terry was unnerved by the warm applause which greeted her and did not recover for some time. Bur Irving, dreadful and cynical as Mephistopheles, dominated the evening. The *Illustrated London News* (26 December), in waxing lyrical about the production, accorded high praise to George Alexander and to Ellen Terry: 'What matter that the Faust cannot realise the fervour and passion of the love-scene'; the *Athenaeum* said that Conway who 'looked, if possible, younger with his flowing beard than after his rejuvenescence—presented none the less a picturesque appearance as Faust, but failed to charge the part with any passion'. *The Times* (21 December) thought Goethe himself undramatic and *Faust* unsuited to the stage:

> . . . To some extent the acting in this case may be at fault. Mr. Conway as
> Faust is a failure. As an old man he is wanting in dignity; as a youthful
> lover he looks trivial, not to say ridiculous, dressed as he is in a bonnet

[270]

and cloak that gives him the air of a petty Highland chief or a moonstruck Jacques.

Godfrey Turner, writing in *The Theatre* (1 January 1886) said, 'Mr. Conway's Faust pleased me more on the first night than his representation seems to have pleased everybody'; but the critics reached unusual unanimity in agreeing that this energetic young actor had failed in a part admirably suited to him. According to Austin Brereton he 'was entirely out of the picture—uninspired, unpoetical, colourless, and essentially modern. It eventually became known that Mr. Conway was suffering from a severe illness, but, of course, the first-night audience was not aware of this misfortune'.[37]

Conway's severe illness was disseminated (or multiple) sclerosis, an insidious and debilitating disease which attacks the nervous system, impairing vision, speech and movement. It usually develops during the earlier part of life (Conway was 36) and may be so mild as to pass unnoticed, or so severe as to cause eventual paralysis and death. It had apparently been creeping upon him for years, and was to continue its course until this handsome, charming, gifted actor became a bed-ridden paralytic. Whether he guessed his fate on this disastrous night there is no saying; and it is equally difficult to determine what effect his illness had on any performance. Certainly he understood the extent of this particular failure because Ellen Terry recorded the unpleasant scene that ensued the following day, when Irving called a rehearsal:

> The company stood about in groups on the stage while Henry walked up and down, speechless, but humming a tune occasionally, always a portentous sign with him. The scene set was the Brocken Scene, and Conway stood at the top of the slope as far away from Henry as he could get! He looked abject. His handsome face was very red, his eyes full of tears. He was terrified at the thought of what was going to happen. The actor was summoned to the office, and presently [H. J.] Loveday [Irving's Stage Manager] came out and said that Mr. George Alexander would play Faust the following night. Alec had been wonderful as Valentine the night before, and as Faust he more than justified Henry's belief in him. After that he never looked back.[38]

With characteristic courage and tenacity Conway went on to several other rôles, playing Lord Archibald in Alfred C. Calmour's *Love's Martyrdom* at the Criterion in 1886 and taking the lead in *Fascination*, a 'New and Improbable Comedy' by Harriett Jay and Robert Buchanan (Novelty Theatre, 6 October 1887). According to Cecil Howard, he 'was but half-hearted as the weak and easily led away Lord Islay' (*The Theatre*, 1 February 1888). He was Frank Blandish in *The Widow*

*Winsome*, an original play by Calmour at the Criterion (27 November 1888), when *The Theatre* commented that he 'appeared to strive hard, but evidently found the material at his command not sufficiently good to call forth his greatest powers—his character was unreal'; but the *Athenaeum* (1 December) thought he 'displayed much earnestness'.

Conway went on to play Philip Selwyn in *A Fool's Paradise* at the Gaiety (12 February 1889); he was married to a fascinating siren who tries to recapture her old lover, Lord Normantower, because he has acquired a title and who poisons herself in the last scene. Just as stagey and improbable was *The Catspaw*, by John Tresahar, first presented as a matinée at Terry's Theatre (24 July 1889). *The Theatre* (2 September) criticised the author for crude dialogue and language 'that is never heard anywhere but on the boards'. Julie Leprallière, in love with Captain Dormain (Conway), actually chloroforms him in order to carry dangerous dispatches herself; but she is shot by a spy in the pay of the Prussians! Dormain leads the complicated life of such a stage character: he is engaged to Adèle Leprallière, with whom Eugène Duval, the spy, is in love: 'Mr. H. B. Conway's acting was full of fire and spirit, and his struggle between gratitude and feeling for the woman who still loved him, and his sense of duty, was finely portrayed'.

In 1891 Conway took several rôles, appearing as Tom Fashion in *Miss Tomboy* an adaptation by Robert Buchanan of Sir John Vanburgh's *Relapse*. He also appeared in *Dick Wilder*. He was Henry Dennis, M.P. in *Diamond Deane*, a moralising play by a young American journalist, W. J. Dam; and Mortimer Mumpleford in *Confusion* by Joseph Derrick, a comedy revived for matinée performances at the Vaudeville, beginning 8 May. *The Theatre* commented on this farce (1 June):

> . . . Mr. Conway has not been seen to such advantage for a long time as in the *rôle* of the madly perplexed husband. . . . The revival was most favourably received, and created shouts of laughter.

Conway also took the lead in *The Honourable Herbert*, by Haddon Chambers, at the Vaudeville on 22 December, playing a cad who is nursed back to health by his wife after being thrown from a carriage in Brighton. *The Theatre* commented:

> H. B. Conway must be forgiven if he was not all that was expected of the Hon. Herbert, for the author had scarcely made it clear whether his hero was really repentant, or intended carrying on his life of profligacy so long as he was not found out.

Conway reappeared in his old part of Captain Fanshawe in a revival of *Saints and Sinners* (Vaudeville, 27 January 1892) and the following year took the lead in *Flight*, an absurd play by Walter Frith at Terry's Theatre (16 February). *The Times* reviewed it, calling it depressing but well acted; but *The Theatre* (1 March) said the play was a 'tomb' for the talent of the company. As Philip Amherst, Conway loses his memory after being hit on the head and is swindled by Ralph Sargent, who tries to get his money and his wife.

This utterly unconvincing piece may well have been his last. His name disappears from the reviews and records of the stage and perhaps at this time, feeling his deadly illness gaining upon him, he decided to get work with the Post Office. He lived for sixteen more years, eventually coming to depend more and more on his wife, who continued throughout with her busy acting career (she made her last appearance in 1925 and died in 1931) and presumably supported them both when encroaching paralysis finally turned him into a bed-ridden invalid. When he died, he had been largely forgotten.[39]

*The Theatre*, which had reviewed most of his performances, had ceased publication in 1897; and only the *Era* and the *Stage* noticed his passing, the latter in a particularly affectionate obituary summing up his achievements and his considerable contribution to the theatre of his day:

> Great sympathy will go out to Miss Kate Phillips, for years one of the brightest and sprightliest of comediennes, on the culmination of a long period of anxiety and devoted nursing in the death, on August 14 [1909], of her husband, H. B. Conway (H. Blenkinsopp Coulson), at the age of sixty. The late 'Harry' Conway, who, on his mother's side, was a kinsman, not a 'lineal descendant', of Lord Byron, was, in the seventies and eighties, one of the most popular and handsome of *jeunes premiers*, and had seemed to have a prosperous career before him up till his unhappy breakdown on the production of Will's *Faust* at the Lyceum in 1885, when, after a few nights, he was succeeded in the title rôle by Mr. George Alexander, promoted from the part of Valentine. This proved to be 'the beginning of the end' in the case of poor Conway, who had previously played the analagous part of Faustus in Gilbert's *Gretchen*, at the Olympic in 1879; and although he appeared for some years more at various theatres and in a good many parts . . . he had, for about a decade and a half past, been the victim of an insidious and ever-encroaching malady, which had rendered him a helpless invalid. . . . [The notice listed his long repertoire and recorded his association with Kate Vaughan and William Farren,] both of whom preceded to the grave this gay and buoyant actor, whose memory will be kept green by playgoers not afraid to be called Victorian.

\*

On 1 November 1879 *The Theatre* reported:

> *Incredible* as it may seem, Mr. Byron has a son eighteen years of age. The young gentleman has a turn for playing in comedy, and has now become an actor by profession under the not inappropriate name of Harryson.

Whether under this appropriate pseudonym or under his own name, John Byron made little impression. *The Theatre* reported his first London stage appearance twelve years later, when he appeared as Wimple in Pinero's *Lady Bountiful*, a new play at the Garrick, criticising the play as derivative and noting:

> Mr. John Byron (son of the [late] Henry J. Byron) and Mr. Gilbert Hare, evidently inherit their respective fathers' talents, and made a most favourable impression on their first London appearances.

He belonged to the Vaudeville company for a time, appearing there on 28 January 1893 in an adaptation by Robert Reece from a German play, *The Governor*. An improbable comedy depending on the acting of David James and William Farren, it had been revived largely on the strength of their performances and was soon replaced by the ever-popular *Our Boys*.

John lived until 1931, but he never realised the promise of his childhood. His beautiful sister, Elizabeth, also went on the stage briefly, but left it to marry Major Henry James Seton (6 December 1888) and died young on 2 September 1897. The profligate, handsome Alfred married Annie Elizabeth, daughter of George Boulton, on 5 February 1885, but he met an early death on 8 July 1891.

Like his brothers and sister, George Frederick, the youngest, disapproved of his father's second marriage and was unreconciled to his stepmother, who died on 18 September 1889. He pursued architecture as a career and emigrated for a while to Florida, where he tried to grow oranges; but crop failures sent him back to England where, in 1892, he was married very happily to Mary Clarissa Gillington, daughter of the Reverend John Maurice Gillington, of Newport, Isle of Wight. As May Byron she wrote books, verses, articles and reviews and her poetry had been praised by Lord Tennyson. She continued to write for such periodicals as *Blackwood's* and *The Spectator*, compiled a book of hymns, wrote a famous adaptation, *Peter Pan in Kensington Gardens*, illustrated by Lucie M. Attewell, and did a series for children, *A Day with . . .* , published by Hodder and Stoughton. Her *Day with Lord Byron* reflects the current attitude to the poet and shows how completely the idea of the exciting, misanthropic, lame nobleman had been established.

May Byron imagined the poet at the Palazzo Lanfranchi (Pisa) in

February of 1822 and joined him at about two o'clock, when his day begins, 'the most notorious personality of his century'. Inevitably he wakes in low spirits, 'in actual despair and despondency' he has termed it: this is partly constitutional and partly the result of feverish brain work. After a meagre breakfast, his lordship discusses ghosts with William Fletcher:

> However, he is laughing as he descends the magnificent staircase,—the reputed work of Michael Angelo,—laughing until the shrill querulous cries of peevish children make him stop and frown. He has allowed the Leigh Hunts, with their large and fractious family, to occupy for the present the ground-floor of the Palazzo; and children are his pet abhorrence. 'I abominate the sight of them so much,' he has already told Moore, 'that I have always had the greatest respect for the character of Herod!' No child figures in any of his poems: his own paternal feeling towards 'Ada, sole daughter of my house and home [*sic*],' is merely a fluctuating sentiment.

Byron then falls into 'sombre meditation' from which he is recalled by his friends—Williams, Medwin, Taafe, and Shelley, who persuade him, 'without much diffficulty', to read some of his poems and then to play billiards with them. As he moves around the billiard table, 'his lameness is distinctly noticeable'.

When Byron rides out, his long sight takes in every detail of scenery, storing it up unconsciously for future reference:

> It is the [night] hour when Byron's brain becomes thronged with a glowing phantasmagoria of ideas that cry aloud for visible expression. He forgets, under the stress of creative impulse, the sources and causes of his inherent melancholy,—the miserable days of his childhood, with a Fury for a mother,—the wound, never to be healed, of his unrequited love for Mary Chaworth,—the inimical wife from whom he is eternally alienated,— the little daughter that he may never hold in his arms,—the beloved sister separated from his side,—the ancestral home of his forefathers now passed into a stranger's hold,—the meteoric glory and total eclipse of his unparalleled popularity in England,—the follies, and worse than follies, which have made him what he is, 'consistent in nothing but his passion and his pride.' These memories, like poisonous exhalations, are banished from his mind, and leave a clear horizon for a while,—a fertile landscape peopled with great words and images. Something akin to inspiration seizes upon him: and he throws himself to work with all the zest and nerve of his impulsive nature.

George Frederick Byron wrote unpublished, unacted plays and at the end of his life (1932) started the autobiography which remains unfinished but which gives such a delightfully detailed glimpse of his boyhood and his father. He seems to have lacked the application for serious work and to have lived in the reflected glory of his clever wife, who had an active and varied career apart from writing. She was the first woman teacher at the Royal Academy of Music. She was the first reader for Hodder and Stoughton, where she was most respected. Imaginative, unworldly, she had the capacity for hard work and shared her father-in-law's ability to write amid noise and interruptions. She worked on the letter-press of Cecil Aldin's dog drawings and corresponded with L. A. G. Strong and other authors. She was interested in her husband's famous family: her 'Ballad of Foulweather Jack' was the best known piece in her book of poems, *The Wind on the Heath*.[40] She was blessed with simple, unpretentious faith and published a little booklet, 'Let Nothing You Dismay', which went through four printings and enjoyed great popularity. She died 5 November 1936, three years before her husband.

The only surviving child of their marriage, Charles Hubert Byron, was born 18 June 1897 at Southbourne, Bournemouth, and educated at Dulwich College, where he went through the Officers' Training Corps and obtained a commission in the Dublin Fusiliers. He volunteered for the newly formed Royal Flying Corps as a single-seater fighter pilot and actually fought air battles with young Count von Richthofen and Herman Goering. After the war he resigned his commission and worked for Lever Brothers, travelling on their behalf up the Congo. Afterwards illness obliged him to return to England, where for many years he was Sales Manager for Westland Aircraft in Yeovil, Somerset, travelling considerably, arranging for the sale of military aircraft to foreign governments, for which his linguistic abilities were useful. He was in the Royal Air Force Reserve and joined up again in the Second World War. He became a Wing Commander and won the American Bronze Star for his work with the Inter-Services Security Board, which planned the secrecy for operation 'Overload', the final allied assault on the Continent. He was RAF representative on the board of five—one for the Navy, one for the Army, one for the RAF, one American, and a Secretary. Above them the Joint Intelligence Committee consisted of three. Above them was Sir Winston Churchill, Minister of Defence and Prime Minister.

After the war Charles Byron returned to civilian life, where he became a lecturer on various historical topics and the Chief Guide and Lecturer at the Royal Pavilion, Brighton. He was a very popular speaker on the history of the Prince Regent's controversial creation. He also had a lifelong interest in the history of English costume and fashion and compiled a series of talks on the subject, illustrating his lectures with colour slides. He travelled extensively to lecture to many groups on such subjects as 'The Story of the Royal Pavilion'; 'Prince and Pavilion:

the Life and Times of the Prince Regent in Brighton'; 'The History of Brighton'; 'Dickensian Brighton'; 'The Story of English Costume and Fashion'. His twelve historical talks on the Early Middle Ages to the Twentieth Century seem to have been entertaining, witty, and informative, and were enthusiastically received.

> The members of this society were absolutely delighted with Mr. Byron's splendid talk. He seemed to have just the knack of knowing how much to give and how much to leave out. . . .     *The London Appreciation Society*

> . . . a delightful entertaining as well as enlightening lecture . . . the highlight of the day . . . what was greatly appreciated . . . was its clarity as well as wit.     *The British Council*

> The members of the Anglo-German Conference were amused, fascinated and impressed. . . .     *The Foreign Office*

> The Queen was so glad to have had the opportunity of coming to the Royal Pavilion at Brighton last Monday, and of being shown round by you [Mr. Clifford Musgrave] and Mr. Byron.     *Buckingham Palace*

In 1928 he had met and, on 25 May 1929 married, Joyce Evelyn, fourth daughter of Thomas Godwin Chance. He had been selecting illustrations for 'Arms and Armour, Costume, and Agricultural Machinery', a proposed article for the *Encyclopedia Britannica*, and she was in charge of thirty girls typing articles for it and she was also responsible for the index. She had lived until then (1917–29) the interesting and varied life of a free-lance-cum salaried journalist and editorial assistant, doing book reviews, publishers' reading, theatrical criticism and other work, and always pursued an interesting career. She was editorial assistant to John Buchan, Deputy Chairman of Reuters, before he became Governor-General of Canada as Lord Tweedsmuir. She was confidential secretary to Lord Beaverbrook and worked with Vernon Bartlett, Assistant to the Chief Editor (Reuter's). After her marriage she helped Bartlett with a book of his radio talks, 'The Way of the World', which became popular under the title *The World our Neighbour*. During the war she worked for Todd, the publishers (later amalgamated with Longman's), where she was highly regarded.

She therefore got on admirably with her remarkable mother-in-law and also remembered with very much affection her father-in-law, who had settled with his wife at Parkstone, Poole, Dorset, where he wrote his fragment of autobiography. Later she remembered:

> I think he wrote the autobiography when he was an old man, in his loneliness. . . . His love for Charles was only second to his love for his wife and I know he was very disappointed not to have any grandchildren, but

he never said a word about this to us—nor did my mother-in-law. We formed a most harmonious quartette. . . .[41]

Charles Byron was a quiet, kind man, as strictly honourable in business as his grandfather and father and adept at intelligent conversation. He was shy and humble and thus never made the most of his talents nor found an outlet for his considerable imagination, which his wife particularly remembered:

> He is the only one of the Byron men whom I've known intimately but he had the romantic mind and the culture of them all. (He was dreaming at one time and I asked him when he woke up what he was dreaming about. 'I've been to the war, with Don John of Austria,' he said enthusiastically. (From Chesterton's poem which re-iterates, 'Don John of Austria is going to the war'.)[42]

That he was a charming, commanding personality, with the family's talent for conversation and letter-writing, is evident from many who knew him and from the testimonials which followed his death on 14 May 1966:

> Your husband was the most charming man we've ever had in this hospital and no one here will ever forget him and his courage and his blue blue eyes.
>
> *The Lady Almoner at the Hospital*

> I was very lucky to know him and privileged rarely. I owe my mental survival to him for those glorious conversations when wide fields were covered . . . the sheer joy and inspiration of his conversation—the breadth, depth and the *simplicity* that was fundamental and the mark of a truly great human being.
>
> *Colleague at the Royal Pavilion*

Henry James Byron's branch of the family apparently ends with his last grandson, since only George Frederick Byron had children.[43]

# · Epilogue ·
## The Fame of His Fathers:
## The Present Byrons

'Far distant he goes, with the same emulation,
The fame of his fathers he ne'er can forget.

That fame, and that memory, still will he cherish;
He vows that he ne'er will disgrace your renown:
Like you will he live, or like you will he perish;
When decayed, may he mingle his dust with your own!'

*On Leaving Newstead Abbey*

RUPERT Byron (the 11th Baron) died on 1 November 1983, and the title passed to his kinsman, Lt-Colonel Richard Geoffrey Byron, DSO, a descendant of the Rev. Richard Byron, the third son of the fourth Lord. We have seen that Admiral Richard, the eldest son of the Rev. Richard, had four sons of whom the Rev. John, the third son, had seven children. Of those seven children, the two boys, John and William Gerard, both became professional soldiers.

John, the eldest son, was born in 1832 and in 1852, at the age of 20, he joined the 34th Regiment of Foot and soon found himself involved in the two major campaigns of the 1850s, the Crimean War and the Indian Mutiny. The Crimean War had broken out in 1853 and in 1854 John was wounded at the siege of Sebastopol and taken prisoner in a sortie by the Russians on the night of 20 December 1854. He suffered considerably from the severe cold during his period of captivity, but in August 1855 English and Russian prisoners were exchanged at Odessa when John, then a lieutenant, was set free and rejoined his Regiment shortly before Sebastopol finally fell early in September. At the conclusion of the Crimean War in 1856, he returned to England only to be sent abroad again the following year after the outbreak of the Indian Mutiny. Along with his brother, William Gerard, he was at the siege of Lucknow which he described in one of his letters as 'not a very happy time'. This was a gross understatement as they suffered extreme privations. At the end of nearly a year, he wrote 'Today we heard the pipers. Thank God the Campbells are coming.'

John Byron's marriage is intriguing. Returning to India after a period of leave, he married in the Cathedral at Cape Town, Susan Amelia Chiappini, an Italian girl, on 24 October 1865. Whether they met and married during the few days when the ship stopped at Cape Town or whether they knew each other before that time is not known but she was by reputation a beautiful girl and John was devoted to her. In 1870, their first and only son, Richard, was born and shortly afterwards, Susan Amelia died of typhoid. John was distraught and erected a monument to her at Trimulgherry in Southern India.

John Byron retired from the Army in 1887 with the rank of Major General and died in 1895 aged 63. In the meantime, his younger brother had also had a successful military career but he died while Colonel with his regiment at the age of 48. After the Indian Mutiny campaign he had seen active service again in the Afghan war from 1878 to 1880, accompanying Sir Frederick Roberts in his celebrated march from Kabul to Kandahar, a distance of 318 miles, which was accomplished in 23 days. In the same year General McGrigor mentioned in his despatch: 'the able manner in which Lt. Colonel Byron commanded his fine regiment.'

Between 1881–82 he served with the Natal Field Force. William Gerard died unmarried on 5th June 1885. There is a memorial tablet to him in Winchester Cathedral.

*

After the death of his mother in India, John Byron's young son, Richard, was sent back to England to spend a very unhappy childhood being brought up by two maiden aunts. After attending what was then known as a Dame's School he was sent to Wellington College and The Royal Military Academy, Sandhurst from where he gained a commission into the King's Royal Rifle Corps. Like his father, Richard was sent out to India soon after joining his Regiment and was stationed in the North-West of India at Rawalpindi. From there, he took part in two North-West frontier expeditions: the Hazar in 1891 and the Chitral in 1893. These campaigns were generally regarded as arduous and unpleasant; the tribesmen were very accurate snipers and had a habit of swooping on the column when least expected. Luck was needed to survive; on one occasion the officer marching alongside Richard was shot through the head and killed.

When this tour of duty came to an end, Richard returned to England and married a Miss Mabel Winter whose father had managed all the legal affairs involving the Nizam of Hyderabad's railway and who was rewarded by a gift of £100,000 on completion—a very large sum of money in those days. Richard Byron's life now took a change of direction; his battalion was asked to find an officer to go to County Cork to be Adjutant to the North Cork Rifles and Richard, probably lured by the hunting prospects in Ireland, volunteered and was appointed. A life of hunting, however, was soon interrupted by the outbreak of hostilities in South Africa and he spent the entire South African War with the North Cork Rifles. There are no details of his activities but it is known that his unit campaigned in the Transvaal, the Orange Free State and the Cape Colony. During the campaign, Richard won the DSO and, although the citation is not known, he was only a Captain at the time and it may be presumed that it was for an act of gallantry in the field as DSO's are not usually won by junior officers. At the end of the War, Richard returned to England to live with his family at Winchester. His eldest son, Richard Geoffrey Gordon, the present holder of the Barony, was born in 1899 and his daughter, Sheila Margaret, in 1903. Richard lived quietly until his death in 1939.

Richard Geoffrey, now the twelfth Lord Byron, known by his second name to avoid confusion with his father, was educated at Eton and Sandhurst during the First World War. Towards the end of November 1918, two weeks after the war had ended, he was commissioned and joined the Fourth Royal Irish Dragoon Guards who at that time were forming part of the Army of occupation in Cologne. After a spell in Ireland, his Regiment, like that of his father and grandfather, was sent to India and stationed at Secunderabad. In 1922 he was appointed ADC to the Governor of Bombay, Sir George Lloyd. He wrote later:

> This was a wonderful opportunity for a young officer and the work, although sometimes daunting, had its funny side also. Once a week, there were dinner parties when forty or fifty important Indian guests would assemble, all with names somewhat unfamiliar to the English tongue. These names had to be learnt by heart and the guests assembled around the ballroom floor prior to introductions to their Excellencies. On one occasion, an important guest, having been introduced by the ADC who was a Grenadier Guards Officer, stepped forward and said 'that is not my name'. Guards Officers are not so easily defeated: 'Yes, it is,' said the ADC and passed on to the next guest.

This colourful appointment came to an end in 1925 and the following year Geoffrey married his first wife, Margaret Steuart. He continued soldiering in India until his Regiment was ordered back to England in 1930 and shortly after this, he was offered and accepted the Adjutancy

*The House of Byron*

of the Duke of Lancaster's own Yeomanry who had their headquarters in Manchester. He recalled later:

> For a regular officer, work with the Territorials is an interesting experience; he is the only professional, being responsible for all training and having to prepare, conduct and review all exercises carried out. The fortnightly camp was a wonderful opportunity to observe the splendid characteristics of the Lancashire man. They were mostly bus drivers or coalminers and yet at the end of a fortnight, were capable of carrying out regimental cavalry drill at the gallop—and enjoying it.

In 1937, Geoffrey Byron took up the position of Military Secretary to the Governor General of New Zealand—Lord Gallway. This was an appointment which meant a lot of travelling throughout New Zealand and, as a result, he formed a deep attachment to the New Zealand countryside.

With the outbreak of the Second World War, this work came to an end and by the time Geoffrey Byron had completed the journey home he found that his Regiment had lost their horses, which had been replaced by light tanks, and were already in France. However, by 10 May—the day the war proper started—he found himself billeted with the vicar in a small village called Vred. Departing hastily to meet the Germans, he left his bicycle and wireless with the vicar. Four years later, after the Normandy invasion, the Regiment, now under his command, found itself near Vred and a visit to the vicar revealed that he was still there. He had managed to hang on to the wireless but had been forced to surrender the bicycle to the Germans!

Like the rest of the British Expeditionary Force, Geoffrey Byron's regiment was forced to evacuate at Dunkirk and during the middle years of the war was involved in the training and preparation which led ultimately to the Normandy Invasion. Landing at H-hour on D-Day in command of the 4th/7th Dragoon Guards, he followed his father's example by winning a D.S.O. during the Normandy campaign.

In 1946, he married for the second time Dorigen Esdaile and had two sons, Richard Noel and Robert (Robin) James. He retired soon after the end of the War and lived in Hampshire until he inherited the Langford Estate on the death of Anna, Lady Byron, the widow of the tenth Lord. He thereafter lived at Langford Hall in Essex and later moved to London where he still lives. In 1983, he inherited the title from Rupert, the eleventh Lord Byron. Because of the complexities of his descent from the fourth Lord, however, he was not immediately able to take his seat in the House of Lords and detailed documentary evidence had to be produced to the Lord Chancellor showing the line of descent from

William, the fourth Lord Byron, and demonstrating that all the lines descending from Admiral, John Byron had come to an end. He was eventually able to take his seat in 1986.

The life of Lord Byron's eldest son, Richard, tragically killed at the age of thirty-seven, encapsulates much of the adventurous spirit of the Byron family.

After leaving Wellington, Richard Byron went to Grenoble University to study French and it was during this time that his love of travel first began to show. Neglecting his studies, he made his way through Italy, Greece and Turkey—if not quite in the style of his most famous ancestor, certainly with all the poet's enthusiasm for new places.

When he returned to England, Richard took up a city job but was never able to settle and after a few years left to continue his travels, thereby beginning a life that in the next fifteen years was to take him to some of the most remote parts of the world. His interest was by and large in the most far-flung places and it was characteristic of him that he always travelled alone so as to be free to stop or move on exactly when he pleased. He never kept a diary or made any written record of his travels—which was a disappointment to his family—but some of his letters, sometimes in diary form, give a glimpse of his experiences.

Crossing Africa by what he called the 'easiest route', he wrote:

*Tuesday 16th* [Feb. 1981]
In the Haggar Mountains . . . up at 5.15 and climb hill to Pere Foucauld's hermitage—a French priest who was murdered by the tribesmen. The desert is safe now but 50 years ago they would have cut your throat. Spectacular sunrise but icy cold . . . we are 9,000 feet here.

*Wednesday 17th*
Looking for a lorry to go south but no luck.

*Thursday 18th*
I find a lorry but we are stopped leaving town because the lorry has no customs pass. Now it is the Muslim weekend and we must wait till Saturday. The driver is impassive but I am nearly berserk.

*Friday 19th*
I spent the day under a tree reading.

*Saturday 20th*
We set out again but after about 2 hours we stopped. Some problem with the lorry. Night by the roadside. The lorry carried wood so we can have a fire.

[ 283 ]

*Sunday 21st*

We leave at 9. The sun is hot now and the wind drives the sand into your face. We stop at 2 and bake bread in the sand.

. . . .

*Tuesday 23rd*

At Agadez. We arrive at 2am at the edge of the town. The driver disappears and I look for somewhere to stay. No sign of a hotel and I am followed by two snarling dogs who track me from the shadows. I take refuge in the courtyard of a house and sleep there till dawn. In the morning I am seen and feel embarrassed, but the people are friendly and bring me some coffee . . .

Another time, travelling in South America he wrote:

I decided to take a shortcut through some open country to the main road which according to my map was about 5 miles. Unfortunately I became lost and it got dark so I decided to spend the night in a tree as somehow this seemed safer than the ground. It must have been the worst night of my life—there were all sorts of animal noises but it was so dark I could see nothing. In the morning I was so cold and stiff for a time I completely lost control of my body. . . .

Several times he was robbed of his belongings—on one occasion suffering a stab wound.

While in England, Richard lived a comparatively quiet life but after a time always became restless to travel again. In January 1985 he set out on what was intended to be a short trip to West Africa to take in a visit to Timbuktu, a place he felt to be of symbolic importance, which a serious traveller could not omit from his itinerary. On 21 February he wrote to his brother:

. . . not without some difficulty I have now finally made it to Timbuktu . . . whether I manage to get away from here remains to be seen. . . .

Before that letter arrived in England, however, news had reached his family that he had been killed when the plane he was leaving on crashed after take off. He was buried in Timbuktu. The family erected a memorial plaque to him at the church in Hucknall where the poet and other Byrons are buried.

Richard never married and on his death his younger brother, Robin, became heir to the title. On leaving Wellington Robin followed the poet's footsteps to Trinity College Cambridge, reading History and Law, and later practised at the Bar in the Chambers of the former Attorney General, Lord Rawlinson. Subsequently he left the Bar and is now a solicitor specialising in maritime law. In 1979 he married Robyn

Margaret Mclean, daughter of John Mclean of Hamilton, New Zealand. They have three daughters, Caroline Anne Victoria, born in 1981, Emily Clare, born in 1984 and Sophie Georgina, born in 1986.

\*

A little over 250 years have passed since the fifth Lord Byron inherited the title from his father and it is a curious fact that since that time only one peer—the seventh Lord—has passed the title to his son. The dearth of male heirs has curtailed many branches of the family and of all the lines which stemmed from the sons of the fourth Lord, it seems that only the present Lord Byron and his younger son, Robin, remain. Whatever the destiny of the family, we may repeat for them the poet's wish for Newstead Abbey long ago, that

> 'Hours, splendid as the past, may still be thine,
> And bless thy future, as thy former day.'

# NOTES

## NOTES TO THE PROLOGUE

1. Letter A. 76, Roe-Byron Collection, Newstead Abbey.
2. The earliest spellings are Burun and Buron, followed by Ber(r)on, Biro(u)n, Birun, and other variations *ad lib.*
3. Cleveland, *Battle Abbey Roll*, III, 357.
4. Kerry, 'Annals of Horestan and Horsley', *Journal of the Derbyshire Archae- ological . . . Society*, X (1888).
5. Thoroton, *Antiquities of Nottinghamshire* (1677), p. 82; quoting from a Register of Lenton Priory then in the possession of Sam Roper of Heanor, now, alas, unknown.
6. Thoroton, *Antiquities*, p. 373.
7. *Ibid.*, p. 355.
8. *V.C.H.*, (*Victoria County History*) Lancashire, II, 113.
9. Farrer, 'Barony of Grelley', *Transactions of the Historical Society of Lancashire and Cheshire*, V, 53, p. 50.
10. For illustration and plan see *V.C.H. Lancashire*, IV, 284, 286.
11. Farrer, *Lancashire Inquests, 1205–1307*, p. 56, says that the Black Book of Clayton and other charters support Richard's claim to precedence. *V.C.H. Lancashire*, IV, 283.
12. P.R.O. (Public Record Office), Cal. Pat. Rolls, 1232–47; Lib. Rolls, 1226–40, 201. The Earls of Chester and Pembroke commanded the English forces during the latter part of Henry III's brief invasion of France, 1230–31. The year was dated from Lady Day, 6 April until 1752, 25 March thereafter. February 1232/3 means February 1233. In 1752 Britain changed from the Julian to the Gregorian calendar (Old Style to New Style). Before that, the British calendar was 10 days behind the continent, 11 days from 1700.
13. P.R.O., Pat. 1292–1301, 364.
14. According to some accounts, Alesia was the second wife of Sir John Byron senior (*V.C.H. Lancashire*, IV, 283). Her marriage to the son seems better supported by contemporary records (*ibid.*, I, 373).
15. Foster, *Some Feudal Coats of Arms*, p. 39.
16. H. Gill, 'Colwick Hall and Church', *Transactions of the Thoroton Society*, *XIX* (1915), 36–37. His authority for the description is not stated.
17. N.B.R. (Nottingham Borough Records), I, 412–21. See also Close and Patent Rolls, *passim.*

18. Quoted in Fishwick's *Rochdale*, p. 338.
19. ˙H. A. Hudson, 'Manchester Cathedral Screens', *Historic Society of Lancashire and Cheshire, Transactions*, LXX, 57–58.
20. H. A. Hudson, *op. cit.*
21. Thornely, *Monumental Brasses of Lancashire*, pp. 41–42 and plate.
22. *Testamenta Eboracensia*, III, 202.
23. But see alternative pedigree in the Visitation of Nottinghamshire (Harleian Society, IV).
24. Collins, *Peerage*, says she married (1) William, son of John Leke; (2) Thomas Walshe of Onlepe, Leicesterhire, Esq. A note by Townely, in his transcript of the Black Book of Clayton, names Walshe and Staunton as her husbands (on Dugdale's authority).
25. Harleian Society, *Lincolnshire Pedigrees*, II, 385. In *Letters of Stephen Gardiner*, ed. J. A. Muller (1933), he is described as 'son of John Gardiner, a reasonably well-to-do clothmaker (d. 1507) and Agnes his wife'.
26. Harland, *Mamecestre*, II, 349, names Sir Edmund Talbot as her first husband. Sir John Assheton died 3 September 1428 (Raines' *Notes to examynacyons towchenge* Cokeye More, *Chetham Miscellanies*, II).
27. P.R.O., Papal Letters, VII, 1427–47, 577–78.
28. *V.C.H. Lancashire*, III, 436, quoting Dugdale's visitation; Harleian Society, *Lincolnshire Pedigrees*, I, 128.
29. The husbands of Jane and Catherine are so named in Collins *Peerage*; earlier references are lacking.
30. *History of Parliament, 1439–1509*; *Biographies*, 147; but statements in this work must be treated with caution. See note 35 below.
31. *History of Parliament, 1439–1509*; Register, 440.
32. J. Harland, ed. *Ballads and Songs of Lancashire* (1865), p. 11.
33. Beaumont, 'Bosworth Field', *Poems*, ed. A. B. Grosart (1869).
34. N.B.R., III, 240, 265.
35. Collins, *Peerage* (1779), VII, 126; Campbell, *Materials for a history of Henry VII*, II, 385; *V.C.H. Lancashire*, IV, 285. The official *History of Parliament* (*Biographies, 1439–1509*, 147) ignores his death and ascribes the transfer of his offices of constable, etc., to Sir Thomas Lovell in 1489 to his fall 'from grace'.
36. N.B.R., III, 308–09; this is the earliest mention yet found of the Byron crest, the origin of which is unknown.
37. Collins, *Peerage* (1779), VII, 127. Like his brother's tomb, the window has disappeared.
38. The dating of the will is self-contradictory: 'the yere of our Lord God m¹ ccccciiijth & ye yere of ye reigne of kyng Henry the vijth after ye conquest xix' (i.e. 1503). See *Testamenta Eboracensia*, IV, 235.

## NOTES TO CHAPTER 1

1. N.B.R., III, 313, 311. The breakfast cost 5*s*. 6*d*.
2. E.g. Harleian Society, IV, *Visitations of Nottinghamshire*, p. 9; Bernard's Pedigree of the Byrons.
3. P. Davenport, *Ralph Lemyngton*, p. 3. Davenport does not, however, mention the Byrons.
4. P.R.O. L. & P., Henry VIII, II, Part 2, 1505.
5. *Ibid.*, III, Part 1, 246.
6. *Hall's Chronicle*, 1809 ed.
7. *H.M.C.* (*Historical MSS Commission*) Middleton, 361.
8. Thoroton calls him Roger. The surname is also spelt Haugh. Booker, Blackley, 113.
9. N.B.R., III, 361.
10. P.R.O., L. & P., Henry VIII, VI, 136, 246–47.
11. *Ibid.*, XI, 223.
12. *Ibid.*, XV, 5.
13. Translated from the original charter at Newstead Abbey.
14. P.R.O., L. & P., Henry VIII, XVII, 526, 557.
15. *H.M.C. Rutland*, IV, 320.
16. P.R.O. L. & P., Henry VIII, XIX, Part 1, 162–63.
17. Proved 5 May 1547 (*Testamenta Eboracensia.*, VI, 228). An angel was then worth between 7*s*. 6*d*. and 8*s*.; a royal = an angel and a half.
18. *H.M.C. Rutland*, I, 67.
19. Bailey, *Annals*, II, 465.
20. Parker, *Correspondence*, 232.
21. Raines, *Stanley Papers*, Part ii, 164–65 (Chetham Society); Booker, Blackley, 184.
22. Earwaker, *Lancashire and Cheshire Wills*, II, 133–36.

## NOTES TO CHAPTER 2

1. Comparatively soon after his death, this sobriquet was mistakenly transferred to his father. The effigies on their respective tombs and the portrait described on p. 39 are sufficient proof of the error, which has nevertheless persisted.
2. That they are so described in 1568 and 1569, before the new owner of Newstead had been knighted, indicates that they had been patronised by his father; see *N.B.R.*, IV, 132, and *Kelly's Notices of the Drama . . . from MSS. of Leicester*, 199, 203.
3. The Vice-Chancellor's letter, mentioned below, gives the date as 24 February; but as the letter is dated 9 February, one of these dates is obviously wrong. Probably the letter was written in March.

4. MS. Lansdowne, xxiv, art. 20; Cooper, Ann., ii, 347–49; Searle, *History of the Queens' College*, 1867, p. 345.

5. Skeffington's will proved 1600. Isabel died between 1625 and 1627. Richard Assheton was born 1557, knighted 1603, and died 1617.

6. Lady Willoughby rode there with Mrs Byron on 12 September 1573: *H.M.C. Middleton*, 432.

7. *H.M.C. Rutland*, I, 106.

8. Lucy Hutchinson, *Memoirs*, p. 57.

9. Tentatively dated 'Aug. 1591?' by the editor of the Rutland MSS. See *H.M.C. Rutland*, I, 294. The recipients were great-uncles of the fifth Earl of Rutland, John being the husband of Dorothy Vernon.

10. After remaining at Newstead more than 330 years, the portrait was removed to Thrumpton Hall, the home of the 10th Lord Byron. It is inscribed: 'Aetatis suae 73 An. Dom. 1599'. It is now the property of the 12th Lord Byron.

11. *H.M.C. Salisbury*, XII, 694.

12. *H.M.C. Salisbury*, XV, 194.

13. Talbot Papers, vol. K, f. 184; text from Lodge, *Illustrations of British History*, III, 156 (contracted words expanded). The date should be 1604.

14. Sir John Harpur of Swarkestone and Breadsall, reputedly one of the richest men of his time in Derbyshire.

15. Hutchinson, *Memoirs*, p. 57.

16. Said by Raine (*Stanley Papers*, II, 166) to be £5,000. I have not seen the original deed, but the particulars given above are recited in Newstead archive no. 11.

17. Newstead archive no. 11: he is described as 'John Byron, junior, of Colwicke ... knight', the earliest mention of his title. Crisp may rightly think he received his knighthood in 1603, at the same time as his father, although only one John Byron is recorded in the list of knights made that year.

18. Hutchinson, *Memoirs*, p. 58.

19. *H.M.C.* Rutland, I, 428.

20. Particulars summarised (field names, etc. omitted) from *C.S.P.D. Calendar of State Papers, Domestic Series*, 190/52, etc.

21. Original letters patent apparently lost; a copy (not quite complete) in book form in the Roe-Byron collection, with bookplate of William Lord Byron (fourth or fifth Baron), dated in pencil: '30th June 13th James 1st 1616' (an error for 1615).

22. *H.M.C. Rutland*, I, 448.

23. Hutchinson, *Memoirs*, pp. 55–56.

24. *Ibid.*, p. 60.

25. The estate became a Manchester Park in 1893.

26. Hutchinson, *Memoirs*, pp. 58–59.

27. Fishwick, *Rochdale*, 26.

28. 'When the first child was borne, the father, mother, and child, could not make one-and-thirty yeares old' (Hutchinson, *Memoirs*, p. 58).

29. Plumptre, *Epigrammaton opusculum*, 1629.

## NOTES TO CHAPTER 3

1. According to some authorities. Morant, *History of Essex*, says that John's heir was his elder brother, Sir William Fitzwilliam; but Sir Nicholas Byron was described as of Gaynes Park at the time of his death.
2. Duncan Gray, 'Historical Notes on Nottinghamshire Coal Mining', *Nottinghamshire Weekly Guardian* (2 December 1944).
3. *Lives of* [*Royalists*], p. 489.
4. On permanent loan from Lt.-Col. W. A. Potter, D.S.O. in Nottingham Public Libraries.
5. I have assumed that Plumptre was punning on the lady's name, and suggesting that she was of undistinguished origin; but other explanations are, of course, possible.
6. The old title of respect, 'Dominus', not necessarily implying knighthood.
7. *C.S.P.D.*, 1639, 55.
8. *C.S.P.D.*, 1640, 106.
9. *H.M.C. Rutland*, I, 521.
10. *C.S.P.D.*, 1640, 493–94.
11. *C.S.P.D.*, 1640, 617: modern copy of a very imperfect original, now wanting, to which the copyist has appended: 'I have thought this imperfect fragment worth preserving on account of the gallant and loyal spirit of this worthy ancestor of one of the most extraordinary men of modern times: of whom it is to be regretted that he has not inherited some portion of that spirit'.
12. Counterpart preserved at Newstead, dated 11 June 1636.
13. *C.S.P.D.*, 1634–35, 200 (and from the original MSS).
14. On 4 March the Constable of Dunham certified that Markham had been put under arrest, but was too infirm and ailing (having been bedridden for two years) to be 'portable to London'. He died about a year later, aged nearly eighty.
15. The distraint of knighthood in 1631, when landowners of a certain status who refused to take up the honour of knighthood, with its duties and expenses, were obliged to compound for their refusal.
16. *C.S.P.D.*, 1635–36, 189–90.
17. It will be remembered that in 1604 the Earl of Shrewsbury had advised Byron's grandfather to remove to Lancashire for reasons of economy.
18. *C.S.P.D.*, 1640–41, 93.
19. *C.S.P.D.*, 1641–43, 265, 269.
20. Lloyd, *Lives of* [*Royalists*], p. 489.
21. By Crisp; not in burial register.
22. *H.M.C. Ormonde*, n.s., II, 201–02.
23. *C.S.P.D.*, 1625–49, 616.
24. *Ibid.*, 1641–43, 51.

## NOTES TO CHAPTER 4

1. Three days earlier his eldest son, Thomas, had been baptised in the Church of St Michael 1e Belfrey, Yorks.
2. *H.M.C. Portland*, I, 85. One doubts the figures, but it may be believed that he was considerably outnumbered.
3. *Collectanea Topographica*, VI, 334.
4. In an execrable hand: British Library Additional MS. 18, 980, I, 80.
5. Lucy Hutchinson, *Memoirs*, 171–72.
6. British Library Additional MS. 18, 980, I, 147.
7. Malbon's *Memorial of the Civil War*, ed. J. Hall (*Record Society of Lancashire and Cheshire*, XIX, 94–95); spelling modernised.
8. Carte's *Collection of Letters, etc.*, I, 34; Phillips, *Memoirs of the Civil War in Wales*, II, 116–18.
9. Letter to M. A. Cursham, 20 August 1831, Nottingham County Libraries.
10. Wood, *Fasti Oxonienses*.
11. See pp. 98–99.
12. A. C. Wood, *Nottinghamshire in the Civil War*, p. 68.
13. *H.M.C. Hastings*, II, 129–32.
14. Lloyd, *Lives of [Royalists]*, pp. 488–89.
15. *Civil War in Nottinghamshire*, p. 92, n. 1.
16. *C.S.P.D.*, 1644–45, 436.
17. Morris, *Siege of Chester*, pp. 186–87.
18. Lloyd, *Lives of [Royalists]*, p. 489.
19. Gardiner, *Hamilton Papers*, 166–68.
20. *Calendar of Committee for Advance of Money*, II, 772, where she is described as 'Lady Ann, Sir Nich. Byron's lady', which may account for the statement that he was twice married.
21. Proved 26 August 1650, *P.C.C.* 135, Pembroke.
22. Lloyd, *Lives of [Royalists]*.

## NOTES TO CHAPTER 5

1. From a letter in the possession of the 12th Lord Byron.
2. He is described therein as *Sir* Ernestus. His father was occasionally, and perhaps correctly, styled Baronet, but he is not in Cokayne's *Complete Baronetage*. The title was also used by Ernestus' son, Edward Byron.
3. And very neatly, too. He describes himself as 'Barronet'.
4. Pepys, *Diary*, 26 April 1667.
5. *Ibid.*
6. Elianor, daughter of Thomas Dutton, widow of Baron Gerard. Her second husband, Robert Needham, 2nd Viscount Kilmorey, died 12 September 1653. Lady Byron is usually said to be her daughter, but as the settlement

on the Needham-Gerard marriage was dated 1636, this is impossible: her mother must have been Needham's first wife, Frances Anderson.

7. His son, born in Chester during the siege, was one of the children there christened Byron. Sir Peter married Elizabeth, third daughter of Gilbert Lord Gerard (first husband of Elianor Lady Kilmorey).

8. See p. 89.

9. *C.S.P.D.*, 1673, 575.

10. See p. 86–87.

11. *C.S.P.D.*, 1661–62, 391.

12. *Calendar of the Treasury Books*, II, Part 1, 1669–72, 237, 572, and index.

13. Harleian Society, *Lincolnshire Pedigrees*, III.

14. *Commons Journals*, IX, 163.

15. *H.M.C. Bath*, I, 58.

16. *H.M.C. Portland*, IV, 96–97.

17. Both buried in the Church of St Mary Magdalen, Bermondsey. *Hackett's Epitaphs*, II, 5.

18. Lucy Hutchinson, *Memoirs*, p. 420.

19. See p. 67. Notice that the reward had somehow grown in the interval.

20. *C.S.P.D.* 1671, 577.

21. *C.S.P.D.* 1672–73, 6.

22. See p. 100.

23. Date of her death unknown.

24. See p. 105.

25. The burial register merely reads 'Esquire Byrion'. He does not appear in the Register of Baptisms.

26. Said by Crisp to have died 1683; perhaps he confused her with her mother, who died the same year.

27. Buried 10 August 1671.

28. Owing, no doubt, to neglect during the Civil Wars and Commonwealth, an account of the deer taken in April 1665 revealed none in Newstead and Papplewick. In 1672 there were 9. There had been 19 red deer in 1635. (*Bromley House Forest Books*, c.c. 266, pp. 149, 209; c.c. 259.)

29. Published in *Carolina: or, Loyal Poems*, by Tho. Shipman, Esq., London, 1683.

30. London, printed for Henry Mortlock at the Phoenix in St Paul's Churchyard and at the White Hart in Westminster Hall, 1682.

31. James II succeeded his brother 6 February 1685.

32. Licence dated 8 September.

33. Pass granted 19 April 1696.

34. The counterpart deed, bearing her shaky signature, is in the Nottingham Public Libraries.

35. To Thomas Coke at Melbourne: *H.M.C. Cowper*, II, 391.

36. Born 14 May 1676.

37. *Wentworth Papers*, 284.

38. Report of the Surveyor-General of H.M. Woods, Trent North, to the Lord High Treasurer, on Byron's Memorial. *Calendar of Treasury Papers*, 1708–14, 599.

39. *Wentworth Papers*, 450; Byron was nearly fifty-two. I have not discovered Frances' age.
40. Buried at Hucknall 24 September.
41. Murray MSS.
42. *H.M.C. Dartmouth*, III, 158.
43. *H.M.C. Portland*, VI, 23.
44. *Anecdotes of Painting*, ed. Wornum (1862), II, 675.
45. Murray MSS.


## NOTES TO CHAPTER 6

1. Marchand, *Byron's Letters and Journals*, X, 208–09.
2. Proved 19 October 1736.
3. The original subscription book in Nottingham County Libraries contains his signature.
4. *History of White's*, II, Part 1, p. 7.
5. James Quin (1693–1766) actor. O'Hara was the family name of Lord Tyrawley, real father of G. A. Bellamy.
6. Born 2 March 1729.
7. Died 1736.
8. A copy bearing his bookplate was offered for sale in 1948.
9. As printed in the *Nottinghamshire Weekly Guardian* (local notes and queries), 26 August 1944; the original publication has not been traced.
10. Ten members were present: Lord Byron, William Chaworth, John Hewett, Frederick Montagu, George Donston, the Hon. Thomas Willoughby, John Sherwin, Sir Robert Burdet, Charles Mellish, and Francis Molyneux.
11. This seems to contradict the advertisement quoted on p. 129.
12. Quotations are from the official report of the trial.
13. Serjeant-surgeon to Kings George II and III; a Baronet in 1778.
14. According to a contemporary newspaper account, Miss R—h, who was pregnant by him, received £10,000, with £25,000 for the child, if a boy, £3,000 if a girl.
15. *Walpole's Correspondence with George Montagu*, ed. Lewis and Brown, II, 148.
16. J. H. Jesse, *George Selwyn and His Contemporaries*, I, 358.
17. *Ibid.*, I, 366.
18. *Ibid.*, I, 371. Lady Falmouth was wife of the 2nd Viscount; Miss Sennisheri remains a mystery.
19. 119 peers returned this verdict; 4 found him Not Guilty on either charge.
20. *Percy Letters*, ed. Brooks, pp. 89–90.
21. *Letters*, ed. Toynbee, VI, 216.
22. Daughter of his sister Isabella, Countess of Carlisle. Lady Frances, who had been engaged to Lord Anglesey the year before, married John Radcliffe.
23. Inn opposite the main entrance to Newstead Park. A lodge was not built until the latter part of the 19th century.

24. Priced catalogue in the possession of Messrs Christie, Manson & Woods.
25. *Correspondence with George Montagu*, I, 299.
26. *H.M.C. Verulam*, 233–34.
27. Leslie A. Marchand, Byron's Letters and Journals, I, 72; see also Doris Langley Moore, *Lord Byron: Accounts Rendered*, p. 63.
28. Undated; Murray MSS.
29. Made 4 January 1785, with five codicils in her own hand added between September 1785 and June 1787, proved 15 July 1788.
30. Murray MSS.
31. *Abbotsford and Newstead Abbey* (1835), p. 180.
32. Augusta Z. Fraser, *Livingstone and Newstead* (1913), pp. 83, 7–8.
33. W. S. Haselden, *Notes & Queries*, VIII (1853), 2–3.
34. *Livingstone and Newstead*, p. 85.
35. *People's Journal*, LVI (23 January 1847), 45–46.

## NOTES TO CHAPTER 7

1. *The Narrative of the Honourable John Byron*, 1768.
2. Pierpont Morgan Library: letter from Margaret Grant MacWhirter to Mrs Byron (see Appendix A), note on accompanying photograph showing memorial column and plaque, 21 January 1936. Mrs MacWhirter sent Mrs Byron a copy of her book, *Treasure Trove in Gaspé and the Baie des Chaleurs*.
3. *Voyage Round the World in His Majesty's Ship the Dolphin*, p. 51 n.
4. *Dictionary of National Biography*.
5. D. A. Stauffer, *Art of Biography*, 1941, I, 208.
6. From Dr Henry Curtis, *Collections for a History of Pirbright*, typescript in the library of the Surrey Archaeological Society; summarised by Miss E. M. Dance.
7. *Sandwich Papers*, I, 74–75. The Parker of this alliterative recommendation became father-in-law of John Byron's daughter, Augusta.
8. *H.M.C. Carlisle*, pp. 388–89.
9. *Sandwich Papers*, III, 182 (19 October).
10. *Thraliana*, I, 407.
11. *Pembroke Papers*, 245, 252, 267, 289.
12. *Barrington Papers*, II, 320–21.
13. 6th Lord Byron's letter to J. J. Coulmann, 12 July 1823; Marchand, *Byron's Letters and Journals*, X, 208. Jean Jacques Coulmann (1796–1873), an Alsatian, was a close friend of Benjamin Constant. He was a great admirer of Byron and made a special trip to meet him in Genoa. The meeting took place on 7 January 1823. For further details, see Kenneth W. Davis 'Lord Byron's Letter to J. J. Coulmann', *Notes & Queries*, June 1982, 29 [227]: 210–11.
14. *Thraliana*, II, 733.

15. D'Arblay, *Diary*, I, 236; Bath, 29 April 1780.
16. *Thraliana*, I, 330 (July 1778), 348 (December 1778).
17. *Ibid.*, 323, 326.
18. D'Arblay, *Diary*, I, 225.
19. *Letters*, II, 344.
20. *Diary*, I, 301; letter to Mrs Thrale, 1 July 1780.
21. *Diary*, I, 257.
22. *Ibid.*, 325.
23. *Letters*, II, 448, 483.
24. *Thraliana*, I, 541.
25. *Letters*, III, 106.
26. To T. Thoroton: *H.M.C. Rutland*, III, 57.
27. From Pirbright; letter in the Pierpont Morgan Library.
28. See p. 180 below.
29. Roe-Byron MS. A. 62, Newstead Abbey.
30. *Thraliana*, II, 739 n.
31. Letter in Pierpont Morgan Library.
32. *Thraliana*, II, 739 (1 April 1789), 734.
33. Quoted in *Thraliana*: Rylands, Eng. Ms. 546.
34. *Walpole's Correspondence with George Montagu*, ed. Lewis and Brown, I, 219.
35. *Cockayne's Complete Peerage*, note by Vickary Gibbs.
36. J. H. Jesse, *Notes on George Selwyn and His Contemporaries*, ed. Lewis, p. 46.
37. Succeeded by his brother as 6th Baronet 1765.
38. See note 36.
39. *Walpole's Correspondence*, I, 219.
40. Ed. *Reliques of English Poetry* (1765); later Bishop of Dromore.
41. *Percy Letters*, ed. Brooks, 1946, pp. 149–51.
42. *Obituaries* published by the Harleian Society, 1899–1901.
43. *Walpole's Correspondence with Mme. du Deffand*, ed. Lewis and Smith, V, 50–51, 61, 163, 85.
44. *Ibid.*
45. *H.M.C. Carlisle*, 497–98.
46. *Anecdotes of Painting*, II, 675.
47. *Percy Letters*, ed. Brooks (1946), p. 154.
48. The 'John, army officer,' who appears in some pedigrees as their second child, is probably confused with George's son, John. Nicols, in his *Literary Anecdotes*, credits Richard with two sons only (V.W.W.). [However, *Alumni Cantabrigienses*, a listing of Cambridge students, tentatively identifies John as probably second son of Richard and records that he died at Haughton; its source is the often unreliable *Gentleman's Magazine* (M.J.H.).]
49. Granger, *Biographical History of England*, 5th ed., 1884, V, 336.
50. Information kindly supplied to V.W.W. by Canon P. J. H. Kirner, Rector of Haughton in 1952.
51. Reproduced by E. Beresford Chancellor in *The XVIIIth Century in London*.

52. To Lady Hardy; Marchand, X, 130.
53. The obituary notice (*Gentleman's Magazine*) describes Isabella as 'Countess Parricini Canelli', more like a travesty of Paravicini than Palavicini.

## NOTES TO CHAPTER 8

1. Murray MSS.
2. Murray MSS.
3. 24 November 1790; Jack Byron's letters in the Lovelace Papers quoted from Doris Langley Moore, *Lord Byron: Accounts Rendered*, pp. 21–42.
4. *Ibid.*, 12 December 1790. The blank is in the original.
5. *Ibid.*, p. 35.
6. Rowland E. Prothero, ed., *The Works of Lord Byron. . . . Letters and Journals*, I, ix.
7. 23 August 1791; Murray MSS.
8. 8 November 1798; Leslie A. Marchand, ed., *Byron's Letters and Journals*, I, 39. Both Professor Marchand and R. E. Prothero (Lord Ernle) thought this letter was addressed to his Aunt Augusta, Mrs Christopher Parker, but she died in 1794. The references to Nottingham and Mrs Parkyns suggest it was written to Mrs George Byron. (V.W.W.)
9. Thomas Moore, who took these lines down from May Gray's dictation, wrongly wrote 'Swan': Swine Green was the street just above Frances Byron's house. Moore's biography of Byron appeared in 1830. (V.W.W.)
10. Like her son, Mrs Byron was a staunch Whig.
11. British Library: Egerton MS. 2,612, f. 43.
12. *Ibid.*, f. 67.
13. 17 November 1803; Murray MSS.
14. Thomas Moore, *Letters and Journals of Lord Byron: With Notices of His Life*, p. 28.
15. 6 February 1806 from 16, Piccadilly; Marchand, I, 88.
16. A full and entertaining account of Byron's finances and debts is given by Doris Langley Moore, *Lord Byron: Accounts Rendered*.
17. *Edinburgh Review* XI (January 1808), 285–89; reprinted in *Byron: The Critical Heritage*, ed. Andrew Rutherford. The reviewer was Henry P. Brougham, well-known lawyer and politician, although Byron never knew this and for some time supposed Francis Jeffrey was the author.
18. 26 April 1808, from Dorant's Hotel; Marchand, I, 165–66. George Anson Byron, eldest son of Captain George Anson Byron, R.N. (died 1793) and Charlotte Henrietta Dallas, succeeded to the poet's title in 1824. The nephew turned out to be a niece, Augusta's first child, Georgiana Augusta, born 4 November 1808.
19. 30 November 1808, from Newstead Abbey to Augusta; Marchand, I, 180.
20. Marchand, I, 218.
21. Marchand, I, 220.

22. Marchand, I, 226–231, esp. 231.
23. Quoted by Doris Langley Moore, *Lord Byron: Accounts Rendered*, 122.
24. Marchand, II, 3–4.
25. Marchand, II, 25.
26. 3 January 1811; British Library: Egerton MS. 2,611.
27. Moore, *Lord Byron: Accounts Rendered*, pp. 145–46.
28. 27 August 1811, to Robert Dallas; Marchand, II, 83.
29. Murray had advertised it for publication on 1 March, but kept it back from sale until the 10th, while he showed sheets from it to increase anticipation. The first edition of 500 copies sold in three days.
30. Mrs Margaret Byron, née Powditch, died 14 September 1813.
31. Information from Thomas Claughton's great-granddaughter. Professor Marchand has the following note (*Byron's Letters and Journals*, IV, 43): 'Chandos Leigh, born in 1791, a landed gentleman of considerable wealth, had just come of age when Claughton entered into contract for the purchase of Newstead Abbey in 1812. His second thoughts or indecisions, or difficulty in raising the money, may have accounted for the delays and procrastinations of Claughton. Byron first mentioned Leigh as the possible purchaser in a letter of July 18, 1813 to Lady Melbourne. . . . Of course, Byron may have been wrong in his conjecture that Leigh was the real purchaser and Claughton only his agent. It is an interesting coincidence that Leigh, who was raised to the peerage in 1839, was not only rich but was also a poet, and an apparent admirer of Byron, for he owned a Phillips portrait of the author of *Childe Harold*.' Blackwell's Catalogue of Antiquarian English Literature (1985), No. A77, listed for sale Chandos Leigh's *Trifles Light As Air*, G. Sidney for F. Benedict, 1813, with this comment: 'Leigh and Byron were schoolfellows at Harrow and later both part of the Holland House set. Their relationship seems to have cooled, though, over the sale of Newstead Abbey.' There follow selective quotations from Byron's letter of 18 July 1813 to Lady Melbourne and 1 February 1814 to Hanson and the comment, 'Leigh is not mentioned in Byron's correspondence after February 1814, and it may be seen . . . that he was buttering-up Byron in 1813 by addressing verse and inscribing volumes of his insipid poetry to him' (pp. 24–25). The volume is inscribed 'To the Rt Honble. Lord Byron from the Author.'
32. Wife of Robert John Wilmot, son of Admiral John Byron's daughter, Juliana, by her second marriage to Sir Robert Wilmot. Wilmot (1784–1841) married Anne Horton in 1806 and changed his name to Wilmot-Horton. He became involved in the burning of his cousin the poet's memoirs and was a friend and confidant of Lady Byron. He eventually became Governor of Ceylon.
33. *Byron's Daughter*, by Catherine Turney (1972). The jacket proclaims 'the first full biography of Elizabeth Medora Leigh—Libby—the child of incest, born as the result of Byron's passionate love affair with his half-sister, Augusta.' Several allusions in Byron's letters suggest that he had a liaison with Augusta, but not that he had a child by her. His much quoted

phrase to Lady Melbourne (25 April 1814), apparently referring to Medora, '—and it is *not* an *"Ape"* and if it is—that must be my fault—' is open to interpretation (see Marchand, IV, 104 and Doris Langley Moore, *The Late Lord Byron*, pp. 301–02; Ada, *Countess of Lovelace*, pp. 101–03). Possibly evidence has been suppressed on the subject of Byron's relations with his sister: a note in the Murray MSS referring to sundry papers belonging to Augusta Leigh indicates that a manuscript, *The Fallen One*, was destroyed 3 March 1892.

34. 24 June 1814; Marchand, IV, 131.
35. 18 and 24 June 1814; Journal entries 30 November, 1 December and 28–30 November 1813; Marchand, IV, 128, 131; III, 227–29.
36. *Medwin's Conversations of Lord Byron* . . ., ed. Ernest J. Lovell, p. 33.
37. Quoted by Leslie A. Marchand, *Byron: A Biography*, I, 368.
38. *Ibid.*, I, 370.
39. Hester Lynch Thrale Piozzi, *Autobiography* . . ., ed. A. Hayward, II, 269–70.
40. 13 November 1814; Marchand, IV, 231.
41. 29 November 1814 to Annabella; Marchand, IV, 236. About a month before this, George Anson Byron borrowed £150 from the poet: Marchand, IV, 213–14.
42. Marchand, VIII, 185 and n. See also *Byron: A Biography*, II, 548–50.
43. Marchand, V, 14. It also had some private sexual significance, briefly discussed by Malcolm Elwin, *Lord Byron's Family*, p. 9.
44. Lady Byron's 'Minutes of Conversation with Ly. C. L. March 27th 1816' are reproduced in full by Moore, *The Late Lord Byron*, Chapter VII.
45. 14 April 1816; Marchand, V, 66; see p. 90 above.
46. Roe-Byron MS., Newstead Abbey.
47. Even Polidori became the subject of a book: Derek Marlowe, *A Single Summer with L.B.: The Summer of 1816* (London: Jonathan Cape, 1969; Penguin ed. 1973).
48. Mary Anne Byron, born 20 March 1817, baptised Marylebone Parish Church.
49. 9 May 1817 to John Murray; Marchand, V, 222.
50. Clare Allegra, born 12 January; baptised 9 March 1817, St Giles-in-the-Fields; Parish Register of St Giles-in-the-Fields.
51. To Augusta, 3 June 1817; Marchand, V, 232.
52. 17 May 1819, from Venice; Marchand, VI, 130.
53. 17 May 1819; Marchand, VI, 129.
54. Circa 10 September 1819; Marchand, VI, 223; 23 August (to Teresa), 215.
55. Roe-Byron MS., Newstead Abbey.
56. 17 May 1824; note from Lady Byron to her solicitor, Mr Wharton, in the Lovelace Papers; quoted by Moore, *The Late Lord Byron*, p. 43; Chapter I is devoted to the burning of Byron's memoirs.
57. Letter dated 19 April 1845 in the collection of James Lees-Milne; first published in *The Byron Journal*, IV (1976), 97. She comments: 'You are

*quite* right about the hair & how could Thorwaldsen so mistake, except from his cramped and Northern idea of what it *ought* to be, instead of what it was. *I* see an error in the ear—it does not sufficiently join on to the Jaw—which was a great peculiarity in his—but—on the whole the head & face delight me. Not so the figure—I cant bear it—but, fancied it was my ignorance—Others have found fault too—who knew him and saw him later than I did. Lord Clare, I hear, said there seemed a *sinking* in the Body. . . . All these reminiscences of your letter & all it gives rise to— occur on the anniversary of his Death!' Smith was head of a large London insurance company. Augusta wanted to borrow money from them.

58. *Daily Telegraph*, 9 May 1969; Marchand, *Byron: A Portrait*, p. 478.

## NOTES TO CHAPTER 9

1. Condensed from William James, *Naval History*, V, 5, 357–60.
2. *H.M.C. Verulam*, p. 182.
3. *The Times*, 5 September 1837: '*Died* on [Saturday] the 2nd. inst., Richard Byron, Esq. Rear Admiral of the White and a companion of the most Hon. Military Order of the Bath'.
4. Lt-Colonel 4th/7th Royal Dragoon Guards (commanding 1941–44); A.D.C. to Governor of Bombay, 1921–22; Military Second to Governor-General and Commander-in-Chief, New Zealand, 1937; served in World War II, 1939–45. He had two sons, both educated at Wellington. See 'Epilogue'.
5. John Byron had died 12 August 1895; his will was proved for £27,785. Ada Blanche and Fanny Lucy Byron died on 7 August 1904 and 29 January 1908, their wills proved for £44,928 and £77,833 respectively.
6. Lovelace Papers, Bodleian Library (L.P.)
7. See p. 167 above and Lovell, *Medwin's Conversations of Lord Byron*, p. 59.
8. L.P.
9. Elwin, *Lord Byron's Wife*, p. 201.
10. 19 January 1816; *ibid.*, pp. 357–58.
11. *Ibid.*, p. 367.
12. Murray MSS., letter to Lord Exmouth.
13. L.P., 9 June 1824.
14. L.P., 16 July 1824, from Bath.
15. Moore, *The Late Lord Byron*, p. 84.
16. *Ibid.*, quoted from L.P., p. 155. Dallas had received money and copyrights from the poet: 'Two Hundred pounds before I was twenty years old. Copyright of Childe Harold £600 Copyright of Corsair £500 and £50 for his nephew on entering the army: in all £1350 . . .': *Ibid.*, p. 117, quoted from Murray MSS.
17. *Diary and Correspondence of Lord Colchester*, III, 345; 5 October 1824.
18. *Diary of Andrew Bloxham*, p. 10.

19. The Hawaiian language was unwritten until the arrival of the American Protestant Missionaries, who created an alphabet first printed in 1826. Place names are therefore variously spelled in the diaries and journals.
20. *Journal of a Residence in the Sandwich Islands*, pp. 339–40, 347.
21. *Ibid.*, pp. 356–58.
22. *With Lord Byron at the Sandwich Islands*, p. 37; such criticisms were discussed in a pamphlet, *An Examination of Charges against the American Missionaries at the Sandwich Islands*, Cambridge, 1827; it declared that the missionaries did not prevent the chiefs from attending the magic lantern show, but advised them to do as they wished, a Saturday evening religious meeting having long been established.
23. 19 April 1826; quoted from L.P. by Moore, *The Late Lord Byron*, p. 156.
24. *Ibid.*, pp. 156–57; letter of 27 April 1826 quoted from L.P.
25. Moore, *Ada, Countess of Lovelace*, p. 184. The rest of their family were Harriet, born 4 December 1826, died 25 June 1828 at Brighton, buried at Epsom; Augustus, born 8 June 1828 at Epsom, who went to Merton College (Oxford), became Rector first of Corton Denham, Somerset (1852–61) and then of Kirkby Mallory (1861–1901); William, born 11 October 1831, who became Rector of Trowell; and another son, John Ralph, born 7 February 1837, who died 30 November 1844 at Leamington.
26. Quoted by Moore, *The Late Lord Byron*, from L.P., 15 March 1828.
27. L.P., n.d. and headed from Dover, 17 March [?1830].
28. Ponsonby, *Lord Henry Ponsonby*, p. 120.
29. Moore, *Ada, Countess of Lovelace*, p. 120; quoted from L.P., 25 October 1842. The MS. of Medora's autobiography is in the Pierpont Morgan Library (New York).
30. Medora's story has been told several times: see Charles Mackay, *Medora Leigh; a History and an Autobiography* (1869); Roger de Vivie de Régie, 'Medora Leigh, La Fille de Lord Byron?', *Revue des Deux Mondes*, XXVI (1 December 1926), 610–653; Catherine Turney, *Byron's Daughter* (1972); the last to be read with caution. Medora's story as it affected Ada is told by Doris Langley Moore in *Ada, Countess of Lovelace* (1977).
31. British Library: Peel Papers, Additional MSS. 40,517, ff. 78–80.
32. British Library: Additional MSS. 43,757, ff. 95–96.
33. Moore, *Ada, Countess of Lovelace*, pp. 356–60.
34. Their story has been told by Elizabeth Longford, *A Pilgrimage of Passion: The Life of Wilfrid Scawen Blunt* (1979).
35. Georgiana Caroline Sitwell, *Two Generations*, I, 106–07.
36. *I Liked the Life I Lived*, pp. 77–79.
37. *The Gorge*, pp. 44–45.
38. *Eton: A Dame's Chronicle*, pp. 128–29.
39. Quoted by Moore, *Ada, Countess of Lovelace*, p. 221.

## NOTES TO CHAPTER 10

1. George Frederick Byron, unpublished unfinished autobiography written in 1932; courtesy Mrs Joy E. Byron.
2. George Rochfort Byron, b. 9 November 1832, d. 19 November 1911; only child of George Byron (1805–1834) and Georgiana Caroline Meiselback; he became a Lieut. in the 63rd Regiment and later joined the Madras Railway Service. He married (1876) Rose, daughter of Frederick Templeton, by whom he had five children.
3. *Four Generations of a Literary Family*, II, 134; much of Chapter 6 is devoted to Henry James Byron. Hazlitt, grandson of the famous essayist, married Henrietta Foulkes and was therefore H. J. Byron's brother-in-law.
4. H. P. Grattan, 'Mr. Byron: A Reminiscence of the Milton Street Theatre', *The Theatre* (1 June 1882), 345–50.
5. Henry J. Byron, 'Pantomimical', *The Theatre* (1 January 1879), 408–10. Of course this panto burlesqued Walpole's novel, *The Castle of Otranto* (1764), itself a parody of the popular Gothic genre.
6. 'My First Play', *The Era Almanack* (1868), pp. 75–76, esp. 76.
7. See Henry J. Byron, 'Bygone Bow Street'; 'Going on the Stage'; *The Theatre Annual*, ed. Clement Scott (1884), 7–10; *The Theatre* (1 October 1879), 130–32; *The Theatre* (1 September 1878), 110.
8. *The Era Almanack* (1868), 76.
9. *The Dickens Theatrical Reader*, pp. 309–10.
10. Letter to W. Davidge, 16 September 1979; Harvard College Library Theatre Collection.
11. *Illustrated London News*, 25 December 1860.
12. Sidney Dark and Rowland Grey, *W. S. Gilbert: His Life and Letters*, p. 9.
13. *The Daily Telegraph*, 3 February 1908; Sir W. S. Gilbert's speech at a complimentary banquet, Savoy Hotel.
14. For *Manfred*'s stage history, see Margaret J. Howell, *Byron Tonight*, (Springwood Books, 1982), Chapter 3.
15. R. J. Broadbent, *Annals of the Liverpool Stage. Manfred*, produced by Charles Calvert, whose version truncated Byron's text much more than Phelps's London version had done, was staged 9 December 1867; on 27 September 1875 a lavish production of Calvert's *Sardanapalus* included in its cast Arthur Wing Pinero, a stock actor destined for fame as a playwright, as Arbaces. For a full account of Calvert's productions, see Margaret J. Howell, *Byron Tonight*, pp. 112–16, 80–89. H. J. Byron protested against the London version of *Manfred*; see p. 248 above.
16. 26 January 1872; letter to an unidentified correspondent in the Harvard College Library Theatre Collection.
17. Hazlitt was married to Martha Foulkes' sister; see note 3 above.
18. 'Actors of the Age', *The Theatre* (1 June 1893), 316–21, esp. 319.
19. *An Architect's Experiences (1897)*, p. 59.
20. See *The Theatre* (1 February 1880), 134; and *The Theatre* (1 April 1879),

157; 'Growls from a Playwright'; 'On Causes of Failure': *The Theatre* (1 January 1880; 1 April 1879), 20–24, 221–24.

21. Letter in Harvard College Library Theatre Collection.
22. George Frederick Byron alone of the immediate family attended his father's funeral. *The Times* reported his eldest son 'at the Cape'. The *Era* obituary listed the chief mourners as Mr George Byron, son of the deceased; Colonel Byron, Mr W. Gayford, Mr Manville Byron, Mr W. Byron, Mr E. W. Garden and Mr A. H. Pearpoint. The last two named were his executors; Pearpoint was his solicitor.
23. Collection of Professor Jane Stedman (both letters).
24. E. J. Goodman, 'Fifty years at the Play', *The Theatre* (1 October 1894), 172–79, esp. 177.
25. Letter in the Lilly Library, Indiana University (Bloomington).
26. *Illustrated Sporting and Dramatic News*, n.d., Harvard College Library Theatre Collection.
27. *Reminiscences of J. L. Toole* (1889), II, 285.
28. *The Theatre* (1 October 1878).
29. *The Story of My Life* (1908), p. 140.
30. *A Player Under Three Reigns*, p. 213.
31. The other children were John Byron Blenkinsopp (1835–1906), who eventually sold Blenkinsopp Castle in Northumberland to his brother and the manor and estate to Mr E. Joicey; William Lisle Blenkinsopp (1840–1911), Captain in the 25th King's Own Borderers and Justice of the Peace; Arthur Blenkinsopp (1841–1905), Vicar of Branxton, Northumberland; Frederick Charles Blenkinsopp (1845–1919), Captain in the Royal Rifles.
32. *The Theatre* (1 April 1879).
33. Odell, *Annals of the New York Stage*, XI, 604.
34. *The Theatre* (1 April 1879).
35. Sidney Dark and Rowland Grey, *W. S. Gilbert: His Life and Letters*, p. 56.
36. George Playdell Bancroft, *Stage and Bar*, p. 49.
37. *The Life of Henry Irving*, II, 86–87.
38. *The Story of My Life*, pp. 239–40.
39. The Death Certificate, signed by W. G. Thorpe, M.R.C.S., gives cause of death as 'Disseminated schlerosis of Spinal Cord, 7 years. Broncho Pneumonia 4 days'. His wife, then living at 30 Hereford Square, South Kensington, was with him when he died at 53 Ritherdon Road, presumably a Nursing Home.
40. See Appendix A.
41. 25 January 1980; letter from Joy E. Byron to Margaret J. Howell.
42. *Ibid*.
43. We have no information about Margaret Ada and May Byron, Henry James Byron's daughters by his second marriage.

# Appendix A

'Foulweather Jack'. A Ballad by May Byron.

Reprinted from *Blackwood's Magazine* in *The Campbellton Graphic*, Campbellton, New Brunswick, 18 July 1935.

Admiral Byron has weighed his anchor,
    And put to sea in a gale;
But deep in his heart is a hidden canker,
    Because of an oft-told tale.
Brave he may be, deny it who can,
Yet Admiral John is a luckless man;
And the midshipmen's mother's cry "Out alack!
My lad has sailed with Foulweather Jack"!

Admiral Byron has hoisted his pennant,
    And steered for Cape Breton shore;
But the surgeon says to the first lieutenant,
    "We shall never see Spithead more!
Weather-beaten and battle-scarr'd,
To Plymouth Hoe or to Portsmouth Hard,
The crews return – but they never come back
Who sign and serve with Foulweather Jack!

"Many a frigate has he commanded,
    In every storm that's blown;
He would fight with a squadron single-handed,
    But his luck is the devil's own;
He loses the wind, he misses the tide,
He shaves the rocks; and his shots go wide;
The fate is curst and the future black,
That hangs o'er the head of Foulweather Jack.

"As for me, I'm a tough old stager,
    Nor care if I sink or swim,
But when I think of the stranded Wager,
    My heart is heavy for him.
Round the world to ruin and wreck

[ 304 ]

He carried his luck on the Dolphin's deck;
If ever a man had the gift and knack;
Of sheer disaster, 'tis Foulweather Jack!"

As a sea-gull's wings o'er the surges flutter,
    In the light of the sunset flame.
There hovered from westward a hasty cutter,
    To speak with the frigate Fame.
"Twenty Parley-voo ships to-day
Lurk and loiter in Chaleur Bay;
Like wolves they gather to make attack
On the ships and convoy of Foulweather Jack.

"Frigates three for your three are biding,
    And of arm'd privateers a score;
Sloops and schooners at anchor riding,
    Are waiting you close in shore;
Where guns are many, and yours are few;
Eight to one they outnumber you;
The wind is slow and the tide is slack,
But you yet may escape them, Foulweather Jack!"

The Admiral stood six foot and over,
    He was stately and stern to see;
But his eyes lit up like those of a lover,
    And merry of mind was he;
And the Byron blood and the Berkeley blood
Burned in his veins like a fiery flood,
And his pulses leaped, and his comely face
Glowed with the pride of a fighting race.

The Admiral laughed with the wind's own laughter,
    And spoke with the sea's own might,
"From danger and death, and what comes after,
No Englishman turns in flight;
They call me unlucky—today you'll learn
How the worst of luck for a time may turn;
We'll rid the seas of this vermin-pack,
And I'll be huntsman!" quoth Foulweather Jack.

The twilight sank and the darkness settled,
    The Admiral frigate led;
She took the waves like a steed high-mettled,
    And this to his men he said;
"Desperate measures for desperate deeds;
And valorous crews for dare-devil deeds:

[ 305 ]

A goodly quarry we have in track—
Clear the decks for action!" says Foulweather Jack.

All through the night were the seabirds soaring
    Shrieking and spared from rest;
All through the night the guns were roaring
    Under the sea-birds' nest.
When morning broke in a glimmer gray,
There was dreadful silence in Chaleur Bay—
Only the crackle of burning decks,
And cries for succour from crowded wrecks.

The Bienfaisant is aground and blazing,
    And sunk is the proud Marchault;
The privateersmen aghast are gazing
    At their vessels that burn a-row;
The staggering smoke that volleys and blows,
Shrouds the shattered Marquis de Marlose,
And the sloops and schooners in rout and wrack
Strew the pathway of Foulweather Jack.

The prisoners question in fear and wonder,
    "What fiend have we fought to-day?
We are burnt and splintered and split in sunder,
    Who boasted him soon our prey.
He grappled and boarded us, one to ten,
But he and his crew are devils, not men;
Curs'd be the hour when we crossed the track
Of this—how do you call him?—Foulweather Jack.'

Admiral Byron has counted his losses,
    And steered for Cape Breton shore;
The haulks and spars that the wild wave tosses,
    Last night they were ships of war.
The wounded men in the cock-pit dim
With feeble voices huzza for him;
"The stars may fall and the skies may crack—
But my luck is broken!" says Foulweather Jack.

# Appendix B

Excerpt from Broadcast Script, 'Shire Talk'; 6:20 p.m. 23 April 1963 by Violet W. Walker.

Recently two portraits of the members of the Byron family in the Stuart period have been acquired by Nottingham Corporation and are at present on view in the Dining Hall of Newstead Abbey. When bought by the Corporation they were attributed to J. O. van Houckgeest, who was a Dutch painter living at the Hague, and the portraits were identified as being those of Sir Thomas Byron and his brother, Sir Robert Byron.

There is another known portrait of Sir Thomas Byron and it was possible to identify the present portrait as being of him. He was a younger brother of John, the first Lord Byron, being born about 1607 and it is known that he commanded the Prince of Wales's Regiment of Horse under the command of the Earl of Cumberland. Knighted at Shrewsbury in 1642, while the regiment was quartered at Oxford in December, 1643, he was attacked and wounded by a captain of his own regiment after some dispute about pay, and after lingering for nearly two months in great pain, died on 5 February 1643/4 (old calendar) and was buried in Christchurch Cathedral, Oxford. His assailant was executed by firing squad a week after the attack, and Thomas's widow, Katherine, continued to help the Royalist cause by acting as a secret service agent. The other painting, which is of an older man, gave cause for doubt as to its attribution and it was felt that it was more likely to be that of Sir Nicholas Byron (Sir Thomas's uncle) rather than Sir Robert Byron, his brother. Nicholas, like his nephews, fought in the Civil War and married the daughter of the Governor of Breda, serving sometime in the Netherlands.

When the portraits were examined it was found that in conditions of oblique light falling on the canvas, the portrait of Sir Thomas Byron showed an inscription lying underneath the top coat of varnish but not much of the inscription was decipherable in ordinary light. The date, June 1631, could be seen on both portraits and on that of Sir Nicholas the inscription 'Houchgeest fecit'. Advice was then sought of the Nottingham Forensic Science Laboratory and with their help on exposure to infra red light much more of the detail of the inscription of the portrait of Sir Thomas was deciphered and the inscription clearly assigned the portrait to Sir Thomas Byron and named him as commanding the Prince of Wales's Regiment of Horse during the Civil Wars, so that the inscription was made sometime after the actual painting was done. On the presumed portrait of Sir Nicholas all that could be deciphered with accuracy were the three letters ICH and this gives strong grounds for presuming

[ 307 ]

that it does in fact represent Sir Nicholas, it being more than likely that the portraits were commissioned by Sir Nicholas about the time of his marriage, and it is known, moreover, that Dutch pictures were handed over by his wife as a security for a loan when the Cavaliers were raising money for the support of King Charles I.

F. C. Tighe,
City Librarian, Curator of
Newstead Abbey.

## Obituaries

### Violet W. Walker, 1900–82

The death occurred in Cumbria on 21st November 1982 of Miss Violet Walker, B.A., F.L.A., a former City Archivist of Nottingham and a committee member of the Society's Record Section for many years. Born in 1900 and a native of Nottingham, she attended Nottingham High School for Girls before proceeding to Royal Holloway College in Surrey, a women's college of the University of London, from which she graduated with a Classics degree in 1923. After a brief spell of teaching at her old school she trained as a librarian at the London School of Librarianship, which included a course in palaeography and archives. She then joined the staff of Nottingham Public Libraries in 1926 initially as a branch librarian but was soon appointed to the position of Reference Librarian in the Central Library. She took an especial interest in the small but growing collection of local historical manuscripts, and when in 1950 a separate Archives Department was created she became its first archivist, also being given responsibility for the reorganisation and repair of the fine and extensive series of city archives housed in the Guildhall. She also undertook much of the curatorial work associated with Newstead Abbey and its collection of Byron manuscripts, which was then administered by the City Libraries. Following her formal retirement in 1966 after forty years' service she returned to the library for two years on a part-time basis helping to compile the monumental catalogue of Nottinghamshire Bibliography.

Her knowledge of local history and its sources was outstanding, aided by a phenomenal memory which frequently enabled her to recall not only the existence of a publication on a particular subject but also its exact position on the shelves. Tragically hampered for most of her adult life by chronic deafness she tended to eschew the public limelight, but she carried out anonymously a great deal of the basic research for a large number of official publications and exhibitions, etc. Her first major academic work was an edition and translation of the fourteenth-century cartulary of Newstead Priory, published in this Society's *Record Series* in 1940. Later achievements were the last two volumes of the *Records of the Borough of Nottingham* covering the period from 1800 to 1900 and published in [the] 1950s, edited jointly with the City Librarian, Duncan Gray. She was responsible for the bulk of the original research for these and also for numerous publications issued under the name of Duncan Gray and others, including his *Nottingham Through 500 Years* (1960), but rarely received the true public recognition which she deserved. However she made several notable contributions to this Society's *Transactions* and *Record Series* in her own right, including a paper on the topography of mediaeval Nottingham and a survey of Nottinghamshire funeral hatchments. An especial interest was the history of Newstead Abbey and the Byron family and her major history of the family which she compiled over several years still awaits publication.

Her standards of scholarship and attention to detail were meticulous, as many an academic discovered to his cost. She maintained a lively mind, a cheerful disposition, and an often impish sense of humour right up until the last, despite overwhelming physical disabilities. Future generations of archivists, librarians, and local historians will be forever in her debt for both her sung and unsung contributions to historical knowledge.

Adrian Henstock
*Transactions of the Thoroton Society of Nottinghamshire,*
Vol. 86 (1982)

*

VIOLET WALKER, Nottingham city archivist from 1949 to 1966, died last November aged 82. The first to hold that appointment, she was a rara avis from the start of her career being also the first woman graduate to be recruited to the city library staff where she was to serve forty years to the day. Rare, too, was her luminous intelligence, her absolute command of her subject, which was at first reference library practice in the post of reference librarian from 1936 to 1949, the result of Duncan Gray's recognition of talent by promoting it to greater responsibility. But her understanding of her materials went deeper than book supply, secondhand as that so often is; it extended into the sphere of primary sources, and so her transition from librarianship to archive administration within the library was inevitable.

To think of her is immediately to recall a woman of subdued power, serene yet buoyant, possessed of an animation sadly absent in so many who profess archival skills. The liveliness of spirit and the composure came from someone in harmony with her materials. She drew life from those dusty records and breathed life back into them; no one ever left her muniment room without a sense of excitement—there was nothing sacrosanct about her department, only a lived significance which was translated into her own work, for example on early Notts elections (she edited the poll book for 1710) and into the histories of Nottingham published under other authors' names but substantially built on her contributions.

One could mention other publications: her edition of the Roe–Byron Collection of books and MSS, a testimony to her sensitive response to the Byron family, its Newstead Abbey home and its ethos; nay, with Byron scholars like Mario Praz and Leslie Marchand she dwelt as an equal. My last memory of her at work was of driving her to remote parish churches as she systematically made her survey of Notts hatchments, and of the ease with which she read them, to her as simple as headlines in a newspaper. Again, the gift of resurrection, the family stories leaping into vivid context as she rapidly transcribed them into her notebook. The result is in the *Transactions* of the Thoroton Society (1965).

Another memory is of her demeanour in the grand houses of the county gentry when in search of fugitive material lurking in their libraries, for the Notts Bibliography, her tact in the face of their ignorance and puzzlement. They were lively encounters, blithe as her touch always was, yet intellectually tough, never losing sight of the objective, paradigms of her lightly held learning and of her fidelity, to her city, to her library, and to her discipline.

David Gerard
*Library Association Record* (January 1983)

Violet Walker's absorbing interest in Byron and his family began in 1936 when she became Librarian-in-Charge of the Reference Library in Nottingham City Library, where there already existed one of the world's largest collections of Byroniana, as yet unclassified and uncatalogued. She created the classification scheme which is still in use, and under her expert guidance the collection was catalogued. At the same time Nottingham had acquired Newstead Abbey, the ancient home of the Byrons, and also a most important collection of Byron manuscripts, books, etc. bequeathed by Herbert Charles Roe. So Violet Walker had the additional task of administering this collection, a job that lasted until her retirement in 1966.

Her researches into the poet and his family began at this time, and lasted for a period of over twenty years. The results of her scholarly investigations are now demonstrated in this monumental history of the Byron family.

I had the great pleasure and stimulating experience of working with her throughout the whole of this period, and my own interest in the Byron family was gained entirely from her inspiration.

Lucy I. Edwards, M.B.E.

# A Selective Bibliography

Excludes manuscript sources, articles or periodicals adequately identified in the footnotes.

*Alumni Cantabrigienses. A Biographical List of All Known Students, Graduates and Holders of Office at the University of Cambridge, from the Earliest Times to 1900.* Compiled by John Venn and J. A. Venn. 10 vols. Cambridge: University Press, 1922–54.

*Alumni Oxonienses: The Members of the University of Oxford 1715–1886.* Arranged, revised and annotated by Joseph Foster. 4 vols. Oxford: Parker & Co., 1888.

Bailey, Thomas. *Annals of Nottinghamshire. History of the County of Nottingham, including the Borough.* 4 vols. London: Simpkin, Marshall & Co.; Nottingham: W. F. Gibson, 1852–55.

———. *Hand-Book to Newstead Abbey.* London: Simpkin, Marshall & Co.; Nottingham: W. F. Gibson, 1855.

Bancroft, George Pleydell. *Stage and Bar: Recollections of George Pleydell Bancroft.* London: Faber & Faber, [1939].

Bancroft, Sir Squire and Marie. *Mr. and Mrs. Bancroft: On and Off the Stage: Written by themselves.* 2 vols. London: Bentley, 1888.

Barrington, The Hon. Samuel. *The Barrington Papers, selected from the letters and papers of Admiral the Hon. S. Barrington and edited by D. Bonner-Smith.* London: Publications of the Navy Records Society, 1937, ff.

Beaumont, Sir John. *Bosworth Field ... with several verses in praise of the author. ...* London: H. Hills, 1710.

———. *The Poems of Sir John Beaumont, Bart., for the first time collected and edited ... by the Revd. Alexander B. Grosart.* London: Fuller Worthies Library, 1869.

Blaquiere, Edward. *Narrative of a Second Visit to Greece, including facts connected with the last days of Lord Byron, Extracts from Correspondence, official Documents, etc.* London: George B. Whittaker, 1825.

Bloxham, Andrew. *Diary of Andrew Bloxham, naturalist of the 'Blonde' on her trip from England to the Hawaiian Islands, 1824–25.* Honolulu: The Museum, 1925.

Boulton, William B. *The History of White's.* 2 vols. London: Hon. A. Bourke, 1892.

Broadbent, R. J. *Annals of the Liverpool Stage. ...* New York: B. Blom, 1969; reprint of the original 1908 edition.

BROMLEY HOUSE FOREST BOOKS. Typescript transcriptions of MSS relating to Sherwood Forest 1329–1676, copied by W. A. Janes at Southwell 5 January– 15 March 1934, in the Local Studies Library, Nottingham County Libraries. The MSS are in Nottingham Subscription Library, Bromley House, Nottingham.

Buchan, Peter. *Ancient Ballads and Songs of the North of Scotland.* Vol. I. Edinburgh, 1875.

Byron, George Gordon (6th Baron). *Byron's Letters and Journals.* Ed. Leslie A. Marchand. 12 vols. London: John Murray, 1973–82.

———. *The Poetical Works of Lord Byron,* in one volume. Ed. Ernest Hartley Coleridge. London: John Murray, 1905.

———. *The Works of Lord Byron: A New Revised and Enlarged Edition, with illustrations: Letters and Journals,* ed. Rowland E. Prothero. 6 vols. *Poetry,* ed. Ernest Hartley Coleridge. 7 vols. London: John Murray, 1898–1904.

Byron, Henry James. *The Comic News; a first class humorous retrospect of the week's events....* Edited by Henry James Byron. Published July to December, 1863.

———. *Mirth.* A Miscellany of wit and humour. Edited by Henry James Byron. London: Tinsley Brothers, 1878.

———. *Our Boys.* A comedy in three acts. New York: H. Roorbach, 1890.

Byron, Admiral John. *The Narrative of . . . the Honourable John Byron . . . containing an account of the great distresses suffered by himself and his companions on the coast of Patagonia from the year 1740, till their arrival in England, 1746. With a description of St. Jago de Chili.... Also a relation of the loss of the Wager man of war, etc.* London: S. Baker & G. Leigh, T. Davies, 1768.

———. *The Wreck of the Wager: The Narratives of John Bulkeley and the Hon. John Byron.* Edited and Introduced by Christopher Hibbert. London: the Folio Society, 1983. Reprint of *A Voyage to the South Seas in the Years 1740–41* by John Bulkeley and John Cummins (1743) and the 1785 edition of Byron's *Narrative.*

Byron, May Clarissa Gillington. *A Day with Lord Byron.* London: Hodder & Stoughton, 1910.

Byron, Nora. *Eton: A Dame's Chronicle.* London: William Kimber, 1965.

Byron, Lord (10th Baron). *The Gorge.* London: John Murray, 1934.


*Calendar of Entries in the Papal Registers (Regesta Romanorum Pontificum) relating to Great Britain and Ireland. Papal Letters....* ed. W. H. Bliss, C. Johnson, J. A. Twemlow. 6 vols. London, 1893, ff.

*Calendar of the Liberate Rolls Preserved in the Public Record Office ... 1226–1240* [*etc.*]. Prepared by W. H. Stevenson, J. B. W. Chapman. London, 1916.

*Calendar of the Patent Rolls Preserved in the Public Record Office....* London, 1901, ff.

*Calendar of the Proceedings of the Committee for Advance of Money, 1642–1656, preserved in the State-paper department of Her Majesty's Public Record Office.* Ed. Mary A. E. Green, *et al.* 3 vols. London: H. M. Stationery Office, 1888.

*Calendar of Treasury Books, 1660–1667, etc., preserved in the Public Record Office.* Prepared by William A. Shaw. London, 1904, ff.

*Calendar of Treasury Books and Papers, 1729–1730, preserved in her Majesty's Public Record Office.* Prepared by W. H. Shaw. 5 vols. London: H.M. Stationery Office, 1897–1903.

*Calendar of Treasury Papers 1556/7–1696 (1720–1728) preserved in her Majesty's Public Record Office.* Prepared by J. Redington, etc. 6 vols. London: Longman & Co., 1868–89.

Campbell, Alexander (Midshipman of *H.M.S. Wager*). *The Sequel to Bulkeley and Cummins's Voyage to the South Seas, or the Adventures of Capt. Cheap, the Hon. Mr. Byron . . . and others, late of His Majesty's Ship the Wager, etc.* London, 1747.

Campbell, W., ed. *Materials for a History of Henry VII.* . . . 2 vols. 1872, 1877. British Library: Department of Printed Books.

Carte, Thomas. *A Collection of Original Letters and Papers concerning the affairs of England, from the year 1641 to 1660 found among the Duke of Ormonde's Papers.* 2 vols. London: A. Millar, 1739.

Chancellor, Edwin Beresford. *The XVIIIth. Century in London. An account of its social life and arts.* London: B. T. Batsford [1920].

Cleveland, Duchess of. *The Battle Abbey Roll. With some account of the Norman lineages.* 3 vols. London: John Murray, 1889.

Cockayne, G. E. *Complete Peerage of the United Kingdom.* 8 vols. Exeter, 1887–98.

Coke, Lady Mary. *The Letters and Journals of Lady Mary Coke.* Ed. Hon. J. A. Home. 4 vols. Edinburgh: David Douglas, 1889–96.

Colchester, Lord. *The Diary and Correspondence of Charles Abbot, Lord Colchester.* Ed. by his son. 3 vols. London: John Murray, 1861.

*Collectanea Topographica et Genealogica.* Series ed. by Sir F. Madden, B. Bandinel, and others; afterwards by J. G. Nichols. 8 vols. London, 1834–43. Esp. VI, 334.

Collins, Arthur. *The Peerage of England; containing a genealogical and historical account of all the peers of England now existing, etc.* 3 vols. London: R. Gosling & T. Wotton; W. Innys & R. Manby, 1735.

———, ———. 9 vols. London, 1779–84.

Compton, Henry. *Memoirs of Henry Compton.* Ed. Charles and Edward Compton. 2 vols. London: Tinsley Brothers, 1879. Vol. II has recollections of Henry James Byron.

Cooper, Charles Henry, ed. *Annals of Cambridge.* 5 vols. Cambridge: Warwick & Co., 1842–1908.

Crisp, Frederick Arthur, ed. *Fragmenta genealogica.* 13 vols. 1899–1909. Ed. of numerous Parish registers.

Dampier, Robert. *To the Sandwich Islands on H.M.S. Blonde.* Ed. Pauline King Joerger. Honolulu: University of Hawaii Press, 1971.

d'Arblay, Madame (Frances Burney). *Diary and Letters of Madame d'Arblay.* Ed. by her niece [Charlotte Frances Barrett]. 7 vols. London: Henry Colburn, 1842–46.

Dark, Sidney, and Rowland Grey. *W. S. Gilbert: His Life and Letters.* New York: B. Blom, 1972. Reprint of 1923 ed.

Davenport, Percy. *Ralph Lemyngton of Loughborough.* Reprinted from 'The Loughburian'. Loughborough: Echo Press, [1935].

[ 313 ]

De Morgan, Sophia Elizabeth. *Threescore Years and Ten.* London: Richard Bentley, 1895.

de Régie, Roger de Vivie. 'Medora Leigh, La Fille de Lord Byron?' *Revue des Deux Mondes*, XXVI (1 Decembre 1926), 610–53.

Dickens, Charles. *The Dickens Theatrical Reader.* Boston & Toronto: Little, Brown, & Co., 1964.

*Dictionary of National Biography (D.N.B.)*

Earwaker, John Parsons. *Lancashire and Cheshire Wills and Inventories at Chester, with an appendix of abstracts of wills, now lost or destroyed....* Ed. J.P.E. Manchester: Chetham Society, 1884.

Elwin, Malcolm. *Lord Byron's Family: Annabella, Ada, and Augusta, 1816–1824.* London: John Murray, 1975.

———. *Lord Byron's Wife.* London: Macdonald, 1962; New York: Harcourt, Brace, & World, 1963.

Evelyn, John. *The Diary of John Evelyn. Now first printed in full from the manuscripts . . . and edited by E. S. de Beer,* etc. 6 vols. Oxford: Clarendon Press, 1955.

Farrer, William, ed. *Lancashire Inquests, Extents, and Feudal Aids.* Lancaster: *Record Society for the Publication of Original Documents relating to Lancashire and Cheshire,* Vol. XLVIII, 1903.

Fishwick, Henry, ed. *The Survey of the Manor of Rochdale . . . made in 1626.* Chetham Society, *Remains,* Vol. LXXI, new series, 1913.

Forbes-Robertson, Sir Johnston. *A Player Under Three Reigns.* London: T. Fisher-Unwin, 1925.

Foster, Joseph. *Some Feudal Coats of Arms and others....* Oxford & London: J. Parker & Co., 1902.

Fraser, Augusta Z. *Livingstone and Newstead.* London: John Murray, 1913.

Gardiner, Samuel Rawson. *The Hamilton Papers: being selections from original letters in the possession of His Grace the Duke of Hamilton and Brandon, relating to the years 1638–1650.* London: Camden Society, 1880.

Gardiner, Stephen (Bishop of Winchester). *Letters of Stephen Gardiner.* Ed. James Arthur Muller. New York: Macmillan, and Cambridge University Press, 1933.

Granger, James (Vicar of Shiplake). *A Biographical History of England, from the Revolution to the end of George I's reign . . . the materials being supplied by the manuscripts left by Mr. Granger, and the collections of the Editor, M. Noble.* 3 vols. London, 1806; 5th ed., 1884.

Hackett, John (of Baliol College, Oxford). *Select and remarkable Epitaphs on illustrious and other persons in several parts of Europe. With translations of such as are in Latin and Foreign Languages, and compendious accounts of the deceased,* etc. 2 vols. MS notes. London, 1757.

Hall, Edward. *Hall's Chronicle, containing the History of England, during the reign of Henry the Fourth, and the succeeding monarchs, to the end of the reign of Henry the Eighth, in which are particularly described the manners and customs of those periods.* Collated with the editions of 1548 and 1550. London: J. Johnson, etc. 1809.

Harland, John, ed. *Ballads and Songs of Lancashire chiefly older than the 19th century.* Edinburgh, 1865.

———. *Mamecestre: being Chapters from the early recorded history . . . of Manchester.* Manchester: Chetham Society, 1861–62.

HARLEIAN SOCIETY.

Vol. IV. *The Visitations of the County of Nottingham in the years 1569 and 1614, with many other descents of the same county.* Ed. G. W. Marshall. London, 1871.

Vol. XXIII. *Allegations for Marriage Licences issued by the Dean and Chapter of Westminster, 1558 to 1699; also for those issued by the Vicar-General of the Archbishop of Canterbury, 1660–1679. Extracted by J. L. Chester . . . and edited by G. J. Armitage.* London, 1886.

Vol. XXIV. *Allegations for Marriage Licenses issued from the Faculty office of the Archbishop of Canterbury at London, 1543 to 1869. Extracted by . . . J. L. Chester . . . and edited by G. J. Armytage.* London, 1886.

Vols XXV, XXVI. *Allegations for Marriage Licenses issued by the Bishop of London, 1520 to 1610 (1611–1628).* Extracted by J. L. Chester and ed. G. J. Armytage. 2 vols. London, 1887.

Vols XLIV, XLIX. *Obituary prior to 1800, as far as relates to England, Scotland, Ireland. Compiled by Sir W. Musgrave and entitled by him 'A General Nomenclator and Obituary'.* Ed. Sir G. J. Armytage. 6 vols. London, 1899, 1901.

Vol. LXIII. *Staffordshire Pedigrees, based on the visitation of that county made by William Dugdale, Esquire, Norroy King of Arms, in the years 1663–1664, from the original manuscript written by Gregory King . . . during the years 1680 to 1700.* Ed. Sir George J. Armytage . . . and W. Harry Rylands. London, 1912.

Vols. L, LI, LII, LIII. *Lincolnshire Pedigrees.* Ed. Canon A. R. Maddison [from materials collected by A. S. Larken]. London, 1902.

Hazlitt, William Carew. *Four Generations of a Literary Family.* 2 vols. London: G. Redway, 1897.

Herbert, Henry. *Letters and Diaries of Henry, tenth Earl of Pembroke and his Circle.* Ed. Lord Herbert. 2 vols. London: Jonathan Cape, 1939.

Hutchinson, Lucy. *Memoirs of the Life of Colonel Hutchinson, written by his widow Lucy.* London: Kegan, Paul, Trench, Trubner & Co., 1904. Dryden House Memoirs; introduction and notes by Harold Child.

Irving, Washington. *Abbotsford and Newstead Abbey.* London: John Murray, 1835.

James, William. *A full and correct account of the chief naval occurrences of the late war between Great Britain and the United States of America. . . .* London: T. Egerton, 1817. Another edition, 2 vols, printed for the author in 1818.

———. *The Naval History of Great Britain, from the Declaration of War by France . . . 1793 . . . to the accesssion of George IV . . . 1820.* 5 vols. London, 1822–24.

Jesse, John Heneage. *George Selwyn and His Contemporaries: with memoirs and notes.* 4 vols. London, 1843–44.

Kelly, William (of Leicester). *Notices illustrative of the drama and other popular amusements, chiefly in the sixteenth and seventeenth centuries, incidentally illustrating*

*Shakespeare and his contemporaries; extracted from the chamberlains' accounts and other manuscripts of the borough of Leicester.* London: J. R. Smith, 1865.

Kendal, Dame Madge. *Dame Madge Kendal, by Herself.* London: John Murray, 1933.

*Letters and Papers, Foreign and Domestic, of the Reign of Henry VIII.* Arranged and Catalogued by J. S. Brewer, *et al.* 34 parts. London: Longman & Co., 1862–1932.

Lodge, Edmund (Norroy King of Arms.) *Illustrations of British History, Biography, and Manners. . . .* 3 vols. London: G. Nicol, 1791.

Lloyd, David (pseudonym of Oliver Foulis, Canon of St Asaph). *Memoires of the Lives, Actions, Sufferings and Deaths of those noble, reverend and excellent personages that suffered by death, sequestration, decimation or otherwise for the protestant religion, and the great principle thereof, allegiance to their soveraigne, in our late intestine wars . . . and from thence continued to 1666. With the life and martyrdom of King Charles I.* London: S. Speed, 1668.

Lovell, Ernest J., ed. *Medwin's Conversations of Lord Byron.* Princeton: University Press, 1966.

Lucas, E. V. 'The Other Byron.' *The Times,* 29 July 1934.

Mackay, Charles, ed. *Medora Leigh; a History and an Autobiography.* London: Richard Bentley, 1869.

Macrae, James. *With Lord Byron at the Sandwich Islands in 1825; being extracts from the ms. diary of James Macrae.* Ed. William F. Wilson. Honolulu, 1922.

Macwhirter, Margaret Grant. *Treasure Trove in Gaspé and the Baie des Chaleurs.* Quebec: Telegraph Printing Company, 1919.

Malbon, Thomas. *Memorials of the Civil War in Cheshire and the adjacent counties. . .* Ed. J. Hall. Manchester: Record Society of Lancashire and Cheshire, XIX, 94–5(1875).

Marchand, Leslie A. Byron: A Biography. 3 vols. New York: Alfred A. Knopf, & London: John Murray, 1957.

———. *Byron: A Portrait.* London: John Murray, 1971.

Mitra, S. M. *Voice for Women without votes, with foreword by Lady Byron.* Guildford, 1914.

Moore, Doris Langley. *Ada, Countess of Lovelace: Byron's Legitimate Daughter.* London: John Murray, 1977.

———. *The Late Lord Byron.* London: John Murray, 1961.

———. *Lord Byron: Accounts Rendered.* London: John Murray, 1974.

Moore, Thomas. *Letters and Journals of Lord Byron: With Notices of His Life.* London: John Murray, 1830; one vol. ed., 1866.

Morant, Philip. *The History and Antiquities of the County of Essex, compiled from the best . . . historians; from Domesday Book, Inquisitiones post mortem, etc.* 2 vols. London, 1768.

Morris, Rupert Hugh. *The Siege of Chester, 1643–46. . . .* Ed. and compiled by P. H. Lawson. Chester: *Journal of the Chester and North Wales Archaeological and Historic Society,* new ser. XXV, 1923.

Namier, Sir Lewis, and John Brooke. *The History of Parliament.* 3 vols. London: H.M. Stationery Office, 1964.

Nash, Eveleigh. *I Liked the Life I Lived. Some Reminiscences.* London: John Murray, 1941.

Nicols, John. *Literary Anecdotes of the Eighteenth Century.* 9 vols. London: printed for the author by Nicols, son, and Bentley, 1812–16.

Parker, Matthew (Archbishop of Canterbury). *Correspondence of Matthew Parker. . . . Letters written by and to him from A.D. 1535 to A.D. 1575.* London: Parker Society, 1853.

Parry, William, *The Last Days of Lord Byron: with His Lordship's Opinions on Various Subjects, particularly on the state and prospects of Greece.* London: printed for Knight and Lacey, Paternoster Row; and Dublin: Westley and Tyrrell, 1825.

Pemberton, T. Edgar. *John Hare, Comedian, 1865–1895.* London: George Routledge & Sons, 1895.

Pepys, Samuel. *The Diary of Samuel Pepys. A new and complete transcription.* Ed. Robert Latham and William Matthews. 11 vols. Berkeley: University of California Press, 1970–83.

*The Percy Letters.* Ed. David Nichol Smith and Cleanth Brooks. 5 vols. Baton Rouge: Louisiana State University Press, 1944–57.

Percy, Thomas (Bishop of Dromore). *Percy's Reliques of Ancient English Poetry.* 3 vols. London: J. Dodsley, 1765; repr. London: J. M. Dent (Everyman's Library), 1906.

Phillips, John Roland. *Memoirs of the Civil War in Wales and the Marches, 1642–1649.* 2 vols. London, 1874.

Plumptre, Huntingdon. *Epigrammaton opusculum duobus libellis distinctum.* London: Thomas Harper & Robert Allot, 1629. Privately printed.

Polidori, John William. *The Diary of Dr. John William Polidori 1816.* Ed. William Michael Rossetti. London: Elkin Mathews, 1911.

Ponsonby, Arthur. *Henry Ponsonby, Queen Victoria's private secretary; his Life from his letters, by his son, Arthur Ponsonby (Lord Ponsonby of Shulbrede).* New York: Macmillan, 1943.

Raines, Francis Robert. *Examynatyons towcheynge Cokeye More temp. Hen. VIII. in a dispute between the Lord of the Manors of Middleton and Radclyffe, with introduction and notes.* Manchester: Chetham Society Miscellanies, II, 1855.

———. *The Stanley Papers (Pt. 2. The Derby Household Books. . . . Pt. 3. Private Devotions and Miscellanies of James, seventh Earl of Derby.)* Chetham Society, *Remains,* etc., Vols XXIX, XXXI, LXVI, LXX, 1853–67.

Robertson, Thomas W. *The Principal Dramatic Works . . . with memoir by his son.* 2 vols. London: S. Low, Marston, Searle & Rivington, 1889.

Rutherford, Andrew, ed. *Byron: The Critical Heritage.* London: Routledge & Kegan Paul; New York: Barnes & Noble, 1970.

Sala, George Augustus. *Living London: Being Echoes Re-Echoed.* London: Remington & Co., 1883.

SANDWICH PAPERS. *The Private Papers of John, Earl of Sandwich, First Lord of the Admiralty, 1771–1782.* Ed. G. R. Barnes and J. H. Owen. London: Publications of the Naval Records Society, LXIX, 1932.

Searle, William George. *The History of the Queen's College of St. Margaret and St. Bernard in the University of Cambridge.* 2 vols. Cambridge: Antiquarian Society, 1867–71.

Shankland, Peter. *Byron of the Wager.* New York: Coward, McCann & Geoghegan, 1975.

Shipman, Thomas. *Carolina; or, Loyal Poems.* London, 1683.

Sitwell, Georgiana Caroline. *Two Generations.* London: Macmillan & Co., 1940.

Stauffer, Donald Alfred. *The Art of Biography in Eighteenth Century England.* Princeton: University Press, 1941.

Stewart, Charles Samuel. *Journal of a Residence in the Sandwich Islands, during the years 1823, 1824; including remarks on the manners and customs of the inhabitants; an account of Lord Byron's visit in H.M.S. Blonde; and a description of the ceremonies observed at the interment of the late King and Queen in the island of Oahu.* Ed. William Ellis. 3rd ed. London: H. Fisher & P. Jackson, 1830.

Stoker, Bram. *Personal Reminiscences of Henry Irving.* 2 vols. London & New York: Macmillan, 1906.

Terry, Dame Ellen. *The Story of My Life.* New York: McLure Co., 1909.

*Testamenta Eboracensia; or, Wills registered at York, etc.* York: Publications of the Surtees Society, IV, XXX, XLV, LIII, LXXIX, CVI, 1836.

Thornely, James L. *The Monumental Brasses of Lancashire.* Hull: Andrews & Co., 1893.

Thoroton, Robert. *The Antiquities of Nottinghamshire.* . . . London: R. White for H. Mortlock, 1677.

Thrale, Hester Lynch (afterwards Piozzi). *Autobiography, Letters and Literary Remains of Mrs. Piozzi (Thrale).* Ed. Abraham Hayward. 2 vols. London, 1861.

———. THRALIANA. *The Diary of Mrs. Hester Lynch Thrale, later Mrs. Piozzi, 1776–1869.* Ed. Katherine C. Balderston. 2 vols. Oxford: Clarendon Press, 1942.

Turney, Catherine. *Byron's Daughter.* New York: Charles Scribner's Sons, 1972.

*The Victoria History of the Counties of England* (V.C.H.) London: A Constable, 1901, ff. Esp. *Lancashire,* ed. William Farrer and J. Brownbill, 1906.

Voignier-Marshall, Jacqueline. *A Modern Byron Expedition to Hawaii.* Sydney: Australian Byron Society, 1982.

Walpole, Horace. *Anecdotes of Painting in England.* . . . New, revised ed. with notes by R. N. Wornum. London: Swan Sonnenschein & Co., 1888.

———. ———. *Collected by George Vertue . . . with additions by the Rev. James Dallaway.* London: Henry G. Bohn, 1849.

———. *The Letters of Horace Walpole, fourth Earl of Orford.* Chronologically arranged and edited with notes and indices by Mrs Paget Toynbee. 19 vols. Oxford: Clarendon Press, 1903–25.

————. *Walpole's Correspondence with George Montagu.* . . . Ed. W. S. Lewis & Ralph S. Brown, Jr. 2 vols. New Haven: Yale University Press; London: H. Milford, Oxford University Press, 1941.

————. *Walpole's Correspondence with Mme. du Deffand.* . . . Ed. W. S. Lewis and Warren Hunting Smith. 6 vols. New Haven: Yale University Press; London: Oxford University Press, 1939.

————. *The Yale Edition of Horace Walpole's Correspondence.* . . . Ed. W. S. Lewis. 39 vols. New Haven: Yale University Press; London: Oxford University Press, 1937–74.

Wentworth, Thomas, Earl of Strafford (of the second creation). *The Wentworth Papers, 1705–1739. Selected from the private and family correspondence of Thomas Wentworth . . . created in 1711 Earl of Strafford.* . . . With a memoir and notes by J. J. Cartwright. London: Wyman & Sons, 1883.

White, Thomas (Captain, R.N.) *Naval Researches; or, a Candid inquiry into the conduct of Admirals Byron, Graves . . . in the actions off Grenada, Chesapeak, etc.* London, 1830.

Wood, Alfred Cecil. *Nottinghamshire in the Civil War.* Oxford: Clarendon Press, 1937.

Wood, Antony à. *Athenae Oxonienses. An Exact History of all the Writers and Bishops who have had their Education in the University of Oxford. To which are added the Fasti, or annals of the said university.* New ed. with additions and continuation by Philip Bliss. London: F. C. & J. Rivington, et al, 1813–20.

# A PEDIGREE OF BYRON

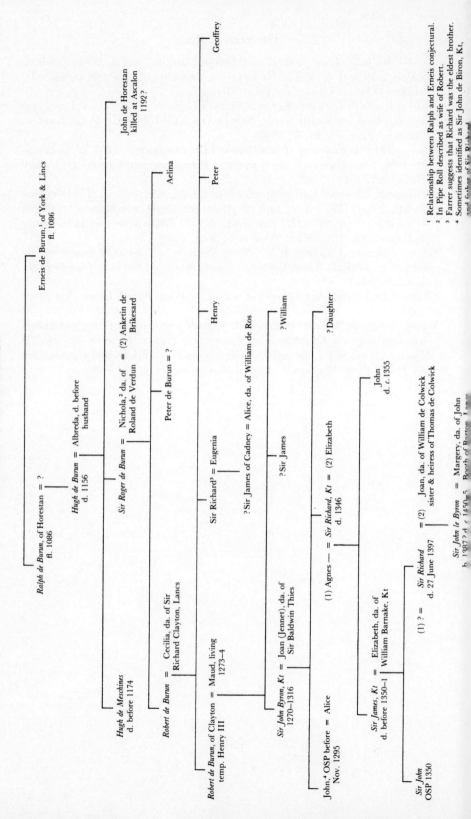

Erneis de Burun,[1] of York & Lincs
fl. 1086

Ralph de Burun, of Horestan = ?
fl. 1086

Hugh de Burun = Albreda, d. before
d. 1156                husband

Sir Roger de Burun = Nichola,[2] da. of = (2) Anketin de
Roland de Verdun      Brikesard

John de Horestan
killed at Ascalon
1192?

Peter de Burun = ?

Aelina          Peter          Geoffrey

Hugh de Meschines
d. before 1174

Robert de Burun = Cecilia, da. of Sir
Richard Clayton, Lancs

Sir Richard[3] = Eugenia          Henry

Robert de Burun, of Clayton = Maud, living
temp. Henry III              1273–4

?Sir James of Cadney = Alice, da. of William de Ros

Sir John Byron, Kt = Joan (Jennet), da. of
1270–1316          Sir Baldwin Thies

?Sir James

?William

?Daughter

John,[4] OSP before = Alice
Nov. 1295

(1) Agnes — = Sir Richard, Kt = (2) Elizabeth
d. 1346

John
d. c.1355

Sir James, Kt = Elizabeth, da. of
d. before 1350–1   William Barnake, Kt

(1) ? =   Sir Richard   = (2)   Joan, da. of William de Colwick
d. 27 June 1397        sister & heiress of Thomas de Colwick

Sir John le Byron = Margery, da. of John
b. 1387? d. c.1450–5   Booth of Barton, Lancs

Sir John
OSP 1350

[1] Relationship between Ralph and Erneis conjectural.
[2] In Pipe Roll described as wife of Robert.
[3] Farrer suggests that Richard was the eldest brother.
[4] Sometimes identified as Sir John de Biron, Kt,
father of Sir Richard

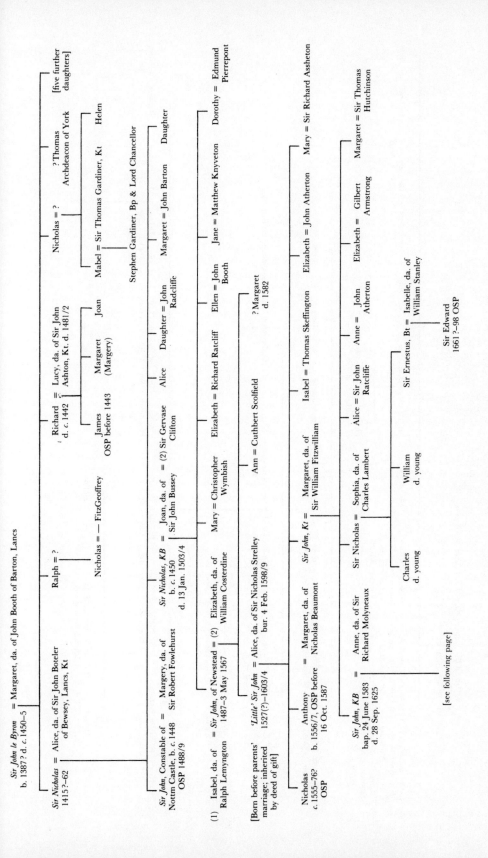

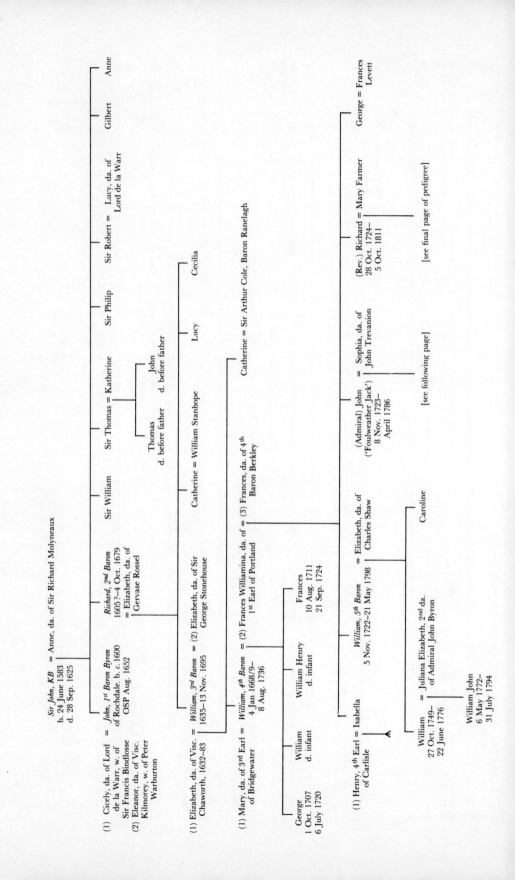

Sir John, KB = Anne, da. of Sir Richard Molyneux
b. 24 June 1583
d. 28 Sep. 1625

(1) Cicely, da. of Lord = John, 1st Baron Byron    Sir William    Sir Thomas = Katherine    Sir Philip    Sir Robert = Lucy, da. of    Gilbert    Anne
de la Warr, w. of         of Rochdale. b. c. 1600                                                              Lord de la Warr
Sir Francis Bindlosse      OSP Aug. 1652
(2) Eleanor, da. of Visc.   = Elizabeth, da. of
Kilmorey, w. of Peter        Gervase Rossel]
Warburton

                                                                         Thomas       John
                                                                    d. before father   d. before father

(1) Elizabeth, da. of Visc. = William, 3rd Baron    Catherine = William Stanhope    Lucy    Cecilia
Chaworth, 1632–83            1635–13 Nov. 1695

(1) Mary, da. of 3rd Earl = William, 4th Baron = (2) Frances Williamina, da. of = (3) Frances, da. of 4th    Catherine = Sir Arthur Cole, Baron Ranelagh
of Bridgewater              4 Jan 1668/9–         1st Earl of Portland              Baron Berkley
                           8 Aug. 1736

George    William        William Henry    Frances                                                                    George = Frances
1 Oct. 1707  d. infant     d. infant      10 Aug. 1711                                                                       Levett
6 July 1720                               21 Sep. 1724

                                                       William, 5th Baron = Elizabeth, da. of    (Admiral) John = Sophia, da. of    (Rev.) Richard = Mary Farmer
                                                       5 Nov. 1722–21 May 1798  Charles Shaw     ('Foulweather Jack')  John Trevanion    28 Oct. 1724–
                                                                                                 8 Nov. 1723–                            5 Oct. 1811
                                                                                                 April 1786

(1) Henry, 4th Earl = Isabella                Caroline                            [see following page]              [see final page of pedigree]
of Carlisle

William = Juliana Elizabeth, 2nd da.
27 Oct. 1749–  of Admiral John Byron
22 June 1776

William John
6 May 1772–
31 July 1794

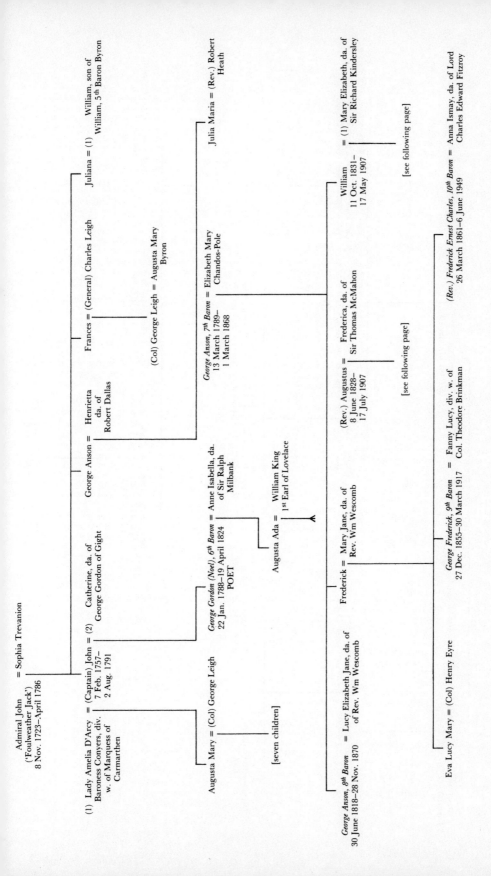

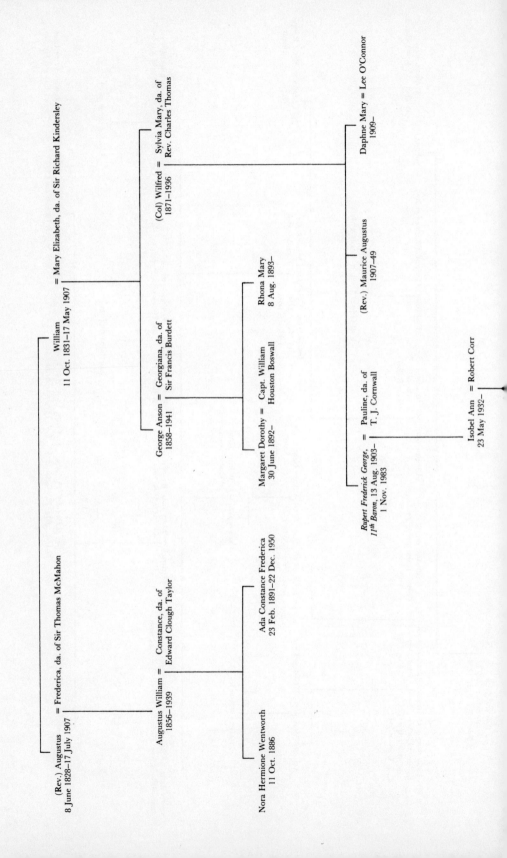

(Rev.) Augustus = Frederica, da. of Sir Thomas McMahon
8 June 1828–17 July 1907

William = Mary Elizabeth, da. of Sir Richard Kindersley
11 Oct. 1831–17 May 1907

Augustus William = Constance, da. of
1856–1939              Edward Clough Taylor

George Anson = Georgiana, da. of
1858–1941            Sir Francis Burdett

(Col) Wilfred = Sylvia Mary, da. of
1871–1936           Rev. Charles Thomas

Nora Hermione Wentworth
11 Oct. 1886

Ada Constance Frederica
23 Feb. 1891–22 Dec. 1950

Margaret Dorothy = Capt. William
30 June 1892–            Houston Boswall

Rhona Mary
8 Aug. 1893–

Rupert Frederick George,
11th Baron, 13 Aug. 1903–
1 Nov. 1983
= Pauline, da. of
T. J. Cornwall

(Rev.) Maurice Augustus
1907–49

Daphne Mary = Lee O'Connor
1909–

Isobel Ann = Robert Corr
23 May 1932–

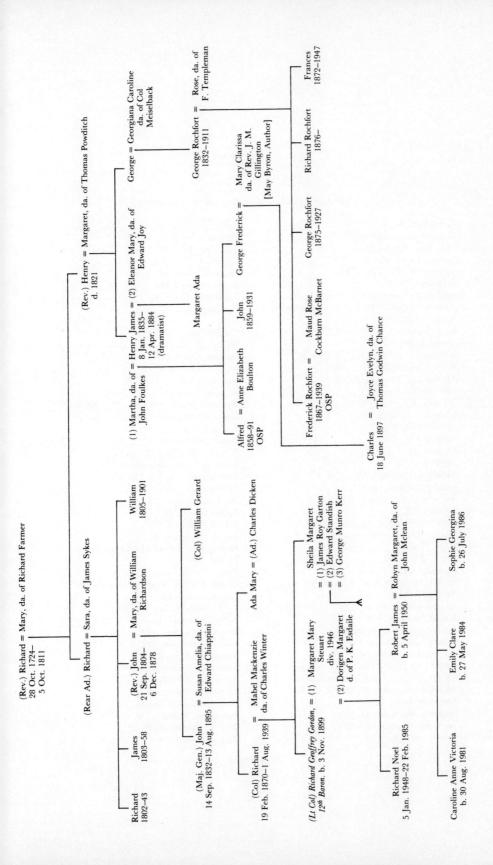

# Index

Proper names and places associated with the Byrons.

# Index

[ 333 ]

[ 337 ]